THE PICKERING MASTERS

G. K. CHESTERTON AT THE *DAILY NEWS*:
LITERATURE, LIBERALISM AND REVOLUTION,
1901–1913

CONTENTS OF THE EDITION

Part I

Volume 1

General Introduction
Columns, Reviews and Letters, 1901–1902

Volume 2

Columns, Reviews and Letters, 1903–1904

Volume 3

Columns, Reviews and Letters, January 1905–June 1906

Volume 4

Columns, Reviews and Letters, July 1906–December 1907

Part II

Volume 5

Columns, Reviews and Letters, January 1908–June 1909

Volume 6

Columns, Reviews and Letters, July 1909–September 1910

Volume 7

Columns, Reviews and Letters, October 1910–December 1911

Volume 8

Columns, Reviews and Letters, January 1912–February 1913
Items from 1916 and 1928

Appendix: Reviews of Chesterton's Books
in the *Daily News*, 1901–1913
Index

G. K. CHESTERTON AT THE *DAILY NEWS*: LITERATURE, LIBERALISM AND REVOLUTION, 1901–1913

Edited By

Julia Stapleton

Volume 5

Columns, Reviews and Letters, January 1908–June 1909

Routledge
Taylor & Francis Group
LONDON AND NEW YORK

First published 2012 by Pickering & Chatto (Publishers) Limited

Published 2016 by Routledge
2 Park Square, Milton Park, Abingdon, Oxon OX14 4RN
711 Third Avenue, New York, NY 10017, USA

Routledge is an imprint of the Taylor & Francis Group, an informa business

© Taylor & Francis 2012
© Editorial material Julia Stapleton 2012

To the best of the Publisher's knowledge every effort has been made to contact relevant copyright holders and to clear any relevant copyright issues. Any omissions that come to their attention will be remedied in future editions.

All rights reserved, including those of translation into foreign languages. No part of this book may be reprinted or reproduced or utilised in any form or by any electronic, mechanical, or other means, now known or hereafter invented, including photocopying and recording, or in any information storage or retrieval system, without permission in writing from the publishers.

Notice:
Product or corporate names may be trademarks or registered trademarks, and are used only for identification and explanation without intent to infringe.

BRITISH LIBRARY CATALOGUING IN PUBLICATION DATA

Chesterton, G. K. (Gilbert Keith), 1874–1936.
G. K. Chesterton at the Daily News: literature, liberalism and revolution, 1901–1913.
Part 2, volumes 5–8. – (The Pickering masters)
I. Title II. Series III. Stapleton, Julia.
824.9'12-dc22

ISBN-13: 978-1-84893-213-5 (set)

Typeset by Pickering & Chatto (Publishers) Limited

CONTENTS

1908

Jan. 04:	A Criminal Head	1
Jan. 11:	Anybody	5
Jan. 18:	'The Fault of the System'. A Word with Mr. R. J. Campbell	9
Jan. 25:	A Somewhat Improbable Story	13
Feb. 01:	'Painting the Green One Red'	17
Feb. 08:	The Whole Elephant	22
Feb. 15:	The Pound of Flesh	25
Feb. 29:	The Name under a Picture	29
Mar. 07:	The Impropriety of Umbrella Stands	33
Mar. 14:	A Case of Comrades	36
Mar. 21:	On Mr. Kipling	40
Mar. 28:	England and Caricature	44
Apr. 04:	The Snob	48
Apr. 11:	On Mrs. Eddy and a New Creed	52
Apr. 18:	The Tower: And Some Remarks on Geography and Character	56
Apr. 25:	The Man who has been There	59
May 02:	The Ballade of a Strange Town	62
May 09:	Humanity: An Interlude	67
May 16:	The Little Birds who won't Sing	72
May 23:	Tommy and the Traditions	76
May 30:	That Cure is better than Prevention	80
June 06:	The Travellers in State	83
June 13:	A Theory of Tyrants	87
June 27:	The Battle of the Barrel Organs	90
July 04:	The Beauty of Buffins	93
July 11:	On Smugglers	96
July 18:	G. K. C.: A Character Study, by A. G. Gardiner.	100
July 18:	Notions and the Nursery	108
July 25:	History versus the Historians	112

Aug. 01:	An Anecdote of Persecution	118
Aug. 08:	Vengeance	122
Aug. 15:	The Vulgar Ghost	126
Aug. 20:	The Russian Tortures (editorial)	130
Aug. 20:	The Sin of Torture (letter by Chesterton)	131
Aug. 21:	'The Sin of Torture' (letter by 'Unconvinced')	134
Aug. 22:	'The Sin of Torture' (letter by H. W. Nevinson)	135
Aug. 22:	The Dickensian	138
Aug. 24:	'The Sin of Torture' (letter by Robert Spence Watson)	142
Aug. 25:	The Sin of Torture (letter by Chesterton)	144
Aug. 26:	The Sin of Torture (letters by H. W. Nevinson, S. T. Rapoport, and H. J. Ayliffe)	147
Aug. 27:	'The Sin of Torture' (letter by H. M. Wallis)	150
Aug. 29:	The Two Noises	153
Aug. 31:	'The Sin of Torture' (letter by Chesterton)	156
Sep. 03:	'The Sin of Torture' (letter by H. M. Wallis)	160
Sep. 05:	The Wheel of Iron	163
Sep. 12:	The Great Cab Crusade	167
Sep. 19:	The Big Thing	171
Sep. 26:	Doubt and the Drama	175
Oct. 03:	The Red Town	179
Oct. 10:	The Burden of Beggars	183
Oct. 16:	A Book of the Day: The Mystery of the Middle Ages (review of G. G. Coulton, *Chaucer and his England*)	186
Oct. 17:	Riot and Decay	191
Oct. 24:	What You Propose	195
Oct. 31:	The Giant	198
Nov. 06:	Books of the Day: The Religion of H. G. Wells (review of H. G. Wells, *First and Last Things*)	202
Nov. 07:	The Long Bow	206
Nov. 14:	The Englishman	210
Nov. 21:	The Queer Memory	213
Nov. 28:	The Thing Indifferent	218
Dec. 05:	How I found the Superman	222
Dec. 12:	On Bluff	226
Dec. 19:	After the Milton Celebration	229
Dec. 26:	The Christmas Boxes	232
Dec. 30:	A Book of the Day: The Democracy of Dickens (review of E. Pugh, *Charles Dickens: The Apostle of the People*)	236

1909 (January–June)

Jan. 02:	The Sacred Suspicion	240
Jan. 09:	On Personalities	244
Jan. 16:	The Three Temples	248
Jan. 23:	The Peril of the Coincidence	253
Jan. 27:	A Book of the Day: A String of Novelists	
	(review of H. Jackson, *Great English Novelists*)	257
Jan. 30:	The Heroic that Happened	261
Feb. 06:	The Vote and the Votary	264
Feb. 13:	Simmons and the Social Tie	268
Feb. 20:	The Divine Detective	272
Feb. 27:	Was Dickens a Socialist?	275
Mar. 06:	The New Tests	279
Mar. 13:	The Real Mob	283
Mar. 20:	On Artificiality	286
Mar. 27:	On Keeping a Dog	290
Apr. 03:	The Three Fools	293
Apr. 10:	Panic	296
Apr. 17:	The Protection of the Bible	300
Apr. 24:	A Cab Ride across Country	303
May 08:	The Pillory	307
May 13:	A Book of the Day: An American view of Mystics	
	(review of R. M. Jones, *Studies in Mystical Religion*)	311
May 15:	Alone in a Cell	315
May 22:	A Great Man	319
May 29:	What is It?	322
June 05:	The Angry Optimist	326
June 12:	The Case for Macaulay	330
June 14:	A Book of the Day: Who was Junius?	
	(review of J. Smith, *Junius Unveiled*)	334
June 19:	The Mystery of a Pageant	338
June 26:	The Evil Day	342

January 4, 1908.

A CRIMINAL HEAD.[1]

When men of science (or, more often, men who talk about science) speak of studying history or human society scientifically they always forget that there are two quite distinct questions involved. It may be that certain facts of the body go with certain facts of the soul, but it by no means follows that a grasp of such facts of the body goes with a grasp of the things of the soul. A man may show very learnedly that certain mixtures of race make a happy community, but he may be quite wrong (he generally is) about what communities are happy. A man may explain scientifically how a certain physical type involves a really bad man, but he may be quite wrong (he generally is) about which sort of man is really bad. Thus his whole argument is useless, for he only understands one half of the equation.

The drearier kind of don may come to me and say, 'Celts are unsuccessful; look at Irishmen, for instance'. To which I should reply, 'You may know all about Celts; but it is obvious that you know nothing about Irishmen. The Irish are not in the least unsuccessful, unless it is unsuccessful to wander from their own country over a great part of the earth, in which case the English are unsuccessful, too'. A man with a bumpy head may say to me (as a kind of New Year greeting), 'Fools have microcephalous skulls', or what not. To which I shall reply, 'In order to be certain of that you must be a good judge both of the physical and of the mental fact. It is not enough that you should know a microcephalous skull when you see it. It is also necessary that you should know a fool when you see him; and I have a suspicion that you do not know a fool when you see him, even after the most lifelong and intimate of all forms of acquaintanceship'.

The trouble with most sociologists, criminologists, etc., is that while their knowledge of their own details is exhaustive and subtle their knowledge of man and society, to which these are to be applied, is quite exceptionally superficial and silly. They know everything about biology, but almost nothing about life. Their ideas of history, for instance, are simply cheap and uneducated. Thus some famous and foolish professor measured the skull of Charlotte Corday[2] to ascertain the criminal type; he had not historical knowledge enough to know that if there is any 'criminal type', certainly Charlotte Corday had not got it. The skull, I believe, afterwards turned out not to be Charlotte Corday's at all; but that is another story. The point is that the poor old man was trying to match Charlotte Corday's mind with her skull without knowing anything about her mind.

But I came yesterday upon a yet more crude and startling example.

****

In a popular magazine there is one of the usual articles about criminology; about whether wicked men could be made good if their heads were taken to pieces. As by far the wickedest men I know of are much too rich and powerful ever to submit to the process, the speculation leaves me cold. I always notice with pain, however, a curious absence of the portraits of living millionaires from such galleries of awful examples; most of the portraits in which we are called upon to remark the line of the nose or the curve of the forehead appear to be the portraits of ordinary sane men, who stole because they were hungry or killed because they were in a rage. The physical peculiarity seems to vary infinitely; sometimes it is the remarkable square head, sometimes it is the unmistakable round head; sometimes the learned draw attention to the abnormal development, sometimes to the striking deficiency of the back of the head. I have tried to discover what is the invariable factor, the one permanent mark of the scientific criminal type; after exhaustive classification I have come to the conclusion that it consists in being poor.

But it was among the pictures in this article that I received the final shock; the enlightenment which has left me in lasting possession of the fact that criminologists are generally more ignorant than criminals. Among the starved and bitter, but quite human, faces was one head, neat but old-fashioned, with the powder of the 18th century and a certain almost pert primness in the dress which marked the conventions of the upper middle-class about 1790. The face was lean and lifted stiffly up, the eyes stared forward with a frightful sincerity, the lip was firm with a heroic firmness. All the more pathetic because of a certain delicacy and deficiency of male force. Without knowing who it was, one could have guessed that it was a man in the manner of Shakespeare's Brutus, a man of piercingly pure intentions, prone to use government as a mere machine for morality, very sensitive to the charge of inconsistency and a little too proud of his own clean and honourable life. I say I should have known this almost from the face alone, even if I had not known who it was.

But I did know who it was – it was Robespierre[3]. And underneath the portrait of this pale and too eager moralist were written these remarkable words: 'Deficiency of ethical instincts', followed by something to the effect that he knew no mercy (which is certainly untrue), and by some nonsense about a retreating forehead, a peculiarity which he shared with Louis XVI. and with half the people of his time and ours.

Then it was that I measured the staggering distance between the knowledge and the ignorance of science. Then I knew that all criminology might be worse than worthless, because of its utter ignorance of that human material of which it is supposed to be speaking. The man who could say that Robespierre was deficient in ethical instincts is a man utterly to be disregarded in all calculations of ethics. He might as well say that John Bunyan[4] was deficient in ethical instincts. You may say that Robespierre was morbid and unbalanced, and you may say the same of Bunyan. But if these two men were morbid and unbalanced they were morbid and unbalanced by feeling too much about morality, not by feeling too little. You may say if you like that Robespierre was (in a negative sort of way) mad. But if he was mad he was mad on ethics. He and a company of keen and pugnacious men, intellectually impatient of unreason and wrong, resolved that Europe should not be choked up in every channel by oligarchies and State secrets that already stank. The work was the greatest that was ever given to men to do except that which Christianity did in dragging Europe out of the abyss of barbarism after the Dark Ages. But they did it, and no one else could have done it.

Certainly we could not do it. We are not ready to fight all Europe on a point of justice. We are not ready to fling our most powerful class as mere refuse to the foreigner; we are not ready to shatter the great estates at one stroke, and put a proud race of peasants upon the land; we are not ready to trust ourselves in an awful moment of utter disillusion in order to make all things seem intelligible and all men feel honourable henceforth. We are not strong enough to be as strong as Danton.[5] We are not strong enough to be as weak as Robespierre. There is only one thing, it seems, that we can do. Like a mob of children, we can play games upon this ancient battlefield; we can pull up the bones and skulls of the tyrants and martyrs of that unimaginable war; and we can chatter to each other childishly and innocently about skulls that are imbecile and heads that are criminal.

I do not know whose heads are criminal, but I think I know whose are imbecile.

Notes

1. *A Criminal Head*: Reprinted in *AD*, pp. 81–6, with minor changes of punctuation.
2. *famous and foolish professor ... Charlotte Corday*: Marie-Anne Charlotte de Corday d'Armont (1768–93) was executed on 17 July 1793 for the assassination of the Jacobin leader Jean-Paul Marat, whom she stabbed to death in his bathtub. The famous painting by Jacques-Louis David called 'The Death of Marat' is in the Royal Museums of Fine Arts of Belgium in Brussels. The 'famous and foolish professor' is the Italian criminologist Cesare Lombroso (1835–1909); Chesterton is referring to his book (written jointly

with William Ferrero) *The Female Offender* (New York: D. Appleton & Co., 1895); there is a photograph of what purports to be Charlotte Corday's skull facing p. 34.
3. *Robespierre*: Maximilien Marie Isidore Robespierre; see 'Reading the Riddle', *DN*, 20 April 1907, Volume 4, p. 208, n. 8 above.
4. *John Bunyan*: see 'A New Study of Swinburne', *DN*, 12 February 1901, Volume 1, p. 14, n. 6, above.
5. *Danton*: George Jacques Danton; see 'Some Reflections on the Strong Man', *DN*, 1 August 1902, Volume 1, p. 362, n. 4, above.

January 11, 1908.

ANYBODY.

The wintry clouds had a queer shape this morning, and the tingle in the air was like the tingle of a string strung too tight; evidently the whole universe had come to a point, and impatiently expected something. Many must have noticed this tense and tingling quality; but I alone understood what it meant. Eternity itself seemed to be asking the time, like the little boys in Battersea Park. But I alone know what is the occasion of this cosmic concentration. It is because a strange and terrible thing is about to happen; one for which the world has been waiting. I am going to agree with 'H. N. B.'[1] I have read through the whole of his letter on blasphemy, and with the best will in the world I cannot find a word in it that is wrong.[2] It is a solemn moment. When I look back at the wonderful and wearisome arguments I have had with 'H. N. B.' I am touched with an emotion as of the approach of evening. I remember how I strove in vain to follow his irrational brilliance. I remember how my heavy and prosaic mind plodded in the path of his galloping love of paradox. I remember how I tried in vain to understand the sparkling assertion that, because nothing mattered, rabbits mattered very much. I remember how I tried, through sleepless nights, to make sense out of the combination of Democracy with moral anarchy; that morality should be settled by everybody, but that everybody had a different morality. But all these wars are over and concluded; and 'H. N. B.' and I have now only to fall on each other's necks; and in that form of physical encounter at least I shall not be wholly at a disadvantage. For 'H. N. B.' and I have simultaneously discovered, to our own marked and mutual astonishment, that we are both Liberals.

I, for one, think it abominable that any man in modern England should be prosecuted for blasphemy. We cannot decide what is religion; how on earth can we decide what is irreligion? What justice can there be in imprisoning the poor man for taking an historical figure whom half of us believe to have been merely human and talking about him as if he was merely human? I refuse as a Liberal to take Christianity for granted as a fundamental of the modern State. But I also refuse as a Christian to take Christianity for granted. It is only people who do not believe in Christianity who take it for granted. As long as I did not believe in it I thought it a most universal, reasonable, and respectable thing. When I disbelieved in Christianity I thought it was the world. It was when I began to believe in it that I found that it was not of the world.[3] And as long as men do not believe in Christianity they will certainly consider it a piece of ordinary decency. But when they come to believe in it they find it is a piece of indecency; of flaming and avenging indecency. Then they feel it as an exposure that has been urgent, even to agony, for all the ages; they feel it as an explosion which at any instant may come. All that the most terrible blasphemer has to say is tame and timid compared with what we have to say. You may sweep the gutters for foul jokes, but you cannot say anything more frightful than that God was made flesh.[4] Piety has anticipated all profanities. All the profane speakers I have ever heard have only been engaged in expounding and elaborating in detail, and perhaps with some dullness, the plain epigram of the Incarnation. The saints made the joke; the blasphemers only explain it. You may laugh if you see fit; but before you were the heavens laughed louder than you, and all the sons of God shouted for joy.[5]

****

It may be alleged, therefore, that my tolerance of blasphemies arises merely from the fact that to me all blasphemies seem very mild. They all seem to me to be, in the most serious and traditional sense of the word, chestnuts; dead and detached chestnuts that have fallen from that living tree of freedom which is also the tree of faith. But I do not think that my objection to prosecutions for blasphemy is merely grounded on this accident of my own indifference. I think that there is a principle in the matter, and that it can be stated. Nay, it shall be stated; it shall be stated now.

Democracy does not rest on the majority, but on the people. The majority is a necessary mechanism for the solution of certain difficulties. But the people is a positive and permanent thing which can be seen as a whole. There is a minority which is a minority, and will probably be in power after the next election; but there is a minority that is really an exception. For instance, there is a very good case (I believe) for bimetallism.[6] There is also a very good case (I could urge it myself if I were quite insincere) for wearing no clothes. There may be quite as few bimetallists as there are Adamites.[7] I can only speak of a small intellectual circle; but in that I have found many people attacking clothes and no people defending bimetallism. But the point is that it is not a question of numbers. The one minority may be as small as the other. But the one minority is of the soul of the people and the other is not. Bimetallism might be instituted without anybody taking much notice. The absence of clothes could not be instituted without everybody taking notice. Now this unfortunate man who has been summoned for blasphemy is also accused of obscenity. In that case, why in the name of wonder did not the authorities prosecute him for obscenity, and not for blasphemy? For between these two things there is exactly the distinction that I have suggested between any odd economic theory and the sudden rejection of clothes. It is not in the least a matter of abstract reason; for an abstract reason it would be quite easy to defend both verbal indecency and physical nakedness. Nor is it a question of the reign of abstract justice; for I could as easily maintain that Christianity is rationally right as any Agnostic could that decency is rationally right. The point is that the whole community does demand the one and does not demand the other. England does believe in decency; England, as England, does not believe in Christianity. To recognise that fact is the first and essential step towards making England believe in it.

****

Now, if there is anyone who thinks that my distinction between public opinion as a whole and the mere triumphant majority is a fallacy or a delusion, I am willing to provide him with what may be called a working test. If you want to know whether a thing is of a mere majority accidentally in power, or whether it is of the people as a people, simply do this. Look at the first man you see in the street, and ask yourself how heavily you would bet that he, a man taken at random, would support the view in question. Do not judge by everybody, for that always means judging by the majority. Do not judge by everybody; judge by anybody. Fix your eye on the man who comes first out of Baker-street Station, and think about him. Bimetallism may have won a wild victory at the polls; but you would not bet that he is a bimetallist. Liberalism may have swept England like a landslide, but you would not bet that he is a Liberal. Christianity may be unconquerably entrenched and enthroned, it may have its Scriptures in all the schools, its public prayers in all the Parliaments. But you would not bet a button that that man believes in Christianity. But you would bet sixpence – nay, ninepence – that he believes in wearing clothes. You would bet that he believes in preserving a certain reticence about sex in the presence of girls or children. Of course, he may happen to have a crank on those subjects; as you tour outside Baker-street Station you may strike the millionth man. If you do you may treat him as something more than an exception – you may feel as if you had forgotten to take your hat off to the Bearded Lady. He is not a minority; he is a monster. And the only way of keeping this distinction is to keep a deep and vigilant reverence for Anybody.

Notes
1. *'H. N. B.'*: Henry Noel Brailsford; see 'What Shall I Eat?', letter to the editor, *DN*, 8 August 1907, Volume 4, p. 277, n. 1, above.
2. *I have read through ... word in it that is wrong*: H. N. Brailsford, 'On Blasphemy', Letter to the editor, *DN*, 9 January 1908, p. 8. The letter protested against the committal for trial of Harry Boulter, a tailor and Secularist lecturer, on the charge of blasphemy. The case had been transferred to the Central Criminal Court and was *sub judice* pending trial. Brailsford was outraged that what may have been a case of indecency, obscenity even, had been treated as blasphemy; he also objected to the absence of publicity surrounding the trial and questioned the motive of the Liberal Government in 'reviving' the persecution of free thought established in the nineteenth century. 'So long as free thought in the eighteenth century was merely the recreation of the polite, the governing classes took no steps to repress it. It was the intimate connection between free thought and revolution which occasioned the orgies of persecution during the reaction of the early nineteenth century ... It is the fear of revolt, the dread of the masses, and not any mere fastidiousness or reverence which causes the police to-day to single out from time to time some obscure street preacher of Atheism for attack'. The *Daily News* took a similar line in an editorial the same day: p. 6. Boulter was found guilty but was spared a jail sentence; he was required instead to provide an affirmation that he would not insult Christianity in public again (*The Times*, 10 February 1908, p. 15). In June 1909 he was jailed for repeating the offence.
3. *not of this world*: See John 17:14: 'I have given them Thy word; and the world hath hated them, because they are not of the world, even as I am not of the world'.
4. *God was made flesh*: See John 1:14.
5. *sons of God shouted for joy*: See Job 38:7.
6. *Bimetallism*: Bimetallists maintain that instead of defining the value of currency in terms of a given weight of a single metal such as gold, it should be defined in terms of the combined weight of two separate metals, normally silver and gold.
7. *Adamites*: Chesterton here uses the term simply to mean 'nudists'; but the Adamites, strictly speaking, flourished in North Africa as a Christian sect between the second and fourth centuries; they adopted nudism and free love as part of their project of recovering the original innocence of Adam and Eve. The idea has had several subsequent revivals: for example, in England between about 1640 and 1650.

January 18, 1908.

'THE FAULT OF THE SYSTEM'.

A Word with Mr. R. J. Campbell.

According to Mr. R. J. Campbell[1] it is morbid to confess your sins.[2] I should say that the morbid thing is not to confess them. The morbid thing is to conceal your sins and let them eat your heart out, which is the happy state of most people in highly civilized communities. But what is really a puzzle is that the upholders of this solitude and self-judgment have a notion that they can do something for social reform. Those whose spirituality is most specially private maintain that in some odd way their morality will be specially public.

I can easily respect the idea of the New Theology, and like all sane men and most mad ones I am concerned about social reform. But it passes the utmost stretch of my imagination to conceive what they have to do with each other. Some have sneered at the New Theology for calling itself new; but it is stranger still that it should regard itself as revolutionary. Mr. Campbell has a quite comprehensible philosophy, but not a philosophy especially akin to practical improvement.

For instance, he is always insisting that evil is a mere emptiness, the absence of something; now this has been held by many sages, but it is not at all useful to reformers. If you have the misfortune to be ruled by a Sultan whose only happiness is cutting off noses, you may call him a negative Sultan; it is a subtle form of Oriental insult; and I quite understand the logical theory on which it rests. But I cannot see why you should be more likely to rebel against a negative Sultan than against a positive Sultan. Mr. Campbell has a right on certain theoretic principles to say that the sin of the tyrant is only 'a shadow where light should be', or a vacancy as yet unfilled with virtue. But I cannot think that the energy of a mob lifting a forest of clenched fists and shouting 'Tyrant!' would be in any way improved for practical purposes if the mob shouted with a thousand throats, 'Vacancy is yet unfilled with virtue. Withdraw!'

As a matter of fact, those Orientals who have been most attached to a half-sceptical pantheism and the relativity of evil have been exactly the people who have never rebelled at all. And, as a matter of fact, the peoples who have rebelled most openly and most successfully have been generally the peoples trained in a very dogmatic and theological conception of sin, such as the English Puritans or the Irish Catholics. Practically, we know that this did occur, and theoretically we should have supposed that it would occur. One would suppose naturally that it would be easier to get angry with a man in a motor-car than to get angry with the absence of a man in a motor-car.

****

It is the same with the New Theology talk about the immanence of God. I understand the idea, but I cannot understand what special good it is supposed to do in Hoxton. If a man is growing very rich on the sale of poisoned gin it would be well, perhaps, to turn his thoughts not so much to the idea that God is perfectly present in him, but rather to the stranger and more mystical doctrine that God is in some ways his superior.

And here again the historical experience supports us; for those mild Eastern civilizations which have most indifference to political improvement have also least sense of a personal and transcendent deity. All Buddhist gods and saints have their eyes shut; they are gazing at the god within. It is a perfectly rational occupation, but it cannot be said either in fact or in theory that it helps them to keep an eye on Mr. Rockefeller.[3]

It is perfectly tenable that religious weapons are of no use in the war of social improvement. But it is quite clear that if any weapons are of use, they are precisely the antiquated weapons. The old theology can be used as an argument for revolution; although it has not always been so used. The new theology, as such, cannot be used at all except as an argument for leaving things alone. It is the only possible result of Mr. Campbell talking to the men who buy peerages and manage the secret fund that they must resist their mad and diseased impulse to confess all their sins. They seem to struggle with that impulse fairly nobly as it is. This hiding of ugly things is the whole disease of England. The whole peril of our public life is that so much of it is private life.

In that case merely to preach that sin is 'a blundering search for God' to a man who has just blundered into a coronet or an oil-trust or a corner in wheat is not likely to improve him much. For the only ultimately evil thing is the motive, the seeking of evil; and if the search is all right, there can be no doubt that the blunders are extremely pleasant. For some individual souls it may be the right optimism; for public life it must be the wrong optimism. It is either innocent of effect or its effect is that Mr. Jay Gould[4] ought not to be ashamed of himself. There is indeed a state of mind in which one may see God in all things not spiritually evil. There is a splendid abstraction in which all the pots and pans are as the bowls before the altar. But, practically, there is a disadvantage in telling the ordinary rich man to look for God in all his furniture; the nearest piece of furniture is so apt to be a looking-glass.

****

Thinkers of this type always reply that we must not think of the fault of the individual sweater or swindler, but of what they call 'The fault of the system'. I believe the system to be the darkest and dreariest hole in which oppressors hid[e] themselves from human anger. We are to allow all men to be as wild and wicked as they please until these wild and wicked men shall erect a mild and unselfish system. We are to refrain from bringing the responsibility home to anybody until some day it simultaneously comes home to everybody. Because it is not easy for any competitive pork butcher at present to be exactly like St. Francis of Assisi,[5] therefore we must ask to dinner and elect to Parliament the pork-butcher who is exactly like Nero;[6] the one particular pork-butcher who butchers men like pork. Our rudest forefathers did not put up with any king, however tyrannical, because all kings had to be a little tyrannical; they did not endure King John[7] until they had completed a Republican system. Having been taught a healthy Christian view of sin, they brought the thing back to the individual. 'The system may be bad, but you at least are worse than the system'.

If we would do this with regard to political and mercantile misconduct the social revolution would really begin in England, as it has already begun in Ireland. The Irish disapproved of landlordism; but they shot the bad landlords. I am not talking here of the ethics of tyrannicide; that is a long business, and stretches from Brutus[8] to Stepniak.[9] But I say their method was right in that they struck the intolerable examples; in that they tracked evil back to its actual source, the human heart.

If we wish to win we must begin with the same simple human passion; an intolerance of startling wickedness. By all means let us reform the system; but let us try to procure a few reformed people to reform it. Let us condemn all people under the[se] conditions in so far as they are parts of a bad society; let us at once condemn them and pardon them. But let us remember that there is the good case in which the man really requires to be protected from the system. And let us realize that there is also the abominably bad case in which the system actually requires to be protected from the man; in which he is actually making it more devilish than the devil intended it to be. Let us attack him by name. Let us cut him in the street. Or, if we really love him and wish him well, and have real charity towards him, let us tell him, not that he has blundered in his search for God, but that he has succeeded alarmingly in his search for Satan; and that he must cut out of his soul cruelty and contempt of the humble.

If we talked like that to three men tomorrow we should see the high turrets of the 'system' beginning to sway in the sky. But as long as we go on cursing the system the system will be perfectly safe.

Notes
1. *Mr. R. J. Campbell*: Reginald John Campbell; see 'Byzantine Influences on Aerated Bread', *DN*, 3 October 1903, Volume 2, pp. 134–5, n. 8 above.
2. *it is morbid to confess your sins*: see *Christianity and the Social Order* (Chapman & Hall, 1908), p. 130.
3. *Mr. Rockefeller*: John Davison Rockefeller (1839–1937), American businessman and philanthropist; co-founder of the first 'trust' company, the Standard Oil Trust and, at the time Chesterton was writing, the world's richest man. He was the first American to amass a fortune of more than a billion dollars.
4. *Mr. Jay Gould*: Jason 'Jay' Gould (1836–92), American railway magnate of dubious business practices. The manipulation of the New York gold market in August 1869 by Gould and his partner James Fisk (1835–72) is usually held to have brought about the financial panic of 24 September 1869 known as 'Black Friday'.
5. *St. Francis of Assisi*: see 'The Mystery of the Mystics', *DN*, 30 August 1901, Volume 1, p. 175, n. 9 above.
6. *Nero*: Nero (Claudius Caesar Augustus Germanicus); see 'A Messenger of Tolstoy', *DN*, 9 September 1901, Volume 1, p. 184, n. 3 above.
7. *King John*: John (1167–1216), King of England, known as 'lackland' and 'Softsword'. His reign was distinguished by military disasters in Normandy and the domestic strife that led to the signing of Magna Carta in 1215; but his reputation as a king of outstanding wickedness is largely due to the hostility of twelfth- and thirteenth-century chroniclers.
8. *Brutus*: Marcus Junius Brutus; see 'The Soul of Charles II', *DN*, 16 July 1901, Volume 1, p. 129, n. 3 above.
9. *Stepniak*: Sergei Mikhailovich Stepnyak (pseudonym of Sergei Mikhailovich Kravchinski) (1852–95) ('Stepniak' is the spelling usually used in English sources): Russian revolutionary and member of the Populist organization 'Land and Freedom'; he assassinated General N. V. Mezentsev, chief of the Russian secret police, in St Petersburg in August 1878, and later lived in Switzerland and England. Among other works he wrote *The Career of a Nihilist* (1889).

January 25, 1908.

A SOMEWHAT IMPROBABLE STORY.[1]

I cannot remember whether this tale is true or not. If I read it through very carefully I have a suspicion that I should come to the conclusion that it is not. But unfortunately I cannot read it through very carefully, because, you see, it is not written yet. The image and idea of it clung to me through a great part of my boyhood; I may have dreamt it before I could talk; or told it to myself before I could read; or read it before I could remember. On the whole, however, I am certain that I did not read it, for children have very clear memories about things like that; and of the books of which I was really fond I can still remember not only the shape and bulk and binding, but even the position of the printed words on many of the pages. On the whole, I incline to the opinion that it happened to me before I was born.

****

At any rate, let us tell the story now with all the advantages of the atmosphere that has clung to it. You may suppose me, for the sake of argument, sitting at lunch in one of those quick-lunch restaurants in the City where men take their food so fast that it has none of the quality of food, and take their half-hour's vacation so fast that it has none of the qualities of leisure; to hurry through one's leisure is the most unbusinesslike of actions. They all wore shiny tall hats as if they could not lose an instant even to hang them on a peg, and they all had one eye a little off, hypnotized by the huge eye of the clock. In short, they were the slaves of the modern bondage; you could hear their fetters clanking. Each was, in fact, bound by a chain; the heaviest chain ever tied to a man – it is called a watch-chain.

Now, among these there entered and sat down opposite to me a man who almost immediately opened an uninterrupted monologue. He was like all the other men in dress, yet he was startlingly opposite to them in manner. He wore a high shiny hat and a long frock coat, but he wore them as such solemn things were meant to be worn; he wore the silk hat as if it were a mitre, and the frock coat as if it were the ephod[2] of a high priest. He not only hung his hat up on the peg, but he seemed (such was his stateliness) almost to ask permission of the hat for doing so, and to apologise to the peg for making use of it. When he had sat down on a wooden chair with the air of one considering its feelings and given a sort of slight stoop or bow to the wooden table itself, as if it were an altar, I could not help some comment springing to my lips. For the man was a big, sanguine-faced, prosperous-looking man, and yet he treated everything with a care that almost amounted to nervousness.

For the sake of saying something to express my interest I said, 'This furniture is fairly solid; but, of course, people do treat it much too carelessly'.

As I looked up doubtfully my eye caught his, and was fixed as his was fixed in an apocalyptic stare. I had thought him ordinary as he entered, save for his strange, cautious manner; but if the other people had seen him then they would have screamed and emptied the room. They did not see him, and they went on making a clatter with their forks, and a murmur with their conversation. But the man's face was the face of a maniac.

'Did you mean anything particular by that remark?' he asked at last, and the blood crawled back slowly into his face.

'Nothing whatever', I answered. 'One does not mean anything here; it spoils people's digestions'.

He limped back and wiped his broad head with a big handkerchief; and yet there seemed to be a sort of regret in his relief.

'I thought perhaps', he said in a low voice, 'that another of them had gone wrong'.

'If you mean another digestion gone wrong', I said, 'I never heard of one here that went right. This is the heart of the Empire, and the other organs are in an equally bad way'.

'No, I mean another street gone wrong', and he said heavily and quietly, 'but as I suppose that doesn't explain much to you, I think I shall have to tell you the story. I do so with all the less responsibility, because I know you won't believe it. For forty years of my life I invariably left my office, which is in Leadenhall-street, at half-past five in the afternoon, taking with me an umbrella in the right hand and a bag in the left hand. For forty years two months and four days I passed out of the side office door, walked down the street on the left hand side, took the first turning to the left and the third to the right, from where I bought an evening paper, followed the road on the right hand side round two obtuse angles, and came out just outside a Metropolitan station, where I took a train home. For forty years two months and four days I fulfilled this course by accumulated habit: it was not a long street that I traversed, and it took me about four and a half minutes to do it. After forty years two months and four days, on the fifth day I went out in the same manner with my umbrella in the right hand and my bag in the left, and I began to notice that walking along the familiar street tired me somewhat more than usual. At first I thought I must be breathless and out of condition; though this, again, seemed unnatural, as my habits had always been like clockwork. But after a little while I became convinced that the road was distinctly on a more steep incline than I had known previously; I was positively panting up hill. Owing to this no doubt the corner of the street seemed further off than usual; and when I turned it I was convinced that I had turned down the wrong one. For now the street shot up quite a steep slant, such as one only sees in the hilly parts of London, and in this part there were no hills at all. Yet it was not the wrong street; the name written on it was the same; the shuttered shops were the same; the lamp-posts and the whole look of the perspective was the same; only it was tilted upwards like a lid. Forgetting any trouble about breathlessness or fatigue I ran furiously forward, and reached the second of my accustomed turnings, which ought to bring me almost within sight of the station. And as I turned that corner I nearly fell on the pavement. For now the street went up straight in front of my face like a steep staircase or the side of a pyramid. There was not for miles round that place so much as a slope like that of Ludgate-hill. And this was a slope like that of the Matterhorn. The whole street had lifted itself like a single wave, and yet every speck and detail of it was the same, and I saw in the high distance, as at the top of an Alpine pass, picked out in pink letters the name over my paper shop.

I ran on and on blindly now, passing all the shops, and coming to a part of the road where there was a long grey row of private homes. I had, I know not why, an irrational feeling that I was on a long iron bridge in empty space. An impulse seized me, and I pulled up the iron trap of a coal-hole. Looking down through it I saw empty space and the stars.

When I looked up again a man was standing in his front garden, having apparently come out of his house; he was leaning over the railings and gazing at me. We were all alone on that nightmare road; his face was in shadow; his dress was dark and ordinary; but when I saw him standing so perfectly still I knew somehow that he was not of this world. And the stars behind his head were larger and fiercer than ought to be endured by the eyes of men.

'If you are a kind angel', I said, 'or a wise devil, or have anything in common with mankind, tell me what is this street possessed of devils'.

After a long silence he said, 'What do you say that it is?'

'It is Bumpton-street, of course', I snapped. 'It goes to Oldgate Station'.

'Yes', he admitted, gravely; 'it goes there sometimes. Just now, however, it is going to heaven'.

'To heaven?' I said. 'Why?'

'It is going to heaven for justice', he replied. 'You must have treated it badly. Remember always that there is one thing that cannot be endured by anybody or anything. That one unendurable thing is to be overworked and also neglected. For instance, you can overwork women – everybody does. But you can't neglect women – I defy you to. At the same time you can neglect tramps and gypsies and all the apparent refuse of the State so long as you do not overwork it. But no beast of the field, no horse, no dog can endure long to be asked to do more than his work and yet have less than his honour. It is the same with streets. You have worked this street to death, and yet you have never remembered its existence. If you had had a healthy democracy, even of pagans, they would have hung this street with garlands and given it the name of a god. Then it would have gone quietly. But at last the street has grown tired of your tireless insolence; and it is bucking and rearing its head to heaven. Have you never sat on a bucking horse?'

I looked at the long grey street, and for a moment it seemed to me to be exactly like the long grey neck of a horse flung up to heaven. But in a moment my sanity returned, and I said 'But this is all nonsense. Streets go to the place they have to go to. A street must always go to its end'.

'Why do you think so of a street?' he asked, standing very still.

'Because I have always seen it do the same thing', I replied, in reasonable anger. 'Day after day, year after year, it has always gone to Oldgate Station; day after ...'

I stopped, for he had flung up his head with the fury of the road in revolt.

'And you?' he cried, terribly. 'What do you think the road thinks of you? Does the road think you are alive? Are you alive? Day after day, year after year, *you* have gone to Oldgate Station ...' Since then I have respected the things called inanimate.

And bowing slightly to the mustard-pot, the man in the restaurant withdrew.

Notes
1. *A SOMEWHAT IMPROBABLE STPRY* Reprinted as 'The Angry Street: A Bad Dream', *TT*(2), pp. 241–8; and 'The Angry Street', *Day Night*, pp. 61–4.
2. *ephod*: An ephod is a kind of priestly vestment or religious object mentioned and described in various places in the Old Testament (e.g. Exodus 28:6–14; 1 Chronicles, 15:27; 1 Samuel 2:28; 2 Samuel, 6:14).

February 1, 1908.

'PAINTING THE GREEN ONE RED'.[1]

We are in peril of not catching sight of the real potential evil in our party system. The evil has generally been stated wrong, as by Lord Rosebery, when he said that it prevented the best men from devoting themselves to politics, and that it encouraged a fanatical conflict.[2] I doubt whether the best men ever would devote themselves to politics; the best men devote themselves to pigs and babies and things like that. And as for the fanatical conflict in party politics, I wish there was more of it. The real danger of the two parties with their two policies is that they unduly limit the outlook of the ordinary citizen. They make him barren instead of creative, because he is never allowed to do anything except prefer one existing policy to another. We have not got real Democracy when the decision depends upon the people. We shall have real Democracy when the problem depends upon the people. The ordinary man will decide not only how he will vote, but what he is going to vote about.

****

It is this which involves some weakness in many current aspirations towards the extension of the suffrage; I mean that, apart from all questions of abstract justice, it is not the smallness or largeness of the suffrage that is at present the difficulty of Democracy. It is not the quantity of voters, but the quality of the thing they are voting about. A certain alternative is put before them by the powerful houses and the highest political class. Two roads are opened to them; but they must go down one or the other. They cannot have what they choose, but only which they choose. To follow the process in practice we may put it thus. The Suffragettes – if one may judge by their frequent ringing of his bell – want to do something to Mr. Asquith.[3] I have no notion what it is. Let us say (for the sake of argument) that they want to paint him green. We will suppose that it is entirely for that simple purpose that they are always seeking to have private interviews with him; it seems as profitable as any other end that I can imagine to such an interview. Now, it is possible that the Government of the day might go in for a positive policy of painting Mr. Asquith green; might give that reform a prominent place in their programme. Then the party in opposition would adopt another policy, not a policy of leaving Mr. Asquith alone (which would be considered dangerously revolutionary), but some alternative course of action, as, for instance, painting him red. Then both sides would fling themselves on the people, they would both cry that the appeal was now to the Caesar of Democracy. A dark and dramatic air of conflict and real crisis would arise on both sides; arrows of satire would fly and swords of eloquence flame. The Greens would say that Socialists and free lovers might well want to paint Mr. Asquith red; they wanted to paint the whole town red. Socialists would indignantly reply that Socialism was the reverse of disorder, and that they only wanted to paint Mr. Asquith red so that he might resemble the red pillar-boxes which typified State control. The Greens would passionately deny the charge so often brought against them by the Reds; they would deny that they wished Mr. Asquith green in order that he might be invisible on the green benches of the Commons, as certain terrified animals take the colour of their environment.

****

There would be fights in the street perhaps, and [an] abundance of ribbons, flags, and badges of the two colours. One crowd would sing 'Keep the Red Flag Flying',[4] and the other 'The Wearing of the Green'.[5] But when the last effort had been made and the last moment come, when two crowds were waiting in the dark outside the public building to hear the declaration of the poll, then both sides alike would say that it was now for democracy to do exactly what it chose. England herself, lifting her head in awful loneliness and liberty, must speak and pronounce judgment. Yet this might not be exactly true. England herself, lifting her head in awful loneliness and liberty, might really wish Mr. Asquith to be pale blue. The democracy of England in the abstract, if it had been allowed to make up a policy for itself, might have desired him to be black with pink spots. It might even have liked him as he is now. But a huge apparatus of wealth, power, and printed matter has made it practically impossible for them to bring home these other proposals, even if they would really prefer them. No candidates will stand in the spotted interest; for candidates commonly have to produce money either from their own pockets or the party's; and in such circles spots are not worn. No man in the social position of a Cabinet Minister, perhaps, will commit himself to the pale-blue theory of Mr. Asquith; therefore it cannot be a Government measure, therefore it cannot pass.

Nearly all the great newspapers, both pompous and frivolous, will declare dogmatically day after day until everyone half believes it that red and green are the only two colours in the paint-box. 'The Times' will say: 'No one who knows the solid framework of politics or the emphatic first principles of an Imperial people can suppose for a moment that there is any possible compromise to be made in such a matter; we must either fulfil our manifest racial destiny and crown the edifice of age with the august figure of a Green Chancellor of the Exchequer, or we must abandon our heritage, break our promise to the Empire, fling ourselves into final anarchy, and allow the flaming and demoniac image of a Red Chancellor to hover over our dissolution and our doom'. The 'Daily Mail' would say: 'There is no halfway house in this matter; it must be green or red. We wish to see every honest Englishman one colour or the other'. And then some funny man in the popular Press would start the sentence with a pun, and say that the 'Daily Mail' liked its readers to be green and its paper to be red. But no one would dare to whisper that there is such a thing as yellow.

****

For the purposes of pure logic it is clearer to argue with silly examples than with sensible ones: because silly examples are simple. But I could give many grave and concrete cases of the kind of thing to which I refer. In the later part of the Boer War both parties perpetually insisted in every speech and pamphlet that annexation was inevitable and that it was only a question whether Liberals or Tories should do it. It was not inevitable in the least; it would have been perfectly easy to make peace with the Boers as Christian nations commonly make peace with their conquered enemies. Personally I think that it would have been better for us in the most selfish sense, better for our pocket and prestige, if we had never done it at all; but that is a matter of opinion. What is plain is that it was not inevitable; it was not, as was said, the only possible course; there were plenty of other courses; there were plenty of other colours in the box. Again in the discussion about Socialism, it is repeatedly rubbed into the public mind that we must choose between Socialism and some horrible thing that they call Individualism; I don't know what it means, but it seems to me that everybody who happens to pull out a plum is to adopt the moral philosophy of the young Horner – and say what a good boy he is for helping himself.[6]

It is calmly assumed that the only two possible types of society are a Collectivist type of society and the present society that exists at this moment and is rather like an animated muckheap. It is quite unnecessary to say that I should prefer Socialism to the present state of things. I should prefer anarchism to the present state of things. But it is simply not the fact that Collectivism is the only other scheme for a more equal order. A Collectivist has a perfect right to think it the only sound scheme; but it is not the only plausible or possible scheme. We might have peasant proprietorship; we might have the compromise of Henry George;[7] we might have a number of tiny communes; we might have co-operation; we might have Anarchist Communism;[8] we might have a hundred things. I am not saying that any of these are right, though I can imagine that any of them could be worse than the present social madhouse, with its top-heavy rich and its tortured poor; but I say that it is an evidence of the stiff and narrow alternative offered to the civic mind, that the civic mind is not, generally speaking, conscious of these other possibilities. The civic mind is not free or alert enough to feel how much it has the world before it. There are at least ten solutions of the Education question, and no one knows which Englishmen really want. For Englishmen are only allowed to vote about the two which are at that moment offered by the Premier and the Leader of the Opposition. There are ten solutions of the drink question; and no one knows what the democracy wants; for the democracy is only allowed to fight about one Licensing Bill at a time.

So that the situation comes to this: The democracy has a right to answer questions, but it has no right to ask them. It is still the political aristocracy that asks the questions. And we shall not be unreasonably cynical if we suppose that the political aristocracy will always be rather careful what questions it asks. And if the dangerous comfort and self-flattery of modern England continues much longer there will be less democratic value in an English election than in a Roman Saturnalia of slaves. For the powerful class will choose two courses of action, both of them safe for itself, and then give the democracy the gratification of taking one course or the other. The lord will take two things so much alike that he would not mind choosing from them blindfold – and then for a great jest he will allow the slave to choose.

Notes
1. *'PAINTING THE GREEN ONE RED'*: See *Macbeth*, II:ii.
   How is't with me, when every noise appals me?
   What hands are here! Ha, they pluck out mine eyes.
   Will all great Neptune's ocean wash this blood
   Clean from my hand? No, this my hand will rather
   The multitudinous seas incarnadine,
   Making the green one red.
2. *The evil ... fanatical conflict*: see 'On a Certain Phrase', *DN*, 14 October 1905, Volume 3, pp. 215–16, n. 2 above.
3. *The Suffragettes ... want to do something to Mr. Asquith*: On 17 January 1908, a number of suffragettes had sought to disrupt a meeting of the Cabinet at the prime minister's residence, 10 Downing Street. Some chained themselves to the railings outside while Mrs Drummond, one of the leaders of the Women's Social and Political Union, gained access to the house by pulling a knob which she thought to be a bell: see 'Women Suffragists and the Cabinet', *The Times*, 18 January 1908, p. 12.

4. *'Keep the Red Flag Flying'*: 'The Red Flag' is a socialist anthem written by the Irishman James Carroll (1852–1929) during the London Dock Strike of 1889. It is sung to the tune of the German carol 'O Tannenbaum' – which is also the tune of the anthem of the State of Maryland.
5. *'The Wearing of the Green'*: see 'Two Bites of the Cherry', *DN*, 5 November 1907, n. 2, Volume 4, p. 219, n. 2 above.
6. *the young Horner ... helping himself*: a reference to the nursery rhyme 'Little Jack Horner':
   Little Jack Horner
   Sat in the corner,
   Eating a Christmas pie;
   He put in his thumb,
   And pulled out a plum,
   And said 'What a good boy am I!'

   It has been suggested that this nursery rhyme originated as a satire on Thomas Horner, steward to Richard Whiting, the last abbot of Glastonbury before Henry VIII's dissolution of the monasteries, who 'pulled out' for himself the 'plum' of the Manor of Mells in Somerset. See I. and P. Opie, *The Oxford Dictionary of Nursery Rhymes*, 2nd edn (1951; Oxford: Oxford University Press, 1997), pp. 234–7. C. Roberts, *Heavy Words Lightly Thrown: the Reason Behind the Rhyme* (London: Granta Books, 2004), p. 3.
7. *Henry George*: Henry George (1839–97), was an American author, politician and political economist who advocated (chiefly in his 1879 work *Progress and Poverty*) the economic theory/ideology called 'Georgism'. The chief tenet of Georgism – the 'compromise' to which Chesterton refers – is that each individual owns what he or she creates but that whatever is found in nature (e.g. land) is the common property of all.
8. *Anarchist Communism*: Anarchist communism (anarcho-communism; libertarian communism) is the variety of anarchism associated particularly with Prince Pyotr Alexeyevich Kropotkin (1842–1921). It advocates the abolition of the state, private property and capitalism in favour of common ownership of the means of production administered by direct democracy – voluntary associations and workers' councils – according to the principle 'from each according to his ability, to each according to his need'. This aphorism comes originally from Karl Marx's *Critique of the Gotha Programme* (1875).

February 8, 1908.

THE WHOLE ELEPHANT.

What makes one nervous about the modern world is that where it is wrong it is wrong in direction; it is taking a splendid fire engine towards York to put out a fire in Brighton. Here, at least, is the main example of this mistake. The modern mind is always trying to be more subtle in order to solve a riddle which it can only solve by becoming more simple. Becoming more simple is itself an abominably difficult business.

There are only two ways of becoming more simple on the spot; one is to have a brick fall on your head and become suddenly quite childish; the other is to be quite extraordinarily good. Both of these methods are rather a nuisance. And as for becoming slowly more simple that necessitates that we should consider the nature of our own complexity.

To use a rough figure, what I mean is this. When first a simple man saw an elephant he had a large but at least a quite complete impression. I do not know what he did. I should think that he laughed. Afterwards when he knew the elephant on easier social terms his analytical faculty was aroused, and, mentally speaking, he cut the elephant up. He noted the fact that his nose was needlessly long; he observed that he had carried into extravagance the conception of having ears to hear;[1] he noticed that two of the teeth were longer than the others, and represented a solid value of ivory.

Primitive man cut up the elephant with his intellect as well as his stone hatchet, and he divided the philosophy of it as well as the carcase among his sons. He advised one to go in for selling ivory; another to specialise in long noses. All this was healthy enough as long as there remained in the mind a clear picture of a complete elephant.

But (if I may continue the symbol) we are in the modern world always trying to be subtle enough to see the grain in the tusks, when we really ought to be trying to be simple enough to see an elephant. We hear of parts of the elephant without realising that any such creature is involved. We hear that fifty pounds of ivory has been landed at Portsmouth; we do not hear that it stuck out of the head of a live animal. We hear that a trunk has been put in the cloak room at King's-cross; we are not told that it is an elephant's trunk. We hear that ten naturalists have been studying a splendid specimen of an elephant's tail; we do not realise that if you pull the tail you discover with some alarm that it is tied on to an elephant.

***

We have grown too subtle to see things at all; we can only see parts of things. And most of our modern intellectualism only increases the evil, because it does not in any sense assist simplicity. For our disease most modern analysis is bad, because it is analysis. It is cutting things up when what we need most is to put them together.

To take but one instance, sociological investigation is now mostly undertaken from the noblest motives; it is no contemptible ideal that makes men with crusades of inquiry or books of statistics seek to classify all the varieties of vice or agony in the English people. But yet this classification misses the point because it is classification. Only in a secondary sense at this moment do we need to see any classifications of the English people.

What we do in the most deadly sense need to see is the English people; to see them as one, and not as many; to see them not as a number of dead species which we may do something with, but as one living species which may quite conceivably do something with us. All talk about the employable and the unemployable, all talk about the capitalist and the proletarian, all talk about the educated and the uneducated, though all of them important discussions in themselves, do at this moment serve chiefly to destroy that image of the English people which has already grown far too faint. We are only cutting up the carcase of England. We do not want more divisions and sub-divisions. What we want is not a new analysis, but the recovery of an old synthesis. We must not go mad on ivory and ears and tails; we must see the elephant and learn again to laugh.

****

If we saw the whole elephant of modern society we should laugh.

If, for instance, anyone wishes to test the complex absurdity to which it has come, I should recommend him to study such a philosophical tangle as the Thaw case.[2] A man named White was killed. He was the kind of man who ought to be killed, if any kind of man ought to be killed. In a simpler and saner community Thaw would not have shot White, for the simple reason that White would have been shot already – by the simple and sane community. In some prehistoric European village it would have been White who was on the village gallows. Thaw would have lived quite happily as the village idiot. But anyhow White, an intolerably wicked man, was killed; and as Carlyle says in dropping the curtain on somebody much better: 'He at least will never through unending ages insult the face of the sun any more'.[3] The man who killed him was an ordinary young fool. I do not suppose that he was mad at all. But if he was mad all his life his sanest moment was when he killed Mr. White; for the act has a perfectly rational motive and explanation. In so far as he is in any sense weak-minded he has exhibited that quality all his life. Then he does something quite reasonable, though wrong, and the authorities decide that it is not so wrong that he must be punished, but is so unreasonable that he must go to a madhouse.

For all the irresponsible things poor Thaw did in the course of his pitiful life he was held responsible. For the one really responsible thing he did he is held irresponsible. And then comes the last touch of this lunatic logic, and I hear that he will probably be released before long even from the asylum.

It requires a huge effort of elemental simplicity to take in all the absurdities of the situation; it is like trying to imagine an elephant when one has not seen him. First you have a frantically silly law that a man who kills another man (on whatever moral provocation) must be killed. Then when one man kills another under obvious moral provocation you say he is not a man at all, but an idiot who cannot help killing people. Then you let the idiot out to kill as many people as he likes.

First you have bad justice; then you have bad science to cure bad justice; and then you have bad administration to cure bad science.

In dealing with such things analysis is no good; it is no good to split hairs. It is no help to settle the exact degrees which divide Thaw from an imbecile or White from a criminal. One must see the whole absurdity simply and suddenly with one explosion of intolerant mirth. One must see the whole elephant, and one must shoot him.

Notes
1. *the conception of having ears to hear*: See Matthew 11:15; Mark 4:9.
2. *the Thaw case*: On 25 June 1906 Harry Kendall Thaw (1871–1947) shot and killed the architect Stanford White (b. 1853), who may or may not have been having an affair with Thaw's wife. At the trial in New York between January and April of 1907 the jury had failed to reach agreement. A second trial had commenced on 6 January 1908. The jury returned a verdict of not guilty on grounds of insanity on 1 February 1908. Thaw was committed to an asylum for an indefinite period. He was released in 1915.
3. *as Carlyle says ... sun any more*: see 'Carlyle, Ruskin, Buchanan, and Kipling', *DN*, 26 June 1901, Volume 1, p. 119, n. 10 above.

February 15, 1908.

THE POUND OF FLESH.

It is recognised that some of the greatest men in literature were plagiarists from much smaller men, and that they even more often borrowed from the stock of popular legends which were composed by nobody in particular. But we generally do less than justice to the value of this outline or framework of the tale that they borrowed. We think too exclusively of the work of the great man and far too little of the great story which was the work of many small men. Above all we omit to observe that the idea and philosophy of the story is generally present in the rude outline as well as in the finished product.

An instance will make the matter more clear. In Professor Raleigh's recent book on Shakespeare that shrewd and effective critic is concerned to explain (very truly on the whole) that it is possible to make too much fuss about the mysteries of Shakespeare, that many of them are accidents, many of them practical limitations of the playwright. But in the course of maintaining this he suggests, I think, that a certain brutality in the mere mechanism of 'The Merchant of Venice' prevented Shakespeare from doing the most delicate spiritual justice to Shylock. He implies that the coarse old tale of the pound of flesh tied Shakespeare down, and prevented him from painting with full sympathy a noble Jew.[1]

If I am right in my memory of Professor Raleigh's meaning, he thinks that Shylock would be finer without the story of Shylock; in that case he does a great injustice to the old story. It is at any rate an injustice that is often done to it. The truth is that the rude story of the pound of flesh is a very spiritual story. Moreover, it was exactly the spiritual story which Shakespeare wished to tell, out of which he wished to draw the full spirituality. No one but Shakespeare could have made the thought explicit; but the thought was implicit in the most jingling old ballad about the merchant and the Jew.

That idea was the profound philosophy of mercy or of charity, which Mr. Belloc has called somewhere 'the appreciation of living things'.[2] In other words, there is a certain kind of sympathy or allowance which is due to organisms, and which cannot be given to the inorganic. There is a sense in which one can be just to a stone; but one could be merciful to a mushroom. When the thing has a life of its own, an interdependence of function, a circulation of power, then it becomes necessary to deal with it sympathetically and not literally, to remember that one thing goes with another, and that one cannot touch parts without injuring the whole.

If you chop a stone in two, you have two halves of a stone; but if you chop a horse in two you only have more horseflesh than you require for any domestic purpose.

****

Now the old tale of the Jew and the merchant of Venice was a satire on that commercial literalism which endeavours to apply hard contract and cruel exactitude to life and to living things.[3] The Jew, as the great, mediaeval symbol of this unchivalrous calculation was represented as saying that he had a legal right to a pound of a man's flesh, and that he would take not a grain more or less. It was useless to point out to him that the pound was a part of an organic life, and that in taking that he was in fact taking more. So at last, when he had rejected all appeals to generosity and commonsense, he was at last routed by the reductio ad absurdum of justice. His own mad logic is pushed one step further, and it destroys his case. He may take flesh if he can manage to take flesh without blood.

The whole legend, even in its baldest and most brutal outline, has the clear voice of Christian morals and European sanity. It is a protest against that pedantry which always becomes inhumanity.

What Shakespeare did was to take this wild tale, to see the mother wit in it, and to develop that into an exalted spiritual wisdom. He was quite as sure that the Jew was wrong as any mediaeval could have been. But he emphasised the wrongness not by making him grotesquely wrong, but by making him splendidly and pathetically wrong. Instead of giving us the comic moneylender of mediaeval farce, he showed us a man mighty in error, whose morality had sublimely gone astray. Shylock, in his own eyes, is asking only for his rights; but he cannot be got to see that when dealing with life it is often possible to take rights and to leave wrongs instead. You not only deduct something, you also add something; you add a wound. Shylock's morality has not enough mysticism to make him see that in touching a living thing he is breaking into a sanctuary where unknown vengeances are hung over his head. And Shylock's philosophy has not enough of what always goes with mysticism, it has not enough *humour* to see that it is silly to talk about owning a part of another man.

****

Shylock's philosophy, the pedantic and inhuman philosophy, is held by many people in our own time, who are as dignified and sincere as Shylock. It is always marked by this inability to apprehend the interdependence between all the parts of a living thing.

When there has been question, for instance, of the suppression of some small nationality I have heard a quite good-natured young English guardsman or squire say 'these people only had to give up their flag which was merely ornamental'. To this I was impelled to reply, 'My good sir, the only thing I ask of you is that you should cut off your head, which I am sure is merely ornamental. The rest of your attractive person will remain in full play; you can salute with your hand and waltz with your legs as before, without this sentimental emblem erected between your shoulders, of which, if you will permit me to say so, I have grown a little tired'.

But, alas, that is the weakness of the Shylock philosophy, for, as the Guardsman lucidly and patiently explained to me, his head, however, useless for the higher purposes, was quite essential to his either drilling or dancing; in short, that I could not take his head without taking his life, which was a much more enjoyable thing. And then I told him that a Christian Commonwealth is an animal of a very funny shape, and it is often hard to say which is the head with the life in it; but, generally, the head is the flag. But I do not think that he quite followed my meaning.

But one may commit this anti-organic crime in many directions, and it concerns us more to realise that we can easily commit it in our arrangements for reforming human society. Do not let us be the dupe of lists and classifications in which Antonio's flesh is put down to Shylock's banking account. Almost every book I find full of a righteous anger against the social evil slips into this bad habit of reckoning by tons or inches instead of by organisms. Like Shylock, it takes humanity by the pound instead of by the person.

Let me take but one case out of a hundred. All rational citizens have long had the thought that certain things ought to be run from the centre, and for all alike. The strongest case, I think, is transit. If a thousand people for a thousand reasons all want to go from Balham to Highgate it must be an advantage to take them all by one responsible system.

But from this certain modern writers, forgetting that they are dealing with living things, deduce the wildest things. They deduce, for instance, that in a better state of society we shall all dine together at a common restaurant. This is to forget all the vital element[s] involved. Men take a tram for Highgate because they want to get to Highgate. But men do not dine because they want dinner. They dine because they want a certain human atmosphere, of repose, of domesticity, of hospitality, and of chosen friends, and they want dinner along with all this. They do not want their pound of flesh or their pound of beans and bacon. They want the spiritual sentiment of a good dinner. If you try to cut that out of humanity you will find (as Shylock did) that you cannot do it unless blood is shed.

Notes
1. *In Professor Raleigh's recent book on Shakespeare ... a noble Jew*: W. A. Raleigh, *Shakespeare* (London: Macmillan, 1907), p. 150. For Raleigh, see 'The Butterfly Again', *DN*, 25 March 1905, Volume 3, p. 68, n. 8 above.
2. *Mr. Belloc ... the appreciation of living things*: 'But, though he [Robespierre] was too absorbed for Pride, he was empty of positive Humility altogether; and Charity (the appreciation of living things, and the salt and good moderator of life) was never granted to him at all': *Robespierre: a Study* (London: James Nisbet, 1901, p. 34.
3. *Now that old tale ... to living things*: Shakespeare's play is adapted largely from the story of Gianetto (Giornata quarta, novella 1) in Giovanni Fiorentino's collection of stories called *Il Pecorone* (1378).

February 29, 1908.

THE NAME UNDER A PICTURE.

A thing may be bad as producing certain effects, or bad as symbolising a certain state of mind. Thus the consequences were vast and terrible when the library at Alexandria was burned.[1] But touching depravity of souls, I can suggest a small thing that was infinitely worse. The silliest and most contemptible thing ever done in a small way was the habit adopted in some picture galleries of putting on the pictures not the traditional names of the painters, but their forgotten family names.

Thus Claude Loraine[2] was called Gelée. Thus Michael Angelo was called Buonarotti. In this act there was concentrated everything that is abominable – pedantry, parvenu vanity, obscurantism, irreverence, lack of humour, tyranny, anarchy, contempt of the poor, tenth-rate culture, pride, vain-glory, and blindness and hardness of heart. The act combined everything that can be bad in being a Tory with everything that can be bad in being a Radical. It blasphemed both tradition and equality. It despised the four august centuries which have called Michael Angelo by that splendid name. It also despised the humble clerk or workman who might have recognised him by it. The authors of this trick took a scrap of second-hand information which anyone can find in a cheap dictionary, and preferred it both to the dignity of the past and the education of the future. It would be very easy (as a silly and supercilious practical joke) to find out the private names of innumerable public figures in history and always refer to them by those names.

****

I could write a whole article about famous people in which not one of them should be recognisable by an ordinary person by his ordinary name. Such an article should combine all the solid analysis of Mrs. Cross[3] with all the volcanic romanticism of Mrs. Nicholls.[4] Its logic should be the logic of Chauvin,[5] its satire the satire of Arouet.[6] On its political side it would show all the cynical good sense of Lord Orford;[7] while its military aspect would have the dash and chivalry of the Duke of Bronte.[8] It would have the political moderation of George Savile[9] combined with the political promptitude of Oliver Williams.[10]

By this simple method we could produce a charming amount of learned confusion in the common mind. We could allude to all well-known Peers by their private surnames, and to all well-known men by their forgotten peerages. We could refer to all great brewers by their original English names and to all great financiers by their original German ones. We could get St. John, Lord Bolingbroke,[11] thoroughly mixed up with St. John the Baptist and be happy. When we came to the Hebrew names in the Old Testament we could have glorious fun, by leaving out the vowels, or something of that kind. But considered as a piece of public education it would be a joke in bad taste.

****

Most modern culture, I fear, has fallen between these two stools; or rather I would have said (had it been grammatical or even logical), fallen between this one stool. For the learned and the democracy are at one. It is the educated who are out of it. Ordinary people call the great sculptor Michael Angelo, because that is his ordinary name. The most penetrating and spiritual personalities also call him Michael Angelo, because to them he is indeed the Angel Michael. It is foolish, indeed, to talk about the paganism of the Renaissance; Michael Angelo was more decisively Christian than any other artist after Christianity; much more Christian than Fra Angelico. His splendid sculpture called 'The Slave'[12] could not have been created in simple slave earning [owning?] times; it represents a huge and heaving human figure struggling to be free. In short, there was a man whose surname was Buonarotti; we have never heard of that name, and it is doubtful if he had ever heard of it himself: I mean as a part of himself. All tradition has called him Michael the Angel because all tradition has felt him to be Michael the Angel. Michael destroyed the devils by smiting them; Michael Angelo destroyed the Titans by creating them. Here then the two essentials of a state are at one. The same words, 'Michael the Angel', would spring to the mouth both of the learned and the quite unlearned man. The literate and the illiterate are combined; and together they sweep the world. But the cultured man is left alone in the middle: for he says 'Buonarotti'.

****

This is so in every case. The best human philosophy is in favour of democracy. But the second best human philosophy is most powerfully and forcibly against democracy. We can see this by studying the modern world, which is full of the second best philosophy. The modern world is full of things which are very good in themselves, but which are, so far as they go, certainly undemocratic.

For instance, the novel, the art of fiction, is really a fine thing, and is quite peculiar to our time. But it is not at all calculated to further democracy. For the novel has for its whole object the separating of man from man; calling this man strong and that man weak, this man misunderstood and that man without understanding. Philosophy, which is dying, was about man; fiction, which is growing, is only about men. The same is true of science; it is a wonderful thing, it is a great glory to mankind. But one cannot say that it tends to advance democracy; on the contrary, its talk is mostly about separating man from man; this man must be good and that man bad.

The same is true of the insistence on some very reasonable things; such as cleanliness and hygiene. They are reasonable, but they are not at all democratic; they are not calculated to bring the classes together. An extreme objection to dirt is hardly the first step to an affection for democracy. All the characteristically modern movements, so far as they go, are anti-democratic movements. Our democracy will die (unless we make quite violent efforts to defend it) just as nearly all democracies have died under the advance of a collective and convenient despotism. I see women walking about with flags and pieces of paper suggesting that women should have votes. Alas! my friends, only for a little while will men have votes. Civilization has taken the turn against us, and unless, as I think, there is something greater than civilization we are lost for ever. But I saw the first hint of it under a picture in a public gallery.

Notes
1. *when the library at Alexandria was burned*: The Royal Library of Alexandria was created during the reign of Ptolemy I Soter (323–283 BC) or possibly during that of his son Ptolemy II (283–246 BC). Its first librarian was the statesman and peripatetic philosopher Demetrius of Phaleron (350–280 BC). The main library was accidentally burnt down by Julius Caesar in 48 BC and some of its contents destroyed. In AD 391 Theophilus, Bishop of Alexandria, determined to eradicate non-Christian institutions, ordered the destruction of its daughter-house called the Serapeum. When Egypt was conquered by the Arabs in 646, what remained of the library was destroyed on the order of Caliph Omar.
2. *Claude Loraine*: Claude Gellée (1600–82) – he took the name Lorraine (also spelt Loraine, as here, and Lorrain) after his native province – was a French Baroque landscape painter; he spent almost the whole of his career in Rome.
3. *Mrs. Cross*: i.e. George Eliot, who acquired her 'ordinary name' of Mrs Cross when she married John Walter Cross in 1880.

4. *Mrs. Nicholls*: ie. Charlotte Brontë (1816–55), English novelist whose 'volcanic romanticism' is most memorably displayed in *Jane Eyre* (1847). She married Arthur Bell Nicholls in 1854.
5. *Chauvin*: i.e. John Calvin (1509–64), Protestant theologian who was born in Picardie, France, but spent almost the whole of his life in Geneva. He developed the system of Christian theology called Calvinism or Reformed theology, as set forth in his *Institutes of the Christian Religion* (1536). Calvin or Calvinus is a Latinized form of the French name Chauvin.
6. *Arouet*: i.e. Voltaire (1694–1778), the French Enlightenment sceptic, satirist, dramatist and historian whose real name was Jean François-Marie Arouet. Among his many works are *The Age of Louis XIV* (1752), *Essay on the Customs and the Spirit of the Nations* (1756) and the satire on the philosophy of Leibniz called *Candide, ou l'Optimisme* (1759).
7. *Lord Orford*: i.e. Sir Robert Walpole, first Earl of Orford; see 'The "Good Man" of the Eighteenth Century', *DN*, 22 March 1901, Volume 1, p. 66, n. 10 above.
8. *Duke of Bronte*: Horatio Nelson received the title Duke of Bronte in Sicily from Ferdinand, King of Naples in 1799, the year after he became a Baron.
9. *George Savile*: George Savile, First Marquess of Halifax (1633–95), was a politician and political writer. Halifax was the anonymous author of *The Character of the Trimmer*, a pamphlet published in 1685 which emphasized the importance of maintaining the centre in English politics, against extremist Whigs and Tories.
10. *Oliver Williams*: Oliver Cromwell (1599–1658), was Lord Protector of England, Scotland and Ireland. Cromwell occasionally used the name Williams after his great-great grandfather Morgan Williams. The latter had married the elder sister of Thomas Cromwell, minister of Henry VIII who was responsible for the dissolution of the monasteries; as a beneficiary of confiscated church land, Morgan Williams changed his name to Cromwell (J. Morrill, *ODNB*).
11. *St. John, Lord Bolingbroke*: Henry St John, first Viscount Bolingbroke (1678–1751), was a politician, diplomatist and author. Bolingbroke associated Toryism with patriotism rather than Jacobitism; as author of the pamphlet *The Idea of the Patriot King* in 1738, he supported the Prince of Wales in his dispute with his father, George II, in an attempt to undermine Robert Walpole.
12. *His splendid sculpture called 'The Slave'*: There are six 'Slaves' by Michelangelo, originally conceived for the tomb of Pope Julius II (1443–1513) in Rome; two of them are now in the Louvre, Paris, and four in the Accademia di Belle Arti, Florence.

March 7, 1908.

THE IMPROPRIETY OF UMBRELLA STANDS.[1]

The other day my friend Phipps was showing me over his Utopia, which is just behind the tennis court. He is so enormously rich that he can afford to have an Utopia of his own, and need not wait for the course of social evolution, which certainly seems to me to be a disgustingly slow affair. In fact, in his set, where everybody is enormously rich, it has become quite natural and necessary to have an Utopia, just as it is to have a stable or a library or a billiard room or a wine cellar or a garage. For this reason several people on an excellent paper called the 'New Age' called out to me quite recently in indignant astonishment, 'Where is your Utopia?'[2] and seemed quite surprised that I did not possess one of these ordinary little luxuries or conveniences.

Phipps's Utopia consists entirely of his footmen, of whom, however, there is a whole army – which is right enough logically speaking, for footmen were obviously intended to go in armies like horsemen. His footmen are not made to powder their heads; in fact, they are forbidden to do it, though they want to do it very much. They are all made to dress in artistic corduroys and have pointed beards, as if these were a sort of uniform of minor poets. They are made to live in beautiful surroundings, which they hate (and so should I), and to stand about the room in dégagé attitudes, which they consider, with much justice, to be at once disreputable and affected.

But I have no space to tell you much about my friend's Utopia, more especially because my mind has been filled with one awful fact about it. Phipps is a man with a heart of gold, and what is much more extraordinary in his economic circumstances, with a brain of good ordinary metal. It is not unusual (in the frantic chaos and anarchy of our economic system) to find a successful man who has virtue. But to find a successful man who has intelligence is almost carrying the principle of coincidence too far. Yet I have found Phipps.

****

When I write a book like one of Mr. Wells's books I will describe the Utopia of Phipps: how everything was carried to the inhabitants through a system of long pipes, one for sunlight and one for moonlight and one for starlight, and how easily the smell of the sea or the smell of roses could be turned on, and how free the people were to choose between ordinary air and more hygienic atmospheres. But I listened quite respectfully while Phipps, who has a real reasoning power, explained all this reasonably; and I was not moved until I came to one thing. At one of the entrances to the paradise I found a row of objects which, after a few moments of horrible uncertainty, I perceived to be umbrella-stands filled with umbrellas and walking-sticks. Then I took hold of Phipps furiously, and said: 'Is this the end of all your analysis? Is this the end of all your detailed criticism of the modern state? You have separated everything from everything. You have separated a man from his origin as a man. You have separated sunlight from the sun. And yet you perpetuate this unnatural, conventional connection between umbrellas and walking-sticks!'

'Oh, of course', said Phipps, glancing at me with slight wonder, 'the men leave their sticks and umbrellas here before they go into the Utopia'.

'Then your Utopia is done for', I said, 'for it has misunderstood the whole nature of man. You could not find two things more unlike in this world, more opposite in their aim and substance, than a walking stick and an umbrella. A cloud and a camel are more like each other than a walking stick and an umbrella. A cigar and St. Paul's Cathedral are more like each other than a walking stick and an umbrella. You are misled by the mere fact that they go into about the same space. A red pillar-box and Napoleon Bonaparte would go into about the same space. But now I know that all your revolutions are only the extension of our conventions. You would class sticks and umbrellas together just as you class men and women together, because you have not thought for an instant what either of them *are*. If you had you would have abolished umbrella stands even before you wrecked the Bank of England'.

Somewhat to my surprise I found that the glance of my friend Phipps was still an inquiring one, so I started again to explain.

'Don't you see', I said, 'that if your people were really happy they would take their walking sticks into Utopia, but leave their umbrellas outside. An umbrella is purely practical. A walking stick is purely poetical. An umbrella is a necessary evil. A walking stick is an unnecessary good. A man hides under an umbrella because he feels frightened, even if it is only of being washed. But a man carries a walking stick because he feels brave, because he feels inclined to fight anybody for twopence. The consequences arising from this distinction are enormous. The peril of rain is a common peril, and therefore we might conceivably have a common umbrella; an umbrella like St. Paul's Cathedral. In fact on rainy Sundays I have noticed that many people do use St. Paul's Cathedral as an umbrella. But you cannot fancy men having a common walking stick. You cannot imagine a walking stick as tall as the cross of St. Paul's laboriously lifted by two hundred men. To say the least of it, the gesture is its point. But a walking stick is only a gesture. It is the mere elongation of the human finger for the purpose of making the gesture more emphatic. But you cannot have a communal gesture, a social or public gesture. On the other hand, an umbrella is simply a roof, or house. And I have no objection to a house being a public-house'.

'All this', replied Phipps, with a friendliness which was creditable under the circumstances, 'all this seems rather fantastical as an objection to putting sticks and umbrellas in the only place where they will go; you do not, I imagine, seriously maintain that my Utopia will fail because I have not appreciated the metaphysical nature of walking sticks'.

'Yes', I answered, 'your Utopia, when it is smashed, will be smashed with a walking-stick. It is exactly these things – so subtle and, as it seems to you, so silly – that have destroyed all societies, and that will destroy yours. You will fall by classing things together that do not go together; you will probably end by calling a towel-horse a quadruped. The objection to all your Utopias is that you have understood the umbrella, but have not understood the walking-stick. You have understood those institutions to which a man retreats for protection, and you have proposed, very rightly, to make them accessible to all. But you have not understood those institutions to which a man looks for expansion, those institutions which are the expression of his own loneliness and liberty. You are right enough to communalise the umbrella; if ever I walk under an umbrella (which God forbid) it would certainly give me great pleasure if some State official were holding it over me. But no State official shall hold my walking-stick; it shall break a few heads before we come to that'.

Phipps saw me out of the seventh west gate of the Utopia, but I noticed with some disappointment that the inquiring look was still in his eyes.

Notes

1. *THE IMPROPRIETY OF UMBRELLA STANDS*: The distinction between walking-sticks and umbrellas at the heart of this essay provides the basis of 'The Umbrella Stand', *What's Wrong with the World?* (1910), part 5, ch. 2.
2. *Several people on an excellent paper called the 'New Age'... Where is your Utopia?*: see G. B. Shaw, 'Belloc and Chesterton', *NA*, 15 February 1908, p. 310; Shaw was echoing H. G. Wells. For the *New Age*, see the 'The Sentimentalism of Zarathustra', *DN*, 15 December 1906, Volume 4, p. 115, n. 1 above.

March 14, 1908.

A CASE OF COMRADES.[1]

There was once a lady of a very beautiful character (delicate, yet decisive, for that is the definition of a lady) who asked me whether I did not believe in the possibility of a simple comradeship between the sexes. Being somewhat in a corner, I replied that, as I understand the word comradeship, I did not.

I gave some of my reasons. I did not give my first and firmest and most unhesitating reason, which was this: that I knew quite well that if I had treated that lady herself for four consecutive minutes as a comrade she would have ordered me out of the house. But I gave some other reasons. I remarked that comradeship was a quite special thing; that it was quite different from friendship. I said (and this, oddly enough, I believe to be profoundly true) that a man can be the friend of a woman, but not her comrade. For friendship implies individuality; whereas comradeship really implies the temporary subordination, if not the temporary swamping, of individuality. Friends are the better for being two; but comrades are the better for being two million.

****

In the Greek grammar, which I learnt with difficulty and forgot with ease, there was one thing, I remember, which would by itself prove that the Greeks were a great people. I mean the fact that there is in Greek a dual as well as a plural. Two is quite different from any other number, just as one is quite different from any other number: that truth is the basis of marriage. When I knew there was a Greek dual I could easily realize that the Greeks gave philosophy to the world.

My concern here is that comradeship is essentially plural. Now, women are not plural. The very word 'women' has about it, I think, a sort of bad taste: it smacks of polygamous Turks or tired and cynical men-about-town. There are no such things as women. There is only the woman you are at this particular moment afraid of or in love with, or inclined to reverence or inclined to assassinate. I think a real crowd of women would be like fifty suns or half a hundred moons – it would be weaker for its numbers. The sun would not have room to shine.

In any case, what I had to say about comradeship to this particular lady was tolerably clear. I merely pointed out that comradeship is a particular sort of human association; and the essential paradox of it is this: that it is at once violent and cool. People talking in twos talk gently, because they feel emphatically: people talking in tens or twenties talk emphatically, because they do not care a dump about anything. Friendship becomes comradeship when you have forgotten the presence of your friend. You are addressing the abstract thing, the club, which, when two or three are gathered together (of the male sort at least) is always in the midst of them.[2] Men's debating clubs have a pedantic phrase which exactly expresses this truth: they talk of 'speaking to the motion'. It is true; men do speak to a motion, not about it: they talk to a topic. Women talk to each other; that is why their conversations are frightfully fascinating, but too terrible for us to listen to for long without running away.

Do you remember how Thackeray cries out, 'O les laches que les hommes!' when George Warrington and Lord Castlewood rush from the room merely because the young American girl has begun a sweet satiric conversation with old Beatrix Esmond?[3] It is almost the truest thing in Thackeray. Our sex is not strong or bold enough to endure that agony of directly personal conversation in which women are supreme. We must have a topic – an impersonal one. And as I told my admirable lady friend, a male friend becomes a comrade when one has forgotten him. To forget a male friend is only to behave like a comrade. But to forget a woman friend is only to behave like a cad. She is herself; he is the club.

But if either that lady or any other lady really wants to know whether she and her sex should share masculine camaraderie; whether they would really be stronger and happier by doing so; whether, in short, we are in such a matter keeping them out of something they would naturally enjoy, I am just now in a position to enlighten them, by giving them an instance, realistically exact and universally typical, of what our masculine comradeship really is.

****

If any lady wants to know what she is letting herself in for if she goes in for Comradeship, what really happens when comrades meet together, this is what happens. It happened yesterday morning. I was breakfasting with a mob of graduates and undergraduates of one of our great Universities, and the whole company was broken up into groups of two or three extravagantly engaged in some argument. I myself was engaged in two arguments. I was trying to prove to an Agnostic on my right that there was such a place as Heaven, and to an Imperialist on my left that there was such a place as England: when suddenly all our minor clamours were cloven with a monstrous and crashing noise from the other end of the table. Ten men were talking at once, three were beating on the table in pure passion, one was screaming above the din, and then (as is common in such crises) there was, for an instant, an unmeaning silence, and then the voice of one of the best orators of the Union rose, piercing and pathetic, throbbing up to the echoes of the roof, alone.

'I do not say that the corridor ran the whole length of the train. What I say, what I say emphatically and with the full responsibility of my intellect, is that it ran on the left-hand side of our carriage. And I know that I speak the truth'. We all rushed to the spot. I dropped England with one hand and Heaven with the other. I craned my neck to find out what it was all about. It was about this very profound and urgent question: Whether when three persons present travelled to Scotland about two years ago in a luncheon car, the shape of that car had been such that there was a corridor down the left-hand side or a kind of passage down the middle. Only three persons present had ever seen the car, and they could not agree; but we soon took it out of their puny hands. We argued it in the abstract. We discussed whether in the nature of things the passage would have been in the middle. I founded a sect of my own, midway between the Orthodox Passagist and the Extreme Corridorians' position. Some held that the nature of the luncheon should be taken into account in all evidence of the shape of the luncheon car. We made maps of the car with forks and spoons on the table, and little lumps of sugar to show where the people sat. The whole discussion took nearly two hours.

But, indeed, temporal measurements cannot express its length, for we talked as if we were the immortal gods and had all eternity before us: for to be outside time is one of the strange elements of fraternity. We were only interrupted by some academic custom, which required that the Union officials should be photographed. And even then one of them moved. He kept on quivering and stirring until the photographer broke into a pathetic complaint. Then he, in return, broke out, 'I never denied that there was a case for the corridor at the side. What I said –'. But we crushed him, reluctantly. All this is, to the best of my recollection, quite true.

****

I fancy that I do not see any very approving expression on the faces of my lady friends. They are not moved by this Homeric war. They feel, perhaps, that the question of whether one luncheon car two years ago was of a particular shape was not an urgent question. They feel that when argued by eighteen noisy youths for two hours it might even have become a tiring question. O mightiest of all things, O mothers of the gods, they are only little things that you do not understand, only a few sports and follies of the stags of the herd. Be you content as you are secure: you understand everything except comradeship.

Notes
1. *A CASE OF COMRADES*: Reprinted in *AWD*, pp. 18–21.
2. *When two or three ... midst of them*: See Matthew 18:20: 'For where two or three are gathered together in my name, there am I in the midst of them'.
3. *Thackeray cries out ... Beatrix Esmond?*: *The Virginians* (1857–9) ch. 73.

March 21, 1908.

ON MR. KIPLING.

Mr. Rudyard Kipling, always admirable in describing travels, has been making, in 'The Morning Post', another attempt to understand the English people.[1] He cannot explain that; but he does explain a great deal. His misunderstanding of England is due to the accident of India, where he thought he was studying the English as compared with foreigners, where he was really studying the European as compared with Orientals. In Asia one realises Europe; it is in France and Germany that one realises England.

Imperialism cannot be so entirely un-English as it looks at first sight to an Englishman. It must draw some sustenance from the original stuff of the English, who, of all white men, hated Imperialism the most. Superficially, as a matter of common sense, it is quite clear that Imperialism is anti-English; the point is not worth arguing. The one quite distinctive thing about England has been that almost alone among Christian countries it has never had the vision of the Eagle and the Imperial Crown.[2] The primary English trait was a sort of cosy contempt for Caesarism and the great dreams of centralisation. A man who does not know this simply does not know the smell and taste of England. He could not tell a German thought from an English with his eyes shut, as they say of connoisseurs. Such men are commonly Imperialists, either because, like Lord Milner, they have really left their own country, or, like Lord Beaconsfield, have never had a country. So much is plain enough. But, after all, as I have said, there must be some English element in Imperialism or it could not have made even its superficial conquest or obtained its brief and dying influence. Aliens did most of the business, but, surely, not all. I was always convinced that Imperialism had some English element concealed about it somewhere, and when I read Mr. Kipling's article I suddenly saw what it was.

Genuine Englishmen must hate Imperialism as a force, but we can almost love it as a weakness. And it is, after all, a weakness, and in some ways quite an

English one. But I owe the revelation of this to Mr. Kipling, to whom I also owe thanks for so much merely literary pleasure.

****

This is the way the weakness works, or, rather, the way in which it shirks. Our nation is one of the four or five great peoples which make up the European power. When England was really a great nation, it compared itself with other great nations. But Imperialism means simply this: that England invents a lot of small nations to compare herself with. Instead of thinking about the noble and dangerous Commonwealths which are at once our rivals and our brethren, we think about our children, because they are small copies of ourselves. We think of the Colonies, in short, and write solemnly about them, as Mr. Kipling does, because we feel safer in that mental world than in the keen mental world of the Europe to which we really belong. Thus Mr. Kipling will say, with inimitable gravity, 'A man told me once – but I never tried the experiment – that each of our Four Races light and handle fire in their own way'.[3] Thus also he will speak of the Seven Seas,[4] or the Seven Nations, or the Seventeen Bloods, or what not – all with awful capital letters.

There is something pathetic in this attempt to invent an old world legend in a hurry, to put up at the last moment a pre-historic tradition that does not arise out of history. There are no Four Races. There are no such things, even spiritually, as the Seven Nations of the Empire. But there are such things spiritually as the Seven Champions of Christendom,[5] and one of them called St. George. There is also such a thing as the Dragon, and St. George still has it in him to conquer it; but the point is that if St. George is going to keep up his credit among the other Champions, who are gentlemen like himself, he must really kill it. But he can keep up his credit with his own children and dependents by merely telling them stories about how it was killed. We are safe to make some impression on crude and half-baked peoples of our own blood, merely because we are bound to be in certain ways more civilized than they. But we cannot hope to be more civilized than the Europeans who are our equals; we cannot hope to be more civilized than civilization. Therefore if we are to impress Europe (as we have frequently done in the past) it must be by doing something strikingly worthy of a high civilization, something that our equals have not done. Thus, we impressed Europe by Shakespeare, by Nelson and the naval legend, and by the fact that we practically founded the science of political economy. But it is a great bother to found a science and to write as well as Shakespeare. On the other hand, it is not difficult to found Colonies (they found themselves), and it is very easy to write rather better than Colonial poets.[6]

Imperialism is the pleasure of living with one's inferiors. It is true, of course, that Mr. Kipling and other Imperialists pretend that the Colonies are England's superiors, but they do not think so in their hearts, for the simple reason that nobody could. But those who with weak vanity play the patron always do have this magnanimous affectation; hardly any man is such a cad as to feel at ease among fools and tell them so. When Addison

> Gave his little Senate laws,
> And sat attentive to his own applause –[7]

he also complimented his protégés and ranked Tickell as a poet much higher than he deserved.[8] So in the cosy Anglo-Saxon club there is no offensive domination of the central and civilized country; but that country has a pleasant feeling all the same that no one in the company can possibly claim to be more central or more civilized. It will contain no element vitally disturbing or dangerously different, nothing to remind us of the arts or arms of our rivals, of stronger revolutions or of subtler creeds.

****

So I was happy, for I had found something English in the thing after all – the English quality of cosiness, horribly over-done and degenerate, but still recognisable.

But we have dreamed too long. We must return to the real world, where there are real nations with real armies, not toy nations with toy armies. We must think about the serious European system to which we belong, and not think exclusively about this half-fanciful system which is supposed to belong to us. And the more we do think the more we shall see that in the last resort we shall stand or fall as an ordinary European nation, helped by whatever we have in us of ordinary Christian courage and ordinary Christian common sense, helped by our own power to feed a people, to keep an exchequer, or to fight a campaign; but helped very little indeed by scattered settlements in odd corners or by visions from the verge of the world. On the best estimate these Colonies of ours are in their childhood; on the worst, in their second childhood. In neither case can we safely talk of them as if they were champions of gigantic might.

I am very fond of Fleet-street, but I am not satisfied with it. I notice occasional traces of dirt, and objects which appear to be ragged little boys; I am aware that some of the journals are disgusting, and some of the journalists more so. But I should not be content if a man were to say to me in a tea-shop in Fleet-street: 'Yes, this heart of London may be dim and cruel, but away on the mountains of Brixton a race of young giants are dancing and wrestling in the sun. In the freer air of Wimbledon men are become as gods. The people of Ealing have re-entered Eden, and naked heroes with tossing golden hair stand on the peaks of Upper Tooting. Do not take this narrow view of London; think of the new nations which are ever pressing forward beyond West Hampstead and beyond South Croydon, conquering the wild earth for man'. I should say to him: 'No, my friend. We have all sinned, and our city is in the deuce of a mess; but this *is* our city. The heart of the Empire is in a bad way; but this *is* the heart of the Empire. In the hour of plague or riot I will not call on the gods of Wimbledon, because I do not believe in them. I once met a man from Brixton and he was not a giant. In all our dirt and agony I will still call on what is best in London, and what is best is here. I will find all that can save us between the column of Nelson and the cross of St. Paul's; I will lift up my eyes to Ludgate-hill, from whence cometh my help.'[9]

Notes

1. *Mr. Rudyard Kipling ... understand the English People*: 'Letters to the Family', 2, *Morning Post*, 19 March 1908, p. 7; reprinted in *Letters of Travel* (1892–1913) (London: Macmillan & Co., 1920). For Rudyard Kipling, see 'A Kipling Reader', *DN*, 21 February 1901, Volume 1, p. 31, n. 3 above.
2. *The one quite distinctive thing ... the Eagle and the Imperial Crown*: From 1889 to 1918 the coat of arms of the German Empire was an eagle surmounted by a crown.
3. *Thus Mr. Kipling will say ... light and handle fire in their own way*: See n. 1 above.
4. *the Seven Seas*: A reference to Kipling's book of verse, *The Seven Seas* (London: Methuen, 1897).
5. *Seven Champions of Christendom*: The expression comes from Richard Johnson's *Famous Historie of the Seaven Champions of Christendom* (1596); the Seven Champions are St George, St Andrew, St Patrick, St Denys, St James Boanerges, St Anthony the Lesser and St David – the patron saints of England, Scotland, Ireland, France, Spain, Portugal and Wales.
6. *it is very easy to write rather better than Colonial poets*: See 'Patriotic Poetry', *DN*, 29 November 1901, Volume 1, pp. 278–81 above.
7. *Gave his ... own applause*: Slightly misquoted from Alexander Pope's 'Epistle to Dr Arbuthnot' (1734); and the lines are not obviously about Addison:
    Dreading even fools, by flatterers besieged,
    And so obliging, that he ne'er obliged;
    Like Cato, give his little senate laws,
    And sit attentive to his own applause;
    While wits and templars every sentence raise,
    And wonder with a foolish face of praise: –
    Who but must laugh, if such a man there be?
8. *Tickell ... deserved*: Thomas Tickell (1685–1740), was a minor English poet and Whig apologist who owed most of his success to Addison's patronage. There is a not uncomplimentary biography of him in Johnson's *Lives of the Poets* (1779–81).
9. *lift ... help*: See Psalm 121:1: 'I will lift up mine eyes unto the hills, from whence cometh my help.'

March 28, 1908.

ENGLAND AND CARICATURE.[1]

———

English literature (by which I mean the literature of England, not the journalism of the British Empire) has extracted and emphasised one very splendid thing; you never hear of it in patriotic speeches or in books about race or nationality, but it is the great contribution of the English temperament to the best life of the world. So far as it can be defined, it may be called the humane use of caricature. It consists in calling a man ugly as a compliment. If we wish to appreciate it we must remember the part played by satire and epigram in the largest part of human literature. Almost everywhere laughter has been used as a lash; if revelations were made about a man's wig or wooden leg, an enemy had done it. Men reminded a man maliciously of his bodily weakness, especially if it was a set-off against his worldly power.

Take, for instance, the case of two of the greatest riders and conquerors among the children of men. Julius Caesar[2] was bald, and he could not cover it with all his laurels. It was always morally as well as physically his unprotected spot. His enemies could say: 'You have conquered Gaul, but you are bald. You have faced Pompey in arms and Cicero[3] in argument, but for all that you are bald'. And he felt it himself, I think, for he was a vain man; the head of Caesar was like the heel of Achilles.[4]

Take, again, that huge hunter and fighter who hurled himself on shore at Hastings and created our country by a raid: William the Norman.[5] If ever a man might have regarded himself as successful his name was William of Falaise. But in his later years (like many other great men) he grew rather stout, and when a Frenchman made a joke about it William went mad with vanity and violent shame. The mountain quivered to its foundations. He struggled into the saddle, and led a crusade against the Comic Frenchman: shouted like a man possessed that he would burn cities and waste provinces to wipe out the insult, and passing like a pillar of fire at night across the perishing land, brought his own wild life to an end, was deserted by all men, died and stank upon the stones.[6]

****

Such is the power of one really vulgar joke to pull down the mighty from their seat.[7] And for such purposes it is bitter but wholesome; it is right that some slave should whisper the 'hominem memento te'.[8] He who seems more than man, ought to be reminded that he is only man. It should be done, even if it can only be done by telling him that he is less than a man – less by a leg or so. It is quite right that the poor man who has no hat should publicly comment on the fact that the rich man has no hair. But, though it redresses the balance, it does not bring about the purest state of feeling. We do not reconcile by pointing out the balance and distribution of glass eyes and wooden legs in all classes of the community. It produces equality, but hardly fraternity. And in some literatures it has run riot until it became utterly devilish, and men have earned as much shame by inventing physical epigrams as if they had invented physical tortures.

It is just here, however, that the most characteristic English literature, from Chaucer to Dickens, has its singular glory. It is as coarse as any literature; but it is far less malignant than most. The young fool in 'David Copperfield' said that he would rather 'be knocked down by a man with blood in him than picked up by a man without';[9] and understanding 'blood' not as gentility, but as generosity, I incline to agree with him. Certainly, if what I wanted was kindness, I would rather be knocked down by Fielding[10] than picked up by Voltaire. The only really harsh English writer was not English. For Swift[11] was an Irishman, and a very typical Irishman – disdainfully courageous, consistent yet perverse, above all like his countryman, Mr. Bernard Shaw, inhuman through the very sincerity of his humanitarianism. But this is a digression, which is repugnant to my feelings. The point is that this English literary style, coarse and yet kind, has done more than anything else to create the possibility of a genial grotesque. As I have said, Julius Caesar was bald and tried to cover his baldness with laurels. But Mr. Pickwick was bald and we feel that his head would be defaced by laurels. Nay, we feel that his head would be defaced by hair. We like him eternally bald.

****

Similarly, as I said, William the Conqueror (like the man in the 'Bab Ballads')[12] 'owned his chief and only grief was being very bulky';[13] he was fat, and furious when reminded of it. But, again, Mr. Pickwick was fat; but we do not wish him otherwise. Rather we feel that his rotundity is like the rotundity of the world; that he is swelling till he takes on the enormous curves of the universe. 'Phiz'[14] dwelt upon the baldness of Pickwick and the fatness of Pickwick because he liked him and them. The satirists of most societies would have insisted on these points as being the weak points of some bad man; but 'Phiz' insists on them as if they were the strong points even of a good one. The French prince called William fat because he had had too much of him. But Dickens made Pickwick fat because you cannot have too much of a good thing. In this matter, however, the pictures of 'Pickwick' are even more important than the letterpress. And, indeed, it will commonly be found that the English love of clear comicality for its own sake will be seen better in the old, clear, comic illustrations by 'Phiz' and Cruikshank[15] than in any other place. Close your eyes and call up before your mind, say, an old English illustration of an angry admiral with a wooden leg. The wooden leg is insisted on, but not with contempt, and yet, again, not with commiseration. It is insisted on with gusto, as if the Admiral had grown his wooden leg by the sheer energy of his character. In any ordinary satire, in any ordinary sentimentality, the point would be that the Admiral had lost a leg. Here it is rather the point that he has gained a wooden leg.

I had intended to extend this article until it included the Other and Darker side of the picture and to point out to you how this English geniality has been twisted into snobbishness, and how a catastrophe will come if we are any longer content with that falsification. But I find I must put this off at least until next week, when (for all I know) the catastrophe will have occurred.

Notes
1. *ENGLAND AND CARIACATURE*: Reprinted in *LL*, pp. 139–42, excluding the parentheses in the first sentence and excluding also the last paragraph.
2. *Julius Caesar*: Gaius Julius Caesar (100 BC–44 BC), 'twas a Roman General and statesman who conquered Gaul (51 BC) and invaded Britain (54 BC).
3. *faced Cicero in argument*: Marcus Tullius Cicero (103 BC–43 BC), was a Roman philosopher, statesman and lawyer. Cicero was initially an opponent of Caesar's, fearing that Caesar's political and military activity would undermine the Republic and the Senate; though they were reconciled after 48 BC.
4. *the heel of Achilles*: i.e., the head of Caesar was a point of weakness. It was prophesied of the infant Achilles that he would die in battle from an arrow in the foot. His mother Thetis dipped him in the waters of the Styx, which were supposed to confer invulnerability; but because she held him by his heel the waters did not touch it, and he was killed by a poisoned arrow shot by Paris that struck him there. The story comes from the unfinished *Achilleid* (1:122–122; 269–270; 480–481) of Publius Papinius Statius (*c.* AD 45–96).
5. *William the Norman*: William I, King of England and Duke of Normandy (1027/8–87), was born at Falaise. He invaded Britain in 1066, defeating King Harold at the Battle of Hastings, and claiming the English Crown in accordance with his belief that he was the rightful heir to Edward the Confessor.
6. *But in his later years ... died and stank upon the stones*: The story that William besieged and burnt the town of Mantes in 1087 because he was so angry that King Philip I of France had described him as looking like a pregnant woman is in William of Malmes-

bury's *Gesta regum Anglorum* (1125) (ed. and trans. by R. A. B. Mynors, R. M. Thomson and M. Winterbottom) (Oxford: Oxford University Press, 1998). It was during the siege that William suffered the injuries (by falling from his horse) from which he died on 9 September 1087.

7. *pull down the mighty from their seat*: see Luke 1:52.
8. *it is right that some slave should whisper the 'hominem memento te'*: Tertullian, *Apologeticus* 33: 'Respice post te: hominem te memento' ('Look behind you: remember that you are [but] a man').
9. *The young fool ... picked up by a man without*: *David Copperfield*, ch. 25, 'Good and Bad Angels'.
10. *Fielding*: Henry Fielding; see 'The "Good Man" of the Eighteenth Century', *DN*, 22 March 1901, Volume 1, p. 66, n. 7 above.
11. *Swift*: Jonathan Swift; see 'The Kipling Reader', *DN*, 21 February 1901, Volume 1, p. 31, n. 1 above.
12. *Bab Ballads*: See 'The Divine Parody', *DN*, September 9, 1901, Volume 1, p. 179, n. 4 above.
13. *'owned his chief ... very bulky'*: A Discontented Sugar Broker', *The Bab Ballads* (London: Routledge, 1898), p. 139:
    > His knocker advertised no dun,
    > No losses made him sulky,
    > He had one sorrow – only one –
    > He was extremely bulky.
    > A man must be, I beg to state,
    > Exceptionally fortunate
    > Who owns his chief
    > And only grief
    > Is – being very bulky.
14. *'Phiz'*: 'Phiz' was the pseudonym of Dickens's illustrator Hablot Knight Browne (1815–82).
15. *Cruikshank*: George Cruikshank (1792–1878), was an English caricaturist and political cartoonist; he illustrated Dickens's *Sketches by Boz* (1836), *The Mudfog Papers* (1837–8) and *Oliver Twist* (1838).

April 4, 1908.

THE SNOB.

This article is only the peroration of my article last week. It seems to be quite in the noblest rules of oratory that the peroration should be a little longer than the speech. But last Saturday I suggested that English caricature had really discovered a certain secret. It does manage to exaggerate a man without insulting him. It manages to elongate his nose without pulling his nose. But it would be disastrously wrong to praise this quality, or even to mention it, without blaming it also.

And I fear it is unquestionable that the same force which causes us to possess the most genial caricature in the world leads us also to possess the most inefficient caricature in the world: a caricature which is quite useless for almost all purposes of political reform. To us caricature is a toy; we have entirely forgotten that it can be a weapon. None of the arrows of modern English satire ever hit the people at whom they were aimed – because they were not aimed at them. English exaggerations come not out of a just hatred, but out of a sort of unjust love. The satirist ends by liking the caricature more than he dislikes the person caricatured. Dickens began by being bored by some pompous American, but he ended by being delighted with the pompous American – with Mr. Elijah Pogram, an American of his own invention.[1] In men like Dickens this mixture of malice with a sort of mad charity is a splendid thing, and can do little but good.

But in later developments the weakness of this English method has been shown; and especially in this, that it has lent its assistance to the evolution of the snob. For the snob really was evolved, like all nasty things. It is a good general rule that bad things are evolved like vermin; but good things are created, like the chemicals for killing vermin. Leave any object to itself, and you will not be leaving it to death. You will be leaving it to the basest form of life; in a week or a year the cast shoe will lie swarming with insects, the neglected society will be swarming with snobs.

Under a strict aristocracy there are no snobs. There are slaves, perhaps – that is a matter of definition – but snobs in the true sense there can hardly be. For snobbishness implies a certain doubt and uneasiness in the snob; it implies that combination of external push with internal insecurity which is the essence of all vulgarity. The serf may be dignified because he has his own position: he is an equal inferior. But the snob is an inferior equal. It is essential to the snobbish soul that it should be on equal terms with the great without feeling equal to them. The snob's delight is to rise high and have all the time the secret joy, the purple ecstacy [sic] of feeling low. In this matter there is a distinction very important to remember. We naturally picture the noble war of this world as being between idols and ideals. But in one way an idol is much better than an ideal. If you have a dangerous idol, you will only worship it, and you must worship something. But if you have a dangerous ideal, you will not only worship it, you will imitate it. If you have a crocodile for an idol, you are a heathen, but still a man. But if you have a crocodile for an ideal, you may seek to get rid of manhood.

There is a great difference between making a thing a god and making it an ideal; for idealisation implies imitation. An Egyptian in old time could make a cat his god; but he did not mew. He could offer awful adoration to the cat and prostrate himself in the twilight of its temple, and then come out again a warrior, royal and erect, ready for the chariot and the charge of battle. He did not come out on all fours. So long as we worship something because we cannot resemble it we are comparatively safe; no sun worshipper tries to shine like the sun. But when we worship something because we ought to resemble it then there enters that dangerous thing called Christianity, which is the worship of something which is a marvel, but also a model.

Now the snob is the romantic slave, the slave as idealist. He dreams of becoming like the thing that he worships. In systematically oligarchical communities he has no such dream, because the thing cannot be done. I do not lie awake at night and weep because I am not the king; because that post is beyond possible social ambition. Or, to take a more honourable example. I take off my hat to ladies; yet I feel no degradation in doing so. This is because, allowing for the most adventurous career, I imagine that I shall never be a lady. But if one's respect for a woman were mixed up with the idea of some day being a woman, another and perilous element would appear – probably the element of snobbishness. I should begin to imitate the attitudes and the costume of women – which would be disastrous. Yet this is the whole trouble of the snob. The snob has made the prince of this world not merely his god to be worshipped, but his ideal to be imitated. He does not merely go on all fours before the cat; he goes on all fours because the cat does. He does not merely offer his riches to the rich man; he offers them to show that he also is rich.

This was the tragic sin of England in the nineteenth century; this may be her tragic punishment in the twentieth. The issue between sacred aristocracy and sacred democracy was put before her by the [French] Revolution, and she had not the courage to choose. We might have chosen equality and led the world; we might have chosen inequality, consistent and disciplined inequality, and hardly have produced a single snob. Inaccessible aristocrats are forgotten as outcasts are forgotten. Or, if you like to put it so, they are forgotten as angels are forgotten. If the castle of hereditary nobility had been kept completely guarded and sealed, we might have forgotten altogether the foolish garrison inside. For a fortress completely closed is only like a hill; a mere bulky feature in the landscape. If, on the other hand, we had surrendered the fortress of the few and let the people enter it, we might now be the first influence in Europe. But in an evil hour we took that maddest of courses, a middle course; we allowed it to be known that a back door was open in the rear of the premises if any desperate burglar desired to enter by it. The result was what might have been expected. Several desperate burglars did enter by it, and are now peers of the realm. But all the sane, masculine, modest people stopped outside. Yet, however sane and modest they were, they could not help dreaming of that open door. And in their dreams they became snobs.

****

And while the brain of every English class is hag-ridden with this hideous romance of social advancement, while the agony of every man is not so much that he belongs to his class, but rather that he does not belong to his class, but half belongs to the class above it, the whole thing is completed by the abuse of the old English kindly caricature. 'Punch' and other comic papers describe a monstrous snob who does not exist for the delight of all the mild snobs who do exist. Sir Gorgius Midas in the old 'Punch' pictures can be enjoyed uproariously by any parvenu.[2] For the very first thing that a real parvenu does is to avoid being like Sir Gorgius Midas. The real vulgarian does not have crimson plush cushions or a son who calls himself 'Enery. He finds it quite necessary and quite easy to have artistic upholstering for his house and academic polishing for his son. The evil is not in what he does, but in what he desires. He has a mythology of this world; he looks up to those above him as gods whom he may possibly join. He does exactly that one unpardonable thing which neither the great blasphemers nor the great saints have done – he takes this world quite seriously.

Notes
1. *the pompous American ... of his own invention*: '[T]he Honourable Elijah Pogram, Member of Congress; one of the master-minds of our country, sir' is introduced in chapter 34 of *Martin Chuzzlewit*.
2. *Sir Gorgius Midas ... parvenu*: Sir Gorgius Midas the plutocrat is one of the characters invented for *Punch* by George du Maurier. On not being made a peer Sir Gorgius said: 'Why, it's enough to make a man turn *Radical*, 'anged if it ain't, to think of sich services as mine bein' rewarded with no 'igher title than what's bestowed on a heminent Sawbones, or a Hingerneer, or a Littery Man, or even a successful Hartist!' (*Punch*, 15 May 1880).

April 11, 1908.

ON MRS. EDDY AND A NEW CREED.

It cannot be too often repeated that if we are to love our enemies we must fight them. Sincere strife is a process of purification; it cleanses us from hate. Many modern writers have sneered at the celebrated command of Christ on this subject; but then these modern writers are men whose affections and aversions are alike in a meaner world. They have no enemies; they have only tiresome friends – friends whom they discuss in an unfriendly spirit. The man who is noble enough to have enemies is already almost noble enough to love them. Bad blood is not created by fighting, but rather by the absence of fighting; the foulest epidemic on earth is a frustrated dispute. This idea of the safety-valve of argument used to be an old Liberal doctrine; but its actual effect among us has been falsified in quite a curious way. The old idea of liberality was that it was a good thing that all the creeds should dispute freely;[1] the new idea of liberality is that there should be no creeds to dispute. The old English Protestant (whom I admire to the verge of idolatry) said, 'I refuse on Liberal principles to boil this poisonous Papist, though I feel very much inclined to do so'. But the new English Protestant practically says, 'I am no longer a Protestant, and under these circumstances I think it is like his cheek to go on being a Papist'.

****

The case of Mrs. Eddy has been recently stirred up in this paper by the pen of my friend Mr. Conrad Noel[2] and by others. Superficially, Mrs. Eddy cannot, at any rate, be accused of omitting the intolerant element of religion. Her anathemas, though not quite comprehensible verbally, at least leave us with no tendency to mistake the thing for a benediction. If you enter her priesthood as a passionate adorer you are pretty certain to find yourself one fine morning being described as the beast with seven horns. I can imagine nothing more dangerous than to be Mrs. Eddy's follower, except, indeed, to be her leader. But it is not with any of these secondary and detailed matters in the Christian Science controversy that I am concerned here. I am concerned only to point out that the case of Mrs. Eddy is one of the strongest cases of the proposition that we grow bitter, not through disputing dogmatically, but through not disputing dogmatically. The modern world thinks that there is something arid, pompous, and arrogant about an impersonal dogma; therefore controversialists, being forbidden to be impersonal, are obliged to be personal. I can remember when orthodox Liberal speakers were practically forbidden to denounce Mr. Chamberlain[3] for being an Imperialist; the natural and soothing result was that they denounced him for being a cad. We are discouraged from discussing the theory, so we have to discuss the practice – and the practitioners.

In the same way we are not allowed to discuss Mrs. Eddy's doctrine; so we have to discuss Mrs. Eddy. Personally I do not much care for either of them; but there is this great difference – that Mrs. Eddy's heresy seems to me a great and vast error, while she herself seems a trifling error, a mere clerical error, so to speak. She is a small person, but to do her justice, she has made a big mistake. I have a suspicion that most of the real heretics were small persons who made big mistakes. But in our present mental atmosphere we are only allowed to discuss the person; we are not allowed to discuss the mistakes. That is, we are not allowed to discuss them violently, with intellectual battery and bloodshed, which is the only satisfactory way of discussing anything.

****

A man in a modern magazine, a man in Parliament, a man in the intellectual atmosphere of our society (now, thank God, dying), is always discouraged, often prevented, from attacking any beliefs with bitterness or abhorrence. He is forbidden to say that a certain creed is shameful, or detestable, or devilish. The only result is that he says that the man who holds it is shameful and detestable and devilish; and tries to make out that it is the man's own fault. We are always blaming a man for spoiling an idea; we never really dare to blame an idea for spoiling a man. And the strongest and strangest evidence of this reluctance to attack the dangerous dogma itself, this disposition to fall back on the personal accidents, is the case of Mrs. Eddy; the mere fact that she has in practical fact been attacked only along the personal line. Christian Science has crept silently into hundreds of English homes, into thousands of American; sooner or later it was inevitable that the idea should be fought. And yet the idea was not fought; when the first movement came from the other side it was not against the idea, but against the person.

The cultivated people of our time will generally tend to say of Christian Science that it is a grand and pure philosophy preached, perhaps, by unbalanced or unpleasant people. But I, for one, should say exactly the opposite. I say that Christian Science is a mean and disgusting philosophy, preached by people who are quite nice – preached, in fact, by many of my personal friends. They are all right; it is only their creed that comes from hell. I use the phrase quite calmly and quite literally. The doctrine that pain and death are not real at all, except in so far as their victims are cowardly enough to submit to them, is a diabolical doctrine, obviously calculated to produce all the purely diabolical qualities such as intellectual cruelty and contempt for the weak. To tell any man that it is his own fault that he has the toothache is to cease to be a Christian while uttering eight words. If there is one thing that is against the whole trend and tide of Christianity, it is any method which permits the man called strong to triumph over those whom he calls weak-minded. Christ came on earth to smash the man who felt himself strong. And He did in the most effective and final manner smash the man who felt himself strong; for He opposed to him the God who felt Himself weak. Human beings henceforward were not to be humiliated by the limitations of pain and death; for Deity itself has admitted them.

Christian Science says that pain is not a reality. Christianity says that pain is so great a reality that even the Creator could feel it. Christian Science says that a man need not think of death at all. Christianity says that even God thought of it with awe. And the ethical results of the two principles have been exactly what might have been expected. Marred by a million other mistakes, betrayed and tortured through the agony of eighteen centuries, Christianity has never lost its strongest and most distinctive note, the physical note; the talk of the body and the blood. Ever since the Crucifixion a certain actuality, and, therefore, a certain sanctity, has clung round the hard pain of prosaic men. Men in misery were sometimes, in hours of impatience, dismissed as nuisances who could not be cured. But they were never despised as cowards who ought to have cured themselves. Even in the refusal there was pity; therefore, even in the pity there was respect. And while Christianity has run for so many centuries and Christian Science not yet for one, yet Christian Science also has already produced its own tone of manners and even its own type of face, a type of face which provokes the Christian to experiments upon the reality of the body.

Notes
1. *The old ideal of liberality ... dispute freely*: Chesterton no doubt has in the back of his mind here John Stuart Mill's *On Liberty* (1859), in which precisely this free discussion of 'all the creeds' is commended. One suspects that in less haste he would have said 'the old idea of liberalism' rather than 'liberality' in this sentence.
2. *The case of Mrs Eddy ... pen of my friend Mr. Conrad Noel*: C. Noel, 'The Founder of Christian Science', *DN*, 1 April 1908, p. 4. Noel was reviewing a book by Lyman P. Powell

entitled *Christian Science: The Faith and the Founder*. He was not impressed by Powell's analysis of the weaknesses of the 'faith'; the 'real value of the volume', he claimed, lay in demonstrating that Mrs Eddy relied heavily on the work of others – principally, Phineas Quimby – in developing 'Christian Science'; this she had denied in her book *Science and Health* (1875). For Conrad le Despenser Roden Noel; see 'A Memory of the Last General Election', *DN*, 1 July 1905, Volume 3, p. 142, n. 6 above.

3. *Mr. Chamberlain*: Joseph Chamberlain; see 'The Decline of Satire', *DN*, 14 February 1902, Volume 1, p. 341, n. 9, above.

April 18, 1908.

THE TOWER.

And Some Remarks on Geography and Character.[1]

I have been standing where everyone has stood, opposite the great Belfry Tower of Bruges, and thinking, as everyone has thought (though not, perhaps, said), that it is built in defiance of all decencies of architecture. It is made in deliberate disproportion to achieve the one startling effect of height. It is a church on stilts. But this sort of sublime deformity is characteristic of the whole fancy and energy of these Flemish cities. Flanders has the flattest and most prosaic of landscapes, but the most violent and extravagant of buildings. Here Nature is tame; it is civilization that is untameable. Here the fields are as flat as a paved square; but, on the other hand, the streets and roofs are as uproarious as a forest in a great wind. The waters of wood and meadow slide as smoothly and meekly as if they were in the London water-pipes. But the parish pump is wild and carved with all the creatures out of the wilderness. Part of this is true, of course, of all art. We talk of wild animals, but the wildest animal is man. There are sounds in music that are more ancient and awful than the cry of the strangest beast at night. And so also there are buildings that are shapeless in their strength, seeming to lift themselves slowly like monsters from the primal mire, and there are spires that seem to fly up suddenly like a startled bird.

****

This savagery even in stone is the expression of the special spirit in humanity. All the beasts of the field are respectable: it is only man who has broken loose. All animals are domestic animals: only man is ever undomestic. All animals are tame animals: it is only we who are wild. And doubtless, also, while this queer energy is common to all human art, it is also generally characteristic of Christian art among the arts of the world. This is what people really mean when they say that Christianity is barbaric and arose in ignorance. As a matter of historic fact, it didn't: it arose in the most equably civilized period the world has ever seen.

But it is true that there is something in it that breaks the outline of perfect and conventional beauty, something that dots with anger the blind eyes of the Apollo and lashes to a cavalry charge the horses of the Elgin Marbles. Christianity is savage, in the sense that it is primeval: there is in it a touch of the nigger hymn. I remember a debate in which I had praised a militant music in ritual; and someone asked me if I could imagine Christ walking down the street behind a brass band. I said I could imagine it with the greatest ease: for Christ definitely approved a natural noisiness at a great moment. When the street children shouted too loud, certain priggish disciples did begin to rebuke them in the name of good taste. He said: 'If these were silent, the very stones would cry out'.[2] With those words He called up all the wealth of artistic creation that has been founded on this creed. With those words He founded Gothic architecture. For in a town like this, which seems to have grown Gothic as a wood grows leaves, anywhere and anyhow, any odd brick or moulding may be carved into a shouting face. The front of vast buildings is thronged with open mouths, angels praising God, or devils defying Him. Rock itself is racked and twisted until it seems to scream. The miracle is accomplished; the very stones cry out.

But though this furious fancy is certainly a speciality of men among creatures, and of Christian art among arts, it is still most notable in the art of Flanders. All Gothic buildings are full of extravagant things in detail; but this is an extravagant thing in design. All Christian temples worth talking about have gargoyles; but Bruges' Belfry is a gargoyle. It is an unnaturally long-necked animal, like a giraffe. The same impression of exaggeration is forced on the mind at every corner of a Flemish town. And if anyone asks 'Why did the people of these flat countries instinctively raise these riotous and towering monuments?' the only answer one can give is: 'Because they were the people of these flat countries'. If anyone asks 'why the men of Bruges sacrificed architecture and everything to the sense of dizzy and divine heights?' we can only answer: 'Because Nature gave them no encouragement to do so'.

****

As I stare at the Belfry, I think with a sort of smile of some of my friends in London who are quite sure of how children will turn out if you give them what they call 'the right environment'. It is a troublesome thing, environment, for it sometimes works positively and sometimes negatively, and more often between the two. A beautiful environment may make a child love beauty; it may make him bored with beauty; most likely the two effects will mix and neutralize each other. Most likely, that is, the environment will make hardly any difference at all. In the scientific style of history (which was recently fashionable, and is still conventional) we always had a list of countries that had owed their characteristics to their physical conditions.

Thus, Spaniards (it was said) are passionate because their country is hot; Scandinavians adventurous because their country is cold; Englishmen naval because they are islanders; Switzers free because they are mountaineers. It is all very nice in its way. Only unfortunately I am quite certain that I could make up quite as long a list exactly contrary in its argument, showing that nations always went point blank against the influence of their geographical environment. Thus Spaniards have discovered more continents than Scandinavians, because their hot climate discouraged them from exertion. Thus Dutchmen have fought for their freedom quite as bravely as Switzers, because the Dutch have no mountains. Thus Pagan Greece and Rome and many Mediterranean peoples have specially hated the sea because they had the nicest sea to deal with, the easiest sea to manage. I could extend the list for ever. But however long it was, two examples would certainly stand up in it as pre-eminent and unquestionable. The first is that the Swiss, who live under staggering precipices and spires of eternal snow, have produced no art or literature at all, and are by far the most mundane, sensible, and businesslike people in Europe. The other is that the people of Belgium, who live in a country like a carpet, have, by an inner energy, desired to exalt their towers until they struck the stars.

As it is therefore quite doubtful whether a person will go specially with his environment or specially against his environment I cannot comfort myself with the thought that the modern discussions about environment are of much practical value. But I think I will not write any more about these modern theories, but go on looking at the Belfry of Bruges. I would give them the greater attention if I were not pretty well convinced that the theories will have disappeared a long time before the Belfry.

Notes
1. *The Tower: And Some Remarks on Geography and Character*: Reprinted as 'The Tower', *TT* (2), pp. 109–14.
2. '*He said: 'If these were silent ... cry out*': Luke 19:40.

April 25, 1908.

THE MAN WHO HAS BEEN THERE.

It happens from time to time during some Colonial quarrel or frontier war that a timid and cruel type of journalist urges the practical necessity of methods of barbarism in a war with barbarians. He urges that our racial superiority gives us a claim to dispense in such a case with civilized formulae.

To put the matter more shortly, he urges that because we are white men we have a right to behave like black men. Thus Lord Kitchener permitted the monkeyish obscenity of defiling a grave.[1] Thus in Natal rebellions and such things it is not uncommon to hear it openly said that the British Colonist should kill prisoners. On the same principle (no doubt) in a naval war with the Cannibal Islands the British admiral ought to eat prisoners.

Whenever these things are done or proposed, and whenever they revolt (as naturally they always do) the clean instincts of ordinary white people, it is always hastily said by way of defence of them that they are recommended by the people on the spot. Those who know Zulus best (we are informed) are strongly in favour of torturing them. Those who are really intimate with Kaffirs recommend skinning them alive as the only tactful course. To this superficiality one would be content to reply that such a man was evidently a great deal too intimate with Kaffirs, and had long lost any right even to be argued with as an Englishman. But in truth this argument from the man geographically on the spot, this argument from local opinion has in it an equally obvious, but a much larger and more important fallacy. There is really very little intellectual value in being physically in a place if you are not part of its life and do not see it from the inside. If you are not in the community it is little use to be in the country. If you have neither the luck to be born in England nor the imagination to understand it (and it requires a most Titanic imagination to understand England) you will not really learn much by merely landing in England. British Imperialists and British Unionists trust the tale of the British garrison in India because it is in India; they trust the tale of the Unionist garrison in Ireland because it is in Ireland. But I wonder how many of them would take their policy for Great Britain from the Frenchmen in Leicester-square.

****

In the town of Bruges, from which I have just come, there is a remarkable collection of men on the spot. There are many Englishmen there, studying with philosophic breadth and tenderness the subtleties of Belgium and all the strange things within the circle of the French civilization. They are amazing people, the English at Bruges. There are men of our blood there who have been in that exile for forty years, who will die in a strange land (a dreadful notion, I think), whose bodies are now built up of Flemish bread and Flemish beer. And those men know no more of Flanders than when they left Finsbury Park – probably without paying the rent. They still feel nothing but a few inconveniences, such as they would feel in a day's trip to Boulogne. They never feel the great differences, good or bad, that are behind these inconveniences. They will tell you that the peasants are rude and suspicious. It has never once (in all those years) flashed across their minds that the peasants are rude and suspicious because the peasants are prosperous and free, that they have no squire to teach them deference, and that this grumble of indifference is the reverberation of the French Revolution. They will tell you that the Popish priests have coarse faces. They never think of adding that this is because the priesthood is democratic in its origin. Never once do they fancy for an instant that there may be in the English way of doing things anything singular or questionable; anything anti-civic in our ladder of social ranks, anything unphilosophic in our clatter of sects, anything hateful in our swollen towns, or pitiful in our perishing villages. They see nothing odd in these English things – nay, they see nothing English in them. To them these English things are still simply the order of Nature, though they have not seen the order of Nature for thirty years.

The enlightened and advanced will immediately take one of their insolent short cuts and call the English in Bruges stupid. But they are not stupid in the least: ordinary people are never stupid, though extraordinary people are sometimes silly. Their talk when it is good English gossip, about old English acting or political anecdote, is as pleasant as any in the world: they know as much as I about Parliament, and much more about cricket. The only things they know nothing about are the stones they walk on and the air they breathe.

****

The real explanation of this enigma of exile is quite different: something deeper and more dignified in human nature. It does not arise from human stupidity, but rather from human thought. It arises from this: that every man sees everything in the light of his own theory of things. One does not see Bruges, but a theory of Bruges. The English tourists in Bruges err not through their dulness, but through their excessive and morbid intellectuality. They force their own meaning on everything they see; they do not ask what a thing means, but what they mean by it. They have always held a certain historical and ethnic system, in which England bulked very big as prosperous and practical, while France and Flanders looked very small and were dreamy and decadent. Therefore they see a French peasant with the eye of faith. They see him as poor and comatose: though to the eye of flesh he is quite obviously as rich as a nigger-driver and working like a nigger. The actual physical face of a Flemish Catholic priest is generally good and stupid. But if one of the Bruges English were to write a romance about a Catholic priest he would make his face intelligent and wicked. For so intelligent and so wicked are the faces of priests in the noble twopenny romances of beautiful Battersea, from which we are exiles.

A child will draw a pig seen sideways with two eyes: because he *knows* a pig has two eyes. His philosophy is stronger than his senses. A primitive artist will draw a distant tree as big as one near to him, because he *knows* it is as big. His philosophy is stronger than his senses. So a Protestant will see all Catholic countries as decaying, and vice versa: because the divine intellect and its great conclusions are greater than material things; because religion is the only interpretation of facts. Religion alone gives any sense to the senses.

And now you will say that, after all, I am only an Englishman in Bruges, and am probably not quite right. To which I answer that I am the only Englishman in Bruges who does not think he is quite right: therefore probably I am not quite wrong.

Notes
1. *Thus Lord Kitchener ... defiling a grave*: After his victory at the Battle of Omdurman (2 September 1898) Kitchener ordered the destruction of the tomb of the Mahdi – the first leader of independent Sudan – as a reprisal for the death of General Gordon. The Mahdi's body was burned and his ashes thrown into the Nile.

May 2, 1908.

THE BALLADE OF A STRANGE TOWN.[1]

My friend and I, in fooling about Flanders, fell into a fixed affection for the town of Mechlin or Malines. Our rest there was so restful that we almost felt it as a home, and hardly strayed out of it.

We sat day after day in the marketplace, under little trees growing in wooden tubs, and looked up at the noble converging lines of the Cathedral tower, from which the three riders from Ghent, in the poem, heard the bell which told them they were not too late.[2] But we took as much pleasure in the people, in the little boys with open, flat Flemish faces and fur collars round their necks, making them look like burgomasters, or the women, whose prim oval faces, hair strained tightly off the temples, and mouths at once hard, meek, and humorous, exactly reproduced the late mediaeval faces in Memling[3] and Van Eyck.[4]

But one afternoon, as it happened, my friend rose from under his little tree, and, pointing to a sort of toy train that was puffing smoke in one corner of the clear square, suggested that we should go by it. We got into the little train, which was meant really to take the peasants and their vegetables to and fro from their fields beyond the town, and the official came round to give us tickets. We asked him what place we should get to if we paid 5d. The Belgians are not a romantic people, and he asked us (with a lamentable mixture of Flemish coarseness and French rationalism) where we wanted to go.

We explained that we wanted to go to fairyland, and the only question was whether we could get there for 5d. At last, after a great deal of international misunderstanding (for he spoke French in the Flemish and we in the English manner), he told us that 5d. would take us to a place which I have never seen written down, but which when spoken sounded like the word Waterloo pronounced by an intoxicated patriot: I think it was Waerlowe. We clasped our hands and said it was the place that we had been seeking from boyhood, and when we had got there we descended with promptitude.

For a moment I had a horrible fear that it really was the field of Waterloo; but I was comforted by remembering that it was in quite a different part of Belgium. It was a cross-roads, with one cottage at the corner, a perspective of tall trees like Hobbema's 'Avenue',5 and beyond only the infinite flat chessboard of the little fields. It was the scene of peace and prosperity; but I must confess that my friend's first action was to ask the man when there would be another train back to Mechlin. The man stated that there would be a train back in exactly one hour. We walked up the avenue, and when we were nearly half-an-hour's walk away it began to rain.

****

We arrived back at the cross-roads sodden and dripping, and, finding the train waiting, climbed into it with some relief. The officer on this train could speak nothing but Flemish, but he understood the name of Mechlin, and indicated that when we came to Mechlin Station he would put us down, which, after the right interval of time, he did.

We got down, under a steady downpour, evidently on the edge of Mechlin, though the features could not easily be recognised through the grey screen of the rain. I do not generally agree with those who find rain depressing. A shower-bath is not depressing; it is rather startling. And if it is exciting when a man throws a pail of water over you, why should it not also be exciting when the gods throw many pails? But on this soaking afternoon, whether it was the dull sky-line of the Netherlands or the fact that we were returning home without any adventure, I really did think things a trifle dreary. As soon as we could creep under the shelter of a street we turned into a little café, kept by one woman. She was incredibly old, and she spoke no French. There we drank black coffee and what was called 'cognac fine'. 'Cognac fine' were the only two French words used in the establishment, and they were not true. At least, the fineness (perhaps by its very ethereal delicacy) escaped me. After a little my friend, who was more restless than I, got up and went out, to see if the rain had stopped and if we could at once stroll back to our hotel by the station. I sat finishing my coffee in a colourless mood, and listening to the unremitting rain.

****

Suddenly the door burst open, and my friend appeared, transfigured and frantic.

'Get up!' he cried, waving his hands wildly. 'Get up! We're in the wrong town! We're not in Mechlin at all. Mechlin is ten miles, twenty miles off – God knows what! We're somewhere near Antwerp'.

'What!' I cried, leaping from my seat, and sending the furniture flying. 'Then all is well, after all! Poetry only hid her face for an instant behind a cloud. Positively for a moment I was feeling depressed because we were in the right town. But if we are in the wrong town – why, we have our adventure after all! If we are in the wrong town we are in the right place'.

I rushed out into the rain, and my friend followed me somewhat more grimly. We discovered we were in a town called Lierre, which seemed to consist chiefly of bankrupt pastrycooks, who sold lemonade.

'This is the peak of our whole poetic progress!' I cried enthusiastically. 'We must do something, something sacramental and commemorative! We cannot sacrifice an ox, and it would be a bore to build a temple. Let us write a poem'.

With but slight encouragement, I took out an old envelope and one of those pencils that turn bright violet in water. There was plenty of water about, and the violet ran down the paper, symbolizing the rich purple of that romantic hour. I began, choosing the form of an old French ballade; it is the easiest because it is the most restricted:

> Can Man to Mount Olympus rise,
> And fancy Primrose Hill the scene?
> Can a man walk in Paradise
> And think he is in Turnham Green?
> And could I take you for Malines,
> Not knowing the nobler thing you were?
> O Pearl of all the plain, and queen,
> The lovely city of Lierre.
>
> Through memory's mist in glimmering guise
> Shall shine your streets of sloppy sheen,
> And wet shall grow my dreaming eyes,
> To think how wet my boots have been.
> Now if I die or shoot a Dean –

Here I broke off to ask my friend whether he thought it expressed a more wild calamity to shoot a Dean or to be a Dean. But he only turned up his coat collar, and I felt that for him the Muse had folded her wings. I re-wrote:

> Now if I die a Rural Dean,
> Or rob a bank I do not care,
> Or turn a Tory. I have seen
> The lovely city of Lierre.

'The next line', I resumed, warming to it; but my friend interrupted me.

'The next line', he said, somewhat harshly, 'will be a railway line. We can get back to Mechlin from here, I find, though we have to change twice. I dare say I should think this jolly romantic but for the weather. Adventure is the champagne of life, but I prefer my champagne and my adventures dry. Here is the station'.

****

We did not speak again until we had left Lierre, in its sacred cloud of rain, and were coming to Mechlin, under a clearer sky, that even made one think of stars. Then I leant forward and said to my friend in a low voice:

'I have found out everything. We have come to the wrong star'.

He stared his query, and I went on eagerly: 'That is what makes life at once so splendid and so strange. We are in the wrong world. When I thought that was the right town, it bored me; when I knew it was wrong, I was happy. So the false optimism, the modern happiness, tires us because it tells us we fit into this world. The true happiness is that we don't fit. We come from somewhere else. We have lost our way'.

He silently nodded, staring out of the window, but whether I had impressed or only fatigued him I could not tell. 'This', I added, 'is suggested in the last verse of a fine poem you have grossly neglected –

> Happy is he and more than wise
>   Who sees with wondering eyes and clean
> This world through all the grey disguise
>   Of sleep and custom in between.
> Yes; we may pass the heavenly screen,
>   But shall we know when we are there?
> Who knew not what these dead stones mean,
>   The lovely city of Lierre'.

Here the train stopped abruptly. And from Mechlin church steeple we heard the half-chime: and Joris broke silence with 'No bally hors d'œuvres for me: I shall get on to something solid at once'.

L'ENVOY.[6]

> Prince, wide your Empire spreads, I ween,
>   Yet happier is that moistened Mayor,
> Who drinks her cognac far from fine,
>   The lovely city of Lierre.

Notes
1. *THE BALLADE OF A STRANGE TOWN*: Reprinted in *TT* (2), pp. 265–72.
2. *in the poem ... they were not too late*: Browning, 'How they Brought the Good News from Ghent to Aix' (1838):

> 'Twas moonset at starting; but while we drew near
> Lokeren, the cocks crew and twilight dawned clear;
> At Boom, a great yellow star came out to see;
> At Düffeld, 'twas morning as plain as could be;
> And from Mecheln church-steeple we heard the half-chime,
> So Joris broke silence with 'Yet there is time!'

3. *Memling*: Hans Memling [also Memlinc or Hemling] (*c.* 1430–94), was a Flemish painter who produced religious paintings and portraits. Among his works are the *Tryptych of Sir John Donne* (Chatsworth) and the *Mystic Marriage of St Catherine* (Bruges, St John's Hospital).
4. *Van Eyck*: Jan Van Eyck (*c.* 1390–1441), was an early Flemish painter and one of the first artists to master the technique of oil painting. His works included *The Marriage of Giovanni Arnolfini and Giovanna Cenami* (National Gallery).
5. *Hobbema's 'Avenue'*: Meindert Hobbema (1638–1709), was a Dutch landscape painter; Chesterton is referring to his 'The Avenue at Middelharnis', now in The National Gallery, London.
6. *L'Envoy*: This poem is not included in *CP*.

May 9, 1908.

HUMANITY: AN INTERLUDE.[1]

Except for some fine works of art, which seem to be there by accident, the City of Brussels is like a bad Paris, a Paris with everything noble cut out, and everything nasty left in. No one can understand Paris and its history who does not understand that its fierceness is the balance and justification of its frivolity. It is called a city of pleasure; but it may also very specially be called a city of pain. The crown of roses is also a crown of thorns. Its people are too prone to hurt others, but quite ready also to hurt themselves. They are martyrs for religion, they are martyrs for irreligion; they are even martyrs for immorality. For the indecency of many of their books and papers is not of the sort which charms and seduces, but of the sort that horrifies and hurts; they are torturing themselves. They lash their own patriotism into life with the same whips which most men use to lash foreigners to silence. The enemies of France can never give an account of her infamy or decay which does not seem insipid and even polite compared with the things which the Nationalists of France say about their own nation. They taunt and torment themselves; sometimes they even deliberately oppress themselves. Thus, when the mob of Paris could make a government to please itself, it made a sort of sublime tyranny to order itself about. The spirit is the same from the Crusades or St. Bartholomew[2] to the apotheosis of Zola.[3] The old religionists tortured men physically for a moral truth. The new realists torture men morally for a physical truth.

Now Brussels is Paris without this constant purification of pain. Its indecencies are not regrettable incidents in an everlasting revolution. It has none of the things which make good Frenchmen love Paris; it has only the things which make unspeakable Englishmen love it. It has the part which is cosmopolitan – and narrow; not the part which is Parisian – and universal. You can find there (as commonly happens in modern centres) the worst things of all nations – the 'Daily Mail' from England, the cheap philosophies from Germany, the loose novels of France, and the drinks of America. But there is no English broad fun, no German kindly ceremony, no American exhilaration, and, above all, no French tradition of fighting for an idea. Though all the boulevards look like Parisian boulevards, though all the shops look like Parisian shops, you cannot look at them steadily for two minutes without feeling the full distance between, let us say, King Leopold[4] and fighters like Clemenceau[5] and Deroulède.[6]

****

For all these reasons, and many more, when I had got into Brussels I began to make all necessary arrangements for getting out of it again; and I had impulsively got into a tram which seemed to be going out of the city. In this tram there were two men talking; one was a little man with a black French beard; the other was a baldish man with bushy whiskers, like the financial foreign count in a three-act farce. And about the time that we reached the suburb of the city, and the traffic grew thinner, and the noises more few, I began to hear what they were saying. Though they spoke French quickly, their words were fairly easy to follow, because they were all long words. Anybody can understand long words, because they have in them all the lucidity of Latin.

The man with the black beard said: 'It must that we have the Progress'.

The man with the whiskers parried this smartly by saying: 'It must also that we have the Consolidation International'.

This is the sort of discussion which I like myself, so I listened with some care, and I think I picked up the thread of it. One of the Belgians was a Little Belgian, as we speak of a Little Englander.[7] The other was a Belgian Imperialist, for though Belgium is not quite strong enough to be altogether a nation, she is quite strong enough to be an empire. Being a nation means standing up to your equals, whereas being an empire only means kicking your inferiors. The man with whiskers was the Imperialist, and he was saying:

'The science, behold there the new guide of humanity'.

And the man with the beard answered him: 'It does not suffice to have progress in the science; one must have it also in the sentiment of the human justice'. This remark I applauded, as if at a public meeting, but they were much too keen on their argument to hear me. The views I have often heard in England, but never uttered so lucidly and certainly never so fast. Though Belgian by nation they must both have been essentially French. Whiskers was great on education, which it seems is on the march. All the world goes to make itself instructed. It must that the more instructed enlighten the less instructed. Eh, well then, the European must impose upon the savage the science and the light. Also (apparently) he must impose himself on the savage while he is about it. To-day one travelled quickly. The science had changed all. For our fathers, they were religious, and (what was worse) dead. To-day humanity had electricity to the hand; the machines came from triumphing; all the lines and limits of the globe effaced themselves. Soon there would not be but the great Empires and confederations, guided by the science, always the science.[a]

Here Whiskers stopped an instant for breath; and the man with the sentiment of human justice had 'la parole' off him in a flash. Without doubt Humanity was on the march, but towards the sentiments, the ideal; the methods moral and pacific. Humanity directed itself towards Humanity. For your wars and empires on behalf of civilization, what were they in effect? The war, was it not itself an affair of the barbarism? The Empires, were they not things savage? The Humanity had passed all that; she was now intellectual. Tolstoy[8] had refined all human souls with the sentiments the most delicate and just. Man was become a spirit: the wings pushed ...

****

At this important point of evolution the tram came to a jerky stoppage; and staring around I found, to my stunned consternation, that it was almost dark, that I was far away from Brussels, that I could not dream of getting back to dinner; in short, that through the clinging fascination of this great controversy on Humanity and its recent complete alteration by science or Tolstoy, I had landed myself Heaven knows where. I dropped hastily from the suburban tram and let it go on without me.

I was alone in flat fields out of sight of the city. On one side of the road was one of those small, thin woods which are common in all countries, but of which, by a coincidence, the mystical painters of Flanders were very fond. The night was closing in with cloudy purple and grey; there was one ribbon of silver, the last rag of the sunset. Through the wood went one little path, and somehow it suggested that it might lead to some sign of life – there was no other sign of life on the horizon. I went along it, and soon sank into a sort of dancing twilight of all those tiny trees. There is something subtle and bewildering about that sort of frail and fantastic wood. A forest of big trees seems like a bodily barrier; but somehow that mist of thin lines seems like a spiritual barrier. It is as if one were caught in a fairy cloud or could not pass a phantom. When I had well lost the last gleam of the high road a curious and definite feeling came upon me. I had heard a lot about Humanity in the tram. Now I suddenly felt something much more practical and extraordinary – the absence of humanity: inhuman loneliness. Of course, there was nothing really lost in my state; but the mood may hit one anywhere. I wanted men – any men; and I felt our awful alliance over all the globe. And at last, when I had walked for what seemed a long time, I saw a light too near the earth to mean anything except the image of God.

I came out on a clear space and a low, long cottage, the door of which was open, but was blocked by a big grey horse, who seemed to prefer to eat with his head inside the sitting room. I got past him, and found he was being fed idly by a young man who was sitting down and drinking beer inside, and who saluted me with heavy rustic courtesy, but in a strange tongue. The room was full of staring faces like owls, and these I traced at length as belonging to about six small children. Their father was still working in the fields, but their mother rose when I entered. She smiled, but she and all the rest spoke some rude language, Flamand,[9] I suppose; so that we had to be kind to each other by signs. She fetched me beer, and pointed out my way with her finger; and I drew a picture to please the children; and as it was a picture of two men hitting each other with swords, it pleased them very much. Then I gave a Belgian penny to each child, for, as I said on chance in French, 'It must that we have the economic equality'. But they had never heard of economic equality, while all Battersea workmen have heard of economic equality, though it is true that they haven't got it.

I found my way back to the city, and some time afterwards I actually saw in the street my two men talking, no doubt still saying, one that Science had changed all in Humanity, and the other that Humanity was now pushing the wings of the purely intellectual. But for me Humanity was hooked on to an accidental picture. I thought of a low and lonely house in the flats, behind a veil or film of slight trees, a man breaking the ground as men have broken from the first morning, and a huge grey horse champing his food within a foot of a child's head, as in the stable where Christ was born.

68–9a   This remark I applauded ... science, always the science.] in *TT* (2) appears as a separate paragraph.

Notes

1. *HUMANITY: AN INTERLUDE*: Reprinted in *TT* (2), pp. 187–94.
2. *St. Bartholomew's*: a reference to the St Bartholomew's Day massacre of 23 August 1572; see 'In the Place de La Bastille', *DN*, 5 May 1906, Volume 3, p. 360, n. 5 above.
3. *the apotheosis of Zola*: a reference to Zola's role in initiating the campaign for the release of Captain Alfred Dreyfus in 1898; see 'A Short Comment on Crime', *DN*, 16 November 1907, Volume 4, p. 345, n. 7 above.
4. *King Leopold*: Leopold II (Louis Philippe Marie Victor) (1835–1909), was King of the Belgians. Chesterton's comment about not 'fighting for an idea' is perhaps a reference to Leopold's creation, in 1876, of *L'Association Internationale Africaine*. The Association had ostensibly humanitarian ideals and objectives but it rapidly became an instrument of Belgian economic interests in Africa.
5. *Clemenceau*: Georges Eugène Benjamin Clemenceau (1841–1929), was a French statesman; a leading spokesman for French Radicals in the House of Deputies in the 1870s, Clemenceau went on to become a journalist who championed the cause of Dreyfus. In

1906 he succeeded Ferdinand Sarrien as Premier. Although his government was defeated in 1909 he became a national leader during the First World War, a symbol of resistance to German aggression. He became president in 1917 and played a central role in the Paris Peace Conference of 1919. Chesterton continued to admire Clemenceau after the War: see 'Clemenceau and the Barbarians', review of H. M. Hyndman, *Clemenceau: the Man and his Time* (London: Grant Richards, 1919), in *New Witness*, 11 April 1919, pp. 480–1.

6. *Deroulède*: Paul Déroulède; see 'Heroic Wit', *DN*, 12 May 1906, Volume 3, p. 365, n. 6 above.
7. *Little Englander*: This expression was in common journalistic use at the time of the Second Boer War to denote those anti-imperialists who wished to see 'England' extend no further than the borders of the United Kingdom.
8. *Tolstoy*: see Leo Tolstoi (Count Lev Nikolayevich Tolstoy) 'The Good Man of the Eighteenth Century', *DN*, 22 March 1901, Volume 1, p. 67, n. 13 above.
9. *Flamand*: 'Flamand' is the French word for 'Flemish', which is not a 'rude language' but the form of Dutch that is the official language of Belgium. Chesterton's problem is that French is the language most commonly used in and around Brussels; everyday Belgian Dutch – 'Tussentaal' – would no doubt have been as incomprehensible to him as it is to most people.

May 16, 1908.

THE LITTLE BIRDS WHO WON'T SING.¹

On my last morning on the Flemish coast when I knew that in a few hours I should be in England my eye fell upon one of the details of Gothic carving of which Flanders is full. I do not know whether the thing was old, though it was certainly knocked about and indecipherable, but at least it was certainly in the style and tradition of the early Middle Ages. It seemed to represent men bending themselves (not to say twisting themselves) to certain primary employments. Some seemed to be sailors tugging at ropes; others, I think, were reaping; others were energetically pouring something into something else. This is entirely characteristic of the pictures and carvings of the early thirteenth century, perhaps the most purely vigorous time in all history. The great Greeks preferred to carve their gods and heroes doing nothing. Splendid and philosophic as their composure is there is always about it something that marks the master of many slaves. But if there was one thing the early mediaevals liked it was representing people doing something – hunting or hawking, or rowing boats or treading grapes, or making shoes or cooking something in a pot. 'Quidquid agunt homines, votum, timor, ira voluptas'.² (I quote from memory.) The middle ages is full of that spirit in all its monuments and manuscripts. Chaucer retains it in his jolly insistence on everybody's type of trade and toil. It was the earliest and youngest resurrection of Europe, the time when social order was strengthening, but had not yet become oppressive; the time when religious faiths were strong, but had not yet been exasperated. For this reason the whole effect of Greek and Gothic carving is different. The figures in the Elgin marbles, though often reining their steeds for an instant in the air, seem frozen for ever at that perfect instant.³ But a mass of mediaeval carving seems actually a sort of bustle or hubbub in stone. Sometimes one cannot help feeling that the groups actually move and mix, and the whole front of a great cathedral has the hum of a huge hive.

****

But about these particular figures there was a peculiarity of which I could not be sure. Those of them that had any heads had very curious heads, and it seemed to me that they had their mouths open. Whether or no this really meant anything or was an accident of nascent art I do not know; but in the course of wondering I recalled to my mind the fact that singing was connected with many of the tasks there suggested, that there were songs for reapers reaping and songs for sailors hauling ropes. I was still thinking about this small problem when I walked along the pier at Ostend; and I heard some sailors uttering a measured shout as they laboured, and I remembered that sailors still sing in chorus while they work, and even sing different songs according to what part of their work they are doing. And a little while afterwards, when my sea journey was over, the sight of men working in the English fields reminded me again that there are still songs for harvest and for agricultural routines. And I suddenly wondered why if this were so it should be quite unknown for any modern trade to have a ritual poetry. How did people come to chant rude poems while pulling certain ropes or gathering certain fruit, and why did nobody do anything of the kind while producing any of the modern things? Why is a modern newspaper never printed by people singing in chorus? Why do shopmen seldom, if ever, sing?

If reapers sing while reaping, why should not auditors sing while auditing and bankers while banking? If there are songs for all the separate things that have to be done in a boat, why are there not songs for all the separate things that have to be done in a bank? As the train from Dover flew through the Kentish gardens, I tried to write a few songs suitable for commercial gentlemen. Thus, the work of bank clerks when casting up columns might begin with a thundering chorus in praise of Simple Addition:

> Up my lads, and lift the ledgers, sleep and ease are o'er.
>   Hear the Stars of morning shouting: 'Two and Two are Four'.
> Though the creeds and realms are reeling, though the sophists roar,
>   Though we weep and pawn our watches, Two and Two are Four.

And then, of course, we should need another song for times of financial crisis and courage, a song with a more fierce and panic-stricken metre, like the rushing of horses in the night:

> There's a run upon the Bank –
>   Stand away!
> For the Manager's a crank and the Secretary drank, and the Upper Tooting Bank
>   Turns to bay!
> Stand close: there is a run

> On the Bank.
> Of our ship, our royal one, let the ringing legend run, that she fired with every gun
> Ere she sank.

****

And as I came into the cloud of London I met a friend of mine who actually is in a bank, and submitted these suggestions in rhyme to him for use among his colleagues. But he was not very hopeful about the matter. It was not (he assured me) that he underrated the verses, or in any sense lamented their lack of polish. No; it was rather, he felt, an indefinable something in the very atmosphere of the society in which we live that makes it spiritually difficult to sing in banks. And I think he must be right; though the matter is mysterious. I may observe here that I think there must be some mistake in the calculations of the Socialists. They put down all our distress not to a moral tone, but to the chaos of private enterprise. Now, banks are private; but post-offices are Socialistic: therefore I naturally expected that post-office would fall into the collectivist idea of a chorus. Judge of my surprise when the lady in my local post-office (whom I urged to sing) dismissed the idea with far more coldness than the bank clerk had done. She seemed, indeed, to be in a considerably greater state of depression than he. Should anyone suppose that this was the effect of the verses themselves, it is only fair to say that the specimen verse of the Post Office Hymn ran thus:

> O'er London our letters are shaken like snow,
> Our wires o'er the world like the thunderbolts go.
> The news that may marry a maiden in Sark,
> Or kill an old lady in Finsbury Park.

Chorus (with a swing of joy and energy):

> Or kill an old lady in Finsbury Park.

And the more I thought about the matter the more painfully certain it seemed that the most important and typical modern things could not be done with a chorus. One could not, for instance, be a great financier, and sing; because the essence of being a great financier is that you keep quiet. You could not even in many modern circles be a public man and sing; because in those circles the essence of being a public man is that you do nearly everything in private. Nobody could imagine a chorus of money-lenders. Everyone knows the story of the solicitors' corps of volunteers who, when the Colonel on the battlefield cried 'Charge!' all said simultaneously, 'Six-and-eightpence'.[4] Man can sing while charging in a military, but hardly in a legal sense. And at the end of my reflections I had really got no further than the sub-conscious feeling of my friend the bank-clerk – that there is something spiritually suffocating about our life; not about our laws merely, but about our life. Bank-clerks are without songs not because they are poor, but because they are sad. Sailors are much poorer. As I passed homewards I passed a little tin building of some religious sort, which was shaken with shouting as a trumpet is torn with its own tongue. *They* were singing anyhow; and I had for an instant a fancy I had often had before: that with us the super-human is the only place where you can find the human. Human nature is hunted, and has fled into sanctuary.

Notes
1. *THE LITTLE BRIDS WHO WON'T SING*: Reprinted in *TT* (2), pp. 195–201.
2. *Qtuidquid ... voluptas*: Juvenal, *Satires* 1:1:85: 'Whatever men do, their prayers, fear, anger, pleasure ...'.
3. *he Elgin marbles*: The 'Elgin Marbles', now in the British Museum, were removed from the Acropolis of Athens by Lord Elgin, British Ambassador to the Ottoman Empire, between 1801 and 1812. Since then various accidents – including misguided attempts to clean them – have seriously damaged the marbles. Repeated attempts by the Greek government to have them returned to Athens have so far met with no success.
4. *'Six-and-eightpence'*: Six shillings and eight pence – a third of a pound in pre-decimal English currency – was traditionally the Solicitor's fee for sending a letter.

May 23, 1908.

TOMMY AND THE TRADITIONS.¹

A little while ago I was trying to convince the writers and readers of an excellent Socialist paper that the democracy was very decent after all.² I did not succeed. The Socialist writers and readers were really delightful, and even playful people; but they could not swallow such a paradox as the statement that the poor are really right and the rich really wrong. In those quarters (in consequence) there has ever since been a disposition to connect my name with gin, a drink which I dislike, and with wife-beating, a pastime for which I lack the adequate energy. I have often wondered whether it would be worth while to try and explain again why I think that the poor are really quite right; and I was suddenly precipitated into the enterprise this morning. The impulse was only this – that as I walked past a dreary row of dwellings I heard a slatternly woman say to a very big child, 'Now, Tommy, run away and play'. She did not say it brutally, but with a hearty and healthy impatience, such as is natural to her sex.

****

I want to make one more attempt to revive the dead tradition of democracy by discussing what was involved in that remark. First we must get it into our heads that a thing can be a superstition and still be true. Ten thousand people may recite a thing as a lie, and it may still be a truth, in spite of their saying it. Thus Liberalism is true; but many Liberals are mere myths. Christianity can be believed; but some Christians are quite incredible. A hypocrite can hand on a truth. The Whigs of the early eighteenth century handed on the theory of liberty and self-government, though there was practically not one of them who was not a dirty courtier and a corrupt tyrant. The fashionable French priests of the later eighteenth century handed on the tradition of Catholicism, though there was hardly one of them who was not an atheist. But when democracy came it was glad the Whigs had kept the tradition of Algernon Sydney.[3] When the Catholic revival came it was glad the French clergy had kept the tradition of St. Louis. Therefore when I say that the poor have the right tradition I do not mean necessarily that they are going on in exactly the right way. I do not even mean that they think they are going on in the right way. As a matter of fact, they don't. The great difficulty is to persuade the poor that they are as right as they are.

I mean that just as there was an important truth in the Whig Parliaments even when they were corrupt, just as there was an important truth in the Christian religion even when the Christians did not think so, so there is a truth which the poor possess in their misery and confusion, which we do not possess in our largest schemes of social reform. The point is not that they have gone specially right; but that they have stayed tolerably right while we have gone specially wrong.

I have often urged instances of this. For the sake of clearness I will repeat one of them only. The very poor are always despised and rebuked because of their fuss and expenditure on funerals. Only to-day I saw that a public body refused aid to those who had gone any length in such expenditure. Now I do not mean that their crape is my abstract conception of robes of mourning, or that the conversation of Mrs. Brown with Mrs. Jones over the coffin has the dignity of 'Lycidas'.[4] I do not even say that educated people could not do it better. I say that they are not trying to do it at all. Educated people have got some chilly fad to the effect that making a fuss about death is morbid or vulgar. The educated people are entirely wrong on the fundamental point of human psychology. The uneducated people are entirely right on the point.

****

The one way to make bereavement tolerable is to make it important. To gather your friends, to have a gloomy festival, to talk, to cry, to praise the dead – all that does change the atmosphere, and carry human nature over the open grave. The nameless torture is to try and treat it as something private and casual, as our elegant stoics do. That is at once pride and pain and hypocrisy. The only way to make less of death is to make more of it. The poor have this blind tradition, and will not be torn away from it. They do it in a bad social system; they do it in a bad way; but they have all humanity behind them, and in the noise and heat of their houses of mourning is the smoke of the baked meats of Hamlet[5] and the dust and echo of the funeral games of Patroclus.[6]

Now take a more cheerful instance: the poor have, in practice, a certain view of work and play. And it is the right view; the root view of all mankind. I do not mean that their work and play are better; they are not. They do not play specially well; and they work as little as they can, and so should I in their shoes. What they have got right is the philosophy; the original principle of the thing. They differ from us and from the aristocracy (pardon the distinction) simply in this; that their work is work and their play is play. Work is doing what you do not like; play is doing what you like. The whole point of work is law; the whole point of play is liberty. There should be hours of labour, and they should be laborious; there should be hours of freedom, and they should be free.

*****

That sounds simple enough: but the educated classes cannot understand it. The educationalists cannot understand it. The public schools cannot understand it. The whole English upper class is built on the negation of it. A gentleman is taught to treat half his work as play (diplomacy, Parliament, finance), and then to treat more than half his play as work, by training for matches and bursting blood vessels in a race. He is taught to play at politics and work at cricket. At the English schools (as Mr. Maurice Baring[7] sketched very cleverly in an article the other day),[8] a game has practically ceased to be a game: it has become a specially dull lesson, where boys are bored by having to look interested. But the athletic school is not alone to blame: the intellectual educationalists are quite as bad. They want to make children's play significant and instructive. They arrange children in Pre-Raphaelite patterns. They make them dance ethically or yell aesthetically. They want to follow children when they play and make their games useful. They might as well follow them when they sleep, and make their dreams useful. Play is a rest, like sleep.

The woman who said 'Run away and play' to Tommy on the doorstep was the weary guardian of an eternal commonsense. Probably Tommy had a bad time sometimes: probably she made him work: but at least she did not make him play. She let him play. He fed on loneliness and liberty. That hour of play at least was not Froebel's contribution[9] or Dr. Arnold's contribution[10] to Tommy. That hour was Tommy's contribution to Tommy. I do not know whether I have succeeded, or ever shall succeed, in conveying what I mean about these people, and how they hold a battered shape of truth, while we hold perfected forms of error. But at least my work for this Friday evening is done. I shall run away and play.

Notes
1. *TOMMY AND THE TRADITIONS*: Reprinted in *LL*, pp. 134–8.
2. *I was trying to convince ... decent after all*: 'On Wells and a Glass of Beer', *NA*, 25 January 1908, p. 250. The controversy was joined by Shaw in an article that famously coined the term 'Chesterbelloc' to characterize Chesterton and Belloc as two ends of a pantomime horse: 'Belloc and Chesterton', *NA*, 15 February 1908, pp. 309–11; for Chesterton's reply, see 'The Last of the Rationalists: A Reply to Mr. Bernard Shaw', 29 February 1908, pp. 348–9.

3. *Algernon Sydney*: Algernon Sidney [Sydney] (1623–83), was a republican political theorist, soldier and opponent of King Charles II of England. His *Discourses Concerning Government* – a long and ill-organized work that has been overshadowed by the more succinct *Second Treatise* of John Locke – is an argument for government by consent against the absolutist 'patriarchal' ideology of the Royalist author Sir Robert Filmer. After the Restoration the *Discourses* were held to be treasonable, and Sidney was allegedly involved also in the 'Rye House Plot' to assassinate Charles II. He was executed for treason on 7 December 1683.
4. *'Lycidas'*: 'Lycidas' is an elegy by John Milton, dedicated to his friend Edward King who was lost at sea in 1637.
5. *baked meats of Hamlet*: *Hamlet*, I.ii:

    Thrift, thrift, Horatio! the funeral baked meats
    Did coldly furnish forth the marriage tables.

6. *funeral games of Patroclus*: Homer, *Iliad*, book 23.
7. *Mr. Maurice Baring*: Maurice Baring (1874–1945), was an English poet, journalist, essayist and novelist, the fifth son of Edward Charles Baring, first Baron Revelstoke, of the Baring banking family. After an early and unsuccessful career in the diplomatic service, Baring became a journalist, covering the Russo–Japanese war in 1905 for the *Morning Post* and afterwards remaining with the paper as its correspondent in St Petersburg. He developed an abiding sympathy for the Russian people and became an authority on their literature and culture. He and Chesterton became close friends in about 1908. Baring was received into the Roman Catholic Church in 1909, and served with distinction in the First World War in the Royal Flying Corps (R. Speaight, rev. A Peach, *ODNB*).
8. *At the English schools ... an article the other day*: 'The Cricket Match: An Incident at a Private School', reprinted in *Orpheus in Mayfair and Other Stories and Sketches* (London: Mills & Boon, 1909).
9. *Froebel's contribution*: Friedrich Wilhelm August Fröbel (Froebel) (1782–1852), was a German educational theorist who developed the idea of the 'kindergarten'. His educational theories owe much to the earlier work of Johann Heinrich Pestalozzi (1746–1827). It is probably the influence of Froebel that Chesterton has in mind when he refers in the previous paragraph to 'intellectual educationalists'.
10. *Dr. Arnold's contribution*: Thomas Arnold (1795–1842), was an English educationalist and historian, and the father of Matthew Arnold. He was the headmaster of Rugby School 1828 to 1841, and is celebrated in Thomas Hughes's *Tom Brown's Schooldays* (1857).

May 30, 1908.

THAT CURE IS BETTER THAN PREVENTION.

I know no worse maxim in its practical effects at the present day than the maxim that 'Prevention is better than cure'.[1] Of course it is strictly true in the abstract. If we could foresee all possible evils a long time before they happened and could modify or avert them without exertion and without harming anything or anybody, obviously of course we should be glad to do so. But this is exactly what is impossible. All our anticipations of the things that are not certain tend of necessity to disorganize the things that are certain. It is possible, for instance, that I may at some time or other catch my finger in a door. The modern professors and scientists, the modern philosophers of hygiene, sociology, eugenics, and all the rest of it, take this possibility and advise me accordingly.

They are divided into two intellectual groups; those who want me to give up doors and those who want me to give up fingers. To take down all the doors in my house, including the front door, would undoubtedly prevent them from pinching me, but I cannot admit that my comfort would really be increased. Chopping off all my fingers with a hatchet would certainly prevent their ever being pinched; but I do not concede in such a case that prevention is better than cure. The whole question touching prevention is whether it does or does not create a morbid atmosphere in attempting to anticipate evil. Does it [one?] become miserable through dreaming of misery? For to be always in good health under doctor's orders is only to be an immortal invalid. To be kept always well is really to be always ill. For the essential of the invalid is not danger, which is the pride of the hero, or pain, which is the pride of the martyr; it is limitation, the being tied by the leg to an unnatural life.

Many hygienic enthusiasts of our time want to think of every man as a patient; but I should like to think of every man as an agent. Prevention is *not* better than cure. Cure is healthy; because it is effected at an unhealthy moment. Prevention is unhealthy; because it is done at a healthy moment. It is not better that I should always shut my eyes for fear of going blind; it is not worse that I should wait for some sign of blindness before going to an oculist. It is not better that I should prevent a wild buffalo from grazing in my garden by poisoning all the grass. It is much better that I should wait for the buffalo and then endeavour quietly and humbly to *cure* the buffalo – most probably with a gun.

****

For this reason I have always had an instinct against all the forms of science or morality which professed to be particularly prescient and provisional. Some beautiful idealists are eager to kill babies if they think they will grow up bad. But I say to them: 'No, beautiful idealists; let us wait until the babies do grow up bad – and then (if we have luck) perhaps they may kill you'.

On the same principle I have always been an anti-vivisectionist, but of so peculiar a kind that both parties hate my position with pure intellectual hatred. All my friends who are vivisectionists would like to vivisect me; and all who are anti-vivisectionists would like to anti-vivisect me; which hurts even more. I deny the whole doctrine that animals have equivalent rights with men; and when I say that 'H. N. B.'[2] leaps out of his lions' den. But I also say that one ought not to do horrible things except in horrible situations; one ought not to do them in cold blood or upon a conjecture. It would be highly excusable, to say the least of it, for a man to beat somebody who had insulted his wife; but it would be highly inexcusable for him to go about partially beating whom he thought (from the tone and arrangement of their features) might some day insult his wife. In short, it would be highly inexcusable for him to go about with a big stick applying the principle that prevention is better than cure.

So I have always felt about any extreme hurting of animals. It is one thing to do something dreadful because you are desperate; it is quite another thing to do it because you habitually look forward to despair. If my head were between the jaws of a crocodile (which you will be glad to hear is not the case), I would stab the crocodile in any place I could, without any anatomic analysis of his feelings; and this might easily amount to all that can possibly happen in vivisection. But then, having your head between a crocodile's jaws can be called, without affectation, an abnormal situation. If in perfect peace and the possession of great wealth, I then bought fifty crocodiles and cut them about in such a way that they never could hold my head with any undue firmness, then I should think myself a nasty fellow. For I should be trying to prevent bites instead of curing them.

It is bad enough to be bitten by a mad dog and to go mad. It is worse to be all your life mad with the fear of that madness.

****

I think this point sufficiently important to emphasise just now because we are soon going to have a great stir about the reform in our criminal system. It wants reform about as much as anything ever did in the world. It is cold, coarse, unnatural, full of a sort of emptiness which is one of the most awful forms of evil, a form which a friend of mine well described in a verse by saying 'The voids of Hell expand enormously around'.³ It is quite inadequate to say that in such systems there is no human pity. It is far worse than that; in such systems there is no human anger; there is no human revenge. If we even hated our convicts we should be far nearer to loving them. It would be much more tolerable if a prisoner was flogged as a libeller is horsewhipped, out of pure personal vengeance. We confound too often the words cruel and inhuman. But to be inhuman is worse than to be cruel. To be inhuman means that you can no longer be even so human as to be cruel. Our penal system is partly cruel; but it is pre-eminently inhuman. Any attempt, therefore, to break it up must be very important and valuable, and should certainly be among the essential tasks of any Liberal Government.

But there is in the atmosphere of the whole question exactly this evil possibility: that in reconsidering and reshaping our criminal system we may give way to this pestilent principle of a scientific prevention in place of a moral cure. The theory of the indeterminate sentence requires the most vigilant watching. Our prisons easily become inhuman places. Our police magistrates and officials easily become inhuman people. The indeterminate sentence may mean that these things have an indeterminate right to continue their inhumanity.

Notes
1. *'Prevention is better than cure'*: For the context of this essay, see 'A Theory of Tyrants', *DN*, 13 June 1908, p.89, n. 8, below.
2. *'H. N. B.'*: Henry Noel Brailsford; see 'What Shall I Eat?', letter to the editor, *DN*, 8 August 1907, Volume 4, p. 277, n. 1 above.
3. *a friend of mine ... enormously around*: Hilaire Belloc, 'The Prophet Lost in the Hills at Evening', reprinted in D. Cecil (ed.), *The Oxford Book of Christian Verse* (Oxford: Clarendon Press, 1940), p. 520.

June 6, 1908.

THE TRAVELLERS IN STATE.[1]

The other day, to my great astonishment, I caught a train; it was a train going into the Eastern Counties, and I only just caught it. And while I was running along the train (amid general admiration) I noticed that there were a quite peculiar and unusual number of carriages marked 'Engaged'. On five, six, seven, eight, nine carriages was pasted the little notice: at five, six, seven, eight, nine windows were big bland men staring out in the conscious pride of possession. Their bodies seemed more than usually impenetrable, their faces more than usually placid. It could not be the Derby, if only for the minor reasons that it was the opposite direction and the wrong day. It could hardly be the King. It could hardly be the French President. For though these distinguished persons naturally like to be private for three hours, they are at least public for three minutes. A crowd can gather to see them step into the train and there was no crowd here or any police ceremonial.

Who were these awful persons, who occupied more of the train than a bricklayers' beanfeast, and yet were more fastidious and delicate than the King's own suite? Who were these, that were larger than a mob, yet more mysterious than a monarch? Was it possible that instead of our Royal House visiting the Tsar he was really visiting us? Or does the House of Lords have a beanfeast? I waited and wondered until the train slowed down at some station in the direction of Cambridge. Then the large, impenetrable men got out, and after them got out the distinguished holders of the engaged seats. They were all dressed decorously in one colour; they had neatly cropped hair; and they were chained together.

****

I looked across the carriage at its only other occupant, and our eyes met. He was a small, tired-looking man, and, as I afterwards learnt, a native of Cambridge;

by the look of him, some working tradesman there, such as a journeyman tailor or a small clock-mender. In order to make conversation I said I wondered where the convicts were going. His mouth twitched with the instinctive irony of the poor, and he said: 'I don't s'pose they're goin' on an 'oliday at the sea-side with little spades and pails'. I was naturally delighted, and pursuing the same vein of literary invention, I suggested that perhaps dons were taken down to Cambridge chained together like this. And as he lived in Cambridge, and had seen several dons, he was pleased with such a scheme. Then when we had ceased to laugh we suddenly became quite silent; and the bleak, grey eyes of the little man grew sadder and emptier than an open sea. I knew what he was thinking, because I was thinking the same, because all modern sophists are only sophists, and there is such a thing as mankind. Then at last (and it fell in as exactly as the last note of a tune one is trying to remember) he said: 'Well, I s'pose we 'ave to do it'. And in those three things, his first speech and his silence and his second speech, there were all the three great fundamental facts of the English democracy, its profound sense of humour, its profound sense of pathos, and its profound sense of helplessness.

****

It cannot be too often repeated that all real democracy is an attempt (like that of a jolly hostess) to bring the shy people out. For every practical purpose of a political state, for every practical purpose of a tea-party, he that abaseth himself must be exalted.[2] At a tea-party it is equally obvious that he that exalteth himself must be abased, if possible without bodily violence. Now people talk of democracy as being coarse and turbulent: it is a self-evident error in mere history. Aristocracy is the thing that is always coarse and turbulent: for it means appealing to the self-confident people. Democracy means appealing to the diffident people. Democracy means getting those people to vote who would never have the cheek to govern: and (according to Christian ethics) the precise people who ought to govern are the people who have not the cheek to do it. There is a strong example of this truth in my friend in the train. The only two types we hear of in this argument about crime and punishment are two very rare and abnormal types.

We hear of the stark sentimentalist, who talks as if there were no problem at all: as if physical kindness would cure everything: as if one need only pat Nero[3] and stroke Ivan the Terrible.[4] This mere belief in bodily humanitarianism is not sentimental; it is simply snobbish. For if comfort gives men virtue the comfortable classes ought to be virtuous – which is absurd. Then, again, we do hear of the yet weaker and more watery type of sentimentalist: I mean the sentimentalist who says with a sort of splutter, 'Flog the brutes!' or who tells you with innocent obscenity 'what he would do' with a certain man – always supposing the man's hands were tied.

This is the more effeminate type of the two; but both are weak and unbalanced. And it is only these two types, the sentimental humanitarian and the sentimental brutalitarian, whom one hears in the modern babel. Yet you very rarely meet either of them in a train. You never meet anyone else in a controversy. The man you meet in a train is like this man that I met: he is emotionally decent, only he is intellectually doubtful. So far from luxuriating in the loathsome things that could be 'done' to criminals, he feels bitterly how much better it would be if nothing need be done. But something must be down. 'I s'pose we 'ave to do it'. In short he is simply a sane man, and of a sane man there is only one safe definition. He is a man who can have tragedy in his heart and comedy in his head.

****

Now the real difficulty of discussing decently this problem of the proper treatment of criminals is that both parties discuss the matter without any direct human feeling. The denouncers of wrong are as cold as the organizers of wrong. Humanitarianism is as hard as inhumanity.

Let me take one practical instance. I think the flogging arranged in our modern prisons is a filthy torture; all its scientific paraphernalia, the photographing, the medical attendance, prove that it goes to the last foul limit of the boot and rack.[5] The cat[6] is simply the rack without any of its intellectual reasons. Holding this view strongly, I open the ordinary humanitarian books or papers and I find a phrase like this, 'The lash is a relic of barbarism'. So is the plough. So is the fishing net. So is the horn or the staff or the fire lit in winter. What an inexpressibly feeble phrase for anything one wants to attack – a relic of barbarism! It is as if a man walked naked down the street to-morrow, and we said that his clothes were not quite in the latest fashion. There is nothing particularly nasty about being a relic of barbarism. Dancing is a relic of barbarism. Man is a relic of barbarism. Civilization is a relic of barbarism.

But torture is not a relic of barbarism at all. In actuality it is simply a relic of sin; but in comparative history it may well be called a relic of civilization. It has always been most artistic and elaborate when everything else was most artistic and elaborate. Thus it was detailed [and] exquisite in the late Roman Empire, in the complex and gorgeous sixteenth century, in the centralised French monarchy a hundred years before the Revolution, and in the great Chinese civilization to this day. This is, first and last, the frightful thing we must remember. In so far as we grow instructed and refined we are not (in any sense whatever) naturally moving away from torture. We may be moving towards torture. We must know what we are doing, if we are to avoid the enormous secret cruelty which has crowned every historic civilization.

The train moves more swiftly through the sunny English Fields. They have taken the prisoners away, and I do not know what they have done with them.[7]

Notes
1. THE TRAVELLERS IN STATE: Reprinted in *TT* (2), pp. 211–17.
2. *he that abaseth himself ... exalted*: See Luke 14:11.
3. *Nero*: Nero (Claudius Caesar Augustus Germanicus); see 'A Messenger of Tolstoy', *DN*, 9 September 1901, Volume 1, p. 184, n. 3 above.
4. *Ivan the Terrible*: Ivan IV Vasilyevich (1530–84), called 'Grozny', was Grand Prince of Moscow from 1533 and Tsar of Russia from 1547 (the sobriquet 'Grozny', usually translated as 'Terrible', really means something like 'awesome').
5. *the flogging arranged in our modern prisons .. boot and rack*: Flogging in British prisons was finally abolished by the Criminal Justice Act, 1967.
6. *the cat*: a reference to the cat o' nine tails, a multi-tailed whip used to inflict severe physical punishment. It originated in the Royal Navy and Army and it became a method of judicial punishment in Britain and elsewhere.
7. *taken the prisoners away ... done with them*: See. John 20:13.

June 13, 1908.

A THEORY OF TYRANTS.[1]

I have come to be convinced of late of a certain theory of the nature of tyranny.[2] It may be right or wrong, but I think it is at least worthy of thought in connection with a highly interesting matter. Broadly speaking, the common theory of tyranny has been this: That men have groaned under some system for centuries, and have at last rebelled against it. But I think that men have actually done quite otherwise; they have rebelled against the system against which they have not groaned. But the matter is so mixed and also so acute that I may be permitted to state it in a more explanatory manner.

Let us take, for the sake of argument, the two risings against tyranny most commonly considered in current literature – the English rebellion of the early seventeenth century and the French Revolution. According to the common theory, Charles I. should have been the heir of at least twenty intolerable despots. The truth is that he was the heir of one tolerable despot (who had not quite effected despotism), and beyond that everything was different. Queen Elizabeth was not tolerable, and she was not tolerated. In so far as she was endured she was adored. Cavaliers and Puritans alike looked back to her reign (most mistakenly, doubtless, but most certainly) as a midsummer of popular monarchy.

In short the English Puritans did not rebel against an old system; whatever else it was it was not old. Even if Charles I. had been a much worse king than he was there would not have been enough time for him to have created a complete and cruel tradition against the tradition of Elizabeth. A few years before Charles' head was cut off, most Englishmen would have died to keep Elizabeth's on. If you turn to the case of the French Monarchy before the French Revolution you will find exactly the same thing. A very short time before the Revolution the French Monarchy was the generally accepted French symbol. The King before Louis the Guillotined was Louis the Well-Beloved.[3] The Monarchy (in France as in England) became the most unpopular thing very soon after it had been the most popular thing. There was no weakness, there was no long decline: the defeat of the thing followed swiftly on its first victory. Charles I. was not the last of the English despots. He was one of the first of the English despots – only there happened to have been no more of them. Encouraged by the arrogance and popularity of Elizabeth, who had stood for patriotism and Protestantism and the defiance of Spain, Charles tried to work with Elizabethan England and found that Elizabethan England was not there. It was not too old to last, it was too new to last.

Louis XVI. was not the last of a line of unpopular kings. On the contrary, he was the first of a line of popular kings to be unpopular.

****

I can only explain all this by my private theory of tyrants; which is this. Men do not rebel against the old; rather they rebel against the new. They turn upon something when they find that it has them in a trap. They do not revolt against something that has been unpopular. They revolt (and very rightly) against something that has been popular. They hated Charles I. because they had loved Elizabeth. They killed Louis XVI. because they had been killed for Louis XIV. In fact, this is probably what is meant by that seemingly meaningless phrase, the fickleness of the mob. It probably means that the mob is quicker than other people in discovering that man has walked into a man-trap. England went mad with joy for the English Monarchy, because the Armada had not conquered England. And then England suddenly went mad with rage because it discovered that (during that exciting interlude) the English Monarchy had conquered England. We had escaped the snare of Philip; we walked into the snare of Elizabeth; we broke out of the snare of Charles I.

This is the essential mark of tyranny: that it is always new. Tyranny always enters by the unguarded gate. The tyrant is always shy and unobtrusive. The tyrant is always a traitor. He has always come there on the pretence that he was protecting something which people really wanted protected – religion, or public justice, or patriotic glory. Men staring at the Armada did not watch the King; so they strengthened the King. Later when they watched the King they unconsciously strengthened the aristocracy. Again, when they attacked the aristocracy, they did not watch the big merchants who were attacking it – and who wanted watching. All tyrannies are new tyrannies. There are no such things really as old tyrannies; there are hardly any such things as old superstitions.

For instance, the decorous Victorian woman is hardly as old as Victoria; she is much newer than Sophia Weston,[4] or Portia,[5] or Rosalind.[6] You do not know a tyranny until it is on top of you; until it has you in a trap. The tyrant is not present until he is omnipresent.

****

There is one moral to these evident facts of history. When you look for tyrants, do not look for them among the obvious types that have oppressed men in the past – the king, the priest, or the soldier. If you do you are merely looking at the Spanish Armada while England is being turned into a despotism behind your back. Monarchy was once a popular organ; yet it was turned against the people. Remember that newspapers are popular organs that may be turned against the people. Whatever the new tyrant is, he will not wear the exact uniform of the old tyrant. The new tyrant may wear any uniform; he may wear the beard of Dowie[7] or the skirts of Mrs. Eddy. But if you ask me, I think it most likely that the new tyrant will wear the uniform of an ordinary prison official announcing that the sentence of 7845 had better be indefinitely prolonged.[8]

Notes
1. *A THEORY OF TYRANTS*: Reprinted in *AWD*, pp. 99–101, excluding the penultimate paragraph and the final two sentences.
2. *I have come to be convinced ... tyranny*: See note 8, below, for the occasion of this essay.
3. *Louis the Well-Beloved*: Louis XV was commonly called '*le Bien-aimé*' after his recovery from a serious illness in 1747; public prayers had been offered for his recovery all over France. But the implication is that he was well beloved of God, not the people.
4. *Sophia Weston*: Presumably he means Sophia Western, Squire Western's daughter in Fielding's *Tom Jones* (1749).
5. *Portia*: The heroine of Shakespeare's *Merchant of Venice*.
6. *Rosalind*: The heroine of Shakespeare's *As You Like It*.
7. *Dowie*: John Alexander Dowie (1847–1907), the Scottish evangelist and religious leader who founded the utopian city of Zion, Illinois in 1900. He established there the Christian Catholic Apostolic Church, with himself as First Apostle.
8. *I think it most likely that the new tyrant ... indefinitely prolonged*: The Prevention of Crime Act, 1908 empowered the British courts to pass on 'habitual criminals' a sentence of indefinite 'preventive detention' in addition to the sentence pertaining to the crime of which they had been convicted. The contemporary liberal objections to this provision were (a) that it amounted to punishing an offender twice for the same offence, and (b) that it made the duration of imprisonment depend in effect on the recommendation of prison officials to the Home Office rather than a sentence of the courts. One of the major critics was Hilaire Belloc: see P. Jenkins, 'G. K. Chesterton and Resistance to Positivist Penology', *Law and Justice: The Christian Law Review*, 80–1 (1984), pp. 7–24.

June 27, 1908.

THE BATTLE OF THE BARREL ORGANS.

In a certain line of flats to the south of the river, in which is the residence of an acquaintance of mine (a man of the greatest physical and moral beauty), there has just occurred, or, rather, there is still occurring, an event which I think worth narrating. I think it worth narrating, not because it is extraordinary, but because it is ordinary. It is only one instance of an energy (or, perhaps, a lethargy) that is going on all over England, and has been going on for several centuries. I give it solely as an instance of what is probably happening in every locality, and certainly in every suburb. Let others go in for the unique or the paradoxical – for my part, I love only the commonplace. And I tell this simple tale of modern England and modern London, not because it is a case of the exception: I tell it, on the contrary, because it is a case of the rule – or of the misrule.

I was walking the other day along the front of these mansions of which I have spoken, when I suddenly saw, nailed on to that blameless bulk of buildings, the following mysterious notice: 'Organs and Street Cries Forbidden. – B. L. A.' At first I thought it was a joke, and a merely personal signature – that of Basil Lawrence Aldershaw, or of some other well-known practical joker. But I discover that it is really supposed to be some sort of serious power or authority that has some sort of right to prevent organ-grinders from playing organs. Here is a certain trade which is undoubtedly very popular with the English people, and this trade is suddenly forbidden in a public street. But by whom is it forbidden? Not by the King; not by the police; not by the Parliament; not (as would naturally be supposed) by the Emperor of the Universe; not, of course, by the mere abject savages who have to live in the houses. It is forbidden by the B. L. A.

What on earth is the B. L. A.? What is this power which is so sacredly despotic that it must not even be mentioned except by the dark hint of these dreadful initials. Who is B. L. A., the tyrant? Are we ruled by the Best-Looking Aunt? Is our master the Best Liverpool Astrologer? Are we helpless in the hands of the

Blonde Lady Aeronaut? Or of the Blackest Living Anglo-Saxon? I asked the porter who is charged to look after the flats what it all was, and by what authority they did these things. He didn't know. I asked the policeman. He didn't know. I asked all my neighbours whom I happened to know, approaching the point delicately. I suggested that perhaps they had joined some secret society called the B. L. A. – a society threatening daggers and a vendetta. Perhaps a purely Italian society, to destroy certain particular Italian organ grinders. But they shook their heads. My neighbours never seemed to have heard of the B. L. A. None of them had consented to the notice. Most of them disapproved of it. Those who were stupid did not mind barrel organs. Those who were intellectual, of course, liked barrel organs. I, for instance, adore them to distraction. But I would give up anything, I would even give up barrel organs (with a burst of tears) if the community in which I live, if my neighbours and equals, had objected to them by a decent democratic majority. But my neighbours and equals had never been asked. They did not object: the B. L. A. objected.

****

In some forgotten forest of the past a fence fell down and was put up again ten feet further, enclosing a strip of land. Slowly the common grew as small as the goose on the common. In almost every case the theory of mediaeval justice was against the encroachment; in almost every case the poor man, in theory, could have won his case at law. But the poor never went to the law. The peasant returned at twilight and found a lawless barrier across the path to his home. For a moment he thought of invoking the justice of the King: then, after a pause, he shrugged his shoulders and went home by some other way. And so, step by step, the new avarice ate up England. The squires and the strong thieves stole ceaselessly and silently. The whole process was one of silent and evolutionary impudence. They might have been stopped at any moment. They were not stopped at any moment. So the Howards[1] and the Cecils[2] rose upon the ruins of religion; so the Russells[3] flung their gigantic shadow over the Fens. So was built up the strongest aristocracy of modern times, the aristocracy under which we live; so was created the immense and omnipotent society of the B. L. A. What can it mean – the B. L. A.? How would 'Bluff licks all' do for an explanation?

****

I have since heard a suggestion about the meaning of this extraordinary phrase. I heard it after a heated scene in our road, when an organ-grinder came by and I offered him from one balcony money to stay, while another gentleman from another balcony offered him money to go. Between us, I think, he did well, but eventually he decided to go. England undoubtedly loves the Italian organ-grinder; but what is that when one is condemned by the B. L. A.? I have heard that this means (of all things in the world) 'Betterment of London Association'.[4] These earnest thinkers have discovered that there is something wrong with London – something smelling of money about Park Lane, something faintly suggesting poverty in Poplar. Some say this is due to sweaters, some to priests, some to agitators, some to Protection, some to Free Trade, some to Christians, some to Atheists. But the B. L. A. looks deeper. It sees that all this evil of London is really due to organ-grinders. It is a thought too deep to be followed in this idle fashion. I only know that the organ grinder has turned a corner and started playing in a poorer street. And from the mere jerk and joy of his music I know that he has entered England.

Notes
1. *the Howards*: The Howards entered the ranks of the British aristocracy through John Howard, created Duke of Norfolk in 1483. His descendants fulfilled (and still fulfil) the role of Earl Marshall of England (see 'The Radical', *DN*, 19 January 1907, Volume 4, p. 142, n. 5 above.) and also acquired the titles of Earl of Arundel, Earl of Surrey and Earl of Norfolk. The Norfolks became a prominent recusant family and have remained central to the Roman Catholic laity in Britain.
2. *the Cecils*: The Cecil family has exercised great political influence in Britain since its descent from William Cecil, Lord Burghley, Lord Treasurer of Elizabeth I. His elder son Thomas was created Earl of Exeter and remained at the family home Burghley House, Northamptonshire. Burghley's second son, Robert, created Earl of Salisbury in 1605, built Hatfield House, Hertfordshire, the family seat for his line of the family.
3. *the Russells*: The Russell family, Earls and Dukes of Bedford, owed their preferment to Henry VIII. As a faithful servant of the king, John Russell acquired – and managed to retain on Henry's death – large tracts of church land, including the abbatial estate of Thornley in Cambridgeshire.
4. *'Betterment of London Association'*: The Betterment of London Association was founded in 1902 under the presidency of the artist Sir William Blake Richmond (1842–1921) to campaign against (among many other things, including 'expectorating on public conveyances') smoke and noise pollution in London. Sir William Richmond also founded the Coal Smoke Abatement Society in 1898. Chesterton does not seem to have been alone in regarding The Betterment of London Association as an organization of busybodies: cf. *British Medical Journal*, 24 November, 1906, p. 1513.

July 4, 1908.

THE BEAUTY OF BUFFINS.

It is possible to sympathise with the freaks of the wealthy, so long as they are vulgar. Where there is vulgarity there will most probably be some sort of simplicity[;] as long as the upstart keeps his loud clothes, crying carpets and screaming wallpaper, he has, perhaps, a modest and reasonable self-respect. It is when he begins to go in for art furniture that he does not appreciate that he becomes vulgar in the more vital sense.

I have met many really vulgar people; but only once in one happy hour did I see a really vulgar drawing-room; the real parvenu's drawing-room of 'Punch', with the furniture in crimson and the hostess in magenta. I do not know the man's name (nobody did); but I am sure his heart was of gold, like many other little knick-knacks scattered about that remarkable room. To me the room seemed red hot with sincerity. For the parvenu is not a snob because he is bold and blatant; the parvenu is a snob because he is sensitive and alarmed. Vulgarity is in timidity; even in refined timidity. There is nothing vulgar about courage, even about brutal courage. The upstart is a snob when he is swift to learn the ways of gentlemen, not when he is slow to learn them.

****

So it is with the decisive public actions of the rich, even with their public interferences and public follies. These are always better if they are done plainly on a big scale, and with the stunning force of simplicity. I always felt a warm admiration myself for that celebrated Mr. Buffins (or whatever his name was) who had carved on the sea wall, 'Presented to his native town by John Buffins. The sea is his, and he made it.'[1] Here Buffins exhibited unmistakably the two noblest human qualities I know of; local patriotism and a religious and cosmic gratitude. He merely failed in sufficiently observing a fine shade of syntax and the relative position of words; a matter of much less importance. But there are many other authentic cases of this enormous naivete in the plutocrat, which is by far his most agreeable aspect. In a town I once wandered into in the South-East of England a successful builder had named big blocks of successful buildings after his own babies or young children. A whole huge new street would stand up in the sun bearing the name in large letters, 'Tommy's Villas'. Round the corner, no doubt, the town was overshadowed by some awful pile called 'Little Mabel's Mansions'. Or just outside the town (though I did not look for them) there were probably some densely populated tenements called 'Baby's Buildings', rather taller than the skyscrapers of New York. This is what we may call having the domestic affections on a large scale.

Another man who had them in the same expansive manner was a banker at Oban, who, when the inhabitants of that town were looking in some other direction (probably at a steamer full of tourists), seized the opportunity to erect on the hill behind a building similar in size and conception to the Coliseum at Rome; and was only with difficulty prevented from surmounting it with colossal statues of all his aunts and uncles.[2] I sympathise with that sort of man. The thing might perhaps have somewhat defaced the Highland landscape, but not half so much as some much more refined persons deface it with their shooting boxes[3] and their champagne. The banker's Coliseum occupied a painfully large space compared with any that you and I could afford for the relics of family affection. But it occupied a very small space compared with the spaces of those Highland hills and valleys which a few rich men deliberately keep desolate and inhuman for the sake of games no more serious than battledore and shuttlecock.

****

No; the most endurable kind of plutocracy is this coarse and hearty and open kind, that is proud of its wealth as of a new toy, but proud also of its nearest and dearest as of an ancestral religion. If we are to have plutocracy the more ostentatious it is the better. The most unendurable kind is that which works by illusive gentlemanliness and voiceless intrigue. The worst kind is the B. L. A., of which I spoke last week.[4] In case this is the first (and perhaps the last) time that the reader's eye has fallen on this column I may inform him that in certain parts of our extraordinary civilization some one nails up a notice without leave from God or man, 'Street organs forbidden. – B. L. A.' If you try to discover who B. L. A. is that he should prevent him who has hands from turning a handle, or he that has ears to hear from hearing, you will find that nobody for miles round has the faintest idea. If at last when your hair is white with age and your spirit broken in the British Museum Library you may have deciphered the hieroglyphic, and know that B. L. A. means 'Betterment of London Association', you will discover (as far as I can make out) that it is simply a certain number of private gentlemen with large private incomes and an accidental private dislike of barrel organs. I do not see why I should not put up placards of this kind on my own account.

****

I cannot see why I should not start a quiet little club called 'The Institution of Infinite Improvement', and shut half the streets of London to all the particular people whom I happen to dislike. Thus you would see in one street 'South African millionaires forbidden, I. I. I.' Or in another 'No Irish Unionists allowed down this road, I. I. I.' Or in another 'Professors of Eugenics must go round by the back street, I. I. I.' Or I might decree that they should enter houses by some humbler approach, so that each house should have first a visitors' entrance, then a tradesmen's entrance, and, lowest of all, an Imperialists' entrance.

For all I know the thing would be successful. But frankly I prefer the style of Mr. John Buffins, who writes his own name in full and in very large letters. And if I am ever a rich man (an hypothesis only entertainable for the sake of argument), if I am ever a rich man I mean to be a frightfully vulgar one. 'B. L. A.' is not so honest as Buffins, and is much more autocratic. All that poor Buffins said by mistake seems a comparatively mild boast in the mouth of B. L. A. – that veiled Sultan. The organ-grinders are his and he made them; and I am sure he would have no hesitation in silencing the vulgar clamour of the sea.

Notes
1. *The sea is his, and he made it*: See Psalm 95:5: 'The sea is His, and He made it: and His hands formed the dry land'.
2. *Another man ... aunts and uncles*: McCaig's Tower overlooking Oban Bay was commissioned and designed by John Stuart McCaig. A wealthy philanthropic banker and an admirer of classical architecture, he built the tower as a memorial to his family and a means of employing local craftsmen in the winter months. It was left unfinished when he died in 1902. According to the original plans, it was to have been much taller and to have contained statues of the members of his family in all of the ninety-four arches. Chesterton visited Oban in 1903: see his letter to the editor, 'Wanted: A Programme', *DN*, 18 July 1903, Volume 2, pp. 99–102 above.
3. *shooting boxes*: It should perhaps be explained that 'shooting boxes' in this sense are small country houses used by sportsmen during the grouse shooting season (12 August to 30 November). The building of vulgar examples by wealthy parvenus is satirized in Compton MacKenzie's *The Monarch of the Glen* (1941).
4. *the B. L. A., of which I spoke last week*: see 'The Battle of the Barrel Organs', *DN*, 27 June 1908, pp. 90–2 above.

July 11, 1908.

ON SMUGGLERS.

I was walking along that strip of East Sussex which is flat and marshy, but full of history and the picturesque, where some of the Five Ports[1] are left stranded, where many conquerors are alleged to have come and one not to have come: for I have heard that there is a rustic song that runs in this spirited manner:

> If Bonyparte should find the heart
>   To land on Pevensey Level,
> Then my three sons with their three guns
>   Will blow him to the Devil.

A very fine poem, I think: and involving all that is noble in the idea of a Territorial Army. But as I was walking along the windy flats, broken with sand-ridges and ragged grass, I came upon a coastguard station: or, rather, upon what had been a coastguard station, but was no more. Many of them, I believe, are being abandoned, upon the fantastic and irrelevant ground that they are of no use. As there were no coastguards, I naturally looked round for smugglers. But they seem to have gone away too.

****

I was somewhat cast down by this: and then I remembered joyfully that perhaps, after all, I may live to see smuggling again; real smugglers rolling barrels up these slopes of sand and (let us hope) with pistols in their belts. For if we ever have a revival of tariffs, surely the least we can ask from Providence is a renascence of smugglers. I incline to think that in this fortunate atmosphere of fisticuffs and battered policemen, it would be our duty as Free Traders to take a hand in the desperate trade. I like to think of Lord Courtney,[2] say, in a tasselled cap, with a cutlass. It is agreeable to imagine Sir Henry Fowler,[3] with a knife in his teeth, creeping into a cavern with a barrel marked 'Gunpowder'.

If ever tariffs were revived in an extreme sense smuggling might be carried on on quite a large and imaginative scale; a scale demanding no small talent for disguise and invention. It would require, for instance, a good deal of tact to smuggle a giraffe. Yet one could easily imagine the necessity arising if some of the Protectionist theories of patriotism were ever logically enforced.

I wonder that the Tariff Reformers have never turned their attention to the horrible case of the Zoological Gardens. In that abandoned Arcadia all disguise is thrown off. It is not even pretended that the lions are of English manufacture. The keepers are not even instructed to pretend that the ostriches, flamingoes, and emus are birds out of our own hedgerows. There is the Bactrian camel, whose very name betrays him; nor have the authorities even reached so modest and Balfourian a point of Imperial preference as to give the best buns to the Indian elephant, while severely beating and banging the African elephant.

There arises before my prophetic eye (which is best clarified by winking the other one), a vision of the Imperial Zoological Gardens, tenanted only with the varied types of a self-supporting Empire. There, in the true Imperial manner, all would be peace because nobody would be allowed to criticise anything; the South African lion would lie down with the New Zealand lamb; and the Tasmanian Devil would insist on being called the Tasmanian Angel. Under these circumstances a few bold spirits might attempt to smuggle a giraffe; and, as I say, I think they would find it a delicate proceeding, abounding in social embarrassment and elaborate explanation. A giraffe walking down the street completely covered with brown paper, or canvas, would rather increase public alarm than allay it.

I once had a scheme for smoothing the way of large families to the seaside by putting each child in a box, about the size and formation of the milk cans that stand in rows at railway stations; a box bearing the same rude resemblance to the shape of a child that a violin case does to the violin. There would be something very touching in the sight of Mr. and Mrs. Jones waiting happily for the train, without the usual shrieks and scrambling, while beside them in a row stood rudely pyramidal shapes, proportioned to the different sizes, and tenderly reminding them of the characteristic outline of each of their beloved offspring.

But this expedient, however applicable to a baby, is decidedly awkward in the case of a giraffe. If you did lock up a giraffe in a box appropriate to his shape and size, it is not very easy to say what you could say that it was. A lamp-post, perhaps; but few, even of the wealthy and luxurious[,] take their own lamp-posts with them when they travel. I fear there would be great difficulties in the path of the scientific smuggler who wished to smuggle foreign animals into the Imperial Zoo.

****

Then there is another kind of smuggling that might become common if certain tendencies supposed to be patriotic become dominant in our island. I mean that that might arise from the common attempts to keep out the alien. All very typical or genuine Englishmen have a great preliminary objection to the idea of keeping out the alien; the notion of the open ports and the island of hospitality is one of the two or three very strong and strictly English traditions. Still I can perfectly comprehend any country under certain extreme alien evils excluding all the aliens.

But the extraordinary thing is this; that we do, as a matter of fact, suffer from some real alien evils; and those are exactly the alien evils that nobody proposes to exclude. The man who has partly poisoned the very springs of England is not the poor alien, but the rich alien. The Imperial politicians and editors are very much frightened of the helpless foreigner.[4] But they are not at all frightened of the powerful foreigner; on the contrary, they make him a peer or let him dictate their Colonial policy.[5] Now if there were ever really a national movement for excluding aliens it would certainly be for excluding all aliens, especially those strangers who were strong and rich enough really to hurt us.

In such a case as that what would become of the great Imperialist newspapers and the great Conservative clubs? What could they do, cut off from their necessary supply of Prussian Jews?[6] They would have to smuggle them in secretly, in barrels or something of that sort. Instead of making a box to hold a giraffe, we should be confronted with the subtler problem of making one of such a shape as comfortably to hold a millionaire. There would have to be an underground passage between certain caves by the shore and the cellars of the Carlton Club.[7] Or the alien might be hurriedly knighted on landing, invested with the Garter, and so on, and then afterwards put into the barrel and rolled away. These are matters of detail which I cannot feel myself competent to decide.

I only comfort myself by gazing at the deserted and defenceless coastguard station, and stroll away towards the leaden and silver sea.

Notes
1. *Five Ports*: The 'five ports' – still called in England the 'Cinque Ports' – are Hastings, New Romney, Hythe, Dover and Sandwich. Chesterton is referring specifically to New Romney, which is now more than a mile away from the sea, and Hythe, the harbour of which has been silted up for several centuries.
2. *Lord Courtney*: Leonard Henry Courtney, Baron Courtney of Penwith (1832–1918), was a journalist and politician. A Liberal MP from 1876 to 1900, Courtney served in Gladstone's second ministry. He was a prominent Free Trader and anti-imperialist.
3. *Sir Henry Fowler*: Sir Henry Fowler (1870–1938), was a mechanical engineer and metallurgist. As a gas engineer and works manager to the Midland Railway at Derby, Fowler

advocated super-heated steam and compound expansion to improve locomotive efficiency (G. W. Carpenter, *ODNB*).

4. *The Imperial politicians ... helpless foreigner*: A reference to the Aliens Act of 1905 which introduced moderate controls on immigration into Britain for the first time. The Act empowered the Home Secretary to refuse entrance to 'undesirable immigrants' and deport those who slipped into the country unnoticed. Although a response to pressure to restrict Jewish immigration, the measure was not overtly discriminatory; however, it was ill-framed in judging the acceptability of immigrants by the presence of 'money in their pockets'.
5. *But they are not at all frightened ... Colonial policy*: A reference to Alfred, Viscount Milner; see 'Ballads of the War', 19 April 1901, Volume 1, p. 75, n. 5 above.
6. *What could they do ... Prussian Jews?*: Perhaps a reference to Alfred Beit; see 'Fabian Futilities', *DN*, 30 September 1901, Volume 1, p. 212, n. 4 above.
7. *Carlton Club*: The oldest and most exclusive Conservative club in Britain, the Carlton Club was founded in 1832 to co-ordinate Tory party activity following its defeat over the First Reform Act.

July 18, 1908.

G. K. C.

**

A Character Study.[1]

Walking down Fleet-street some day you may meet a form whose vastness blots out the heavens. Great waves of hair surge from under the soft wide-brimmed hat. A cloak that might be a legacy from Porthos[2] floats about his colossal frame. He pauses in the midst of the pavement to read the book in his hand, and a cascade of laughter descending from the head notes to the middle voice gushes out on the listening air. He looks up, adjusts his pince-nez, observes that he is not in a cab, remembers that he ought to be in a cab; turns and hails a cab. The vehicle sinks down under the unusual burden and rolls heavily away. It carries Gilbert Keith Chesterton.

Mr. Chesterton is the most conspicuous figure in the landscape of literary London. He is like a visitor out of some fairy tale, a legend in the flesh, a survival of the childhood of the world. Most of us are the creatures of our time, thinking its thoughts, wearing its clothes, rejoicing in its chains. If we try to escape from the temporal tyranny, it is through the gate of revolt that we go. Some take to asceticism or to some fantastic foppery of the moment. Some invent Utopias, lunch on nuts and proteid at Eustace Miles'[3] and flaunt red ties defiantly in the face of men and angels. The world is bond, but they are free. But in all this they are still the children of our time, fleeting and self-conscious. Mr. Chesterton's extravagances have some of this quality. He is not a rebel. He is a wayfarer from the ages, stopping at the inn of life, warming himself at the fire and making the rafters ring with his jolly laughter.

Time and place are accidents: he is elemental and primitive. He is not of one time, but of all times. One imagines him wrestling with the giant Skrymir and drinking deep draughts from the horn of Thor;[4] or exchanging jests with Falstaff at the Boar's Head in Eastcheap,[5] or joining in the intellectual revels at the

Mermaid Tavern,⁶ or meeting Johnson foot to foot and dealing blow for mighty blow. With Rabelais⁷ he rioted and Don Quixote and Sancho were his 'vera brithers'.⁸ One seems to see him coming down from the twilight of fable through the centuries, calling wherever there is good company, and welcome wherever he calls, for he brings no cult of the time or pedantry of the age with him.

****

He has the freshness and directness of the child's vision. In a very real sense indeed he has never left the golden age – never come out into the light of common day, where the tone is grey and things have lost their imagery. He lives in a world of romance, peopled with giants and gay with the light laughter of fairies. The visible universe is full of magic and mystery. The trees are giants waving their arms in the air, carrying us all on a magnificent adventure through space. He moves in an atmosphere of enchantment, and may stumble upon a romance at the next street corner. Beauty in distress may call to him from some hollow secrecy: some tyrannous giant may straddle like Apollyon across the path as he turns into Carmelite-street.⁹ It is well that he has his swordstick with him, for one never knows what may turn up in this incredible world. Memory goeth not back to a time when a sword was not his constant companion. It used to be a wooden sword, with which went a wooden helmet glowing with the pigments of Apollo. Those were the days when the horn of Roland echoed again through Roncesvalles, and Lancelot pricked forth to the jousts, and

> Ever the scaly shape of monstrous sin
> At last lay vanquished, fold on writhing fold.¹⁰

Ah, le bon temps quand j'étais – jeune. But he still carries with him the glamour of the morning; his cheek still blanches at Charlemagne's 'What a marching life is mine!'¹¹ I burst in on him one afternoon and found him engaged in a furious attack on a row of fat books, around which his sword flashed like the sword of Sergeant Troy around the figure of Bathsheba Everdene.¹² His eye blazed, his cheek paled, and beads of perspiration – no uncommon thing – stood out on his brow. It was a terrific combat, and it was fortunate that the foe were not as in the leading case of Don Quixote disguised in wine-skins, for that would have involved lamentable bloodshed. As it was, the books wore an aspect of insolent calm. One could almost see the contemptuous curl upon the lip, the haughty assurance of victory. I own it was hard to bear.

****

Adventure is an affair of the soul, not of circumstance. Thoreau by his pond at Walden or paddling up the Concord had more adventures than Stanley had on the Congo, more adventures than Stanley could have. That was why he refused to come to Europe. He knew he could see as many wonders from his own backyard as he could see though he sought for them in the islands of the farthest seas. 'Why, who makes much of miracles'? says Whitman.

> As to me I know of nothing else but miracles...
> To me every hour of the light and dark is a miracle.[13]

Miracles and adventures are the stuff of Mr. Chesterton's everyday life. He goes out on to the Sussex downs with his coloured chalks – in the cavernous mysteries of his pockets there is always a box of pastels though 'the mark of the mint', in his own phrase, may be unaccountably absent – and discovers he has no white chalk with which to complete his picture. His foot stumbles against a mound and lo! He is standing on a mountain of chalk, and he shouts with joy at the miracle, for the world has never lost its freshness and wonder to him.[14] It is as though he discovers it anew each day, and stands exultant at the revelation.

It is a splendid pageant that passes unceasingly before him –

> New and yet as old
> As the foundations of heaven and earth.[15]

Familiarity has not robbed it of its life and magic. He sees it as the child sees its first rainbow or the lightning flashing from the thundercloud. Most of us, before we reach maturity, find life stale and unprofitable –

> a twice told tale
> Vexing the dull ears of a drowsy man.[16]

We are like the blasé policeman I met when I was waiting for a bus at Finchley last Bank holiday. 'A lot of people abroad to-day?' I said interrogatively. 'Yes', he said, 'thousands'. 'Where do most of them go this way?' 'Oh to Barnet. Though what they see in Barnet I can't make out. I never see nothin' in Barnet'. 'Perhaps they like to see the green fields and hear the birds', I said. 'Well, perhaps', he replied, in the tone of one who tolerated follies which he was too enlightened to show. 'There'll be more at the Exhibition, I suppose?' I said, hoping to turn his mind to the contemplation of a more cheerful subject. 'The Exhibition! Well, I was down there on duty the day it was opened, and I never see such a poor show. Oh, yes the gardens; they're all right, but you can see gardens anywhere'. Despairingly I mentioned Hampstead as a merry place on Bank Holiday. 'Well, I never see nothin' in 'Ampstead myself. I dunno what the people go for. And there's the

Garden City there, and crowds and crowds a-going to look at it. Well, what is there in it? That's what I asks. What-is-there-in-it? I never see nothin' in it'.

The world of culture shares the policeman's physical ennui in a spiritual sense. It sees 'nothing in it'. We succeed in deadening the fresh intensity of the impression, and burying the miracle under the dust of the common day – veiling it under names and formulas. 'This green, flowery, rock-built earth, the trees, the mountains, rivers, many-sounding seas: – that great deep sea of azure that swims overhead; the winds sweeping through it; the black cloud fashioning itself together, now pouring out fire, now hail and rain; what *is* it? Ay, what? At bottom, we do not know; we can never know at all. It is not by our superior insight that we escape the difficulty; it is by our superior levity, our inattention, our *want* of insight. It is by *not* thinking that we cease to wonder at it ... This world, after all our science and sciences, is still a miracle; wonderful, inscrutable, *magical* and more, to whomsoever will *think* of it'.[17] It is this elemental faculty of wonder, of which Carlyle speaks, that distinguishes Mr. Chesterton from his contemporaries, and gives him kinship at once with the seers and the children. He is anathema to the erudite and the exact; but he sees life in the large, with the eyes of the first man on the day of creation. As he says, in inscribing a book of Caldecott's pictures for a little friend of mine[18] –

> This is the sort of book we like
>   (For you and I are very small)
> With pictures stuck in anyhow.
> And hardly any words at all.
>
>   ******
>
> You will not understand a word
>   Of all the words, including mine;
> Never you trouble; you can see
>   And all directness is divine –
>
> Stand up and keep your childishness;
>   Read all the pedants' screeds and strictures;
> But don't believe in anything
>   That can't be told in coloured pictures.

Life to him is a book of coloured pictures that he sees without external comment or exegesis. He sees it, as it were, at first hand, and shouts out his vision at the top of his voice. Hence the audacity that is so trying to the formalist who is dominated by custom and authority. Hence the rain of paradoxes that he showers down. It is often suggested that these paradoxes are a conscious trick to attract attention – that Mr. Chesterton stands on his head, as it were, to gather a crowd. I can conceive him standing on his head in Fleet-street in sheer joy at the sight of St. Paul's, but not in vanity or with a view to a collection. The truth is that his paradox is his own comment on the coloured picture.

****

There are some men who hoard life as a miser hoards his gold – map it out with frugal care and vast prescience, spend to-day in taking thought for tomorrow. Mr. Chesterton spends life like a prodigal. Economy has no place in his spacious vocabulary. 'Economy' he might say, with Anthony Hope's Mr. Carter, 'is going without something you do want in case you should some day want something which you probably won't want'.[19] Mr. Chesterton lives the unconsidered, untrammelled life. He simply rambles along without a thought of where he is going. If he likes the look of a road he turns down it, careless of where it may lead to. 'He is announced to lecture at Bradford tonight', said a speaker, explaining his absence from a dinner. 'Probably he will turn up at Edinburgh'. He will wear no harness, learn no lessons, observe no rules. He is himself, Chesterton – not consciously or rebelliously, but unconsciously, like a natural element. St. Paul's School never had a more brilliant nor a less sedulous scholar. He did not win prizes, but he read more books, drew more pictures, wrote more poetry than any other boy that ever played at going to school. His house was littered with books, filled with verses and grotesque drawings. All attempts to break him into routine failed. He tried the Slade School, and once even sat on a stool in an office.[20] Think of it! G. K. C. in front of a ledger, totting up figures with romantic results – figures that turned into knights in armour, broke into song, and added together produced paradoxes unknown to arithmetic! He saw the absurdity of it all. 'A man must follow his vocation', he said with Falstaff,[21] and his vocation is to have none.

And so he rambles along, engaged in an endless disputation, punctuated with gusts of Rabelaisian laughter, and leaving behind a litter of fragments. You may track him by the blotting-pads he decorates with his riotous fancies, and may come up with him in the midst of a group of children, for whom he is drawing hilarious pictures of his toy theatre, the chief child of his fancy and invention. If you cannot find him, and Fleet-street looks lonely and forsaken, then be sure he has been spirited away to some lonely spot by his wife, the keeper of his business conscience, to finish a book for which some publisher is angrily clamouring. For 'No clamour, no book' is his maxim.

Mr. Chesterton's natural foil in these days is Mr. Bernard Shaw. Mr. Shaw is the type of revolt. The flesh we eat, the wine we drink, the clothes we wear, the laws we obey, the religion we affect – all are an abomination to him. He would raze the whole fabric to the ground, and build all anew upon an ordered and symmetrical plan. Mr. Chesterton has none of this impatience with the external garment of society. He enjoys disorder and loves the haphazard. With Rossetti, he might say, 'What is it to me whether the earth goes round the sun or the sun round the earth?'[22] It is not the human intellect that interests him, but the human heart and the great comedy of life. He opposes ancient sympathies to modern antipathies. It follows that Mr. Shaw's weapon is wit, sharp-edged as the east wind, and that Mr. Chesterton's weapon is humour that buffets you like a gale from the west.

****

No man was ever more careless of his reputation. He is indifferent whether from his abundant mine he shovels out diamonds or dirt. You may take it or leave it, as you like. He cares not, and bears no malice. It is all a blithe improvisation, done in sheer ebullience of spirit and having no relation to conscious literature. He is like a child shouting with glee at the sight of the flowers and the sunshine and chalking on every vacant hoarding he passes with a jolly rapture of invention and no thought beyond.

But there is one thing, and one only, about which he is serious, and that is his own seriousness. You may laugh with him and at him and about him. When at a certain dinner, one of the speakers said that his chivalry was so splendid that he had been known to rise in a tramcar and 'offer his seat to three ladies', it was his laugh that sounded high above all the rest. But if you would wound him, do not laugh at his specific gravity: doubt his spiritual gravity. Doubt his passion for justice and liberty and patriotism – most of all, his patriotism. For he is, above all, the lover of Little England and the foe of Imperialism, whose love of country is 'not what a mystic means by the love of God, but what a child might mean by the love of jam'. 'My country, right or wrong!' he cries. 'Why it is a thing no patriot could say. It is like saying, "My mother, drunk or sober". No doubt if a decent man's mother took to drink he would share her troubles to the last; but to talk as if he would be in a state of gay indifference as to whether his mother took to drink or not is certainly not the language of men who know the great mystery ... We fall back upon gross and frivolous things for our patriotism ... Our schoolboys are left to live and die in the infantile type of patriotism which they learnt from a box of tin soldiers ... We have made our public schools the strongest wall against a whisper of the honour of England ... What have we done and where have we wandered, we that have produced sages who could have spoken with Socrates, and poets who could walk with Dante, that we should talk as if we have never done anything more intelligent than found colonies and kick niggers? We are the children of light and it is we that sit in darkness. If we are judged, it will not be for the merely intellectual transgression of failing to appreciate other nations, but for the supreme spiritual transgression of failing to appreciate ourselves'.[23]

******

I sometimes think that one moonlight night, when he is tired of Fleet-street, he will scale the walls of the Tower and clad himself in a suit of giant mail, with shield and sword to match. He will come forth with vizor down and mount the battle steed that champs its bit outside. And the clatter of his hoofs will ring through the quiet of the city night as he thunders through St. Pauls Churchyard and down Ludgate-hill and out on to the Great North-road. And then once more will be heard the cry of 'St. George for Merry England!' and there will be the clash of swords in the greenwood and brave deeds done on the King's highway.

A. G. G.

Notes
1. *G. K. C.: A Character Study*: The author was A. G. Gardiner, at the time editor of the *Daily News*. The piece is reprinted in his collection of biographical essays called *Prophets, Priests and Kings* (London: J. M. Dent & Sons, 1908).
2. *Porthos*: Porthos, Baron du Vallon de Bracieux de Pierrefonds, is one of the 'three musketeers' in Alexandre Dumas's musketeers trilogy; he is represented as being physically very large and a great lover of wine and food – evidently why the comparison suggested itself here.
3. *lunch on nuts and proteid at Eustace Miles*: The Eustace Miles Restaurant was a health food restaurant in Chandos Street near Charing Cross Station, London, opened in 1907; the proprietor, Eustace Miles, was a noted 'real' tennis player who competed in the 1908 Olympic Games. The restaurant became a favourite meeting place for suffragette groups. 'Proteid' was a patent protein powder food supplement marketed by Eustace Miles at his establishment.
4. *wrestling with the giant Skrymir ... Thor*: The reference is to *Gylfaginning*, the first part of Snorri Sturluson's *Prose Edda* (*c*. 1220); see A. Orchard, *Dictionary of Norse Myth and Legend* (London: Cassell, 1997).
5. *exchanging jests with Falstaff ... Eastcheap*: Sir John Falstaff, frequenter of the Boar's Head tavern in Eastcheap, is a comic character who appears in three of Shakespeare's plays: *Henry IV Part 1*, *Henry IV Part 2*, and *The Merry Wives of Windsor*.
6. *joining in the intellectual revels at the Mermaid Tavern*: The Mermaid Tavern near St Paul's Cathedral, London, was the meeting-place of the Friday Club founded by Sir Walter Raleigh in 1603. Its membership included William Shakespeare, Ben Jonson, John Donne and other literary notables; some account of their 'intellectual revels' is in 'Master Francis Beaumont's Letter to Ben Jonson' in *English Poetry 1: Chaucer to Gray* (New York: P. F. Collier & Son, 1909–14).
7. *Rabelais*: François Rabelais; see 'Charles Dickens', *DN*, 8 February 1902, Volume 1, p. 331, n. 14 above.
8. *'vera brithers'*: 'Vera brither' seems to come from Burns's 'Tam o'Shanter':

And at his elbow, Souter Johnny,
His ancient, trusty, drouthy crony;
Tam lo'ed him like a vera brither –
They had been fou for weeks thegither!

Quite why the expression should suggest itself in connection with Don Quixote is not clear!

9. *Some tyrannous giant ... Carmelite-street*: Northcliffe House, headquarters of the Harmsworth Press, is situated in Carmelite Street off Fleet Street, London. In Bunyan's *The Pilgrim's Progress*, Apollyon is the 'foul fiend' who assails Christian on his pilgrimage through the Valley of Humiliation.
10. *Ever the scaly shape ... writhing fold*: William Watson, 'The Purple East: A Series of Sonnets on England's Desertion of Armenia' (1896).
11. *cheek still blanches at Charlemagne's 'What a marching life is mine!'*: Gardiner uses the same trope in *The War Lords* (London: J. M. Dent & Sons, 1915), p. 229, but I have not been able to find its origin.
12. *the sword of Sargeant Troy ... Bathsheba Everdene*: See Thomas Hardy, *Far From the Madding Crowd* (1874), ch. 28.
13. *As to me ... miracle*: Walt Whitman, *Leaves of Grass*, 'Miracles' (1856).
14. *He goes out onto the Sussex downs ... wonder to him*: See 'A Piece of Chalk', *DN*, 4 November 1905, Volume 3, pp. 229–32 above.
15. *New and yet as old ... earth*: not identified
16. *a twice told tale ... drowsy man*: Shakespeare, *King John,* III.iv; cf. *Hamlet*, I.ii.
17. *'This green, flowery, rock-built earth ... will* think *of it'*: Carlyle, *On Heroes and Hero-Worship*, lecture 1.
18. *inscribing a book of Caldecott's pictures ... little friend of mine*: Randolph Caldecott (1846–86), was an artist and book illustrator. Caldecott exploited the new opportunities for colour lithograph printing in the 1870s. He began a long series of Caldecott's Picture Books published by Routledge; these included *John Gilpin* (1878), *The House that Jack Built* (1878), *Babes in the Wood* (1879) and *Ride a Cock Horse* (1884). The books sold in great numbers (J. Hamilton, *ODNB*). The 'little friend' referred to here was probably Gardiner's youngest child, Gilbert, who was Chesterton's godson.
19. *Anthony Hope's Mr. Carter ... probably won't want*: Anthony Hope, *The Dolly Dialogues* (1894), 12: 'An Uncounted Hour'.
20. *once even sat on a stool in an office*: See 'Reading the Riddle', *DN*, 20 April 1907, Volume 4, p. 208, n. 2 above.
21. *A man must follow his vocation ... Falstaff*: Henry *IV Part 1*, IV.ii: 'Why, Hal, 'tis my *vocation*, Hal; 'tis no sin for a *man* to labour in *his vocation'*.
22. *With Rossetti ... sun round the Earth*: See A. G. Gardiner, 'On Losing One's Memory', in *Pebbles on the Shore* (London: J. M. Dent & Sons 1916).
23. *'not what a mystic means ... failing to appreciate ourselves'*: G. K. Chesterton, 'A Gap in English Education', *Speaker*, 4 May 1901, 128–9; reprinted in *The Defendant* (London: Dent, 1901), pp. 165–71.

July 18, 1908.

NOTIONS AND THE NURSERY.

I read the following paragraph in the last issue of this paper:

> There is to be a thoroughly practical sequel to the summoning of Mr. Edwin Collins, of St. John's Wood, for failing to send his children to school. With the help of some influential sympathisers Mr. Collins is to open a 'reformed' school in the neighbourhood of London, and, although the plans are not yet far advanced, it is hoped that the experiment may be in full swing before the end of the summer. Boys and girls will be educated side by side, and will live almost entirely in the open air.[1]

Mr. Collins explains that instead of class rooms there will be class fields and class gardens. 'The class gardens separated from one another by trees and bushes will in some cases be provided with blackboards and school desks'. Also, I suppose, all the trees and flowers far away to the purple horizon will have little tickets tied on to them with their names in English and Latin. And such birds as are permitted to fly freely about will have a wooden label round their necks inscribed with a short bright description of their biological origin and habits. Such additions, at least, could hardly increase the hideous irony of taking a child deliberately into the playground and not allowing him to play. Mr. Collins's children will only associate trees and bushes with routine and compulsion instead of with liberty and initiative. He will not destroy the school-room. He will only destroy the recreation ground.

All the attempts to make lessons entirely pleasant rest on a false psychology, because they have not got hold of the root cause that makes lessons unpleasant. Lessons are not irksome because the surroundings of them are dreary or austere; they are not even irksome because the subjects of them are colourless or inhuman.

When I first learnt lessons they were out of a history book full of the very things that always fascinated me most – fighting and coloured pageantry. I learnt the tales of Bruce[2] and the Black Prince,[3] and liked them so much that I acted them all the rest of the day and (when alone) for the rest of my life. But for all that I hated the hour of work as it arrived every morning with a hatred which I retain heartily to this day.

The basic nuisance of lessons is not that the thing is intrinsically dull; it is that you want to do something else. My own present trade is more amusing than most, but I am cursing this article as fast as I write it, because I have an important appointment with myself on the top of a neighbouring hill that overlooks the flats towards the sea. If a man is in prison he cares very little whether he is imprisoned in the bare cubicles of Holloway or in the romantic caverns of Cornwall; the only objection to prison is that you have to stay there.

And a child cares very little whether he is learning in a schoolroom or in a summer forest. The only thing that is nasty about lessons is that you have to do them, and the only thing that is nice about a summer forest is that you can do what you like in it. If children are to be taught anything systematic at all, from putting their boots on to telling the time by the clock, you cannot get rid of a minimum of reluctance. And if you taught your schoolboys in the Elysian fields you would do nothing but slightly stain with trouble the memory of Elysium.

****

There are many other funny things in Mr. Collins's plan. The bedroom will be 'a cross between a comfortable and hygienic bedroom in an ordinary house and the sleeping accommodation provided for consumptives in sanatoria'; about as ghastly and blood-curdling a compromise as could be suggested to the mind. 'Even the fear of doing something wrong', says Mr. Collins, 'is an unhealthy emotion; it lowers vitality, impairs digestion, and injuriously affects all the powers of both mind and body'; a sentence which I should have admired if it had appeared in 'Punch'.

I am not quite sure what it means; as far as I can see, it means this – that if Tommy is tempted to pinch the baby, and feels the morbid shadow of morality pass momentarily over his soul, he is to remember the superior claims of his digestion and pinch away. This is also good: 'Pupils will not on any account be awakened from sleep, but they will not be encouraged to lie in bed a moment after they are awake'. This seems to me a serious omission. I cannot explain the absence from so well equipped a school of the usual officials (in uniform) whose business it is to go round the dormitories and encourage the pupils to lie in bed. We are also told that 'they will be allowed to eat as much as they like of wholesome food, including meat' – and including jam tarts and cream buns, unless the race is degenerating. Lastly, we have these menacing and awful words: 'The habits of the scholars will necessarily be regulated by some degree of rule; but the rules will be in every direction as elastic as possible'.

****

That last sentence gives away the whole weakness of this kind of well-meaning educational idealism. The people who make it up are not thinking of the happiness of children at all. They are thinking of the intellectual happiness of certain grown-up people in the repetition of certain phrases or the fulfilment of certain social dogmas. They have quite forgotten what a child is like. They would teach him lessons in a field because mature modern people enjoy the beauty of a field; but children enjoy the freedom of a field. Nature answers two quite different needs for the two ages, and these people are unconsciously thinking only of their own needs. The cool air, the quiet colours of green and grey, the healthy silence – all these soothe the tortured nerves of the modern adult. Therefore he would rather read algebra in a field than in a schoolroom. But the child loves the field as a place for emancipation and energy, for adventure and splendid self-will – in a word, as a place for a holiday, not as a place for that foul parody of a holiday which our evil generation calls a 'rest'. In short, the child likes the field for the same reason that he hates the algebra. But the educationists are thinking about the notions that are the children of their brains, not about the noble and nonsensical creatures that are the children of their bodies; therefore they think of a field first in relation to aesthetics and hygiene, under which all are passive, not in relation to liberty and lonely adventures, towards which all must be active.

So, again, with that phrase, that fatal phrase, about 'the rules being in all directions as elastic as possible'. Modern politicians and reformers, weary of many bad laws and of some good ones, have got into a way of talking about the need for rules being pliant and opportunist; this being a common modern craving, down it goes among the ideals of education. But it has nothing in the world to do with children. It is startlingly and almost insanely inappropriate to them. About the most brutal thing you can do to a child, short of knocking it down, is to have a rule and then allow it to be elastic. To relax a rule in one case and straighten it again in another is to combine every kind of cruelty and anarchy; you tempt the child into wrong by safety and you outrage him by capricious vengeance. If the educationist had been thinking about a single living child he would have made it his ideal that the rules should be very few and very mild; but that they must be in every direction as inelastic as possible. Then the child forgets them while he obeys them, as we forget and obey the laws of nature. That is certainly a gain for the joy of the child. But these people are not thinking of the joy of the child; they are thinking (unconsciously of course) of the joy of the reformer.

Lastly, of course, the whole thing is corrupted like most other things in our time by some of the million ramifications of the primary mistake of materialism. The form it takes here is the persistent but extraordinary notion that because a child is physically small he is morally small. Educationists talk as if training the will or joie de vivre of a child were like coaxing some tiny plant from an unfriendly soil. The fact is that a child may be only three feet high, and his will be like a battering ram, and his joy of life like a windmill in a hurricane. A human soul is never a sensitive plant growing spotless in a sheltered garden; a human soul is always a fruitful and terrible tree of life, bearing golden apples, but growing on the brink of a precipice.

Notes
1. *There is to be ... open air*: 'Reformed School ... Novel Open-Air Tuition', *DN*, 17 July 1908, p. 7.
2. *Bruce*: Robert the Bruce (1274–1329), King Robert I of Scotland, led his country in the wars of independence, defeating England militarily at the Battle of Bannockburn in 1314; Scotland gained its independence in the year before his death.
3. *Black Prince*: Edward Plantagenet, known during his life as Edward of Woodstock (1330–76), was the eldest son of Edward III of England; Prince of Wales, Duke of Cornwall and Prince of Aquitaine; heir to the English throne and military commander (he died before his father; Edward III was succeeded by Edward of Woodstock's son, who became Richard II). Edward's military victories at Crécy, Poitiers and Najera earned him much popularity at home. The sobriquet 'Black Prince' is a late invention of uncertain derivation; it occurs for the first time in Richard Grafton's *Chronicle of England* (1568).

July 25, 1908.

HISTORY VERSUS THE HISTORIANS.[1]

In my innocent and ardent youth I had a fixed fancy. I held that children in a school ought to be taught history, and ought to be taught nothing else. The story of human society is the only fundamental framework outside of religion in which everything can fall into its place. A boy cannot see the importance of Latin simply by learning Latin. But he might see it by learning the history of the Latins. Nobody can possibly see any sense in learning geography or in learning arithmetic – both studies are obviously nonsense. But on the eager eve of Austerlitz,[2] where Napoleon was fighting a superior force in a foreign country, one might see the need for Napoleon knowing a little geography and a little arithmetic. I thought that if people would only learn history they would learn to learn everything else. Algebra might seem ugly, yet the very name of it is connected with something so romantic as the Crusades, for the word is from the Saracens.[3] Greek might be ugly until one knew the Greeks, but surely not afterwards. History is simply humanity. And history will humanise all studies, even anthropology.

Since that age of innocence I have, however, realised that there is a difficulty in this teaching of history. And the difficulty is that there is no history to teach. This is not a scrap of cynicism – it is a genuine and necessary product of the many points of view and the strong mental separations of our society, for in our age every man has a cosmos of his own, and is therefore horribly alone. There is no history; there are only historians. To tell the tale plainly is now much more difficult than to tell it treacherously. It is unnatural to leave the facts alone; it is instinctive to pervert them. The very words involved in the chronicles – 'Pagan', 'Puritan', 'Catholic', 'Republican', 'Imperialist', – are words which make us leap out of our armchairs.

No good modern historians are impartial. All modern historians are divided into two classes – those who tell half the truth, like Macaulay[4] and Froude,[5] and those who tell none of the truth, like Hallam and the Impartials.[6] The angry historians see one side of the question.[7] The calm historians see nothing at all, not even the question itself.

But there is another possible attitude towards the records of the past, and I have never been able to understand why it has not been more often adopted. To put it in its curtest form, my proposal is this: That we should not read historians, but history. Let us read the actual text of the time.[8] Let us, for a year, or a month, or a fortnight, refuse to read anything about Oliver Cromwell except what was written while he was alive. There is plenty of material; from my own memory (which is all I have to rely on in the place where I write) I could mention offhand many long and famous efforts of English literature that cover the period. Clarendon's History,[9] Evelyn's Diary,[10] the Life of Colonel Hutchinson.[11] Above all let us read all Cromwell's own letters and speeches, as Carlyle published them.[12] But before we read them let us carefully paste pieces of stamp-paper over every sentence written by Carlyle. Let us blot out in every memoir every critical note and every modern paragraph. For a time let us cease altogether to read the living men on their dead topics. Let us read only the dead men on their living topics.

****

I have just come by accident on a striking case of what I mean. Most modern notions of the earlier and better Middle Ages are drawn either from historians or from novels. The novels are very much the more reliable of the two. The novelist has at least to try to describe human beings; which the historian often does not even attempt. But generally speaking, it is to novels first and then to partisan histories that we owe our impressions of this epoch.

The average modern Englishman's idea of the Middle Ages is a stratification of several modern views of them which might be summarised thus:

1. The Old Romantic View, with its wandering knights and captive princesses. According to this, the Dark Ages were not so much dark as lit exclusively by moonlight. This view was fictitious, but not false; for since love and venture exist in all ages, they did exist in the Middle Ages.

2. The Cheap Manchester View, which Dickens floundered into in his happy ignorance,[13] which enabled the smug merchant to say with a snigger that no doubt it was very romantic for a Jew to have his teeth pulled out;[14] and even to suggest that the feudal heroes took care to lock themselves up in steel and iron before they ventured into battle.[15] To this one obvious answer was to ask the merchant whether the knight was ever as ingloriously safe as his armourer, and whether even his armourer was not a braver man than the merchant who in modern Birmingham lives by making the tools of death.[16]

3. The Rossetti View that the age was one of tender transparencies and sacred perfumes:[17] a strong dose of Chaucer's Miller[18] can be recommended as a desperate remedy for this.

4. The Condescending View; as when Macaulay said of the Pilgrims with the utmost solemnity that in an age when men were too ignorant to travel from curiosity, 'or the desire of gain', it was just as well that they should travel from superstition.[19] I have always delighted in this idea that the ecstatic traveller and the heroic traveller were mere foreshadowings and prophecies of the commercial traveller. The Palmer kissed the Land of Christ,[20] and the Crusader fell with forty wounds at Ascalon,[21] that they might make smooth in the desert a highway for the bagman.

Now Dickens and Rossetti and Macaulay were very great men, and though none of them knew very much about the Middle Ages, their views on that time are bound to be interesting. But there is another humble class of men who might be allowed to tell us something about the Middle Ages. I mean the men who lived in the Middle Ages. There are in existence mediaeval memoirs which are nearly as amusing as Pepys,[22] and much more truthful. In England they are almost entirely unknown. But I am very glad to find that in the Everyman's Library Series Mr. Dent has published the Chronicle of Joinville and the Chronicle of Villehardouin, translated into excellent English by Sir Frank Marzials, under the general name of 'Chronicles of the Crusades'. Let anyone buy this book (it costs 1s.);[23] let him open Joinville's[24] rambling story, and he will find the Middle Age of Macaulay and Rossetti and Dickens and Miss Jane Porter[25] fall from him like a cumbrous cloak. He will find himself among men as human and sensible as himself, a little more brave and much more convinced of their first principles. Joinville reveals himself as innocently as Pepys, and reveals himself as a very much finer fellow. The reader will find it impossible [not] to respect the man; his lumbering punctiliousness about truth, when he explains what part of a scene he saw himself and what he heard reported; his prompt and instinctive veracity, as when St. Louis[26] asked him, 'Is it better to be a leper or commit a mortal sin?' and he answered, 'I would rather commit fifty mortal sins'; his perpetual and generous praise of others in battle; his rooted affections and simple pride in the affection of others for him; his slight touchiness about his dignity as a gentleman, which St. Louis rebuked in him, but which is, even to a shade, the exact touchiness of Colonel Newcome.[27] Above all we must thank him for his picture of the Great King in whom the lion lay down with the lamb. The shafts of St. Louis' judgment fly across the ages and hit the joints in every harness.

I had intended to tell some tales out of this book, but I must at least defer them. But they would all be to the same tune, the tune to which Chaucer's pilgrims walked when the miller with his bagpipes played them out of town. If the eighteenth century was the Age of Reason, the thirteenth was the Age of Commonsense. When St. Louis said that extravagant dress was indeed sinful, but that men should dress well 'that their wives might the more easily love them', we can feel the age that is talking about facts, and not about fads. There was plenty of romance, indeed; we not only see St. Louis giving humorous judgments under a garden tree, we see also St. Louis leaping from his ship into the sea with the shield at his neck and the lance in his hand. But it is not a romance of darkness nor a romance of moonlight, but a romance of the sun at noonday.

Notes
1. *HISTORY VERSUS THE HISTORIANS*: Reprinted in *LL*, pp. 128–33.
2. *Austerlitz*: On 2 December 1805 Napoleon defeated the much larger Russo-Austrian army at Austerlitz after a battle that lasted almost nine hours.
3. *Algebra ... Saracens*: 'Algebra' is derived from the Arabic word *al-jabr*; it was apparently coined by the Islamic mathematician Abu Abdallah Muhammad ibn Musa al-Khwarizmi (*c.* 780–*c.* 850); from whose name, incidentally, the words 'algorism' and 'algorithm' are derived.
4. *Macaulay*: Thomas Babington Macaulay; see 'A Handbook of Tennyson', *DN*, 5 August 1901, Volume 1, p. 150, n. 4 above.
5. *Froude*: James Anthony Froude; see 'Shakespeare's London', *DN*, 20 April 1906, Volume 3, p. 350, n. 3 above.
6. *the Impartials*: By this expression Chesterton probably means the 'school' of source-based, empirical historiography effectively founded by the German historian Leopold von Ranke (1795–1886). At least in principle von Ranke rejected the prevailing 'teleological' approach to historiography – the assumption that history is a narrative of human 'progress' – in favour of the view that each period is unique and should be understood in its own context.
7. *The angry historians ... question*: see also 'A Plea for Partial Historians', *DN*, 17 December 1902, Volume 1, pp. 449–52 above.
8. *Let us read the actual text of the time*: 'An Instructive Patchwork', *DN*, 19 January 1906, Volume 3, pp. 279–82 above.
9. *Clarendon's History*: Edward Hyde, first Earl of Clarendon (1609–74), was a politician and historian. His *History of the Rebellion and Civil Wars in England* was published in 1720. Clarendon's allegiance switched from Parliament to the King during the events that led up to the Civil War. During the War, Clarendon served in the King's Council as Chancellor of the Exchequer.
10. *Evelyn's Diary*: John Evelyn (1620–1706), was a diarist and writer; he commenced the notes from which his *Diary* is drawn at the age of eleven. Written contemporaneously with the diary of Samuel Pepys (see n. 22 below), Evelyn's *Diary* records events such as the deaths of Charles I and Oliver Cromwell and the Great Fire of London at first hand, together with his personal reflections. Extracts from the *Diary* were first published in 1818.
11. *Life of Colonel Hutchinson*: Colonel John Hutchinson (bap. 1615, d. 1664), was a parliamentarian army officer and regicide. *Memoirs of the Life of Colonel Hutchinson* written by his wife Lucy and published after her death became one of the great English biographies.
12. *Cromwell's own letters and speeches, as Carlyle published them*: Thomas Carlyle, *The Life and Letters of Oliver Cromwell* (1845). This work stood in place of the biography

of Cromwell that Carlyle had intended to write, but failed to complete; in 1843 he destroyed the manuscript.

13. *The cheap Manchester view ... happy ignorance*: Although in *Charles Dickens* (London: Methuen, 1906), Chesterton says this: 'But Dickens in his cheapest cockney utilitarianism, was not only English, but unconsciously historic. Upon him descended the real tradition of 'Merry England', and not upon the pallid mediaevalists who thought they were reviving it. The Pre-Raphaelites, the Gothicists, the admirers of the Middle Ages, had in their subtlety and sadness the spirit of the present day. Dickens had in his buffoonery and bravery the spirit of the Middle Ages. He was much more mediaeval in his attacks on mediaevalism than they were in their defences of it' (pp. 159–60). See also 'The Conservatism of Dickens', *DN*, 5 March 1904, Volume 2, pp. 204–6 above.

14. *a Jew to have his teeth pulled out*: The origin of the story of Jewish moneylenders having their teeth pulled out by order of King John is Roger of Wendover (d. 1236), *Flores historiarum* 2:232; and see Dickens, *A Child's History of England*, 3 vols (1852–4), vol. 1, ch. 14.

15. *smug merchant to say ... ventured into battle*: not identified.

16. *the merchant who in modern Birmingham lives by making the tools of death*: This is presumably a reference to the 'Gun Quarter' of the city of Birmingham in England, an area traditionally associated with the manufacture of firearms. A specific merchant Chesterton had in mind may be Dudley Docker (1862–1944), who became a director of the Birmingham Small Arms Company in 1906.

17. *The Rosetti view ... sacred perfumes*: The reference is to Gabriel Dante Rossetti's romantic medievalism as exemplified in the illustrations of Tennyson's poems that Edward Moxon commissioned from him in 1855, and in such paintings as *Beata Beatrix* (c. 1864–70), now in the Tate Gallery; for Rossetti, see 'Art and the Churches', *DN*, 2 January 1902, Volume 1, p. 303, n. 6 above.

18. *a strong dose of Chaucer's Miller*: 'The Miller's Tale', the second of Chaucer's *Canterbury Tales* (c. 1375), is a ribald and vulgar story of cuckoldry evidently intended as a contrast to the first tale, 'The Knight's Tale', an elegant story of courtly love.

19. *The Condescending View ... superstition*: Rather a misrepresentation of Macaulay, *History of England*, vol. 1, ch. 1: 'In times when men were scarcely ever induced to travel by liberal curiosity, or by the pursuit of gain, it was better that the rude inhabitant of the North should visit Italy and the East as a pilgrim, than that he should never see anything but those squalid cabins and uncleared woods amidst which he was born'.

20. *The palmer kissed the land of Christ*: A palmer (*palmarius* or *palmerius*) was a Christian pilgrim who had visited the holy places in Palestine and brought back a palm leaf folded into a cross (in the way that is still done in Europe on the Sunday before Easter). One suspects that Chesterton has in mind the palmer Wilfrid of Ivanhoe in Scott's *Ivanhoe*.

21. *Ascalon*: Ascalon or Ashkelon is a coastal city in Israel; the battle fought there on 12 August 1099 is usually regarded as the last battle of the First Crusade (1096–9).

22. *Pepys*: Samuel Pepys (pronounced 'Peeps') (1633–1703), was an English naval administrator and Member of Parliament who became Chief Secretary to the Admiralty under Charles II and James II; the diary that he kept between 1660 and 1669 is an important primary sources for the history of the English Restoration period.

23. *But I am very glad to find ... (it costs 1s)*: *Chronicles of the Crusades* by Villehardouin and De Joinville, translated with an introduction by Sir Frank Marzials (London: Dent, 1908). Chesterton's reference to this edition of the works was omitted from the reprint of the essay in *Lunacy and Letters*.

24. *Joinville*: Jean, Sire de Joinville (1224–1317), was a chronicler and biographer of Louis XI ('St Louis'). Joinville accompanied Louis on the Seventh Crusade (1248–54) and shared his imprisonment; he was opposed to the King's subsequent and final crusade (the Eighth Crusade) and declined to participate in it. His *Histoire de St Louis* (1304–9) is both a biography of Louis IX and a chronicle of the Seventh Crusade. It was written at the request of Jeanne of Navarre and dedicated to her son, the future King Louis X of France.
25. *Miss Jane Porter*: Jane Porter (bap. 1776, d. 1850), was a novelist. Born in Durham but educated in Edinburgh, she absorbed the romance of Scottish legend; through family connections, she was acquainted with Walter Scott. She attained some success as a writer of historical novels before the popularity of the genre declined in the 1820s; her most successful works were *Thaddeus of Warsaw* (1803), inspired by the Polish patriot Kosciusko, and *The Scottish Chiefs* (1804), based on William Wallace and Robert Bruce (D. McMillan, *ODNB*).
26. *St. Louis*: Louis IX, King of France; see 'Shelley, Mr. Salt, and Humanity,' *DN*, 4 February 1902, Volume 1, p. 323, n. 11 above.
27. *Colonel Newcome*: Colonel Thomas Newcome was one of the two main characters in Thackeray's novel *The Newcomes* (1853–5).

August 1, 1908.

AN ANECDOTE OF PERSECUTION.[1]

In my remarks last week I said that there were many tales in Joinville's reminiscences of St. Louis which would be worth retelling;[2] I will, however, be reasonable, and retell only one of them. I will tell it with strict reference to the record; I will only expand it in so far as obvious inference and historical circumstances are clear in the case; whenever I am ornamenting it I will say so; and anybody can buy the book for a shilling and bowl me out. But it is a tale which seems to me to tell in the most vivid and everyday style how it is in practice that persecution arises. It is common talk in these days that we ought to be imaginative if only in order to be charitable. If a man commits forgery we must try and understand his temptations and his original trend. But no such mercy is generally shown to the enthusiast for ideas. The sins of the intolerant are seldom considered with any intellectual tolerance. It seems that we are to find excuses for the crimes of bad men; but not for the crimes of good men.

Wherever we have read history (and most of us, I am glad to say, have read it only in historical novels) we have noticed one class of statements or allegations. I mean simply incredible allegations; statements that cannot be believed. For instance, it cannot be believed (at least, I cannot believe it) that the French Jacobins who ran the Terror were diseased and hysterical doctrinaires. They fought all Europe and beat it; the thing is impossible. It cannot be believed that the Irish are a weak and superstitious people; they give us our best judges and soldiers;[3] they have forced us to give them back their land;[4] they nearly forced us to give them back their country. Now exactly in this sense it is impossible to believe the ordinary modern version of the position of the Jew in the Middle Ages. Whatever else the Jew was, he was important. If he had really lived like Isaac in 'Ivanhoe'[5] he could not have been important; he could not have been at all. A man from whom anybody could steal money would not have any money to steal. A man utterly outlawed must perish. Now I will tell a little tale out of Joinville.

An Anecdote of Persecution

****

The Monastery of Our Lady at Cluny[6] was prosperous and charitable; when the snow was on the ground in winter it showed a maze of footprints of the poor folk who came to its doors. Most of these, of course, were not only poor, but of a plain rank; but it sometimes happened that a man of good estate was so impoverished as to receive such aid. Among the many figures familiar at the door was one especially, who crawled to it more slowly than the others, for he was crippled and hung upon a crutch. He was an old knight with white hair, quite disabled, and entirely penniless; but his eyes (I think) were fierce and restless, as are the eyes of all those whose activity has been shifted from the body to the mind. His clothes were dropping off his back; he was a perfect gentleman, and very much of a nuisance.

Now it happened that he came to the Monastery on a day that was somewhat solemnly set apart for one of those intellectual tournaments which the men of the Middle Ages loved as much as bodily tournaments. The Abbot was presumably something of a philosopher as well as a philanthropist, and he was liberal in his mental interests as well as liberal with his corn. In the exact words of Joinville's Chronicle, 'There was a great disputation between clergy and Jews at the Monastery of Cluny'. That single sentence knocks flat for ever the whole picture and conception of the mediaeval Jew which we all have from Scott's romances or from general report. Ignorant fools who insult a strange sect merely because it is strange do not arrange public debates to give it a chance of explaining itself. People bent on rooting out a tribe ruthlessly like rats or weeds do not invite the heads of the tribe to make speeches about themselves on a platform. The truth is, of course, that the mediaevals, like all other sane human beings, started with a preference for reasonable argument and peaceable settlement. It is always afterwards, if at all, that these excellent intentions break down. And they did, unfortunately, break down in the philanthropic and philosophical Monastery of Cluny; as you shall hear.

****

I think we can call up some rude and dim conception of the scene. The architecture, I think, would still be Norman with the low, almost sullen arch, and short, almost brutal columns; for though no date is given to the story, the Gothic can hardly have been greatly spread. Such laymen as were present would be people of all conditions; and while there would be more initial ceremony of precedence between these classes, there would be far less practical shyness or contemptuous shrinking than at the present day. Prominent, and probably in a row, would sit the Christian theologians, eager with the eagerness of all men who live much with their own sex in schools and clubs and universities for an unending war of words. Like all men who have a complete theory of things, they would be fretting and on fire with the chance of expounding it, many of them stirring and stamping. For men who have much to say are more nervous than men who have nothing to say.

Over against them, probably calmer, probably more prosperous in appearance, certainly more observant of all that was going on, would sit the great Rabbis of the mysterious race. In their hands they would hold parchments undecipherable to all the children of the West; but their very faces would be more undecipherable parchments. Their smiles would seem carved like hieroglyphics. Into that place of plain arches and Latin logicians with shaven heads they brought the memory of things cloudy and monstrous, as of many-headed cherubim or winged bulls walking enormous in the desert. For though both theologies were by this time twisted and elaborate, each worked back like a tangled tree to its original root. All the arabesque of Rabbinical riddle and commentary referred eventually to the ultimate Jewish idea: the idea of the awful distance between man and God.[7] All the roaring and grinding syllogisms of the schoolmen were tools and symbols of the awful union of God and man. The Jewish angel had ten eyes or twelve wings to express the idea that if even we saw the beauty or wisdom of God it would seem to us outrageous or frightful. The Christian angel often had two wings only in addition to eyes and two arms; to show that human beauty and dignity were divine realities which would survive and break the doors of death. Two sublime creeds were in collision: the creed that flesh is grass,[8] and the creed that flesh was God. And at the moment, before any of the philosophers could move the old man of the crutch stood up and asked to speak.

Joinville in his Chronicle gently says that this was received 'with doubt'. Human life is so startlingly the same in all ages that one can see the scene as clearly as if it were a modern meeting in a corrugated iron hall at Croydon, when some peppery and impracticable Colonel insisted on addressing the meeting. One can imagine the whispers between the Abbot and his chief supporters. 'If he speaks there will be a row', and the unanswerable answer, 'If we stop him there will be a worse row'. The assembled philosophers, who had been about to pose the Rabbis with the awful rationalism of mediaeval argument, 'Why do you believe in God if He is not manifest?' or 'Could anyone believe in Heaven except through revelation?' stood for a moment aside. The old cripple said, 'At least you admit that Our Lady was the mother of God'.

The Rabbi who was addressed smiled, perhaps, that rich smile which some find repulsive even when it is benevolent, and said that he did not admit this. The old man said steadily, 'Then if you do not love Our Lady you were very silly to come into her house'. He plucked the crutch from under his arm, and, whirling it suddenly aloft, caught the Jew with a stunning crack behind the ear, bringing him to the ground. Instantly, of course, there was a scuffle, and the Jews were driven from the place. The Abbot rushed up to the old Knight and told him in no measured terms that he had made a horrible fool of himself. The old gentleman, still panting and blowing, no doubt from his exertion, told the Abbot that he thought him the greater fool of the two. Thus unfortunately ended the great experiment of religious inquiry in the Monastery of Cluny. I leave it to anyone to say whether it is not as human a tale as any that might have happened in Surbiton during the Boer war.

Notes
1. *AN ANECDOTE OF PERSECUTION*: Reprinted in *AWD*, pp. 102–5.
2. *In my remarks last week ... worth retelling*: see 'History Versus the Historians', *DN*, 25 July 1908, pp. 114–15 above.
3. *our best judges and soldiers*: An example of the Irish judge is Lord Russell of Killowen; see 'The Life of Lord Russell of Killowen', *DN*, 18 November 1901, Volume 1, pp. 267–71 above; an example of the Irish soldier is Arthur Wellesley, First Duke of Wellington (1760–1852).
4. *forced us to give them back their land*: A reference to the Irish Land Act (1903); see 'The Delusion of Race', *DN*, 26 November 1904, Volume 2, p. 330, n. 1 above.
5. *Isaac in 'Ivanhoe'*: Isaac of York is the persecuted Jewish moneylender in Scott's *Ivanhoe* who is distinguished by his love for his daughter Rebecca and his kindness to Ivanhoe. Eventually he and his daughter flee to Spain to escape persecution.
6. *The monastery of Our Lady at Cluny*: A Benedictine abbey at Cluny in Burgundy, founded in 910 by William I, Count of Auvergne.
7. *all the arabesque ... awful distance between man and God*: Here and in the remainder of this paragraph Chesterton is alluding to the esoteric tradition of Rabbinic Judaism called Kabbalah, the central text of which, the Zohar, first appeared in Spain in the thirteenth century, though it is traditionally said to have been composed in the second century by a Rabbi called Shimon bar Yochai.
8. *flesh is grass*: See Isaiah 40:6.

August 8, 1908.

VENGEANCE.

The whole object of literature is to prevent truths becoming truisms. We must not only keep our truths but keep them alive; we must not only guard our truths, but feed them. It is quite possible to regard something for ten years as a truism and still to jump into the air with astonishment on discovering that it is true. I always believe in the theory that the poor are ordinary human beings. But I shall never forget the moment of shattering astonishment when I discovered that they really were. If we have omitted to examine and test any stock idea in our heads we ought not to refrain from testing it merely because we are certain that it is true. It may be true, and we may not know how true. There is, perhaps, in our world a little too much of the practice of poring over new ideas until they become old. We require a little of the practice of poring over old ideas until they become new.

Here is a case of a phrase we must all of us have often used; a phrase that has a thought in it, only that it is used quite thoughtlessly. The phrase I mean is this: 'Punishment should not be vindictive; it is only for the protection of society'. When next we use this phrase let us stop and think about it for five minutes, unless, of course, we are using it in the middle of a political speech, when so long a reflective pause would be rather a strain on the audience.

****

What is it that is really evil about revenge? Certainly not that it is selfish; there is nothing immoral merely in pleasing oneself; it is selfish to read Virgil; it is selfish to get up and see the sun rise. Not that it is violent or destructive; it cannot be wrong to redress wrongs; Sir Galahad was violent and destructive.

The evil of vindictiveness is the same as that of every other sin; it is that in some extraordinary way it tends to destroy the soul, to blacken and eat up the whole nature. This is really the whole quarrel between the moralists and the immoralists. A celebrated decadent wrote, 'The only way to get rid of a temptation is to yield to it'.[1] Yet that unhappy man himself was a complete contradiction of his own epigram; his life narrowed and darkened to a dungeon because he was unable to get rid of the hideous desires that he had satisfied. Yielding to a temptation is like yielding to a blackmailer; you pay to be free, and find yourself the more enslaved. The reality of sin arises, in fact, from the same truth which makes the reality of human poetry and joy. It arises from the fact that the smallest thing in this world has its own infinity. A mouse has an eternity of truth tied on to its tail. A prisoner in an empty cell has been known to occupy himself for decades with the natural history, philosophy, and morality of a single mouse.

Now just as a good man can find everlasting joy in looking at a mouse, so it is possible for a bad man to find everlasting joy in torturing a mouse. It is not true that cutting off its tail is a mere episode and that the man passes on to pat his children or say his prayers. The truth is that having cut off the mouse's tail is the first suggestion of the artistic interest of cutting off its ears. The hellish happiness renews itself, and has an infinity of its own.

That is the whole point of the position of sin in human psychology, and that is the whole point of the peril of revenge. Hatred is bad not because it is personal or destructive, but because it narrows the soul to a sharp point. It is not merely that Jones desires the death of Brown. Under certain circumstances, instantaneous or impersonal, he might justly desire it. The evil is that the death of Brown becomes the whole life of Jones. The violent man, in short, tries to break out; but he only succeeds in breaking in. He breaks into smaller and smaller cells of his own subterranean heart till he is suffocated in the smallest, and dies like a rat in a hole.

But a whole people can hardly die like a rat in a hole. It is not very likely that an entire nation will go mad upon one point of morbidity. A million city men with black hats and bags will not all be dreaming at the same moment of how they may poison Brown. Therefore we must first remember that the public acts done by a whole people, though they may be fierce and tragic, will hardly be vindictive in this stagnant, secretive, and poisonous sense. The people may be a butcher; but the people can hardly be an assassin. You may happen to think the killing of Charles I. As lawless or cruel as the killing of his friend Buckingham.[2] But you will hardly deny that Bradshaw,[3] with all his bitterness, was in a more open and bracing frame of mind than Felton[4] fingering the knife in his pocket and brooding over his private wrongs.

While assenting, therefore, to the ultimate proposition that punishment must not be mere vengeance, we have to point out first that it never is mere vengeance in the sense that mere vengeance can corrupt and weaken an individual soul. And, second, we have to point out that in continually repeating without reflection that it must not be vindictive, we lay the foundations of another evil more cruel than vengeance itself. There is no fear of modern English punishment being excessively revengeful; it has not enough life in it. It is attacking altogether the wrong danger to tell a modern judge that he must not shudder from head to foot with a horror of sin or foam at the mouth with a hatred of individuals. You might as well tell the stonebreaker in the road not to be an iconoclast. You might as well reproach the tax collector with his fanatical Socialism, or earnestly assure the scavenger that he must not value too transcendentally and supremely the mere ideal of hygiene.

The evil in our modern law is not one of barbaric passions, but one of passionless routine. The trouble is not that a lawyer really flies into a passion when he thinks about petty larceny; the trouble is that he never really thinks about it at all. It is not that the authorities have an excessive horror of the idea of sin; it is that they have a quite insufficient horror of the idea of punishment. The professional lawyer punishes more drearily and mechanically than the professional thief thieves. To tell him not to punish from mere vengeance is like telling an oyster not to run too fast. He has about as much vindictive feeling against criminals as a butcher has against oxen and immeasurably less than a gardener has against snails.

Now in this legal atmosphere a burst of decent human vengeance would be an almost unmixed benefit. There is nothing in the least Christian or charitable about not being vindictive. It is Christian to love your enemies, but there is nothing Christian in the mere fact of hurting them without hating them. Real tenderness is really the better, because it is effected with difficulty. But cruelties are not any the better because they are effected with composure. Thus we see that this modern phrase, 'Punishment should not be vindictive', is exactly the wrong phrase; innocent as it seems[,] it puts the matter precisely in the wrong way. Say that we ought to have a flaming charity or a fierce pity, say that we ought to be like the saint who kissed the criminal's severed head or the saint who took the convict's seat in the galleys; say that and you may raise the banner of a really valuable revolt. But to say simply that we must not be vindictive is merely to say that we must not only do a heartless thing, but do it in a heartless manner.

And there is one more point that should be emphasised yet more pointedly. By merely saying that we must not avenge, we make it much easier to punish a poor and feeble class of criminals against whom no sane man can feel vengeful. And we make it much more difficult to punish the only class of criminals on whom we might really wish to be avenged. The prosperous oppressor, the successful swindler may really inflame vindictive feelings; but they escape – because punishment is not vindictive. The desperate tramp, the dreary pickpocket, could not make anyone feel vindictive; but they can be crushed under wheels of iron – because punishment is not vindictive.

In short, the theory that we must not be angry is the very charter of escape for all evil-doers who are strong enough to awaken anger. We are not told to love; that divine and terrible commandment has died with the superstitions of our infancy. But we are told not to hate. And so the tyrant escapes – because he is only hateful.

Notes

1. *A celebrated decadent wrote ... yield to it*: Oscar Wilde, *The Picture of Dorian Gray* (1891), ch. 2. The quotation continues, 'Resist it, and your soul grows sick with longing for the things it has forbidden to itself, with desire for what its monstrous laws have made monstrous and unlawful'.
2. *Buckingham*: George Villiers, first Duke of Buckingham (1592–1628), was a royal favourite. He was distrusted and disliked by Parliament, and was the subject of a remonstrance presented to the King in June 1628. This was rejected by Charles. For the manner of Buckingham's death see note 4 below.
3. *Bradshaw*: John Bradshaw (bap. 1602, d. 1659), was a lawyer, politician and regicide. As Lord President of the court set up to try Charles I in January 1649, Bradshaw delivered the sentence of death to his sovereign.
4. *Felton*: John Felton (d. 1628), was the English soldier who fatally stabbed Buckingham in Portsmouth in 1628. Buckingham was in Portsmouth to monitor the progress of a second fleet to relieve the Huguenots in La Rochelle, a mission that was deeply unpopular in Parliament. Felton bore a personal grudge against the Duke but felt compelled also to rid the nation of a tyrant; immediately after the assassination he declared himself to the assembled crowd, expecting applause. He was hanged at Tyburn and his body taken to Portsmouth where, hung in chains to rot, it became an object of popular veneration: a circumstance that deepened Charles I's mistrust of his subjects. There is a fictionalized account of Buckingham's assassination in Dumas's *The Three Musketeers*.

August 15, 1908.

THE VULGAR GHOST.

I was reading a thick book about the results of spiritualist séances when these foolish reflections came to me from somewhere, perhaps from the spirits. My instinctive feeling about spiritualist séances, I regret to say, is rather like a man's feeling about the infernal regions. I am perfectly willing to believe in them so long as I am not asked to go to them. That things of that class called for ordinary purposes supernatural or spiritualistic do sometimes happen, I have always myself admitted, not as a piece of uncommon experience, but as a piece of common sense. It seems to me likely enough that there should be other personalities besides human personalities, and other modes of communication besides the five human senses. It is not necessary to treat it as something unnatural which becomes a part of Nature merely by being proved. It is one of those things that are natural even before they happen. It is more than proved; it is probable. In such matters one can see the truth a long time before one has found all the facts. To that we can add that the whole tradition and experience of humanity is in favour of it. And nobody has ever very clearly suggested anything against it except the mere fact that the materialist theory of the universe is against it. For there is really very little value in the attack on spiritual phenomena as conducted in detail. It is not very convincing to be told that of ten reported miracles one might barely be a coincidence, one might possibly be a lie, one might be a subjective monomania in the witness, and so on. That might be applied to anything. Take any incident which in its nature occurs rarely and at least in some privacy – such as a Prime Minister being quite drunk – and it would be easy to show that the thing never happened if you had a strong fanatical interest in showing that it could never happen. If you were really trying to prove that the intoxication of Premiers was a physical impossibility, that alcohol had no effect upon the brain cells of a Prime Minister, then you could easily get rid of the ten or twelve reported cases of helpless and incapacitated Premiers, unless you are a much less clever fellow than I take you for. This drunken Prime Minister was a mere figment, a fable originating with the Leader of the Opposition. That drunken Prime Minister was a sort of ecstatic hallucination in the credulous spectator; the fulfilment of his prophetic faith; the result of his yearning and devout desire some day to see a drunken Prime Minister. The third (it would be said) was the case of a highly intemperate auctioneer living in Ladbroke-grove, who bore a general physical resemblance to the Prime Minister. The fourth was no doubt the case of a somewhat eccentric Prime Minister, who, when all by himself, was in the habit of reeling and staggering with the sense of the burden of Empire, and even falling to the ground in the very passionate impotence of patriotism. But if people really talked in this way about the drunkenness of Carteret[1] or the drunkenness of the younger Pitt[2] we should all explode with the observation which a certain mathematician is said to have addressed to the shade of John Milton after reading two pages of 'Paradise Lost'. 'But what are you trying to prove?'[3] What are you driving at? Are you not, as a fact, simply defending this proposition: 'That Prime Ministers cannot get drunk'? So when I hear a man explaining that a ghost might have been a nightmare or a miracle might have been a coincidence, I am not so much interested in the man's explanation as I am in the man's dogma, and his dogma is that the supernatural cannot occur.

Now, after I had been reading for some little time this book of psychical reports, the reader may be surprised to learn that I put it down for a moment, and even began to look at a newspaper. In that newspaper I found, printed quite plainly and placidly, in ordinary printer's ink, the statement that a Leprechaun had been captured in Ireland and taken to the workhouse. Then I suddenly realised whatever it really is that makes me shrink from ordinary spiritualism. The conditions are too elaborate. Men turn down the lights to talk to Plato and Sir Isaac Newton; but God turns down the lights before they can talk to the midnight ghost or the moon-struck fairies. Just as there are some beauties that can only be seen by artificial light, so these spectres can only be seen by artificial darkness. Some people are against ordinary table-rapping spiritualism because it is vulgar; I am against it because it is not vulgar enough. It is over-civilized, and, like all over-civilized things, aristocratic; it clings to tables and private rooms, and all that particularly pompous kind of ritualism which is called 'scientific conditions'. It will not come out into the daylight; it will not even come out into the moonlight. It will not come out and haunt the churchyard, the dark lane or the gallows, as its ghostly fathers did before it. The spiritualistic ghost will not 'walk', which is quite as healthy an exercise for ghosts as for men. In the matter of ghosts I greatly prefer the democratic ghost, the ghost who succeeds in frightening yokels, rather than the ghost who succeeds or fails in convincing professors. I cannot with any pleasure believe in Astral Bodies. But I can believe in the Cock Lane ghost not only with pleasure, but with the greatest intellectual ease. Actually there are less frauds in a lane. But even frauds in a lane seem more tolerable than frauds at a séance; they are a part of the very mystification and romantic crookedness that belongs to one of the lanes of England. It is a long lane that has no spectre. The spectre is more likely to be genuine in such an environment; but even if he is not genuine, he is still somehow more genuine than the 'spirits'. A fraud effected by phosphorescent lights is a thing that stinks in the nostrils like phosphorus. But a turnip ghost is as healthy and sustaining as a turnip.

But, indeed, the case for the ghost of the churchyard against the ghost of the séance has a much deeper root, whose ramifications go down to the ancestral soil of humanity. The superiority of the vulgar ghost is a thing almost too delicate for words to grace. We may, perhaps, put the matter thus: that if the dead can indeed talk with the living, one would expect it to be rather on the basis of what we call ignorance, which often means the main fundamentals of human nature, rather than on the basis of what we call knowledge, which is often only a cheap and very temporary culture. If I could, indeed, hear Cardinal Wolsey[4] talking, I should not expect to hear him talking about Henry VIII. I should expect to hear him talking about somebody of whom no one knows; somebody whom he had loved. If I could meet the ghost of Charles Fox[5] (and I wish I could), I should not expect to meet him by moonlight in the lobbies of the House of Commons, even if I could reasonably expect to meet myself there at that time of night. I should expect to meet him by some country farmhouse, or outside some London lodging with which he had associations that we shall never know. The weakness of so much ordinary spiritualism is that it is mere vulgar history. It always connects Fox with Westminster and Sir Walter Raleigh with Elizabeth.[6] But the strength of popular superstition is that it always connects men with the things they really cared about; the Naboth with his vineyard,[7] the lover with his trysting-place; the miser with his hidden gold. Nothing drives me more towards believing in ghosts than their strong local patriotism; their sense of the sanctity of place. The modern English ghosts have lost that; but how can we wonder? The modern English men have lost it. A little oligarchy of landlords has destroyed the sentiment of the local affections of the living; it is not strange that it has not left any very general sentiment of the local affections of the dead. The common Englishman may not possess any part of England as a man; it may well be that he has not wished to return to it as a shadow. Perhaps, if ever the peasant gets back into the field, the ghost will come back into the lane.

Notes
1. *Carteret*: John Carteret, second Earl Granville (1690–1763), was a British statesman and diplomat. He served as Secretary of State for the Southern Department (1721–4); Lord Lieutenant of Ireland (1724–30); Secretary of State for the Northern Department (1742–4); and Lord President of the Council (1751–63). Contrary to what Chesterton seems to suggest, he never became Prime Minister – possibly because of his notorious

fondness for wine but no doubt also because his interests were predominantly in foreign rather than domestic policy.
2. *the younger Pitt*: William Pitt (1759–1806), was a British statesman. He was Prime Minister and Chancellor of the Exchequer from 1783 to 1801 and from 1804 until his death in 1806. Something of a recluse, Pitt certainly drank a good deal of port under the combined pressure of failing health and office, particularly during the war with France. However, the extent of his dependence on alcohol has been questioned (J. P. W. Ehrman and A. Smith, *ODNB*).
3. *the observation which a certain mathematician ... to prove*: Chesterton is remembering this from an anonymous piece called 'The Confessions of a Cantab', in *Blackwood's Magazine*, 16 (October 1824), pp. 459–67: 'It is related of a late mathematical professor, that being persuaded by a friend to read Milton's Paradise Lost, he went home one evening, took off his coat, and read it through. His friend asked him if he did not think it very beautiful – "Beautiful!" exclaimed the Professor; "why, it's all assertion – the fellow does not *prove* anything from beginning to end"'.
4. *Cardinal Wolsey*: Thomas Wolsey (1470/1–1530), was a royal minister, Archbishop of York, and cardinal. Wolsey became Henry VIII's minister for domestic affairs in 1515, although he fell out of the King's favour when he failed to obtain a divorce for Henry from Katharine of Aragon.
5. *Charles Fox*: Charles James Fox; see 'The Good Man of the Eighteenth Century', *DN*, 22 March 1901, Volume 1, p. 67, n. 19 above.
6. *Sir Walter Raleigh with Elizabeth*: see 'Some Reflections on the Strong Man', *DN*, 1 August 1902, Volume 1, p. 362, n. 3 above.
7. *Naboth with his vineyard*: 1 Kings, 21.

August 20, 1908.

THE RUSSIAN TORTURES [EDITORIAL].

We publish to-day a letter from Mr. G. K. Chesterton,[1] dealing with the hideous disclosures in regard to the treatment of political prisoners in Russia which have twice this week appeared in our columns.[2] On some points Mr. Chesterton holds views which are not ours. On others he holds ours with a difference. When, for example, he qualifies his detestation of the Riga atrocities with the suggestion that 'the instant terror of conspiracy' may be called in to palliate the actions of the police as described in those two articles, we experience no sense of conviction. There is such a thing as the taste, gradually developed, for cruelty as an end in itself; and it seems to us to have been at work in the prison at Riga. But when Mr. Chesterton reminds us that our own record is not over-clean in the matter of prison tortures, he draws attention to a plain but neglected fact. Let me add that the same point has been made in several of the letters received by us expressing the horror felt by every man and woman who read what we have published this week; letters with which we could fill the columns of this paper.

1   *We publish to-day ... letter from Mr. G. K. Chesterton*: see 'The Sin of Torture', letter to the editor, *DN*, 20 August 1908, pp. 131–2 above.
2   *hideous disclosures ... twice this week appeared in our columns*: 'Russian Prisons', 17 August 1908, p. 5; 'The Torture at Riga', 18 August 1908, p. 5.

August 20, 1908.

THE SIN OF TORTURE.[1]

(To the Editor of 'The Daily News'.)

Sir, – Every decent person must be with you in your denunciation of the cruelties in the Russian prisons, and especially must applaud your good sense in disregarding the conventional distinction between flogging, however extreme, and older forms of 'question'. Torture depends, obviously, on the degree of pain; not on the instrument. Extreme flogging is pure torture. It is certainly a strong statement (I don't say too strong) to say that any Government inflicting it is outside the pale. For one of the Governments inflicting it is the present Government of Great Britain. In the same issue with the Russian revelations there was a paragraph in your paper saying that an English prisoner had been condemned to thirty lashes with the cat-o'-nine-tails, one of the most frightful instruments in the history of torture, so frightful that medical arrangements have to be made to prevent a man dying under it.[2] It will be said that at least the English prisoner was tortured for a more terrible offence. No; for substantially the same offence. He had assaulted a warder; that is, he had rebelled against legal, though despotic, authority. The degree of criminality and the type of criminal will probably be similar in both cases. The worst Russians will never be in Russian prisons; and the worst criminals would never be so silly as to attack warders. The mean man is safe, even in gaol; the mean man is safe, even in a revolution. The type of man who defies the warder will be the same that defies the Tsar, that is, he will be a good type, instinctive, unbroken to ignominy, a little unbalanced, and very brave.

Please do not fancy that I am playing the silly game of 'tuquoque'[3] or two blacks and a white, which makes international argument so wearisome. I decline to be oppressed in Brixton because there is worse oppression in Beluchistan. And certainly it is quite as silly to palliate Beluchistan because things are bad in Brixton. I only say, the Russians are in revolt against their horrors; let us be in revolt against ours. The most striking difference between the two national torture-chambers is one that has nothing to do with the degree of cruelty. What startles a Western man about the story told in your columns is the extraordinary chaos and spontaneity of the proceedings. When the examining officer does not like a prisoner's answer he rushes at him and tramples him with his boots. We torture our prisoners, but it never occurred to us to do it by jumping on them. The Russian torturer shrieks like the tortured; he howls 'Down with the Socialist!' No flogger in our prisons would be allowed to offer any philosophical reason for flogging. This order and silence in our gaols vaguely comforts us. But it ought not to comfort us. If the lashes are numerous, it is small comfort that they are numbered. If men half kill other men it is no consolation that they do it calmly. A thumbscrew is none the better for being a bright, well-polished thumbscrew. But there are modern people who would think the rack quite right and scientific if it were worked by electricity.

Torture, wherever it happens, is a thing from hell. I will not risk even the appearance of palliating it. Still, even inhuman things have some human temptation in them, and there are two mental conditions that make torturing men conceivable. One is after a psychological shock, such as that which jars the soul of some old Quaker lady when she first hears a blasphemy or of some innocent lad when he first hears of sexual perversion. Men in a state of horror will do horrible things: modern Americans do them when the black hand touches sex. The other occasion is in the instant terror of conspiracy. Thus, if we know that a hidden bomb could blow up London in an hour, and the only man who knew where the bomb was would not tell us – then the ugly whisper would arise that we might hurt him till he did. Now I mention these two here for a strong reason, which is this: It is just barely possible that the Russian tormentors work under these morbid but still imaginable motives; it is certain that our tormentors have not even these excuses; ours are the worst, if there are any degrees in devilry. It is barely possible that the Russian tyrants are in a panic about hidden bombs; ours only desire to break a man body and soul. It is barely possible that these Russians do feel a mystical horror of an atheist or anarchist or enemy of the Tsar. But none of us (I hope) have any mystical or abstract horror of the idea of hitting a policeman.

But I have left the largest difference to the last. The big and glaring difference is this: In Russia the reformers are at least trying to take prisoners out of the hands that flog. In England many reformers are trying to put prisoners permanently into those hands. In Russia the scourged can defy the scourger, saying, 'Light breaks into these dark places; and I will tell this tale to all the world'. But in England the scourger can answer, 'No, my friend; you won't tell the tale; for a Liberal Government is introducing a Bill which gives me the right to say whether you shall come out to tell it'.[4]—Yours, etc.,

G. K. CHESTERTON.

Notes

1. *THE SIN OF TORTURE*: The letter was a response to exposure in the *Daily News* of the systematic practice of torture in Russian prisons. Based on an account by a former prisoner in the jail at Riga, the newspaper expressed its outrage at a narrative that 'reads rather like some horrid page from Foxe's Book of Martyrs than a contemporary document'. It went on to condemn the despotism that prevailed across the Russian Empire, enabling local governors to arrest and torture citizens without trial: 'The Russian Tortures', 18 August 1908, p. 4. This was all the more sensitive in the light of the Anglo–Russian Entente the previous year. Liberal journalists such as Henry Brailsford had condemned the Entente: see 'Entente with Russia', letter to the Editor, *DN*, 25 May 1907, p. 6.
2. *cat-o'-nine-tails ... dying under it*: The nature of the frequency of use, and impact of 'the cat' was disputed among readers of the *Daily News*: see letters to the editor by H. M. Wallis, 27 August 1908, pp. 150–2 and by Douglas Blackburn, 28 August 1908, p. 3.
3. *silly game of 'tuquoque'*: 'Tu quoque' = 'you too': i.e. you yourself do the thing that you condemn.
4. *'No, my friend ... whether you shall come out to tell it'*: This is a reference to the Prevention of Crime Act (1908); see 'A Theory of Tyrants', *DN*, 13 June 1908, p. 89, n. 8 above.

August 21, 1908.

'THE SIN OF TORTURE'.

(To the Editor of 'The Daily News'.)

Sir, – When you say in your editorial comment on Mr. Chesterton's letter on the Russian tortures[1] that you 'experience no sense of conviction'[2] you express my own views on that startling production in the mildest form of words which human ingenuity could invent. Because there is one case of flogging – to which I am altogether opposed – in an English prison mentioned in a newspaper which is exposing a wholesale system of indescribable brutalities carried on against a whole class in Russia, we are invited to regard ourselves as in some sense the partners of the Russian police in guilt. I do not know whether Mr. Chesterton really holds the opinion which I have just stated, but his letter leaves upon the mind the impression that he does. If so, I venture to think that he stands alone – a situation, however, to which your brilliant contributor is probably by this time quite accustomed. – Yours, etc., UNCONVINCED.

---

1 *Mr. Chesterton's letter on the Russian Tortures*: see 'The Sin of Torture', letter to the editor, *DN*, 20 August 1908, pp. 131–3 above.
2 *When you say ... 'experience no sense of conviction'*: see 'The Russian Tortures', *DN*, 20 August 1908, p. 130 above.

August 22, 1908.

'THE SIN OF TORTURE'.

(To the Editor of 'The Daily News'.)

Sir, – I am glad to say that, as usual, I agree with Mr. Chesterton in many things.[1] I agree that flogging is torture; that the prisoner who attacks a warder is very likely the best of the prisoners, and is certainly not the meanest; that if men half kill other men, it is no consolation that they do it calmly; that torture, wherever it happens, is a thing of hell; and that the indeterminate sentence is an inhumane and dangerous experiment. I also agree that we should be in revolt against our own horrors. We should be in fierce revolt against them, whether in Dartmoor or Natal.

Mr. Chesterton is careful not to risk even the appearance of palliating torture, and no one who follows his work as I do would for a moment suspect him of it. But still, in his anxiety to reveal the full horror of British torture, he suggests two possible excuses for the Russian tortures which appear to me quite untenable. One is psychological shock, the other is instant terror of conspiracy. I think both imply suddenness, nearness of danger, and brevity of time.

The Russian system of torture described in those terrible revelations which you lately published was introduced just after the failure of the rising that I witnessed in Moscow in December, 1905. I heard evidences of it while I was in the Baltic Provinces in January and February, 1906. It was some eight months later that the first tortures were inflicted on the victim who has described the hideous sufferings of himself and many others in your columns. It was a considerable time later – I think almost a year – that the chief torturer was promoted to a more important and lucrative position by the Tsar and M. Stolypin,[2] as a token of their approval. It is now more than two and a half years since the tortures were instituted, and we have evidence that they are still continued: at all events, they were continued a very short time back. We also know that most of the prisoners tortured were arrested on the charge of political offences committed nearly three years ago, and that at Reval and other places the Russian Government is still slowly hanging off the offenders of that time, though all fear of immediate and violent revolution has long been over.

I think there is no place here for psychological shock or instant terror of conspiracy. Such feelings cannot be spread over months and years. During the two years of M. Stolypin's office as Prime Minister the process of torture, exile, and execution has been as cold-blooded and deliberate as any single case of flogging at Dartmoor. It is true that Mr. Stead has attempted what I think you yourself called a curious defence of M. Stolypin and his methods; but then, as I believe, Mr. Stead has been admitted to an interview not only with M. Stolypin, but with the Tsar himself, and some allowance can, perhaps, be made for the influence of those privileges upon his judgment.[3]

Numbers go for something, even in computing cruelty. If Catherine had killed only one Huguenot on St. Bartholomew's Day;[4] if the Duke of Savoy had killed only one Vaudois in the Piedmont;[5] if Abdul Hamid had killed only one Armenian in Constantinople,[6] it would have been bad; but their names would not have been held up to the execration of history. Similarly, the flogging of a Dartmoor prisoner is bad, but it is overwhelmed in the horrors inflicted by the Russian Government upon thousands of victims by torture, imprisonment, exile, and execution, not to mention nameless abominations, during the last two and a half years. If Mr. Chesterton had been with me in Moscow, in the Baltic Provinces, in Poland, and the Georgian districts of the Caucasus, I think he would agree with what I say, - Yours, etc.,

HENRY W. NEVINSON.[7]
4, Downside-crescent, Hampstead.

Notes
1. *I am glad to say ... many things*: a response to 'The Sin of Torture', letter to the editor, *DN*, 20 August 1920, pp. 131–3 above.
2. *M. Stolypin*: Pyotr Arkadyevich Stolypin (1862–1911), was a Russian statesman. As Russia's Prime Minister, Stolypin sought to suppress the revolution of 1905 while addressing the causes of discontent. He was assassinated at the Kiev Opera House by an anarchist revolutionary called Dmitri Bogrov.
3. *It is true that Mr. Stead ... influence of those privileges upon his judgment*: W[illiam] T[homas] Stead, 'The Situation in Russia: Interview with M. Stolypin', *The Times*, 3 August 1908, p. 8. Stead assured his readers that 'provided the great political evolution of the Duma is allowed regular development there is no reason to apprehend a recurrence of the disturbances of 1905 and 1906. The most remarkable evidence which is afforded of this transformation is the fact that at last the Tsar has a Prime Minister whom everyone trusts'. For Stead, see 'A Plea for Philosophical Uniforms', *DN*, 24 October 1903, Volume 2, p. 146, n. 2 above.

4. *If Catherine ... St. Bartholomew's Day*: The St Bartholomew's Day massacre, 1572, is thought to have been instigated by Catherine de Medici, mother of King Charles IX; see 'In the Place de La Bastille', *DN*, 5 May 1906, Volume 3, p. 360, n. 5 above.
5. *Duke of Savoy ... Piedmont*: The Vaudois (usually called 'Waldensians' in English) were a heretical Christian sect founded at Lyon in 1179 by Pierre Valdo. In 1655 the Duke of Savoy commanded the Vaudois – then about 15,000 strong – to attend Mass or forfeit their property. On 24 April an army sent by the Duke to suppress resistance began a general massacre, at the end of which only some 3,000 Vaudois remained alive.
6. *Abdul Hamid ... Constantinople*: a reference to 'Abdul the Damned', i.e. Abdül Hamid II, and the particularly scandalous massacre that took place in western Armenia in May 1904; see 'Paganism and Some Protests', 10 September 1904, Volume 2, p. 292, n. 5 above.
7. *HENRY W. NEVINSON*: Henry Woodd Nevinson (1856–1941), was a journalist, social activist and author. He served as foreign correspondent for a number of Liberal newspapers; he reported on major wars over thirty years from 1897 when he was appointed the *Daily Chronicle*'s correspondent in the Graeco–Turkish conflict. He also helped to organize relief, first in Macedonia in 1903 and then in Albanian in 1911. Among his other reports was one on bonded labour engaged in the production of cocoa in Portugese Angola in 1904–5. He was a leader writer for the *Daily News*, 1908–9, resigning with H. N. Brailsford in protest against the paper's stance on the forcible feeding of suffragettes in prison (H. N. Brailsford, rev. S. Agnew, *ODNB*).

August 22, 1908.

THE DICKENSIAN.[1]

He was a quiet man, dressed in dark clothes, with a large limp straw hat; with something almost military in his moustache and whiskers, but with a quite unmilitary stoop and very dreamy eyes. He was gazing with a rather gloomy interest at the cluster, one might almost say the tangle, of small shipping which grew thicker as our little pleasure boat crawled up into Yarmouth Harbour.[2] A boat entering this harbour, as everyone knows, does not enter in front of the town like a foreigner, but creeps round at the back like a traitor taking the town in the rear. The passage of the river seems almost too narrow for its traffic, and in consequence the bigger ships look colossal. As we passed under a timber ship from Norway, which seemed to block up the heavens like a cathedral, the man in the straw hat pointed to an old wooden figure-head carved like a woman, and said, like one continuing a conversation, 'Now, why have they left off having them. They didn't do anyone any harm?'

I replied with some flippancy about the captain's wife being jealous; but I knew in my heart that the man had struck a deep note. There has been something in our most recent civilization which is mysteriously hostile to such healthy and humane symbols.

'They hate anything like that, that's human and pretty', he continued, exactly echoing my thoughts. 'I believe they broke up all the jolly old figureheads with hatchets and enjoyed doing it'. 'Like Mr. Quilp', I answered, 'when he battered the wooden Admiral with the poker'.[3]

His whole face suddenly became alive, and for the first time he stood erect and stared at me. 'Do you come to Yarmouth for that?' he asked.

'For what?'

'For Dickens', he answered, and drummed with his foot on the deck.

'No', I answered; 'I come for fun, though that is much the same thing'.

'I always come', he answered quietly, 'to find Peggotty's boat.[4] It isn't here'. And when he said that I understood him perfectly.

There are two Yarmouths; I daresay there are two hundred to the people who live there. I myself have never come to the end of the list of Batterseas. But there are two to the stranger and tourist; the poor part, which is dignified, and the prosperous part, which is savagely vulgar. My new friend haunted the first of these like a ghost; to the latter he would only distantly allude.

'The place is very much spoilt now ... trippers, you know', he would say, not at all scornfully, but simply sadly. That was the nearest he would go to an admission of the monstrous watering place that lay along the front, outblazing the sun, and more deafening than the sea. But behind – out of earshot of this uproar – there are lanes so narrow that they seem like secret entrances to some hidden place of repose. There are squares so brimful of silence that to plunge into one of them is like plunging into a pool. In these places the man and I paced up and down talking about Dickens, or, rather, doing what all true Dickensians do, telling each other verbatim long passages which both of us knew quite well already. We were really in the atmosphere of the older England. Fishermen passed us who might well have been characters like Peggotty; we went into a musty curiosity shop and bought pipe-stoppers carved into figures from Pickwick. The evening was settling down between all the buildings with that slow gold that seems to soak everything when we went into the church.

In the growing darkness of the church my eye caught the coloured windows which on that clear golden evening were flaming with all the passionate heraldry of the most fierce and ecstatic of Christian arts. At length I said to my companion: 'Do you see that angel over there? I think it must be meant for the angel at the sepulchre'. He saw that I was somewhat singularly moved, and he raised his eyebrows.

'I daresay', he said. 'What is there odd about that?'

After a pause I said, 'Do you remember what the angel at the sepulchre said?'

'Not particularly', he answered; 'but where are you off to in such a hurry?'

I walked him rapidly out of the still square, past the fishermen's almshouses, towards the coast, he still inquiring indignantly where I was going.

'I am going', I said, 'to put pennies in automatic machines on the beach. I am going to listen to the niggers. I am going to have my photograph taken. I am going to drink ginger beer out of its original bottle. I will buy some picture postcards. I do want a boat. I am ready to listen to a concertina, and but for the defects of my education should be ready to play it. I am willing to ride on a donkey; that is, if the donkey is willing. I am willing to be a donkey; for all this was commanded me by the angel in the stained-glass window'.

'I really think', said the Dickensian, 'that I had better put you in charge of your relations'.

'Sir', I answered, 'there are certain writers to whom humanity owes much, whose talent is yet of so shy or delicate or retrospective a type that we do well to link it with certain quaint places or certain perishing associations. It would not be unnatural to look for the spirit of Horace Walpole at Strawberry Hill,[5] or even for the shade of Thackeray in old Kensington.[6] But let us have no antiquarianism about Dickens, for Dickens is not an antiquity. Dickens looks not backward, but forward; he might look at our modern mobs with satire or with fury, but he would love to look at them. He might lash our democracy, but it would be because, like a democrat, he asked much from it. We will not have all his books bound up under the title of 'The Old Curiosity Shop'. Rather we will have them all bound up under the title of 'Great Expectations'. Wherever humanity is he would have us face it and make something of it, swallow it with a holy cannibalism and assimilate it with the digestion of a giant. We must take these trippers as he would have taken them, and tear out of them their tragedy and their farce. Do you remember now what the angel said at the sepulchre? "Why seek ye the living among the dead? He is not here; He is risen".[7]

With that we came out suddenly on the wide stretch of the sands which were black with the knobs and masses of our laughing and quite desperate democracy. And the sunset which was now in its final glory flung far over all of them a red flush and glitter like the gigantic firelight of Dickens. In that strange evening light every figure looked at once grotesque and attractive, as if he had a story to tell. I heard a little girl (who was being throttled by another little girl) say by way of self-vindication, 'My sister-in-law 'as got four rings aside her weddin' ring!'

I stood and listened for more, but my friend went away.

Notes
1. *THE DICKENSIAN*: Reprinted in *TT* (2), pp. 75–80.
2. *Yarmouth Harbour*: Chesterton means Great Yarmouth in Norfolk, England, not Yarmouth on the Isle of Wight.
3. *Like Mr. Quilp ... poker*: Daniel Quilp is the grotesque villain – a hunchbacked dwarf moneylender – of Dickens's *The Old Curiosity Shop*; see ch. 62 for his beating a ship's figurehead with a poker.
4. *Peggotty's boat*: Daniel Peggotty is a good-hearted fisherman in Dickens's *David Copperfield*; he lives in a converted boat on the beach at Great Yarmouth.
5. *Horace Walpole at Strawberry Hill*: Horatio [Horace] Walpole, fourth Earl of Orford (1717–97), was an author, politician and patron of the arts. Walpole was the youngest son of the Prime Minister Robert Walpole. With his inheritance, Walpole purchased Strawberry Hill, a house with large grounds and views of the River Thames at Twickenham in South-West London. With the assistance of a 'committee of taste', Walpole transformed the house into a 'Gothic castle' that became the basis of the Gothic revival in English art and architecture. There he wrote, among other works, *The Castle of Otranto* (1763) and *Historic Doubts on the Life and Reign of King Richard the Third* (1766) and *The Mysterious Mother* (1768) (P. Langford, *ODNB*).

6. *Thackeray in Old Kensington*: Following his wife's mental breakdown in 1842, Thackeray moved between lodgings in the area of Kensington several times. He wrote to support his family and attended the theatre, clubs and dinner parties to relieve his loneliness. He rented a house in 1846 and purchased another – 2 Palace Green, Kensington – three years before his sudden and unexpected death (P. L. Shillingsburg, *ODNB*).
7. '*Why seek you ... risen*': Luke 24:5.

August 24, 1908.

'THE SIN OF TORTURE'.

(To the Editor of 'The Daily News'.)

Sir, – I am afraid that Mr. Chesterton's letter in your issue of Thursday[1] may divert attention from the great gravity of the articles which you have had upon the tortures in Russia. I should like to point out that he seems to ignore the fact that, in Russia, the tortures are continued over a long period of time in individual cases, and that they are avowedly inflicted for political reasons. It is to some of us no new thing that these tortures exist. It must be at least 16 or 18 years since Stepniak[2] asked me to see certain men from Warsaw who had come over with a terrible account of the way in which the political prisoners were then being tortured. It was especially so with one man who died from the torture. He was very ill when he was imprisoned, and the governor of that day (whose name I regret to have forgotten) had a certain number of men in the cell of this prisoner, whose duty it was to waken him up every hour, or, in certain cases, every two hours; and whatever he said upon being awakened was taken down by a writer there for the purpose.

This was continued night after night. The prisoner was awakened by kicks and blows, and often was in a state of delirium at the time. The object in view was to endeavour to obtain information from him. The fact that this torture existed so long ago entirely does away with the excuses which Mr. Chesterton suggests for the terrible things carried out by the police at the present time systematically, time after time, until they have reduced their victim to an absolutely helpless condition.

There is much more which I should like to say upon this subject, but I must refrain. It surely shows how absolutely impossible it is that the English people generally look with the slightest satisfaction upon any political understandings with Russia at all. I may say that upon the question of our flogging prisoners I am quite with Mr. Chesterton, but I fail entirely to understand how there is the very slightest similarity in the cases, or why one should be brought up at a time when we are properly considering the great evil of the others. I should like to express the gratitude many of us feel to you for the manner in which you have treated the Russian question. – Yours, etc.,

ROB'T SPENCE WATSON[3]
Bensham Grove, Gateshead-on-Tyne,
August 20th, 1908.

Notes

1. *I am afraid ... issue of last Thursday*: a response to 'The Sin of Torture', letter to the editor, *DN*, 20 August 1920, pp. 131–2 above.
2. *Stepniak*: Sergei Mikhailovich Stepnyak; see '"The Fault of the System"', *DN*, 18 January 1908, p. 12, n. 9 above.
3. *Rob't Spence Watson*: Robert Spence Watson (1837–1911), was a solicitor, writer and educationist. A Quaker, Spence was the President of the Newcastle-Upon-Tyne Liberal Association, 1874–97 and of the National Liberal Association, 1890–1902. He played an energetic role in advancing the cause of education in Newcastle, for example through the Literary and Philosophical Society of Newcastle, which he served throughout his life; also in the establishment of Armstrong College, which later became the University of Newcastle. He was President of the Society of Friends for Russian Freedom from 1890 to 1911, and worked with exiles such as Stepniak in drawing attention to Russian autocracy. His books included *Caedmon, the First English Poet* (1874), *The History of English Rule and Policy in South Africa* (1879), and *The Proper Limits of Obedience to the Law* (1887).

August 25, 1908.

THE SIN OF TORTURE.

('To the Editor of 'The Daily News'.)

Sir, – May I, in a spirit of love, inquire (as Mr. Chadband would say)[1] what on earth 'Unconvinced' can possibly mean by talking about 'one case' of the cat-o'-nine-tails?[2] Honestly, his meaning is dark to me. The implication of his actual words is certainly this: that there has only been one case of flogging in English prisons. Of course he can't mean that; but unless he means that, there is no particular point in his letter. Is not English flogging a 'system'? Do not its engines stand ready in all our prisons? Is it not a recognized sentence, constantly passed in law courts? Are not certain bad men known openly as 'flogging Judges'? And cannot the prison authorities flog to their hearts content without any judge at all? There may be fewer floggings in England than in Russia. I say nothing about that; for the excellent reason that neither you nor I know how many there are in England. Some probably are going on at this moment. It is suggested that there are great differences between the Russian and the English police; there are, indeed. And the greatest of all the differences is this: that the Russian police are a long way off. Telling the truth about them will only lead to the agreeable indulgence of a just anger. Telling the truth about the English may lead to offending Judges at dinner parties or obstructing the police in the exercise of their duty. There is a certain class of reformers for whom the rule of perspective is reversed. For them the tyrant grows smaller as he comes nearer. When he is in the wastes of Eastern Europe they loathe him, curse him, denounce him, and defy him. When he comes up their own street they begin to 'disapprove' of him.

I turn with great relief to Mr. Nevinson's excellent letter.[3] He has a right to speak; for he has been in the evil places he denounces, and opposed the Tsar in Russia as well as in Fleet-street. Not only do I always admire Mr. Nevinson, but I do not think there is really much disagreement between us. I never tried to show that Russian tortures as a whole were excused by horror or peril. What I tried to show, and since no one has attempted to deny it, I will say what I did show, was this – that these motives of horror and peril do exist in Russia, however mixed with yet blacker motives, and that they *might* operate in some cases.[3] They do not exist in English prisons, and cannot operate in any cases. A Russian torturer may be maddened by fanaticism or fear; but we *know* that no English torturer has anything to fear or anything to be fanatical about. I do not say that this palliation is general in Russia. I say that this palliation is possible in Russia; and I say it is impossible in England. That, I think, is unanswerable; at any rate, it is unanswered.

And now we come to the one point on which I really contradict Mr. Nevinson. He says that it depends on the size and scale of the cruelty. I say it does not. For the conscience one dead man in a field is worse than a thousand dead men on a battlefield. So for the health of a nation, one wickedness done coolly, without any excuse, is worse than twenty done in the rush of avowedly exceptional emotions. When the French Revolution had its back to the wall it killed thousands of ladies and gentlemen on suspicion of foreign treason; and the nation was rather the better for the clearance. But if there were now an arbitrary rule in Paris that three dukes must be shot every tenth of August, we should feel that France was dead, dead with the dead ceremonial and dead cruelty of China. Englishmen sacked the city and tore the citizens to pieces in the Protestant frenzy of the Gordon Riots;[4] but the frenzy passed – and Catholic emancipation[5] passed too. But if we now had a rule that one High Church curate must be chopped up with a hatchet every quarter-day, we should feel that evil had paralysed a whole people, so that it could not cry out. That is how I feel today. The curate cut-up with a hatchet and without reason is for me a no more monstrous image than the prisoner cut up with a cat-of-nine-tails and without a reason – even a wicked reason. It is torture without the motives or even the pretences of torture – without any fiction of finding a secret or uttering an indignation.

The great masters of massacre of whom Mr. Nevinson speaks are the bogeys, not the real devils, of mankind. The French Revolution is the great outrage on humanity – on the nursery governess's humanity. The Massacre of St. Bartholomew is the chief calamity of history – of bad history. Bloody Mary is the worst English Sovereign – in waxworks.[6] But this kind of killing does not kill the nation. The Bartholomew, wrought by real religious hatred like Cromwell's massacres,[7] was soon followed by enormous national prosperity and unprecedented religious freedom. If you want the stamp of a decaying society, of a state of things that cannot go on, you will find it not in the fierce street-fights of St. Bartholomew, but in some of the isolated executions of the eighteenth century. A man was broken on the wheel, for instance, in the midst of men with powdered heads who were talking about Nature and sensibility.[8] The wheel on which he was broken was a wheel of routine, like the wheel of a clock: the passions that had made such a thing possible were dead. When that happens I really think the clock is running down; and I think it now. If a gang of Socialists killed every Individualist they saw I should think it bad for the murderers, and not (I concede) quite nice for the murdered. But I should not fear for England. But as it is, I feel as if I were living a few years before the Deluge. I feel that we are walking round a sunlit square, talking about art and social reform, exchanging snuff-boxes, smiling, but slightly averting our eyes; for in the middle of the square a man is being broken on the wheel.[9] —Yours, etc.,

G. K. CHESTERTON.

Notes

1. *(as Mr. Chadband would say)*: The sanctimonious parson Mr Chadband is a character in Dickens's *Bleak House* (1852–3).
2. *What on earth 'Unconvinced' ... cat-o'-nine-tails?*: see 'Unconvinced', '"The Sin of Torture"', letter to the editor, *DN*, 21 August 1908, p. 134 above.
3. *I turn ... Mr Nevinson's excellent letter*: see '"The Sin of Torture"', letter to the editor, *DN*, 22 August 1908, pp. 135–7, above.
4. *I do not think there is really much disagreement between us ... in some cases*: The difference between Chesterton and Nevinson concerning the basis of torture in Russia was addressed by the paper's correspondent in Russia, who had visited a Russian prison: torture persisted as a result of the weakness of the administration in Russia in the face of the prison authorities, and 'the Russian character': 'Russian Torture', 2 September 1908, p. 5.
5. *Gordon Riots*: The Gordon Riots were an anti-Catholic uprising of 1780 against the Papists Act of 1778, relieving some of the civil disabilities imposed on Roman Catholics by the Popery Act of 1698. They were called the 'Gordon Riots' because they were fomented by Lord George Gordon (1751–93), who formed the Protestant Association to press for the repeal of the Papists Act. The Gordon Riots are the central episode in Dickens's *Barnaby Rudge* (1841).
6. *Catholic emancipation*. The Catholic Relief Act of 1829 enabled Roman Catholics to sit in Parliament and repealed the Test Act of 1673 and Penal Laws against Catholics in Ireland.
7. *Bloody Mary ... in waxworks*: Queen Mary of England (1516–58) was known as 'Bloody Mary' because, determined to restore Roman Catholicism to England, she had some 300 religious dissenters burnt at the stake between 1555 and 1558.
8. *Cromwell's massacres*: For an example, see 'Mr. Chesterton's Farewell', letter to the editor, *DN*, 4 October 1902, Volume 1, p. 414, n. 8 above.
9. *broken on the wheel ... Nature and sensibility*: 'Breaking on the wheel' was a method of capital punishment that involved tying the victim to a large wagon wheel and beating him (or her) to death with cudgels – a process that could take several hours or even days. The legend is that the fourth-century martyr St Catherine of Alexandria was executed in this way – hence the expression 'Catherine wheel'. Chesterton here probably has no specific instance in mind; his point is simply that, in the right circumstances, brutality can exist unnoticed alongside gentility.
10. *But as it is, I feel as if I were living ... broken on the wheel*: Much of this letter echoes the concerns that Chesterton had raised in previous months about the inhumanity of punishment in modern Britain, not because of its harshness but because of its banality: see 'That Cure is Better than Prevention', *DN*, 30 May 1908, pp. 80–2; and 'Vengeance', *DN*, 8 August 1908, pp. 122–5 above.

August 26, 1908.

THE SIN OF TORTURE.

(To the Editor of 'The Daily News'.)

Sir, – Some day I should much like to discuss the very interesting historic and moral points raised in Mr. Chesterton's letter this morning. But I am glad to say I agree with him on every principle that really matters, and I think it is not the time for us to enter into controversy right in the front of an advancing enemy.

Here is Mr. Stead doing his best to whitewash the Tsar's Government,[1] which supports itself by the hideous means that you have revealed in your columns. Here are other reputed Liberals trying to draw our country year by year into closer agreement with that Government, so that England is already counted as the friend and supporter of an atrocious despotism.[2] And here is the Russian Government itself continuing its course of political execution, exile, and imprisonment without trial, and openly rewarding the fittest agents of massacre and torture.

In the face of such an enemy the only strategy is to strike hard and strike often. It does not seem to me the moment to discuss possible, though unreal, excuses, which the enemy will eagerly grasp as palliations for their infamies. – Yours, etc.,

HENRY W. NEVINSON.
4, Downside-crescent, Hampstead,
August 25.

Sir, – Is it not strange that subtle minds like Mr. Chesterton, who justifies torturers, and Mr. Nevinson, who detests them, should miss the real point of difference between what is going on in English and in Russian prisons? In England flogging is administered for a crime or offence as a punishment. It may be a bad system or a good one. But in Russia, as everyone could read in the articles on the Riga tortures, terrible cruelties are done, even to a child of eight years, with the object of extorting some confession or getting out of the mouth of the victim some information. Is there anything like this going on in England? – Yours, etc.,

S. T. RAPOPORT.
12, Dagmar-road, N.

Sir, – The parallel drawn by Mr. Chesterton between the tortures in the Russian prisons and the flogging of criminals in our own has been ably dealt with by the writer of the letter published in your issue of to-day.[3]

May I point out besides that Mr. Chesterton ignores the distinction that in the one case the punishment is inflicted after a scrupulously fair and careful trial, and mainly with a view to deterrence from violent and brutal crime, while in the other hideous and protracted torture appears to be administered at the mere will of irresponsible police officials, and (apart from sheer lust of cruelty as a motive) solely for the purpose of extorting information which may or may not be in the possession of the victim.

Whatever our shortcomings, past or present, in relation to our methods in dealing with prisoners, the employment of torture to obtain confessions has always, I believe, been condemned both by the letter and the spirit of the law of England.

It would doubtless be possible for Mr. Chesterton, by brilliant manipulation of fanciful analogies, to show that Nero[4] was an enlightened philanthropist, and that John Howard[5] was a monster of selfishness and barbarity, but even he will fail to convince the thinking public that an isolated instance of the punishment of a violent ruffian by flogging after an impartial trial, is on the same plane as the torture practised in Russia by irresponsible police officials upon innocent men, women, and children. – Yours, etc.,

H. J. AYLIFFE.
13, Denmar-hill, S.E., August 24.

Notes
1. *Here is Mr. Stead ... Tsar's Government*: see Nevinson's previous letter, '"The Sin of Torture"', 22 August 1908, pp. 136, n. 3 above.
2. *Here are other reputed Liberals ... atrocious despotism*: most obviously a reference to the role of the Foreign Secretary Sir Edward Grey in sealing the Anglo–Russian entente in 1907.
3. *Ably dealt with by the writer ... to-day*: Robert Spence Watson, 'The Sin of Torture', *DN*, 24 August 1908, pp. 142–3 above.

4. *Nero*: Nero (Claudius Caesar Augustus Germanicus); see 'A Messenger of Tolstoy', *DN* 9 September 1901, note 3, Volume 1, p. 184 above.
5. *John Howard*: John Howard (1726–90) was an English philanthropist and prison reformer after whom the present day Howard League for Penal Reform is named.

August 27, 1908.

'THE SIN OF TORTURE'.

Sir, – On reading Mr. Chesterton's letter in to-day's 'Daily news',[1] a doubt assailed me as to the genuineness of his facts.

'Is not English flogging a system?' asks Mr. Chesterton in his best bloodcurdling manner. 'Do not its engines stand ready in all our prisons? Is it not a recognized sentence constantly passed in law courts? Are not certain bad men known as Flogging Judges? And cannot the prison authorities flog to their hearts' content without any judge at all?'

Grammatically, these are questions. But Mr. Chesterton is not seeking information, he is by way of imparting it by the method interrogative, and ninety-nine out of every hundred of your readers will assume that each question has a fact behind it.

Let us take them seriatim. I deny that flogging is a sentence 'constantly passed'. It is almost as rare as hanging.

'Cannot the prison authorities flog to their hearts' content without any judge at all?' Certainly they cannot. To suggest that such a practice prevails in these islands outsteps the decencies of controversy. This mischievous falsehood will be read in the Colonies, in America, and abroad by thousands who will accept the figment as fact, and will never see the refutation. I assert, circumstantially, that no single prisoner is, or can be, flogged in any English jail at the will of the prison authorities. Let us come to the facts.

Say that a convict attacks a warder. (This is practically the only offence which is ever punished by the lash. A mutineer is liable to it; but, unless he adds violence, or incitements to violence, to his mutiny, he is never flogged.) The striker is charged before the visiting justices – not Government nominees ad hoc, but local magistrates chosen by their fellows upon the Bench for their known firmness and character – these take the evidence in the prisoner's presence, hear his defence, and then may, or may not, suggest corporal punishment (they cannot order it). And this is merely preliminary. Their suggestion, with the evidence, must go to the Home Office for consideration. There it is sometimes set aside altogether, and frequently reduced.

Such are the plain facts; such is routine, prescribed by printed rules, hedged about and guarded at each step in the convict's interest. Is this the orgy of torture represented by Mr. Chesterton – the irresponsible tyrant flogging to his heart's content, secretly, unchecked, and without record kept, so that 'neither you nor I know how many floggings there are in England'?

But what is a prison flogging? The maximum sentence is thirty-six lashes, but in practice the maximum is never inflicted. A public servant of long experience assures me that twenty-four strokes were once inflicted in his presence, and once only. A dozen, or less, I have reason to believe, is more usual. But 'usual' is not the word. Flogging in our prisons is most unusual. In the jail which I visited to-day only three floggings have been inflicted in five years, and one of the three was with the birch. There are at Portland 800 bad cases, yet a period of sixteen months recently elapsed without the cat being used.

But even a dozen lashes might be a serious infliction if given with such an instrument as Mr. Chesterton describes in his first letter. 'The English prison cat', says he, (I quote from memory), 'is one of the most frightful instruments in the history of torture, so frightful that medical arrangements have to be made to prevent a man dying under it.'[2] This description might apply to the Navy cat, used in the early years of the last century, as described by Mr. Silk Buckingham[3] or to the thieves' cat, depicted by Captain Marryat,[4] or to the Roman 'horribile flagellum',[5] but to use such terms about the cat which I saw and handled to-day is grotesque exaggeration.

I will describe it. Bear in mind that each cat is to pattern, and is passed for use by the Home Office. The instrument consists of a handle of light wood, about eighteen inches long, with lashes, say, twice as long, of pliable, softish hemp about as thick as a stout quill. The material is somewhat loosely twisted and of a rather woolly and yielding texture, neither tarred, starched, nor stiffened with brine (as in books). There is not one knot to any of the lashes, they end bluntly without cord or twine crackers, and the only part of them which seemed to me capable of inflicting any considerable pain were the extreme ends, which, to prevent untwisting, were bound for about half-an-inch with unwaxed thread, like a child's bat-handle. The whole thing weighed just eight and a half ounces. The Russian prison whip examined by Mr. Coulson Kernahan[6] weighed nearly 8 lbs.

There is nothing secret about these circumstances; everything about which I have written is accessible. There are tabular statistics which the Government collect and print in volume form. Mr. Chesterton may see them all as I saw them; they are open to the inspection of any seeker for truth. – Yours, etc.,

H. M. WALLIS.
Ashton Lodge, Reading, August 28 [25].

Notes

1. *On reading Mr. Chesterton's letter in to-day's 'Daily News'*: a response to Chesterton's letter to the editor, 25 August 1908, pp. 145–6 above.
2. *such an instrument as Mr. Chesterton describes in his first letter ... dying under it*: see 'The Sin of Torture', letter to the editor, *DN*, 20 August 1908, p. 131 above.
3. *Mr. Silk Buckingham*: James Silk Buckingham (1786–1855), was an author and traveller. After extensive travel across the globe, on the basis of which he wrote several successful travelogues, Buckingham became MP for Sheffield from 1832–7. He used his position to campaign for social reforms, including the abolition of flogging in the army and navy and press-gangs (G. F. R Barker, rev. F. Driver, *ODNB*).
4. *thieves' cat ... Captain Marryat*: Frederick Marryat (1792–1848), was an English naval officer and novelist. He served with distinction in the West Indies, East Indies and the Mediterranean. He began his career as a successful writer of naval adventure stories while still in the navy. His books included *The King's Own* (1830), *Mr. Midshipman Easy* (1836), *The Phantom Ship* (1839), and *The Privateer's Man* (1846). The reference here is to *The Dog Fiend: or Snarleyyow* (1837), ch. 2.
5. *the Roman 'horribile flagellum'*: According to Horace (*Satires* 1:3) the *horribile flagellum* was a whip made of thongs of ox-hide.
6. *Mr. Coulson Kernahan*: Coulson Kernahan (1858–1943) was an English novelist and poet, but he is not meant here. The name 'Kernahan' is a mistake on the part of the correspondent (see Wallis's subsequent letter, 3 September 1908, p. 160 below), and the name Coulson has probably been added without comment by the typographer.

August 29, 1908.

THE TWO NOISES.[1]

For three days and three nights the sea had charged England as Napoleon charged her at Waterloo. The phrase is instinctive, because away to the last grey line of the sea there was only the look of galloping squadrons, impetuous, but with a common purpose. The sea came on like cavalry, and when it touched the shore it opened the blazing eyes and deafening tongues of the artillery. I saw the worst assault at night on a seaside parade where the sea smote on the doors of England with the hammers of earthquake, and a white smoke went up into the black heavens. There one could thoroughly realise what an awful thing a wave really is. I talk like other people about the rushing swiftness of a wave. But the horrible thing about a wave is its hideous slowness. It lifts its load of water laboriously: in that style at once slow and slippery in which a Titan might lift a load of rock and then let it slip at last to be shattered into a shock of dust. In front of me that night the waves were not like water; they were like falling city walls. The breaker rose first as if it did not wish to attack the earth; it wished only to attack the stars. For a time it stood up in the air as naturally as a tower; then it went a little wrong in its outline, like a tower that might someday fall. When it fell it was as if a powder magazine blew up.

****

I have never seen such a sea. All the time there blew across the land one of those stiff and throttling winds that one can lean up against like a wall. One expected anything to be blown out of shape at any instant; the lamppost to be snapped like a green stalk, the tree to be whirled away like a straw. I myself should certainly have been blown out of shape if I had possessed any shape to be blown out of; for I walked along the edge of the stone embankment above the black and battering sea and could not rid myself of the idea that it was an invasion of England. But as I walked along this edge I was somewhat surprised to find that as I neared a certain spot another noise mingled with the ceaseless cannonade of the sea.[a]

Somewhere at the back, in some pleasure ground or casino or place of entertainment, an undaunted brass band was playing against the cosmic uproar. I do not know what band it was. Judging from the boisterous British Imperialism of most of the airs it played, I should think it was a German band. But there was no doubt about its energy, and when I came quite close under it it really drowned the storm. It was playing such things as 'Tommy Atkins' and 'You Can Depend on Young Australia', and many others of which I do not know the words, but I should think they would be 'John, Pat, and Mac, With the Union Jack', or that fine though unwritten poem, 'Wait till the Bull Dog gets a bit of you'. Now, I for one detest Imperialism, but I have a great deal of sympathy with Jingoism. And there seemed something so touching about this unbroken and innocent bragging under the brutal menace of Nature that it made, if I may so put it, two tunes in my mind. It is so obvious and so jolly to be optimistic about England, especially when you are an optimist – and an Englishman. But through all that glorious brass came the voice of the invasion, the undertone of that awful sea. I did a foolish thing. As I could not express my meaning in an article, I tried to express it in a poem – a bad one. You can call it what you like. It might be called 'Doubt', or 'Brighton'. It might be called 'The Patriot', or yet again 'The German Band'. I would call it 'The Two Voices', but that title has been taken for a grossly inferior poem.[2] This is how it began:

> They say the sun is on your knees
>   A lamp to light your lands from harm,
> They say you turn the seven seas
>   To little brooks about your farm.
> I hear the sea and the new song
> That calls you empress all day long.
>
> *(O fallen and fouled! O you that lie*
> *Dying in swamps – you shall not die,*
> *Your rich have secrets, and strange lust,*
> *Your poor are chased about like dust,*
> *Emptied of anger and surprise –*
> *And God has gone out of their eyes.*
> *Your cohorts break – your captains lie,*
> *I say to you, you shall not die.)*

Then I revived a little, remembering that after all there is an English country that the Imperialists have never found. The British Empire may annex what it likes, it will never annex England. It has not even discovered the island, let alone conquered it. I took up the two tunes again with a greater sympathy for the first:

> I know the bright baptismal rains,
>   I love your tender troubled skies,
> I know your little climbing lanes,

Are peering into Paradise.
From open hearth to orchard cool,
How bountiful and beautiful.

(*O throttled and without a cry,*
O strangled and stabbed, you shall not die,
The frightful word is on your walls,
The east sea to the west sea calls,
The stars are dying in the sky,
You shall not die; you shall not die.)

Then the two great noises grew deafening together, the noise of the peril of England and the louder noise of the placidity of England. It is their fault if the last verse was written a little rudely and at random:

I see you how you smile in state
    Straight from the Peak to Plymouth Bar,
You need not tell me you are great,
    I know how more than great you are.
I know what William Shakespeare was,[a]
I have seen Gainsborough and the grass.

(*O given to believe a lie,*
O my mad mother, do not die,
Whose eyes turn all ways but within,
Whose sin is innocence of sin,
Whose eyes, blinded with beams at noon,
Can see the motes upon the moon,
You shall your lover still pursue.
To what last madhouse shelters you
I will uphold you, even I.
You that are dead. You shall not die.)

But the sea would not stop for me any more than for Canute;[3] and as [for] the German band, that would not stop for anybody.

153a sea.] In *TT* (2) is replaced by: surf.
155a I know what William Shakespeare was,] in *TT* (2) is replaced by: I know what spirit Chaucer was,

Notes
1. *THE TWO NOISES:* Reprinted in *TT* (2), pp. 167–71.
2. *I would call it ... grossly inferior poem*: Tennyson, 'The Two Voices' (1833).
3. *Canute*: Canute (Cnut), called 'the Great' (*c.* 985–1035), was the Viking king of Denmark, England, Norway and parts of Sweden. The only story that most people remember about this formidable statesman – that he commanded the sea to turn back and not wet his feet – is very likely apocryphal; it originates with the twelfth-century chronicler Henry of Huntingdon (1080–1160) and is not corroborated by any independent source.

August 31, 1908.

'THE SIN OF TORTURE'.

(To the Editor of 'The Daily News'.)

Sir, – The cat-o'-nine-tails is a cat of nine lives; and so many of your readers are ready to rush to its rescue that I hope you will permit me, as one against many, some more space. I have several things to say to several people. With your permission I will say them personally one by one.

First: To Mr. S. T. Rapoport,[1] who makes the monumental statement that I 'justify' Russian torturers. I said of Russian torture that it came from hell, that all decent people must denounce it, but that there were degrees in devilry. When I bring out my forthcoming work, 'The Life and Letters of S. T. Rapoport', suppose I say the same thing of him. I hope Mr. Rapoport will regard that as a complete 'justification' of him.

Second: To Mr. H. J. Ayliffe,[2] who, with Mr. Rapoport, urges, truly enough, that at least torture is not used in England in order to extract confessions. Precisely; that is what I maintained. It is not used for the original reason which made it, not excusable, but at least intelligible. Mr. Ayliffe also says that we inflict it only after a scrupulously fair and careful trial. He is wrong; in the prison cases the trial, if there is any trial, is private and probably perfunctory; and I have myself heard a Judge threaten a pauper with a flogging, after four minutes of highly irrational conversation. But Mr. Ayliffe must remember that the trial, even if it is careful, can only be careful about the fact of the guilt, not about the magnitude of the guilt or the fitness of the punishment. If we have a law that little boys can be skinned alive for cigarette smoking, it is no comfort that we always find positive proof of the cigarette.

Third: To Mr. H. M. Wallis.[3] It has come at last. I knew it would; and though the subject is somewhat gloomy, I have to resist a strong disposition to laugh. At last we have the inevitable official assurance that all is well, delivered with the same statistical pomposity with which we were assured that Mr. Whitaker Wright was beyond or above the law,[4] and that the Jameson Raid telegrams had nothing in particular written on them.[5] Mr. Wallis suggests to us that a prison is a little paradise, that the police are always tenderly 'safe-guarding the interests' of the convicts, and also (in a passage of extraordinary humour) that the lash is of so light and feathery a description that a stroke of it can, I conceive, almost be regarded as a caress. Mr. Nevinson may take the torture view, as I do, as a piece of common knowledge and common-sense;[6] 'Unconvinced', may disapprove of flogging;[7] you yourself, sir, may feel that our hands are not wholly clean. But the only result of such minor protests is to let down upon all our heads this cataract of whitewash. I will not pursue Mr. Wallis through his long design of answering my questions seriatim; more especially as he forgot to do it. Flogging is a sentence constantly passed. It may be 'almost as rare as hanging'; but if Mr. Wallis thinks that hanging is rare, I can only say that his demand for human lives happens to be higher than mine. It may be that two magistrates, 'chosen for their firmness' (I can see their faces), are present when the prisoner, after some pitiful explanation of his own, is condemned to torture. But if Mr. Wallis thinks that is a trial, he has never thought about what a trial is. The only advantage in a trial is not that magistrates are specially mild or kind; it is that open discussion is a defence of justice. Out of the public eye a magistrate may be cruel, just as a magistrate may be drunk. But I pass all this by; because there is one simple fact which overtops it all. I will not go into any of these details. I will ask a plain question.

This argument is about whether certain cruelties are hidden in English prisons as in Russian and other prisons. Now what would Mr. Wallis think of me if I made it an answer to the Russian revelations that the Russian officials do not confess to them? That in a Russian gaol which I visited the Government representatives [had] told me that flogging was most unusual. That I was then informed that very few floggings had occurred in the last five years. That the Russian police had shown me some kind of stick, and that it did not look as if it would hurt. Of course, Mr. Wallis would instantly reply: 'But you are putting on the judgment seat the very people who are in the dock. We accuse the Russian police, and the only answer you can offer is that they defend themselves'. So I say to Mr. Wallis. Someone accuses the police of cruelty. And the only answer he can give is that they do not accuse themselves. The truth is, of course, that his mind is caught in that iron argument in a circle, which will perhaps for many centuries imprison the English intellect. 'English magistrates and gentlemen are spotless; they say so themselves. And they would not tell a lie, because they are spotless'. Then (with adorable simplicity) Mr. Wallis adds that there is 'nothing secret' about these statements or statistics. He might as well say that there is nothing secret about the proclamations of the Tsar. There never is anything secret about the official version of an affair. One can only judge by accidental facts, inferences which are overlooked. The fact of medical supervision is quite enough for me. If flogging were what Mr. Wallis represents it, one would no more summon a doctor for the flogging of a prisoner than the smacking of a child.

Fourth: To Dr. Spence-Watson.[8] This distinguished man asked me why the subject should be brought forward in the midst of the Russian atrocities. I can answer in one breath. Because I am much more alarmed about England than about Russia. Russia is awake. England is not only going to sleep, under the Wallis lullaby, but like a person poisoned with laudanum, she may be going to sleep for ever. In all countries there are official explanations; only in one country have I ever heard of their being believed. Giving a man thirty lashes for a word or a gesture is possible in all countries; but Mr. Wallis is only possible in our own. All nations have sins, and tyranny may be Russia's; but England's sin is a lack of the conviction of sin.

Fifth: To Mr. Nevinson,[9] to whom I dedicate these last lines, and by whose great spirit I am very willing to be judged. I agree that we must march together against the enemy. But the Tsar is not the enemy. The enemy is the Holy Alliance,[10] the old spirit of an ancient pride and cruelty from which the Revolution only half delivered us. The French Revolution was meant as a signal for a revolution in every land. It meant not that we should hate their tyrants, but that we should hate our own. Russia is marching towards the Bastille. But we are marching away from it. Science and the modern forces are telling us that the Bastille is a good thing. We have committed a military mistake, which may be the end of our whole effort. We have left our own Bastille uncaptured, in our rear. – Yours, etc.,

G. K. CHESTERTON.

Notes
1. *To Mr. S. T. Rapoport*: see S. T. Rapoport, 'The Sin of Torture', letter to the editor, *DN*, 26 August 1908, pp. 147–8 above.
2. *To Mr. H. J. Ayliffe*: see H. J. Ayliffe, 'The Sin of Torture', letter to the editor, *DN*, 26 August 1908, p. 148 above.
3. *To Mr. H. M. Wallis*: see H. M. Wallis, '"The Sin of Torture"', letter to the editor, *DN*, 27 August 1908, pp. 150–2 above.
4. *assured that Mr. Whitaker Wright ... the law*: (James) Whitaker Wright (1846–1904), was an English mining company owner who, after a disastrous speculation in the construction of the Baker Street and Waterloo Railway, embarked on a series of complex financial frauds. Despite pressure on the Government to bring a prosecution against him, it was a creditor who instigated the issuing of a warrant for his arrest. He committed suicide by taking a cyanide pill immediately after being sentenced to seven years' penal servitude. (Ironically enough, Counsel for the prosecution was Rufus Isaacs, who was himself to become embroiled in the 'Marconi Scandal' of 1913; see Chesterton, 'The Honour of Politics', letter to the editor, *DN*, 19 June 1913, Volume 8, pp. 238–9, n. 1 below.)

5. *Jameson Raid telegrams ... written on them*: During the House of Commons inquiry into the Jameson Raid, Cecil Rhodes refused to be drawn over 'missing telegrams' that would have revealed the complicity of the Colonial Secretary, Joseph Chamberlain, in the affair. In exchange, Chamberlain defended the Charter of Rhodes's British South Africa Company. While Rhodes's political career was ruined by the Raid, his commercial interests remained unscathed (S. Marks and S. Trapido, *ODNB*).
6. *Mr. Nevinson ... common-sense*: see H. W. Nevinson, '"The Sin of Torture"', letter to the editor, *DN*, 22 August 1908, (opening paragraph) p. 135 above.
7. *Unconvinced ... disapprove of flogging*: see 'Unconvinced', '"The Sin of Torture"', letter to the editor, *DN*, 21 August 1908, p. 134 above.
8. *To Dr. Spence-Watson*: see Robert Spence Watson, '"The Sin of Torture"', letter to the editor, *DN*, 24 August 1908, pp. 142–3 above.
9. *To Mr. Nevinson*: see H. W. Nevinson, 'The Sin of Torture', letter to the editor, *DN*, 26 August 1908, p. 147 above.
10. *Holy Alliance*: The Holy Alliance was a coalition of Russia, Austria and Prussia created by the Congress of Vienna after the final defeat of Napoleon in 1815. The three states undertook to conduct their domestic and foreign policies in accordance with Christian principles. Especially under the influence of the Austrian statesman Prince Klemens Wenzel von Metternich (1773–1859) the alliance was in practice a highly conservative instrument for resisting and suppressing revolutionary sentiment and activity.

September 3, 1908.

'THE SIN OF TORTURE'.

(To the Editor of 'The Daily News'.)

Sir, – Mr. Chesterton cannot be so blind as he would have us believe.[1] He probably sets some limit to his irresponsibilities; let us hope that this has now been reached. How stands the matter? Whilst inveighing against Russian enormities – and doing it rather well – he capriciously skips aside to charge the whole prison staff of Great Britain with similar abominations. That this excursus was no help to Russian freedom was immaterial; it made good copy, and might even have raised a scare had there been the least modicum of basal fact beneath it. There is none, and that the vivacious Chesterton knows as well as I; and in wantonly libelling a great public service he did ill, and is coming out worse.

Russian and British jails and jailors are not on a parity. Any horror is antecedently credible of theirs, for there is evidence, but is incredible of ours, for there is none. Who has been flogged in any English prison 'to the heart's content of the governor without any judge at all'? And when? and where? This is my challenge, a plain one for Mr. Chesterton. Will he meet it?

Mr. C. has no case. His 'facts' are wrong. The 'cat' he described so harrowingly, the engine of torture dangerous to life, is a figment of his own imagination. It exists in no British prison. But, when I confront him with the real thing, the thing, that is, which he or anyone can handle and weigh, Mr. Chesterton shies at the tangible, visible fact, and falls back upon some instrument of torture (of unknown weight, and apparently forty-five knots) seen in use by a Mr. Nevinson, some ten years since, *in the Transvaal in the days of Oom Paul.*

This Mr. Chesterton calls 'taking the torture view as a piece of common knowledge and common-sense'.

Each of us is liable to a slip of the pen; in my previous letter I wrote Kernahan when I meant Kennan.[2] But Mr. Chesterton's divagations from veracity are amazing and difficult to explain. Relying upon an exuberant fancy, he has made statements which I have exposed. What does he [do]? Substantiate? Withdraw? In no wise. He 'resists a disposition to laugh'. All the officials are untrustworthy; Mr. Wallis is an official, ergo –. This is the substance of Mr. Chesterton's reply. My evidence is swept aside as a thing of no worth; yet he slates me in a hundred lines of fine, florid rhetoric. But I am not an official; simply a business man, without Government bias or connection. But were I the hireling scribe of the Home Office, whose clumsy official denials set Mr. Chesterton roaring, what of the rest? Are *all* English jail governors, chaplains, doctors, and warders in a conspiracy of silence? Are *all* visiting justices 'cruel, and even drunk', when Mr. Chesterton's eye is off them? And what of the convicts themselves when released? Surely they could a tale unfold? Has *one* – merely one – alleged that he has been flogged by the jail authorities 'to their hearts' content', etc.?

I am asking myself what has this man to go upon. Apparently he is fishing for evidence in support. Having no data of his own, and having rejected mine, he is driven to go 'upon accidental facts'. Having begun by asserting secrecy, he gets it from me that a doctor is always present. (In two cases that I knew of, the medical men were general practitioners called in from outside. Both were known to me.) 'This is enough', cries Mr. Chesterton, changing front. 'If flogging were what Mr. Wallis represents it [as], why summon a doctor?' The answer is: Because the Home Office regulations so order. But, save us! what an argument! Secrecy proved cruelty; what was done without witnesses was obviously cruel. But secrecy had to be given up, and forthwith the mere presence of a doctor proved the cruelty just as well, proved it indubitably to any unprejudiced mind, albeit the man was there to prevent it.

And this from the Master of the Art of Controversy, who a paragraph earlier is found lecturing me for arguing in a circle!

Your readers will observe that in my two letters, I have adduced facts, exploded fallacies, but offered no opinions of my own upon the question of prison flogging. Nor am I about to do so now. Mr. Chesterton has misrepresented my views (which he knows nothing about), and has garbled and travestied my statements, which he had under his eyes; that is his method.

But life (and your columns) are too short for exposing the protean shifts and disingenuities of Mr. Chesterton. 'What would Mr. Wallis think of me?' he asks. Better not press that question. Yours, etc.,

H. M. WALLIS.
Ashton Lodge, Reading, Sept. 1.

Notes
1. *Mr. Chesterton ... have us believe*: see 'The Sin of Torture', letter to the editor, *DN*, 31 August 1908, pp. 156–9 above.

2. *Each of us is liable ... Kennan*: George Kennan (1845–1924), was an American explorer noted for his travels in the Kamchatka and Caucasus regions of Russia. Originally a supporter of the Tsar's government, he espoused the cause of revolution following his return to America after his third visit to Russia in 1886. He campaigned for the release of Russian political prisoners and on behalf of persecuted minorities in the Russian empire. (Coulson Kernahan had pointed out the mistake in a letter to the editor, 31 August 1908, p. 4.)

September 5, 1908.

THE WHEEL OF IRON.

―――

While I am dwelling like a brooding dove with exquisite placidity upon this column I am told that I am having a violent row in some other column. I will make no inquiries of that sordid quarrel; I will not ask about the provocation or the declaration of war. This is the declaration of peace. Elsewhere in this paper a gentleman has been in a state of just fury because he thought I said he was an official.[1] I never said so; as Mr. Lammle said to Mr. Fledgeby, the just anger of a gentleman has sent the blood boiling to his head so that he did not hear me.[2] I never said he was an official; he is far too innocent. I did say that he could call no evidence on behalf of the officials except the evidence of the officials themselves. I shall go on saying this, at agreeable intervals, during my life until somebody answers it. But this little quarrel as far as I am concerned is drawing to its close; and I only desire to wind up by stating the truth as well as the termination of the matter.

Now the really interesting truth is this. When any kind of quarrel arises between tyrants and rebels (that is rulers whom the subjects call tyrants and the subjects whom the rulers call rebels) it is at once apparent that there must be on both sides an argument in a circle. In Ireland (to take an instance) the Orange garrison declare 'The Nationalist peasants say the police are cruel; but then Catholics are such liars'. The Nationalists declare 'The Orangemen say the police are not cruel; but then Orangemen are such hypocrites'. The gentleman with whom I have recently parted, with tears and embraces, in another part of this paper, seems to have darkly adumbrated the idea that I am in a circular argument as well as he. But of course I am. We all are. We either hate all the convicting judges merely because they convict; or we hate all the convicts merely because they are convicted.

****

The usual course in England is to assume that all prisoners as such are likely to be wrong in England; but that all policemen as such are likely to be wrong abroad. If any convict assaults any warder in Russian prisons, we feel that he is probably right; if any warder assaults any prisoner in our prisons, we feel he is probably right. The circular argument is so natural and obvious. The worse the judge the more he will be inclined to over-punish. The worse the criminal the more he will say he was over-punished. This is the original iron circle by which all oppression was possible. No one ever tortured good men; they tortured bad men who would not confess that they were bad. No one ever defied a court of justice; he defied a court of injustice which would not confess that it was unjust. That is what I meant when I said (so much to the distress of my friend elsewhere) that in these things one must judge by external and even accidental clues. The heretics who defend sexual manias will never admit that they are anything but chaste. The Inquisition which tears them with red-hot pincers will never admit that it is anything but merciful. The ordinary police detective will always believe that the ex-convict is a scoundrel who is trying to get back to scoundrelism. The ordinary ex-convict will always believe that the detective is a spy who is trying to get him back to prison. Practically speaking, there is considerable foundation for both views. In the recent controversy my opponent innocently asked why the convicts do not denounce the public servants if the public servants oppress them. There are many answers, including the answer that the convicts do. But the principal answer to my adversary is simply this: that if the convicts did denounce the officials he would be the first to say, 'Will you take the word of a gaol-bird against a reputable public servant?' No; the authorities have not only got the convicted labourer under the stick; they have got him in a cleft stick. If he calls his masters good he confesses that he is bad. If he calls his masters bad then that only shows how bad he is.

Some have found it touching and reassuring that whatever is done in prisons has some sort of bewildered assent from a county magistrate. Have these people ever seen a county magistrate? I will not say that he is frequently a fool; for that statement, though true, is unphilosophical. I will ask whether anyone between the four seas of Britain knows any reason why he should not be a fool, why he should not be cruel, profligate, cowardly, and a liar. If there are any processes in the selection of a J.P. preventing any of these probabilities, I have yet to learn what they are. That J.P.'s have constantly behaved as all these things I pass as too obvious for comment; for what interests me here, as I say, is not fact, but theory. The same sort of silly, red-faced young man appears all over England in the dock as a poacher and [the same sort of old gentleman appears][3] on the bench as a magistrate. Neither has passed any test or proved any virtue. The poacher has been slightly more successful in picking up rabbits than the gentleman in picking up law, but both proceedings have been unscientific and quite untested. The only difference is that the rich fool can in practice get the poor fool arrested and imprisoned and tortured. The last touch of humour is that the torture of the poor fool is supposed to have a kind of halo of innocence because it has the consent of the rich fool. That, at least, is all I have been able to gather from the legal explanations offered to me. I have tried in vain to discover any approved merit in the magistrate, except that he is the magistrate. In fact, the main philosophy of the English rulers seems to be expressed in that sound old song of theirs about the Duke of York. When they are up they are up; and when they are down they are down.[4] That seems to be the whole circular logic of the matter.

****

Now what interests me is this: is there any way out of this iron circle of confidence that has created all the tyrannies? Some old criminals were silenced by being killed. The modern criminals are silenced by being disgraced. That is a matter of detail. No one will credit the prisoner – because he has been in prison. No one will accept his account of gaol – because he has been there. He is disbelieved because he knows. Is there any way of breaking out of this circular trap? There is, I think, one which is at least worth trying. I mean democracy; the direct consultation of the people. If the opinions of the criminal and the judge are obviously discredited, let us ask what is actually the opinion of one actual poor woman with whom I was speaking to-day[; it?] was this: 'Whichever way we turn we go into prison'. One thing I have always noticed when I talked to any of the poor about Battersea; that I heard a voice which is utterly new and unknown in the government of this country. If ever the English people enter England they will enter it as something entirely new. They will be a surprise to the capitalist, but more of a surprise to the Socialists. It would take a long time to express all the tones of the voice I mean. But this is certain; that anyone who understands the poor understands the police; and understands them well enough to laugh at all this discussion. I have seen the police being brutal to the poor collectively in the street. How should I believe they will be tender to them separately in the cells? I have heard magistrates being impatient and indecent in open court. Why should I believe that they will be unnaturally cautious and chivalrous in a secret tribunal behind soundless walls? I know it is very shocking to suggest anything evil about the governing system of England. It is true that the overwhelming majority of the actual English people agree with me. But that counts for very little – as yet.

Notes

1. *Elsewhere ... he thought I said he was an official*: see H. M. Wallis, "'The Sin of Torture'", letter to the editor, *DN*, 3 September 1908, p. 161 above.
2. *As Mr. Lammle ... hear me*: See Dickens, *Our Mutual Friend*, ch. 5.

3. *[same sort of old gentleman appears]*: these words have been interpolated in accordance with the sense of the paragraph.
4. *sound old song of theirs ... they are down*: The English nursery rhyme to which Chesterton refers may well have a satirical origin, as many nursery rhymes do; possibly it 'celebrates' the ignominious defeat of Prince Frederick, Duke of York and Albany (1763–1827), at the Battle of Tourcoing in 1794:

> Oh, The grand old Duke of York,
> He had ten thousand men;
> He marched them up to the top of the hill,
> And he marched them down again.
> And when they were up, they were up,
> And when they were down, they were down,
> And when they were only half-way up,
> They were neither up nor down.

September 12, 1908.

THE GREAT CAB CRUSADE.

———

The question of cabs (unlike that of prisons) is one which I have considered from the inside. In fact I have in preparation an important historical and antiquarian monograph, called 'The Cab in All Ages'. It is so voluminous and exhaustive that only a faint idea of it can be given even by quoting its synopsis: 'Fossil Cabs – Persian legend of the Origin of Cabs – Quadrigae, Should They be Translated Four-wheelers? – The Cab in Christian Art – Prophesy of Merlin, did it refer to Motor-Cabs? – The Hansom Cab, or Two is Company – Compared with Universalist Ideal of Omnibus – War between Taximeter Cabs and Hansom Cabs – Regrettable Incidents during the Struggle'. I abbreviate the summary of this contribution to learning, because it is only with the last phase of it that I am here concerned. The truth is that I cannot find a publisher who will take my monograph on the cab, which is in only fourteen volumes, so I propose to print some of the last and most exciting passages of it in this paper. And I select the passage which describes the conflict between Hansoms and Taxi-cabs,[1] with some account of the great orators and soldiers to whom that contest gave birth.

****

The first important phase in the controversy occurred, of course, when a Select Committee of Taximeter Drivers (in uniform) met and composed their celebrated manifesto: which, in echo of Dr. Johnson's pamphlet on American taxes,[2] they entitled 'Taximetration No Tyranny'. This was answered in a brilliant and amusing, though somewhat too free-spoken, article called 'Handsome Is As Hansom Drives',[3] written by a witty, but slightly intoxicated, cabman in the neighbourhood of Farringdon-street. After this exchange of epigrams feeling ran high on both sides; and that civil war in England which public men had feared (and which wise men had prayed for) broke out abruptly over this question of cabs.

The opening speech of the leader of the taxi-cab party was justly regarded as a very learned and powerful performance. The speaker was obviously a scientific man; his speech was full of long words from Latin and Greek; he dropped his h's a good deal, but then so did the Latins and the Greeks. The substance of his speech remained essential, and, as some thought, unanswerable. On the largest philosophical grounds he justified the automobile. The earth itself (he said in a fine passage) is an automobile. You worship (he cried with passion) the State that rules itself. Should you not worship also the cab that moves itself? The new powers of science were present. The driver of a taxi-cab ought to drive it with the sense that he was letting loose all the secret energies of the universe. That is (the speaker hastened to add) so long as he did not do so when he was driving it through St. James's Park. There was no limit to the miracles of science; there was nothing which one could not ask of it. Science had invented a machine that could calculate better than a man.[4] Was it unreasonable that science after that should invent a machine that could run better than a horse? (Taximeter cheers.) It was really an argument between the old England and the new England, and the new England would win. The speaker resumed his seat amid loud applause, having spoken for two hours and a quarter, and the taximeter clock (which he wore round his neck as an ornament) registering nine and sixpence.

****

But the debate was destined to be a war of giants. The splendid opening speech of the taximeter champion was easy to remember; the reply of the representative hansom cabman (a man of the name of Gumm) was impossible to forget. He began by saying that as far as he was concerned the new England was not England at all. (Hansom and Fourwheeler cheers.) He could imagine Shakespeare driving a hansom (cries of 'Withdraw') – but not driving a taxicab. (Laughter.) The last speaker had said that we might ask anything of science, and that a machine could do anything. 'Very well', cried Mr. Gumm, in a voice that rang in the rafters, 'let science discover a motor-cab that can find its way to my house when I am drunk'. (A long and thoughtful silence, followed by furious Hansom Cab cheers.) The last speaker had troubled them with some terribly long words, and with much that he should be inclined to call pedantry. But he also, even he (Mr. Gumm) had some knowledge of history. What did European history really mean? It meant chivalry. (Cheers.) What did chivalry really mean? It meant horses. (Loud and continued cheering.) All the great adventures, from Alexander the Great to Napoleon, had depended upon this ancient alliance between the two noble animals – the horse and the man. Whenever he (Mr. Gumm) drove out his horse in the morning, gave it fodder, or led it to a water trough, he (Mr. Gumm) remembered that he was doing for his horse exactly what Lannes[5] had done on his last night before Wagram and Lion Heart[6] before he stormed Jerusalem. (Loud cheers, mingled with cries of historical criticism.)

****

It is impossible to follow into much further detail the course of this interesting debate. I am compelled to pass over the speech of the Leader of the Fourwheelers, who regarded motor-cabs as a judgment upon hansoms for having only two wheels, and that of the smart young intriguer of the taximeter group who endeavoured to surround and isolate the hansoms by creating a Fourwheel Coalition. The driver of a motor-cab (yellow with green stripes) observed that if a motor was a system of wheels and circles so was the whole universe a system of wheels and circles. The driver of a fourwheeler from Highgate was understood to reply (but, indeed, his utterance appeared thick and incoherent) that the only creatures that were really made in the shape of wheels and circles were the creatures that you swallowed in a drop of water, if you were fool enough to drink any. Were there time or space I should be only too pleased to give a full account of the great conference on this subject, if only because it was the last conference that was held. Next morning, as everyone knows, the yellow motor-cabs published an ultimatum.

The red motor cabs accepted the situation, and the omnibuses declared a benevolent neutrality. Thus the other side had no choice, and the romantic charge of the Piccadilly hansoms was the result. It was supposed at first that the superior force and impact of a motor could always crush another cab; but in this, as in so many other cases, the experts were found to have made a miscalculation. The cabmen from Hammersmith Broadway, enrolled under the name of The First Chiswick Charioteers, soon adopted a manoeuvre which was entirely successful at the battles of Brompton and Sloane-square, and was only with difficulty evaded even on the tragic field of Clapham Junction. They trained their horses to swerve so as exactly to avoid the rush of the motor, and then, rearing on their hind legs, to kick out the brains of the chauffeur: a trick that seldom failed. But if once I begin telling you of these old, forgotten battles I shall go on for ever. You have something better to do than to listen to an old man like me, telling the true tales that are already so rapidly being forgotten.

Notes
1. *conflict between Hansoms and Taxi-cabs*: 'Taxi cab' is a contraction of 'taximeter cabriolet', a 'taximeter' being the 'clock' that calculates the fare for a specific time/length of journey. Chesterton is referring to the rivalry between the traditional horse-drawn han-

som and four-wheeler cabs and the new motor cabs that became increasingly common in London in and after 1903. He evidently enjoyed the idea of a civic war in London, having already worked it up into his novel *The Napoleon of Notting Hill* (1904).

2. *Dr. Johnson's pamphlet on American taxes*: The pamphlet was called 'Taxation no Tyranny: an Answer to the Resolution and Address of the American Congress', and was written in 1775.

3. *'Handsome Is As Hansom Drives'*: In Oliver Goldsmith's *The Vicar of Wakefield* (1755) Dr Primrose's wife, describing her children, says: 'they are as heaven made them, handsome enough, if they be good enough; for handsome is that handsome does'; but in some form the proverb 'handsome is as handsome does' is much older than this. Chaucer's Wife of Bath says: 'That he is gentil that doth gentil dedis' (*Wife of Bath's Tale*, line 6752).

4. *Science had invented ... a man*: No doubt Chesterton means Charles Babbage's 'difference engine'; see 'The Apology of a Partisan', *DN*, 21 October 1905, Volume 3, p. 220, n. 3 above.

5. *Lannes*: Jean Lannes (1769–1809), was the first Duc de Montebello, first Sovereign Prince de Sievers and Marshal of France; he was one of Napoleon's most distinguished generals.

6. *Lion Heart*: Richard I (1157–1199), King of England from 1189 until his death, was commonly called 'Coeur de lion'; during the Third Crusade (1189–92) he led the crusaders' unsuccessful attempt to recover Jerusalem.

September 19, 1908.

THE BIG THING.

At rare intervals in my life I have been forced reluctantly (and, as it were, crying for mercy) into the thing called controversy. And there are certain general considerations about truth in this medium which I should like to offer. The chief is this: that most arguments are not about what is true, but about what is important, if true. Sanity does not consist in seeing things; madmen see things more clearly than other people. Sanity consists in seeing the big things big and the small things small. A man can have this sense of proportion even if he is wrong; nay, a man can have it even if he is lying. There are such things as credible lies. A man can tell a cock-and-bull story and still remember that a cock is very much smaller than a bull. If I were to say that the Mayor of Battersea had burnt his boots because they did not fit his feet, it would be (I am sorry to say) a lie. But if I were to say the Mayor of Battersea had burnt his feet because they did not fit his boots then it would be more than a lie, it would be an unlikely thing. For feet are more important than boots. Spiritually (though not always materially) feet are bigger than boots. Christ said this, as He said nearly everything: Is not the body more than raiment?[1]

****

Here is one case: A few days ago Mr. Holiday wrote in this paper a very able letter in answer to a lecture by Professor Ridgeway, who had urged that we ought to let the poor perish to procure the survival of the fittest.[2] Mr. Holiday pointed out perfectly and precisely all the fallacies of fact in this argument. He showed that the phrase 'the fittest' has no moral meaning. 'The survival of the fittest' is a silly phrase; because it only means the survival of those that can survive. He also showed (what badly needs showing) that to leave the poor in economic anarchy is to insure the survival of the unfit – if anything can ensure it. Darwinism might be an argument for massacring the poor; it is no argument at all for neglecting them.³ If you exterminate them they will not breed; if you neglect them they will breed more than anybody else.

All these incidental arguments Mr. Holiday urged quite admirably. Yet I could never have urged all those arguments, because I could never have had the patience. The thing is too obscenely absurd. The notion that we must give up justice and mercy and the whole human tradition because of one fancy about our physical origins is to me a notion so startlingly and shockingly silly that I look at its exponent as at a man suddenly drunk in a drawing room.

But if I overcome the obvious virile instinct to burst out laughing or to go away, if I make myself examine the ground of my own contempt, I find it to be this: that the professor in question is cutting his feet to fit his boots. Or, rather, instead of changing his boots, he is trying to change the world he walks on. He has no sense of which is the big thing and which the little. Human society is the big and certain thing; pre-human evolution is the small and fanciful thing. To talk of 'humanity's place in evolution' is to be foolish and topsy-turvy. We do not know that there was any evolution in the sense that we know that there is humanity. Some men hold they are the children of apes; some that they are the children of Adam, or of Wrath,⁴ or of Mumbo-Jumbo.

These are creeds. But all men know that they are men; all men know that they belong to a positive human society, with rules of justice and mercy, and that they cannot even conceive themselves as belonging to anything else. We belong to a club which is so old that nobody knows anything about its origin. We only know that in this club alone we can get our meals; in this club alone we can meet our friends; in this club alone we can sleep or argue or organize or pray. This club holds endless debates about everything – stars, boots, biology, sacraments, Alps, origins. Among the many minor things our human club discusses (for the fun of the thing) is how the club itself arose. The question is all the more interesting because nobody can answer it; the origins are in the fog of the utterly forgotten. Still, it is amusing to guess, and this guess or that guess is fashionable at any given time. At one time the club accepts the view that it was founded by a Mr. Adam. At another time it records a vote that it was probably an affiliated branch of the Monkeys' Club. But these discussions of the forgotten origin are meant to amuse the club. No one ever dreamt of their being allowed to destroy it. Yet they would certainly destroy the Human Club if once they meant that we were to be rude to the members or stingy to the waiters.

****

This is the strongest instance I know of the big thing against the small; that Humanity is the huge house that I live in, while Evolution is a small but interesting animal which has quite recently asked to be domesticated in it. But there are many other instances of the same error, the failure to see which is the small thing and which the big. And the trouble is that modern English people are generally so completely concentrated on the small thing that they are quite startled if they are reminded of the big one. In numerous cases I could mention the thing which everyone called the important thing was exactly the thing that was not important.

Thus, over the Transvaal war, people said that the important point was whether the Transvaal was under a tyranny. But that was not the important point. The important point was whether England was under a tyranny. Was England controlled by a few financiers, or confused by a few newspapers? It may be that President Kruger[5] was a scoundrel; I never knew the old gentleman. But for me the interesting question was not whether one foreign farmer on the under side of the world was a scoundrel, but whether the people who ran my own country were at that moment being scoundrels. Was the newspaper on my breakfast table written by scoundrels? Was my income tax levied by scoundrels? Was the great imperial effort of my countrymen undertaken at the command and in the interest of scoundrels? I investigated the facts, and came with some sadness to the lasting conviction that it was. There may have been a conspiracy against England by the Boers; that we shall never know. But there was a conspiracy against England by the international financiers; that we know, and know for ever.

So it is with the idea about which I have recently engaged in these columns. Some people supposed that the question was whether Russian tortures are worse than English. That is not the point at all. The point for us is whether English tortures are worse than Englishmen know they are. The big sin ought always to be the nearest sin; that is, our own. If we are really fighting that, then we may fight anything else, however small. But if we fight the small thing first – then we have fled from fighting the big one. The man who sees nothing wrong in himself is the one man who is really wrong. He who wanders through the universe trying to find someone worse than himself, will find that he cannot find one.

Notes
1. *Is not the body more than raiment?*: Matthew 6:25: 'Therefore I say unto you, Take no thought for your life, what ye shall eat, or what ye shall drink; nor yet for your body, what ye shall put on. Is not the life more than meat, and the body than raiment?'
2. *A few days ago Mr. Holiday ... survival of the fittest*: Professor William Ridgeway (1858–1926) was a distinguished classical scholar of Irish birth who founded the Cambridge School of Anthropology. He was knighted in 1919. He had addressed the meeting of the British Association on the subject of the application of zoological laws to mankind at its meeting in Dublin on 3 September 1908. Holiday's letter was published on 16 September 1908, p. 4; this in turn was prompted by another letter that was critical of Ridgeway: W. Percy Winter, 'The Goal of Evolution', 9 September 1908, p. 4.
3. *The survival of the fittest ... neglecting them*: Contrary to what is so often supposed, the expression 'the survival of the fittest' was coined not by Charles Darwin but by Herbert Spencer in his *Principles of Biology* (1864) (see 'The Great Pessimist', *DN*, 7 June 1901, Volume 1, p. 98, n. 4 above). Darwin initially gave only qualified approval to the term

(see F. Burkhardt et al., *The Correspondence of Charles Darwin* (Cambridge: Cambridge University Press, 2004), vol. 14, Introduction).

4. *or of Wrath*: See Ephesians 2:3: 'Among whom also we all had our conversation in times past in the lusts of our flesh, fulfilling the desires of the flesh and of the mind; and were by nature the children of wrath, even as others'. What Chesterton perhaps has in mind by 'Some men hold they are the children ... of Wrath' is the Calvinist doctrine of predestination, in support of which this text and the two verses following it are customarily cited.

5. *President Kruger*: Stephanus Johannes Paulus [Paul] Kruger; see 'A Study in Modern Oligarchy', *DN*, 20 February 1903, Volume 2, p. 12, n. 2 above.

September 26, 1908.

DOUBT AND THE DRAMA.

The somewhat gloomy views expressed in this paper on the state of the English drama[1] are a good thing in one way; since if they err they err on the opposite side to the general modern English error. The true evil of Jingoism[2] has yet to be adequately analysed. It is too much assumed that it consists in uttering boasts or telling lies; but in truth it need not be verbally aggressive or even verbally false. A man may mention nothing but facts; and the evil may be that he selects all the facts with the single motive of self-praise. A man has no need to say that Adam was English, or that all Englishmen are ten feet high. He need only fill his book or speech with certain facts: it is true that England rules India; it is true that Sir Isaac Newton was an Englishman; it is true that the English squares did not break at Waterloo; it is true that London is very large; it is true that England had fine sailors; it is true that Milton was a poet of merit; it is true that the Zoological Gardens is an amusing place. But if we wish to see the motive of a man who says all these things and says nothing else we have only to imagine the method adopted in a private case.

Suppose that my name is Gilbert Keith Chesterton; suppose that I live in Battersea; suppose I have certain peculiarities. And suppose I filled my articles with nothing but remarks like this, 'The great Lord Bolingbroke[3] lived at Battersea; there is an intellectual stamp about all the inhabitants of the place. Pope[4] wrote the Essay on Man at Bolingbroke House; the Battersea air is highly favourable to fine poetry. John Burns[5] lives at Battersea; the note of the place is the combination of practicality with poetry. It is remarkable how many great men have been called Gilbert – Sir Humphrey Gilbert,[6] W. S. Gilbert,[7] Gilbert Burnet, Gilbert White.[8] It is also noticeable that some of the noblest human beings have Scotch middle names – as James McNeil Whistler[9] or Miss Lillias Campbell Davidson,[10] who writes stories in 'The Daily News'. I have also observed that many great men were tall, Edward I,[11] Thackeray,[12] Mr. Balfour.[13] I have further noted that many great men are fat, William the Conqueror, Charles Fox, Mr. Corney Grain'.[14] If I went on talking like that I think you would begin to get a trifle sick of it, and would say, 'My dear Sir, your conversation is highly disconnected, and your historical facts seem to be selected in a most singular manner. But it seems to me that you have a motive in mentioning all of them, and the only motive I can attribute to you is a desire to show what a fine fellow you are'. So there is no need for the Jingo to be loud or mendacious; he has only to mention a number of disconnected facts, or rather of facts only connected by the common motive of national self-flattery.

****

Now it is certainly a fortunate thing that in the case of the drama educated people have generally taken up a somewhat humbler and saner attitude. No one says that our plays must be good because we are the country of Shakespeare. Yet that is not really, by any means, more absurd than saying that our Navy must be glorious because we are the country of Nelson or that our Empire must be strong because it is the Empire of our fathers. About the drama at least we have begun to sit on forms instead of resting on laurels. It may be a somewhat decadent sign to begin the reconstruction of the Empire with the famous distribution of bread and circuses,[15] especially as we give the people more circuses than bread. Still the matter is a genuine one, and may occupy us while we are waiting for the revolution and better things.

It is the distinction of the best dramatic critics today that they really are critical; and this is a distinction indeed. Books, pictures, political speeches in our time are not criticised at all; they are damned with faint praise or else praised with faint damns – private ejaculations of the critic's disdain or indifference to his own dreary trade. But dramatic critics like Mr. Baughan and Mr. Max Beerbohm[16] do really set up a standard and urge men in some manner to rise to it, a thing not done at all in the rest of our public life. I may regret perhaps that this fierce fastidiousness should have fastened on the mimic world rather than the real one. I may wish that Mr. Baughan would for one moment take his eagle eye off the actors and fix it on the audience, especially on the audience in the stalls. I wish that instead of merely explaining to actor-managers how men really behave he could apply the process elsewhere and explain to prominent politicians and Privy Councillors how men really behave. I may wish that such vivid and sincere minds were not only occupied with a comedy at St. James's, but also with the farce at St. Stephen's.[17] In short, I may wish that instead of merely urging dramatists to imitate life we could give them some sort of life to imitate. But that is no reason why one should not be on the side of anything that is in any department fighting for manliness and self-criticism.

****

So far as I could judge the discussion, it largely turns upon one confusion. The new critics are always asking for plays with ideas in them. But when one comes to examine the matter one generally finds that by ideas they mean a certain sort of new ideas, called by some fads. By truths they mean truths which have not become current in public talk, which are not domesticated in literature. Many of them ask in a wondering way why melodrama is so popular. I can tell them on the spur of the moment, and without the least hesitation. Melodrama is popular because of its profound truth; because it goes on repeating the things which humanity has really found to be central facts. This endless repetition profoundly annoys the irritable artist inside you and me. But it ought to profoundly please the realist. This sentence contains a split infinitive, of which I am very proud. The melodrama is perpetually telling us that mothers are devoted to their children; because mothers are devoted to their children. Humanity may for a time grow tired of hearing this truth; but humanity will never grow tired of fulfilling it. The melodramas say that men are chiefly sensitive upon honour and their personal claim to courage. Men are. It bores one to hear one's honour reiterated; but it would startle one to hear it denied. Now the modern critics seems to mean (when they talk of ideas) some ideas other than, or even opposite to, these old and certain ideas; but surely they are wrong. In so far as the melodrama is really bad it is not bad because it expressed old ideas; it is bad because it so expresses them as to make them seem like dead ideas. We do not want thought in our plays so much as life – for life makes all old thoughts new thoughts. A poem on Spring in a penny magazine is not dull because it is a poem about the Spring. If it were really about the Spring it would be splendid and startling every year.

Notes

1. *The somewhat gloomy views ... English drama*: This column was prompted by E. A. Baughan's article 'The Drama: Plays for the Public', *DN*, 19 September 1908, p. 2. Baughan maintained that the public was ill-served by theatre managers in Britain, who underestimated the intelligence of theatregoers. Melodramas had enjoyed a revival to appease the 'Philistine' critics of popular journalism. Baughan ventured to predict that a 'dramatist who could write a play of genuine emotional power would not have to meet his public halfway'. There were several letters by readers on the subject: see 'The Public and the Drama', letters to the editor, 23 September 1908, p. 4; and 25 September 1908, p. 3. On Edward Algernon Baughan, see 'Mr. Baughan and the Basket', *DN*, 9 July 1904, Volume 2, p. 256, n. 1 above.
2. *Jingoism*: for the origins of Jingoism, see 'The Indispensable Fire', *DN*, 4 May 1907, Volume 4, p. 216, n. 3 above.
3. *Lord Bolingbroke*: Henry St John, first Viscount Bolingbroke; see 'The Name Under a Picture', *DN*, 29 February 1908, p. 32, n. 11 above.

4. *Pope*: Alexander Pope; see 'The Decline of Satire', *DN*, 14 February 1902, Volume 1, p. 341, n. 4 above.
5. *John Burns*: John Elliot Burns; see 'The Bad Manners of the Well-Bred', 18 July 1902, Volume 1, p. 354, n. 3 above.
6. *Sir Humphrey Gilbert*: Sir Humphrey Gilbert (1537–83), was a soldier and navigator, the half-brother of Sir Walter Raleigh. He is remembered for his campaign of military subjugation in Ireland in 1569 and the establishment of Newfoundland as British territory in 1583. This was after receiving letters patent from the queen to 'discover and possess' remote 'heathen lands'. Earlier, he had made the case for a North-West passage over America to the Pacific.
7. *W. S. Gilbert*: Sir William Schwenk Gilbert; see 'The Cryptogram Again', *DN*, 6 May 1901, Volume 1, p. 85, n. 13 above.
8. *Gilbert White*: Gilbert White (1720–93), was an English naturalist. He devoted himself to the history of natural history around Selborne, Hampshire, where he was a curate. His *The Natural History and Antiquities of Selborne*, written in epistolary style, was published in 1788.
9. *James McNeill Whistler*; James Abbott McNeill Whistler; see 'Two Great Tories', *DN*, 1 August 1903, p. 106, n. 2 above.
10. *Miss Lillias Campbell Davidson*: Lillias Campbell Davidson (*c.* 1865–*c.* 1950), was a writer and novelist. The British Library Catalogue lists twenty-five books published by her, including *Hints to Lady Travellers at Home and Abroad* (1889), *Handbook for Lady Cyclists* (1896), *Catherine of Braganza, Infanta of Portugal and Queen Consort of England* (1908) and *Children of Liberty* (1935).
11. *Edward I*: Edward I (1239–1307), King of England, Lord of Ireland, and Duke of Aquitaine.
12. *Thackeray*, William Makepeace Thackeray; see 'The Soul of Charles II', 16 July 1901, Volume 1, p. 129, n. 6 above.
13. *Mr. Balfour*: Arthur James Balfour; see 'The Bad Manners of the Well-Bred', *DN*, 18 July 1902, Volume 1, p. 354, n. 4 above.
14. *Mr. Corney Grain*: Richard Corney Grain (1844–1895), was an entertainer. A failed barrister, Grain joined the German Reed entertainment group in 1870. A large man, he had exceptionally large and expressive hands (J. Knight, rev. Nilanjana Banerjee, *ODNB*).
15. *bread and circuses*: Panem et circenses – 'bread and circuses', denoting superficial entertainments to keep the population pacified – is an expression that originates with Juvenal, *Satires* 10. Possibly Chesterton is here referring to the popular festivities of Empire Day (24 May), established in 1904 (see 'What is it?', *DN*, 29 May 1909, pp. 322–5 below).
16. *Mr. Max Beerbohm*: Henry Maximilian Beerbohm; see 'The Life of Stevenson', *DN*, 18 October 1901, Volume 1, p. 236, n. 7.
17. *the farce at St. Stephen's*: i.e. at the Palace of Westminster (the 'Houses of Parliament'); until 1834 the Commons met in the medieval St Stephen's Chapel, now incorporated into the Palace as St Stephen's Hall; the clock tower commonly (but erroneously) called 'Big Ben' is St Stephen's Tower.

October 3, 1908.

THE RED TOWN.[1]

When a man says that democracy is false because most people are stupid, there are several courses which the philosopher may pursue. The most obvious is to hit him smartly and with precision on the exact tip of the nose. But if you have scruples (moral or physical) about this course, you may proceed to employ Reason, which in this case has all the savage solidity of a blow with the fist. It is stupid to say that 'most people' are stupid. It is like saying 'most people are tall', when it is obviously that 'tall' can only mean taller than most people. It is absurd to denounce the majority of mankind as below the average of mankind.

Should the man have been hammered on the nose and brained with logic, and should he still remain cold, a third course opens: lead him by the hand (himself half-willing) towards some sunlit and yet secret meadow and ask him who made the names of the common wild flowers. They were ordinary people, so far as anyone knows, who gave to one flower the name of the Star of Bethlehem and to another and much commoner flower the tremendous title of the Eye of Day. If you cling to the snobbish notion that common people are prosaic, ask any common person for the local names of the flowers, names which vary not only from county to county, but even from dale to dale.

****

But, curiously enough, the case is much stronger than this. It will be said that this poetry is peculiar to the country populace, and that the dim democracies of our modern towns at least have lost it. For some extraordinary reason they have not lost it. Ordinary London slang is full of witty things said by nobody in particular. True, the creed of our cruel cities is not so sane and just as the creed of the old countryside; but the people are just as clever in giving names to their sins in the city as giving names to their joys in the wilderness. One could not better sum up

Christianity than by calling a small white insignificant flower 'The Star of Bethlehem'. But then, again, one could not better sum up the philosophy deduced from Darwinism than in the one verbal picture of 'having your monkey up'.[2]

Who first invented these violent felicities of language? Who first spoke of a man being 'off his head'? The obvious comment on a lunatic is that his head is off him; yet the other phrase is far more fantastically exact. There is about every madman a singular sensation that his body has walked off and left the important part of him behind.

But the cases of this popular perfection in phrase are even stronger when they are more vulgar. What concentrated irony and imagination there is, for instance, in the metaphor which describes a man doing a midnight flitting as 'shooting the moon'? It expresses everything about the runaway; his eccentric occupation, his improbable explanations, his furtive air as of a hunter, his constant glances at the blank clock in the sky.

No; the English democracy is weak enough about a number of things; for instance, it is very weak in politics. But there is no doubt that the democracy is wonderfully strong in literature. Very few books that the cultured class has produced of late have been such good literature as the expression 'painting the town red'.

****

Oddly enough, this last Cockney epigram clings to my memory. For as I was walking a little while ago round a corner near Victoria I realised for the first time that a familiar lamppost was painted all over with a bright vermillion, just as if it were trying (in spite of obvious bodily disqualifications) to pretend that it was a pillar-box. I have since heard official explanations of these startling and scarlet objects. But my first fancy was that some dissipated gentleman on his way home at four o'clock in the morning had attempted to paint the town red and only got as far as one lamppost.

I began to make a fairy tale about the man; and, indeed, this phrase contains both a fairy tale and a philosophy; it really states almost the whole truth about those pure outbreaks of pagan enjoyment to which all healthy men have often been tempted. It expresses the desire to have levity on a large scale which is the essence of such a mood. The rowdy young man is not content to paint his tutor's door green: he would like to paint the whole city scarlet. The word which to us best recalls such gigantesque idiocy is the word 'mafficking'. The slaves of that saturnalia were not only painting the town red; they thought that they were painting the map red – that they were painting the world red. But, indeed, this Imperial debauch has in it something worse than the mere larkiness which is my present topic; it has an element of real self-flattery and of sin. The Jingo who wants to admire himself is worse than the blackguard who only wants to enjoy himself. In a very old ninth century illumination which I have seen, depicting the war of the rebel angels in heaven, Satan is represented as distributing to his followers peacock feathers – the symbols of an evil pride. Satan also distributed peacock feathers to his followers on 'mafficking' night.

****

But taking the case of ordinary pagan recklessness and pleasure seeking, it is, as we have said, well expressed in this image. First, because it conveys this notion of filling the world with one private folly; and secondly, because of the profound idea involved in the choice of colour. Red is the most joyful and dreadful thing in the physical universe; it is the fiercest note, it is the highest light, it is the place where the walls of this world of ours wear thinnest and something beyond burns through. It glows in the blood which sustains and in the fire which destroys us, in the roses of our romance and in the awful cup of our religion. It stands for all passionate happiness, as in faith or in first love.

Now the profligate is he who wishes to spread this crimson of conscious joy over everything; to have excitement at every moment; to paint everything red. He bursts a thousand barrels of wine to incarnadine the streets; and sometimes (in his last madness) he will butcher beasts and men to dip his gigantic brushes in their blood. For it marks the sacredness of red in nature, that it is secret even when it is ubiquitous, like blood in the human body, which is omnipresent, yet invisible. As long as blood lives it is hidden; it is only dead blood that we see. But the earlier parts of the rake's progress are very natural and amusing. Painting the town red is a delightful thing until it is done. It would be splendid to see the cross of St. Paul's as red as the cross of St. George, and the gallons of red paint running down the dome or dripping from the Nelson Column. But when it is done, when you have painted the town red, an extraordinary thing happens. You cannot see any red at all.

****

I can see, as in a sort of vision, the successful artist standing in the midst of that frightful city, hung on all sides with the scarlet of his shame. And then, when everything is red, he will long for a red rose in a green hedge and long in vain; he will dream of a red leaf and be unable even to imagine it. He has desecrated the divine colour, and he can no longer see it, though it is all around. I see him, a single black figure against the red-hot hell that he has kindled, where spires and turrets stand up like immobile flames: he is stiffened in a sort of agony of prayer.

Then the mercy of heaven is loosened, and I see one or two flakes of snow very slowly begin to fall.

Notes
1. *THE RED TOWN*: Reprinted in *AD*, pp. 63–8, with minor changes of punctuation.
2. '*having your monkey up*': i.e. being angry.

October 10, 1908.

THE BURDEN OF BEGGARS.

There is one thing worse even than hypocrisy, and that is needless hypocrisy. If a man has robbed Buckingham Palace, if he has vanished through a side door, and fled down a side street, if he has jumped over a wall, hidden in a coal cellar, emerged with a false beard, given a false address, cheated policemen, and escaped from prison, then it does not soothe, but rather exaggerates, our irritation to discover in the end that he has stolen nothing but a trouser button. To conceal is always offensive; but to conceal what one might safely confess is intolerable. Yet this is a very common modern habit; to be a hypocrite not only about discreditable, but about quite pardonable things. A man takes a quite venial sin, and pretends that it is a virtue. A man takes a tiny weakness and pretends that it is a great strength.

There are many cases of this; the most obvious is the case of the thing called pessimism. Pessimism is simply a very defensible mood, fixed and perpetuated until it becomes an indefensible philosophy. There is nothing wicked about being weary; a man who has worked decently has as much right to be weary as to be sleepy. But the pessimist is the man who is too pompous to confess that the weariness is in himself; he will not own to being sleepy. It is not wrong to yawn; but it is wrong to neglect to make a ritual gesture which indicates that the act is a private one. So it is not wrong to yawn over everything, but it is wrong to give a great gape and pretend that one has swallowed the universe. The pessimist could afford to confess his flying sadness, and then simply shrug his shoulders. But he prefers to fling his melancholy upon the enormous shoulders of the everlasting universe. He will call the boisterous birds and beasts and the whole blazing cosmos tiresome rather than say simply that he is tired.

With us every innocent weakness is represented as a strength. In modern England if a statesman is deaf they talk about his firm refusal to listen to flatterers. If he is dumb they talk about his manly reticence and contempt of needless oratory. If he is lame they dwell on the fact that he is never in a hurry.

But there is one form of this making a bad boast out of a harmless fatigue of which I must confess that I have an especial dislike. I mean the form which pretends that promiscuous charity can be despised because it is easy; while subscribing hospitals and such institutions should be essayed because it is difficult and heroic. The exact opposite is really the truth. Scientific charity is perfectly easy; it means the quickest and easiest of all actions – signing a cheque. Promiscuous charity is really difficult; it means the most dark and terrible of all human actions – talking to a man.

****

The obvious and perfectly just objection to beggars is that they are a nuisance. I do not mind a man turning beggars away, because it is impossible to deal with them. I do not in comparison mind his bellowing oaths at them or setting his dog on to them, because it is impossible to deal with them. But I do very much object to his pretending that he rejects them because it is so easy to deal with them. Personally, I have a hearty dislike for hard work of every description; and I know no harder work than really to talk to all the poor men you meet. I do not despise a man because he breaks down under the daily torture of giving personal help to the poor. But I do object to him if, after having broken down under it as a torture, he pretends that he despises it as a frivolity. Obviously it is much easier to be benevolent by scientific theory than to be benevolent by personal practice; for the very excellent reason that there are about four million poor people, whereas there are (thank God) only about four hundred philanthropic theories.

For my part, I will freely admit (and I know very well that in the present intellectual fashions I merely fling down a challenge), for my part, I believe in giving money to beggars in the street as they stand. I know all the accepted objections to the act. I know that many old ladies have said that they gave a poor man money, and almost immediately afterwards 'saw him go into a public-house'. Given our existing conditions, this is exactly like saying: 'I lent two hundred pounds to Captain Crackenthorpe from South Africa; I followed him across London in a cab and distinctly saw him go into an hotel'.

I know the more general objection; that one can 'never know' whether the man is honest. Alas! That is bitterly true and can never be answered. I can never know whether any man is honest. I can never know whether I am honest; in my more solemn moments I incline to the belief that I am not. But this I will say with no special hesitation. I am more certain of the honesty of a certain type of beggar than I am of the honesty of a certain type of rich man, who fills the committees of most philanthropic institutions. I know more about one beggar whom I have seen than about ten guinea-pig peers whom I have never seen and never want to see. The beggar may deceive me, but he has to do it with a human eye, which may fail him, not with a prospectus, which will mechanically do his will. It is often hard to keep a stiff face; but institutions keep stiff of themselves. Still, I return to the original compromise; by all means let it be at the tenth beggar that you lose your temper. But do not let it be at the tenth beggar that you find your political economy.

October 16, 1908.

A BOOK OF THE DAY.

The Mystery of the Middle Ages.

'Chaucer and His England'. By G. G. Coulton, M.A. Methuen and Co. 10s.6d. net. [1908].

Much of Mr. G. G. Coulton's[1] learned and fascinating book, called 'Chaucer and His England', appears to be written with a notion of taking the gilt off the gingerbread in our estimate of the Middle Ages. Now I have not the smallest objection to people taking the gilt off gingerbread, for the simple reason that I like gingerbread much better than gilt. And I have feasted on the rich, solid, and sustaining gingerbread of mediaeval virtue and commonsense quite enough to be very glad to see it despoiled of mere tinsel decoration. The mediaeval civilization, at its best, was not an earthly paradise; and many of its best spirits spoke of it rather as a purgatory. The men of the fourteenth century had their own special sins and sorrows as we have ours. Individual cruelties and revenges were easier than with us; though this was due not so much to bad laws as to bad roads. Philosophy was too arid, one might say too rationalistic. A pardonable, but excessive, habit of treating all physical knowledge as a mere joke or hobby left nations open to real scourges of physical evil. In morals these men thought too much of rules and too little of exceptions. In art they perfected colouring, while they grossly neglected drawing.

The Relative Virtues.

But one condition is of adamantine necessity. If a man is comparing that age with this age, he ought to know this age; it is not enough that he is vastly learned about that one. Every criticism of the fourteenth century ought to be also a criticism of the twentieth. Now it is exactly here that the whole difference between the two comes in. The fourteenth century had huge sins: it had not the one peculiar sin of the twentieth; the sin of taking oneself as the standard of everything. Chaucer never said that he was the heir of all the ages,[2] or that Nimrod[3] and Nero,[4] Abraham and Brutus,[5] were good or bad according as they were like Geoffrey Chaucer. He was perfectly willing to admit that his century might be degenerate or have wandered God knows where. If he criticized Chaucerian London he compared it with the New Jerusalem;[6] we only compare Chaucerian London with our London.

Now this vice of taking our own goodness and happiness for granted, which is the chief fault of modernity, is almost the only fault of Mr. Coulton. I do not blame him for seeing the gaps in Chaucer's age, but I do blame him for not seeing the gaps in his own. At the risk of dwelling too long on one point, I will give one strong example of this vision and this blindness. In warning the reader (justly enough) against taking the old chivalry entirely at its own valuation, he says: 'And without treason to Chaucer or his age we may frankly admit that his perfect knight is only younger brother to Colonel Newcome, and that Froissart[7] himself can show us no figure so deeply chivalrous as the Lawrences[8] or the Havelocks[9] of our later Indian wars'.

Now in this paragraph Mr. Coulton shows that he is himself as much bamboozled and blinded by his own society and century as if he had swallowed all the tallest talk in Froissart. Buried in that paragraph is the unconscious confession of the two great virtues in which the fourteenth century towers above our own. Take first the name of Colonel Newcome. It is perfectly true that Newcome was as gentle and magnanimous as Chaucer's knight, though not more so. But that is not the first thing that springs to my mind if I connect the Colonel with the Canterbury Pilgrimage. The first and most arresting fact is simply this – that Colonel Newcome would never have gone on the Canterbury Pilgrimage at all. He would have refused to dine with a cook, a miller, a ploughman, and a vulgar woman in a common public-house. He would have been disgusted, as he was with Fielding, for taking him into 'the servants' hall'.[10] At the best he would have been proud and embarrassed, as he was when Clive introduced him to the son of a butler.[11] Thus, when Mr. Coulton wrote down the words 'Colonel Newcome', he held unconsciously the clue to a real fact and mystery of the Middle Ages; but he let it slip.

Paternity v. Equality.

The real difference between the old Knight and the modern Colonel is simply that the modern Colonel is the more exclusive aristocrat of the two; not, perhaps, in theory, but unquestionably in feeling and practice. In short, one of the sins of our time is that the classes have been sundered by something worse than hatred – shyness, which is a shameful fear. Chaucer's Knight talks and laughs with every class in England, not only without embarrassment, but without condescension; as if it were quite natural they should mix. A modern gentleman would feel as a modern gentleman feels alone with a housemaid. Somehow, God knows how, for some cause, God knows what, these people had Fraternity, even when they had not Equality.

And, again, Havelock and Lawrence should have given the author a clue to the real comparison. Doubtless they were very fine men; but let it be remembered that (in comparison to Froissart) we only know the fine side of them. We only know of them through patriotic newspapers or family biographies; which the modern fashion forbids to report hesitations, infidelities, and skeletons in the cupboard. In a modern book on Lawrence we have only the matured decision and the official justification. Now Froissart will show you a king as a complete man, from his first rage to his last repentance. If a modern Edward ultimately decided to spare the burghers of Calais[12] we should never hear in the Court histories even the whisper of his first fury; Froissart gives you the old men standing shivering in their shirts. Rightly or wrongly, those who suppressed the Indian Mutiny are accused of an awful inhumanity; perhaps it was palliated by the Sepoy cruelties;[13] but it is not faced in the official books. But the old chronicler faces every cruelty of the Black Prince,[14] as he faces every outburst of penitence or charity. In short, the other great merit of the Middle Ages, as compared with to-day, is that its chroniclers had a habit of telling the truth; and that (like all really truthful men) they thought telling 'the whole truth' more important even than telling 'nothing but the truth'.

It is not so unfair as it looks to make a criticism of this book turn on the pivot of this paragraph: first, because nearly all Mr. Coulton's paragraphs are interesting enough to have essays written on them; and, second, because this one really sums up the spirit of the book. The summary of the whole really is that Mr. Coulton knows twenty times more than I do about the age of Chaucer, but that, unfortunately, Mr. Coulton knows not half as much as I do about the age of Mr. Coulton. Hence, while his positive judgment may be infallible, his comparative is often false. Occasionally, however, Mr. Coulton is wrong, not through misunderstanding mediaevalism or modernism, but through misunderstanding everlasting human nature. The fourteenth century was an age of revolutions, and no one can understand revolutions who writes this, 'The tramp on the high road is not appreciably unhappier for knowing that his nothingness is contrasted nowadays with Mr. Carnegie's millions[15] instead of de la Pole's thousands'.[16] I repudiate and deny this implication with all the most horrible energies of the human soul. What makes revolt is not pain, but wrong. If we are all eating ships' biscuits on a raft it may be the will of God; but if one of us is putting away pâtéde-foie-gras and champagne, I come to the conclusion (as I do with the modern world) that the devil is in it somewhere.

Notes

1. *Mr. G. G. Coulton*: George Gordon Coulton (1858–1947), was a medieval historian and controversialist. Educated at the University of Cambridge, where he took an aegrotat degree, religious doubts led him to abandon his intention of a career in the Church. After an unhappy spell as a schoolmaster he turned to research into medieval history, while supporting himself through the coaching establishment he set up with a friend in Eastbourne. A translation of Salimbene's *Cronica* in 1907 and the book on Chaucer here under review laid the foundation of his reputation as a medievalist. Like Chesterton, he set much store by the use of original documents, though to strengthen rather than undermine the professional historian (See 'History versus the Historians', *DN*, 25 July 1908, pp. 112–17 above). He was appointed to a lectureship at Cambridge in 1911, remaining at the University until his retirement in 1934. A stickler for 'truth' in history and also a defender of modern culture, he courted controversy, targeting Roman Catholic historians such as Cardinal Gasquet in particular (H. Summerson, *ODNB*). He clashed with Chesterton following Chesterton's radio talk in 1935, 'The Liberty that Matters'. The talk was published in the *Listener*, 19 June 1935, pp. 1029–30, 1063. The correspondence between Chesterton, Coulton and others ran until December 1935.
2. *the heir of all ages*: see Tennyson, 'Locksley Hall' (1835):

    Mated with a squalid savage – what to me were sun or clime?
    I the heir of all the ages, in the foremost files of time –

3. *Nimrod*: The son of Cush, grandson of Ham, and great-grandson of Noah; 'a mighty one in the earth' and 'a mighty hunter before the Lord', 'the beginning of his kingdom was Babel, and Erech, and Accad, and Calneh, in the land of Shinar'. See Genesis 10:8–10.
4. *Nero*: Nero (Claudius Caesar Augustus Germanicus); see 'A Messenger of Tolstoy', *DN*, 9 September 1901, Volume 1, p. 184, n. 3 above.
5. *Brutus*: Marcus Junius Brutus; see 'The Soul of Charles II', *DN*, 16 July 1901, Volume 1, p. 129, n. 3 above.
6. *New Jerusalem*: One suspects that Chesterton has borrowed this term from Walter Thornbury's *Old and New London* (1878), vol. 1, ch. 51, 'Chaucer's London': 'You will find him [Chaucer's Clerk], be sure, on his knees on the cold floor, before some humble City altar, heedless of all but prayer, or at the lazar-house on his knees, beside some poor leper, and pointing through the shadow of death to the shining gables of the New Jerusalem'.
7. *Froissart*: Jean Froissart (*c.* 1337–*c.* 1405), was a medieval French chronicler; his *Chroniques* (first printed in four volumes in 1498) is a major primary source of our knowledge of the history of England and France between 1322 and 1400.
8. *Lawrences*: Sir George St Patrick Lawrence (1804–84), Twas an army officer who served with much courage in the First Anglo–Afghan war and helped to secure the arsenal at Ajmer during the Indian Mutiny; his brother, Sir Henry Montgomery Lawrence (1806–57), was an army officer who also served in Afghanistan and the two Anglo–Sikh wars, and was killed in the Indian Mutiny while attempting to secure Lucknow against the rebels.

9. *Havelocks*: Like his brother, Sir Henry Havelock (see 'Some Reflections on the Strong Man', 1 August 1902, Volume 1, p. 362, n. 5 above), William Havelock (1793–1848), was an army officer. He served in the second Anglo–Sikh War of 1848–9, during which he fell mortally wounded after a desperate charge against the Sikhs.
10. *He would have been disgusted ... 'the servant's hall'*: See Thackeray, *The Newcomes*, ch. 4.
11. *At the best ... son of a butler*: *The Newcomes*, ch. 12.
12. *If a modern Edward ... Calais*: After his victory at the Battle of Crécy, Edward III of England, having laid siege to Calais, offered to spare the city if six of its leading citizens would surrender themselves to him. When the six duly did so, after an eleven-month seige, the king spared their lives at the intercession of the Queen, Philippa of Hainault. Rodin's famous sculpture at Calais commemorates the event; the story is in book one of Froissarts *Chroniques*.
13. *the Indian Mutiny ... Sepoy cruelties*: for the origins of the Indian Mutiny, see 'Wisdom and Wax Fruit', *DN*, 4 July 1903, Volume 2, p. 92, n. 8 above. Among the Sepoy cruelties were those committed in the notorious siege of Cawnpore in June/July 1857; the British retaliated when they regained control of Delhi in September and also following the signing of the peace treaty in July 1858.
14. *Black Prince*: see 'Notions and the Nursery', *DN*, 18 July 1908, p. 111, n. 3 above.
15. *Mr. Carnegie's millions*: Andrew Carnegie (1835–1919), was a steel magnate and philanthropist. Born in Scotland, his family emigrated to the United States in the depression in the linen trade in 1848. Carnegie's business interests in steel production amassed him one of the largest fortunes in the world: $447 million in 1900 on selling his share in the recently formed United States Steel Corporation (G. Tweedale, *ODNB*).
16. *de la Pole's thousands'*: Sir William de la Pole (d. 1366), was a financier and merchant. De la Pole and his brother Richard (died 1345) were wealthy wool merchants of Hull who did much to finance the wars of Edward III.

October 17, 1908.

RIOT AND DECAY.

Recently there has been a considerable growth of that game which has been picturesquely defined as 'making a scene'. Several persons, including Mr. Frank Smith,[1] Mr. Grayson,[2] and a few ladies,[3] have made scenes in the very centre of our political life. My own instinctive sympathies are entirely with the people who make a scene. I cannot imagine any trade more supreme and heroic than the trade of a professional scene painter. To make a scene is to be a dramatist; even if it is only Scene I. And in the present pungent dilemma of wealth and poverty no one can reasonably expect to create anything except Scene I. After all, the English people is the hero of the play; and only when he enters will there be the actual explosion of applause. Nevertheless, for a specific reason, I sympathise with the people like Mr. Grayson. I cheerfully concede that Mr. Grayson is, if possible, even more unlike an ordinary English labourer than are most of the Labour members. I admit that in his protest, in which the majority of the Labour members did not follow him, the majority of the labouring classes would probably not have followed him either. Nevertheless, there is an aspect of this matter which appears to be entirely neglected.

****

It is always assumed that making a scene in a club will spoil the club. But as a matter of fact it all depends upon what condition the club happens to have reached. If the club is at its best, a scene may spoil it; but if it is at its lowest and weakest, a scene may revive it and (what is not without its importance) advertise it. Granted that we all love our club, it still depends upon our view of its necessities whether we help it with a benediction or with a bomb. All the objection to mere rows is based ultimately upon this idea: that constitutions only break up when someone breaks them up. But this is unphilosophical; there is such a thing as corruption, the law of death in our members.[4] The very smallest things which hint of corruption, which is death from within, are immeasurably worse than even the largest things which hint of danger, which is death from without.

For instance, I should be annoyed if I were pursued by a large tiger all the way down Fleet-street. But I should be infinitely more horrified if I were pursued by one small churchyard worm all the way down Fleet-street. The tiger at the worst would come to tell me that I should shortly die. The worm could only come to tell me that I was already dead. And in practice the only nations that have really died completely are those that have died quietly. Everyone knows when Athens was conquered, and everyone knows the old tag that she conquered her conqueror.[5] Everyone knows when Florence died, and everyone knows that she is not dead. But we cannot put any finger upon the exact moment when Venice became unimportant; we only know that she is unimportant. We have no historical certainty that Sparta ever died. We only have the moral certainty that she is dead.[6]

****

The truth is that every self-respecting institution anticipates its own destruction, but not its own decline. If you worship with sacred sincerity at an altar you may expect that altar to be destroyed; you may expect it to be desecrated; but you cannot expect it to be ignored. Take one of those pleasant, solemn, florid fellows who, in the end of the Middle Ages, took chivalry and heraldry quite seriously; Froissart,[7] for instance. Froissart could easily have believed that the peasants would rise and destroy all knighthood and all pictured pedigree; would split all the shields, rip up all the pennons, and drag all the crests and feathers in the mire. This really seemed likely in his time;[8] and I wish to heaven it had happened. But the one thing Froissart never could have understood or believed was this, that heraldry should remain, but should remain unimportant. He could have imagined plebeians tearing in pieces the sacred person of a herald; but he could not have conceived the idea of a patrician being slightly ashamed of being a herald at all. Yet certainly every modern gentleman of that rank would shake either with shame or laughter upon being reminded that he was known in public as a Red Dragon or a Portcullis, or even a Blue Mantle. Froissart, in short, could have imagined that heraldry might be destroyed; but it has not been destroyed. But he could never have imagined what has really happened. He never could have fancied that heraldry would be at once preserved and forgotten.

We, the modern English, have the same beautiful blindness. We dream of our institutions being ruined by popular hatred; but we never dream of what is the real possibility, that our institutions may be preserved and protected by popular contempt. Six hundred years after Froissart's time there is still a Heralds' College;

only it is entirely unimportant. Six hundred years from our time there may still be a House of Commons; only it may be even more unimportant than it is now. Now that all chivalry is dead there is still a man called Garter King-at-Arms. So in that time, when all representative government is dead, there may still be a man called the Prime Minister. Our modern Parliamentary system shows just now the possibilities of becoming a pure oligarchical ritual. Parliamentary procedure is developing all those characteristics of solemn and baffling complexity which characterised the ranks and blazonings of Froissart. That which had once been the art of chivalry was corrupted into the science of heraldry. So in our time the regulations which were once made to ensure the convenience of speakers are now employed to ensure the impossibility of speech. They were once the rules of debate. Now they are simply rules against debate. If this is what is rudely symbolised in the resistance of Mr. Grayson and Mr. Smith, I very strongly sympathise with them. Our modern English danger does not lie in the possibility of Parliament being insulted; it lies in the probability of Parliament being, within a very short time, despised. The danger is not that the House of Commons will suddenly cease by being wrecked. The danger is that the House of Commons will go calmly on until it is not even worth wrecking. The vision in front of us is not that of a Parliament surrounded by monstrous mobs with bludgeons and torches. The far more plausible vision is that of a Senate of solemn and powerless old gentlemen still debating at enormous length, and with exquisite tact and gravity, the things over which they have no control, as they did under the last despots of Rome.

Notes
1. *Mr. Frank Smith*: Francis [Frank] Samuel Smith (1854–1940), was an English Salvationist. He joined the Salvation Army in the late 1870s and quickly rose to the rank of Commissioner. With General William Booth, he promoted the Salvation Army's cause in America in 1884; he also made fact-finding trips to Holland, Denmark and Sweden and contributed many ideas to Booth's *In Darkest England and the Way Out* (1890). Smith was elected to the London County Council for a second time in 1907, his aim being to organize the Labour members into a separate grouping from the Progressives (M. Brodie, *ODNB*). On 14 October 1908, he disrupted a Council meeting by persisting in bringing forward a resolution that had been ruled out of order by the Chairman. First the galleries were cleared of supporters and then Smith himself was removed from the chamber. The meeting for the day had to be adjourned with no business transacted: *The Times*, 15 October 1908, p. 11.
2. *Mr. Grayson*: (Albert) Victor Grayson (b. 1881), was an English socialist politician. He was elected to Parliament as an Independent Labour Party candidate in a by-election in Colne Valley, near his native Manchester, in 1907, though without Labour Party support. Mistrusted by the Parliamentary Labour Party for his revivalist style, he flouted parliamentary procedure twice in October 1908 in calling for a debate on unemployment. Before being removed from the Chamber on 15 October, he denounced Labour MPs as traitors to their class. He was defeated at the general election of January 1910. His

controversial career ended with his unexplained disappearance in 1920, shortly after he had accused Lloyd George of selling political honours through an agent called Maundy Gregory. He was last seen entering Gregory's house on 28 September 1920 (D. Howell, *ODNB*). See D. Clark, *Victor Grayson: Labour's Lost Leader* (London: Quartet Books, 1985); and R. Groves, *The Strange Case of Victor Grayson* (London: Pluto Press, 1975).

3. *a few ladies*: A reference to the Women's Social and Political Union, which organised a 'rush' on the House of Commons on 13 October 1908. A large number of arrests were made and three leaders of the Union – Emmeline Pankhurst, Christabel Pankhurst and Flora Drummond – were arrested on warrants issued by magistrates for conduct liable to cause a breach of the peace. Emmeline Pankhurst was sentenced to three months in prison. One suffragette managed to get into the Commons chamber and was making her way towards the Speaker's Chair before being ejected: *The Times*, 14 October 1908, p. 9c.

4. *the law of death in our members*: See Romans 7:5: 'For when we were in the flesh, the motions of sins, which were by *the Law*, did work in *our members* to bring forth fruit unto *death*'; and v. 23: 'But I see another law in my members, warring against the law of my mind, and bringing me into captivity to the law of sin which is in my members'.

5. *the old tag ... conquered her conqueror*: The 'old tag' is at Horace, *Epistulae* 2:1:156–7: 'Graecia capta ferum victorem cepit et artis intulit agresti Latio' ('Conquered Greece has captured her fierce victor and brought her arts into rustic Latium').

6. *the only nations that have really died completely ... she is dead*: The point in this paragraph about conquered nations conquering their conquerors in turn was made in 'Mr. Shaw's Escape', *DN*, 20 July 1907, Volume 4, pp. 262–5 above.

7. *Froissart*: Jean Froissart; see 'The Mystery of the Middle Ages', *DN*, 16 October 1908, p. 189, n. 7 above.

8. *in his time*: i.e. at the time of the 'Peasants' Revolt' of 1381, recorded in book 2 of Froissart's *Chroniques*.

October 24, 1908.

WHAT YOU PROPOSE.

It would be very thoughtful and suggestive (only unfortunately quite untenable), to maintain that the self-satisfaction of the English is well represented by the fact that they are the one nation which prints the first personal pronoun with a big 'I'. The word egoism comes from the Latin; nevertheless, no Latin ever spelt 'ego' with a large 'E'. A Frenchman may say, with the most frightful violence, 'Monsieur, je demands la parole', but he does not say it with a big 'J'. As a simple school in modesty and self-criticism, I should suggest that we should sometimes put the small letter for ourselves and the large letter for our neighbour. By all means let us say, 'As an Englishman I despise you and your Latin civilization'. But let us sometimes try the experiment of seeing how it looks when you write it: 'As an Englishman i despise You and Your Latin civilization'. If you look steadily at that small 'i' you will find that it gives you a cold and curious shock, which is the beginning of the salvation of England.

However this may be, I have become heartily sick of the word 'I' in these articles. You will reply (with your old rapidity in repartee) that you were sick of it a long time before I was. I agree with you. There was once a jolly lady who hated me as she hated poison or democracy, and who carefully counted the number of times that the word 'I' occurred in one of my articles in this column. I have forgotten the circumstances; but I think the number was either 23 or 73. So I propose to make a reform in this matter. If you object to my egotism, as you very reasonably may, I will no longer say of one my convictions that I hold it. I will say that You hold it. I will not say of an adventure that I actually went through it. I will say that you [*sic*] actually went through it. My articles shall not be any longer a mere autobiography; they shall be the official biography of yourself. Doubtless, indeed, the strange wild aristocracy of the modern world has very largely arisen from the habit of merely saying about a thing 'I think so'. As things go in modern thought, it is a very bold and solid thing even to be able to say 'This is true; I believe it'. But how much more brazenly and substantially brave it would be to be able to say of something, 'This is true; and You believe it'.

****

This is, of course, one of the old arguments for democracy, that there are some things that I can affirm about you as much as about myself, because they are really common to mankind. Therefore, for the remainder of this article I am not going to tell you what I think but what you think. Suppose we are confronted with any great modern principle or proposal, with any political proposal, such as that, for instance, criminals should be kept in prison until they are medically cured of their crimes. Now upon this question you feel strongly. You feel (and very rightly) that one particular principle is wholly neglected here. And when you consider the conditions of modern politics you make a plain offer.

This matter of the medical treatment of crime is one which any sensible citizen can quite easily test for himself. The theory of the new criminologist is this: that sin is merely a malady which can be cured by certain processes and conditions. If a man persistently throws bombs into the window, or throws children out of the window, there is some specific course of treatment which may make him moderate his pleasures in this respect. It is scientifically possible (they say) to feed him, drug him, starve him, cool him, boil him, amuse him, intoxicate him, or torture him out of the habit of taking life. Very well. It is an important and intelligible opinion, and is held by many good and able men, such as Mr. J. M. Robertson.[1] But it has one initial query or complaint about it; and that is this, that by the nature of the case this treatment can only be meted out in 99 cases out of 100, to the most impotent stratum of society, to the class called the criminal class. And the criminal class really means those who can safely be treated as criminals, even if they happen to be innocent. Sometimes as a humanitarian taunt, sometimes God help us, as a scientific fancy, it has been suggested that criminals should be vivisected for the sake of experiment. But the debate is really idle. Criminals are vivisected for the sake of experiment. All these police proposals have in them the essential principle of vivisection; that mistakes will not so much matter if they are written only in the blood and fibres of some baser or more foolish creature. The idea of self-government is almost dead among us. I mean the idea that self-government is the same as self-control. No modern lawgiver making a law ever thinks even for one wild moment that he is making a law against himself. A legislator no more dreams that he might some day be a thief than a vivisectionist dreams he might some day be a rabbit.

We are, therefore, confronted with this dilemma. Here is a very interesting scientific theory, the theory that sin can be cured by peculiar conditions. Here is the disadvantage; the somewhat disgusting fact that the theory is being, or may be, tried by brute force on the most helpless part of humanity merely because it is helpless. Vaccination was tried at least upon some considerable number of individuals before it was forced on the people. If a man of science really wishes to prove that a certain chemical compound is not a poison, then the general sense of honour (not to mention the general sense of humour) suggests that he should try it first on himself. If this new medicine of the scientific treatment of sin is really valid, let us not try it on our slaves, like a dirty Oriental despot. Let us try it on ourselves, like a decent European doctor. Let us seriously ask ourselves whether we should ever admit this scientific principle in the case of our own temptations or our own immoralities.

****

Now it is just here that You come in, with Your splendid solution. You, the solid and central citizen, you the pillar that upholds the State, you the sane ordinary man, you know that the most cruel blunders, the most pitiless collapses of life, generally come from things beyond the reach of the law. A wife deliberately clattering the spoons may easily be worse than a burglar stealing them. A dog who bites will be far less a problem than an aunt who backbites. Obviously, therefore, the solution for the present is simple. Before this medicinal cure of crime is admitted into public life let it be proved to be successful in private life. Private wrongs are smaller in extent, often worse in character; let us begin with them. Let us offer to the universe the awful spectacle of one entirely purified uncle. Let us prove that we have taught someone, if only one errant grandmother. Apply science to sin in your own actual lives. Create the conditions (the perfect scientific prison conditions) which will finally cure the snobbishness of Cousin George. Tell me that you have found a Treatment that will stop the scandal-mongering of Aunt Eliza. Try it first (like Sapolio)[2] in the family. Then when it has succeeded with yourselves I will begin to believe that it deserves the noble name of science; till then I shall continue to call it the oppression of the poor.

Notes
1. *Mr. J. M. Robertson*: John Mackinnon Robertson; see 'Iconoclast', *DN*, 1 August 1906, Volume 4, p. 24, n. 3 above.
2. *Sapolio*: 'Sapolio' was a kind of soap popular in England and America before World War II. The product apparently succeeded because of the vigour and ingenuity of the American advertising executive Artemas Ward (1848–1925). 'Try it First' was one of the slogans associated with it.

October 31, 1908.

THE GIANT.[1]

I sometimes fancy that every great city must have been built by night. At least, it is only at night that every part of a great city is great. All architecture is great architecture after sunset; perhaps architecture is really a nocturnal art, like the art of fireworks. At least, I think many people of those nobler trades that work by night (journalists, policemen, burglars, coffee stall keepers, and such mistaken enthusiasts as refuse to go home till morning)[2] must often have stood admiring some black bulk of building with a crown of battlements or a crest of spires and then burst into tears at daybreak to discover that it was only a haberdasher's shop with huge gold letters across the face of it.

****

I had a sensation of this sort the other day as I happened to be wandering in the Temple Gardens towards the end of twilight. I sat down on a bench with my back to the river, happening to choose such a place that a huge angle and façade of building jutting out from the Strand sat above me like an incubus. I dare say that if I took the same seat to-morrow by daylight I should find the impression entirely false. In sunlight the thing might seem almost distant; but in that half darkness it seemed as if the walls were almost falling upon me. Never before have I had so strongly the sense which makes people pessimists in politics, the sense of the hopeless height of the high places of the earth.[3] That pile of wealth and power, whatever was its name, went up above and beyond me like a cliff that no living thing could climb. I had an irrational sense that this thing had to be fought, that I had to fight it; and that I could offer nothing to the occasion but an indolent journalist with a walking-stick.

Almost as I had the thought, two windows were lit in that blind, black face. It was as if two eyes had opened in the huge face of a sleeping giant; the eyes were too close together, and gave it the suggestion of a bestial sneer. And either by the accident of this light or of some other, I could now read the big letters which spaced themselves across the front; it was the Babylon Hotel. It was the perfect symbol of everything that I should like to pull down with my hands if I could. Reared by a detected robber, it is framed to be the fashionable and luxurious home of undetected robbers.[4] In the house of man are many mansions;[5] but there is a class of men who feel normal nowhere except in the Babylon Hotel or in Dartmoor Gaol. That big black face, which was staring at me with its flaming eyes too close together, that was indeed the giant of all epic and fairy tales. But, alas! I was not the giant killer; the hour had come, but not the man. I sat down on the seat again (I had had one wild impulse to climb up the front of the hotel and fall in at one of the windows), and I tried to think, as all decent people are thinking, what one can really do. And all the time that oppressive wall went up in front of me, and took hold upon the heavens like a house of the gods.

****

It is remarkable that in so many great wars it has been the defeated who have won. The people who were left worst at the end of the war were generally the people who were left best at the end of the whole business. For instance, the Crusades ended in the defeat of the Christians. But they did not end in the decline of the Christians; they ended in the decline of the Saracens. That huge prophetic wave of Moslem power which had hung in the very heavens above the towns of Christendom, that wave was broken, and never came on again. The Crusaders had saved Paris in the act of losing Jerusalem. The same applies to that epic of Republican war in the eighteenth century to which we Liberals owe our political creed. The French Revolution ended in defeat: the kings came back across a carpet of dead at Waterloo. The Revolution had lost its last battle; but it had gained its first object. It had cut a chasm. The world has never been the same since. No one after that has ever been able to treat the poor merely as a pavement.

These jewels of God, the poor, are still treated as mere stones of the street; but as stones that may sometimes fly. If it please God, you and I may see some of the stones flying again before we see death. But here I only remark the interesting fact that the conquered almost always conquer.[6] Sparta killed Athens with a final blow, and she was born again. Sparta went away victorious, and died slowly of her own wounds. The Boers lost the South African War and gained South Africa.

And this is really all that we can do when we fight something really stronger than ourselves; we can deal it its death-wound one moment; it deals us death in the end. It is something if we can shock and jar the unthinking impetus and enormous innocence of evil; just as a pebble on a railway line can stagger the Scotch

Express. It is enough for the great martyrs and criminals of the French Revolution, that they have surprised for all time the secret weakness of the strong. They have awakened and set leaping and quivering in his crypt for ever the coward in the hearts of kings.

****

When Jack the Giant Killer really first saw the giant his experience was not such as has been generally supposed.[7] If you care to hear it I will tell you the real story of Jack the Giant Killer. To begin with, the most awful thing which Jack first felt about the giant was that he was not a giant. He came striding across an interminable wooded plain, and against the remote horizon the giant was quite a small figure, like a figure in a picture – he seemed merely a man walking across the grass. Then Jack was shocked by remembering that the grass which the man was treading down was one of the tallest forests upon that plain. The man came nearer and nearer, growing bigger and bigger, and at the instant when he passed the possible stature of humanity Jack almost screamed. The rest was an intolerable apocalypse.

The giant had the one frightful quality of a miracle; the more he became incredible the more he became solid. The less one could believe in him the more plainly one could see him. It was unbearable that so much of the sky should be occupied by one human face. His eyes, which had stood out like bow windows, became bigger yet, and there was no metaphor that could contain their bigness; yet still they were human eyes. Jack's intellect was utterly gone under that huge hypnotism of the face that filled the sky; his last hope was submerged, his five wits all still with terror.

But there stood up in him still a kind of cold chivalry, a dignity of dead honour that would not forget the small and futile sword in his hand. He rushed at one of the colossal feet of this human tower, and when he came quite close to it the ankle-bone arched over him like a cave. Then he planted the point of his sword against the foot and leant on it with all his weight, till it went up to the hilt and broke the hilt, and then snapped just under it. And it was plain that the giant felt a sort of prick, for he snatched up his great foot into his great hand for an instant; and then, putting it down again, he bent over and stared at the ground until he had seen his enemy.

Then he picked up Jack between a big finger and thumb and threw him away; and as Jack went through the air he felt as if he were flying from system to system through the universe of stars. But, as the giant had thrown him away carelessly, he did not strike a stone, but struck soft mire by the side of a distant river. There he lay insensible for several hours; but when he awoke again his horrible conqueror was still in sight. He was striding away across the void and wooded plain towards where it ended in the sea; and by this time he was only much higher than any of the hills. He grew less and less indeed; but only as a really high mountain grows at last less and less when we leave it in a railway train. Half an hour afterwards he was a bright blue colour, as are the distant hills; but his outline was still human and still gigantic. Then the big blue figure seemed to come to the brink of the big blue sea, and even as it did so it altered its attitude. Jack, stunned and bleeding, lifted himself laboriously upon one elbow to stare. The giant once more caught hold of his ankle, wavered twice as in a wind, and then went over into the great sea which washes the whole world, and which, alone of all things God has made, was big enough to drown him.

Notes

1. *The Giant*: Reprinted in *TT* (2), pp. 123–9; and *DayNight*, pp. 45–8 (from the fourth paragraph, 'When Jack the Giant Killer really ...').
2. *those mistaken enthusiasts ... morning*: The allusion is to a popular song by Oliver Ditson (1811–88) the chorus of which is:

   For we won't go home till morning,
   We won't go home till morning,
   We won't go home till morning,
   Till daylight does appear.

3. *high places of the earth*: See Micah 1:3: 'For, behold, the Lord cometh forth out of His place, and will come down, and tread upon the high places of the earth'.
4. *Reared by a detected robber ... undetected robbers*: One assumes that Chesterton is referring to the Savoy Hotel on the Strand; 'Babylon Hotel' is a resonance of Arnold Bennett's novel *The Grand Babylon Hotel* (1902), in which the hotel is a thinly-disguised version of the Savoy. The Savoy, which opened in 1889, was built by the impresario Richard D'Oyly Carte: not, as far as one can tell, 'a detected robber'. Perhaps Chesterton is remembering the dismissal in 1897 of the manager, César Ritz, the famous chef Auguste Escoffier and the *maître d'hôtel* Louis Echenard, who had apparently conspired to defraud the hotel of a large sum of money.
5. *In the house of man are many mansions*: See John 14:2.
6. *conquered almost always conquer*: See 'Riot and Decay', *DN*, 17 October 1908, p. 194, n. 6 above.
7. *Jack the Giant Killer ... generally supposed*: The earliest printed version of this English folk-tale was produced (as *The History of Jack and the Giants*) by J. White of Newcastle in 1711; no doubt the oral tradition is much older. See I. and P. Opie, *The Classic Fairy Tales* (Oxford: Oxford University Press, 1974, repr. 1992).

November 6, 1908.

BOOKS OF THE DAY.

The Religion of H. G. Wells.

'First and Last Things'.[1] By H. G. Wells. Constable.

It is honestly true to say of Mr. Wells'[2] books that they do a man good. Nay, they almost make a man good, for half an hour or so. Those of us who have some disposition to be swashbucklers in journalism are merely roused to further violence and vanity by other swashbucklers. When Mr. Bernard Shaw tries in a genial way to bully me, I am merely moved to bully him back, with an even more brutal geniality. I do not choose to be bullied, even by my best friends. But I am quite willing to be shamed, and there are moments when Mr. Wells thoroughly shames me. Large and luminous as his intellect is, I think his intellect is less exceptional and admirable than the beauty of his moral temper. He combines a plodding, explanatory patience with a prompt and perfect sense of honour, which leaps back from a real lie as if stung. This book is Mr. Wells' complete statement of his views, and passes from the largest metaphysic to the last points of morals and manners. In the course of this book Mr. Wells utters some scepticism about the ideals of justice and of chivalric honour. This is very funny, because justice and honour make a sort of mental music through the whole book, as if the sentences were set to a silvery tune. He will not use the word God in the impersonal sense in which millions of modern people use it, because he feels that it is not quite chivalrous to do so. He writes down a criticism of Christ which ought to seem blasphemous to any Christian, but which does not seem so in the least, because it is so plain that the writer is not trying to blaspheme, but only trying to think – or, it may be, trying to confess, trying in any case to tell the truth. The only possible excuse for ever talking about style is that the most superficial thing sometimes reveals the most fundamental; Mr. Wells' style simply smells of fair-play and a hospitable head and heart whose doors stand open to conviction. This book has explained to me for the first time what journalists mean by the two words 'brilliant' and 'solid'.

Mr. Wells' reputation is, like many other good things, a paradox. He is still being praised as a pillar of everything that he hates. Mr. Wells is still regarded as the hard, scientific writer, the champion of bleak and astronomical rationalism. The truth is that Mr. Wells spends all his time in banging and battering reason; it is the one thing he detests. I am a bit of a mystic myself, but I utterly refuse to relegate the rational faculty to the gutter into which Mr. Wells would like to trample it. If Mr. Wells had talked about human reason in a mediaeval pulpit as he talks about it in this book all the theologians of the day would have thought he had gone mad with mystical theology. No Bishop excommunicating a heretic ever expressed his contempt for 'mere human reason' in such terms as this. 'The mind of man may be primarily only a food-seeking, danger-avoiding, mate-finding instrument, just as the mind of a dog is, just as the nose of a dog is, or the snout of a pig'. No country vicar rebuking the scepticism of the village shoemaker ever attacked rationalism, merely for being rational, so frankly as Mr. Wells does when he says, 'The thinking mind seems clearer than it is, and is more positive than it ought to be'. The country vicar will quite agree with Mr. Wells that 'The thinking mind', especially that of the shoemaker, is 'more positive than it ought to be'. I may be allowed to say in passing that there is surely a fallacy here. We cannot possibly learn from biology that thought is unreliable, for that simply means learning that learning is unreliable. We reach biology by reason, and biology must be just as unreliable as the reason by which we reach it. A man's mind may be as stupid as the snout of a pig; but in that case, how can it even be certain that the snout of a pig is stupid?

The Thinker as Artist.

But all this is quite unfair to Mr. Wells, because he is not preaching either reason or science. His whole object at present is to dethrone science in favour of art. He desires to create a kind of artistic test of thought instead of the scientific one. If not himself a poet he is counsel for the poets. His whole object in this book and in most recent ones has been to back up the poets against the philosophers. If I might venture to summarise the meaning of this much greater master of summary I should be inclined to say that Mr. Wells' main doctrine is this: that a picture of Battersea Park is much truer than a map of Battersea Park. The picture gives the essential fact about the park – its business. A picture gives all the half-tones, all the softness of outline, all the fringes that fade away. It is the vice of a map (Mr. Wells would say) that in order to make things roughly true it must make them harshly true. When the bishop and the vicar kick away human reason they profess to appeal to something beyond it. Mr. Wells appeals (rather more vaguely) to what he calls Beauty, an ultimate feeling of the poetical proportions of things, such a feeling as a man has who hews out a statue. The thesis of this book might roughly be called the plea of Proportion against Reason.

If one might offer any criticism of so suggestive and generally sound a book I should be disposed to say that wherever Mr. Wells is wrong he is wrong by his own test, on almost every point on which he differs from the old Christian morality he also differs from the new Wells philosophy; that is, he fails to apply it properly. I will give only two instances of what I mean. Thus, after urging art and instinct against mere logic, he goes on to say in substance that he does not understand the old idea of justice, and can attach no importance to it. He tries to make out that it is only a sort of hurried and bewildered good nature. Now, it is exactly here that primal, impenetrable emotion might have put him right. We all *feel* that justice is a fine thing, and never finer than when it goes against all impulses of liking. I know that Mr. Wells would at once admire any man who was doing strict justice to someone whom he hated. We feel for certain that a god is never so godlike as when he is giving the devil his due. Justice is not a cold thing; it is one of the hottest, fiercest, and most fundamental of the buried fires of our being. Mr. Wells would have gone right here if he had really followed Beauty; for there is nothing so beautiful as an honest grocer. But in this matter of justice he fell away, and flirted with the lowest type of logic. There is another example which is not so easy to explain; yet I will attempt to explain it.

Food for Controversy.

If Mr. Wells were really judging by Beauty and Proportion he would not talk in the way he does about everything changing at every minute. He seems really to say in some places that one cannot apply an adjective to a noun at all. I cannot say of a horse that it is four-legged, because everything is always changing. Now, it is true that the horse had no legs when he was an embryo; and it is true that he will have an enormous number of legs when he is running about in the form of maggots. And it is even true that some slight changes (such as lameness) happen to his legs during his normal lifetime. But if we are talking about Proportion, about the thing that an artist sees, then exactly the thing that an artist sees is not the continuous mutability of the horse, but his very startling immutability all the time that he is a horse. If art and instinct are any use at all it ought to be their business to point out that there is no comparison at all between the microscopic changes of maturity on the one hand, and on the other the rapid rush of development and the abrupt collapse of decay. If we go by Proportion rather than Reason, the truth is that a horse for all solid purposes stubbornly remains a horse. The artist ought to see the elements of changeableness in a thing, because it is the biggest element. He may well leave it to the sophist to see the element of change.

There is one other element on which I should feel inclined to quarrel a little with Mr. Wells, but it is really too large a matter to be discussed here. I do not like all this about the Race. I am not one leg of a centipede; but a man who can love other men, dead and unborn. Mr. Wells is always regarding everyone as a means to an end which is some vague vigour in the Race. Now, of course, every man can be considered as a means, and not as an end, just as every man can be considered as a tradesman and not as a customer. You can define Mr. Wells as a man who writes books to please me. You can define me as a man who writes books to please (or bore) Mr. Wells. But after all, books are meant to be read. The goal, the ideal of the whole universe is a pleased Wells and a grinning, satisfied Chesterton. The aim, in other words, is not the Race, but the making of the largest possible number of people good and happy, here or hereafter. The ultimate fact is not service, but what the mediaeval philosophers called 'Fruition' – the beatitude of souls.

Notes
1. *First and Last Things: A Confession of Faith and Rule of Life* (London: Constable, 1908). Wells presented Chesterton with a copy of the book, which is now in the British Library, annotated by Chesterton.
2. *Mr. Wells*: Herbert George Wells; see 'The Worship of the Insect', *DN*, 7 March 1903, Volume 2, p. 21, n. 3 above.

November 7, 1908.

THE LONG BOW.[1]

I find myself still sitting in front of the last book by Mr. H. G. Wells, I say stunned with admiration, my family says sleepy with fatigue.[2] I still feel vaguely all the things in Mr. Wells's book which I agree with; and I still feel vividly the one thing that I deny. I deny that biology can destroy the sense of truth, which alone can even desire biology. No truth which I find can deny that I am seeking the truth. My mind cannot find anything which denies my mind ... But what is all this? This is no sort of talk for a Saturday article. This is no stuff for a Christian democracy on the eve of a half-holiday.[a] Let us change the subject; let us have a romance or a fable or a fairy tale.

****

Come, let us tell each other stories. There was once a king who was very fond of listening to stories, like the king in the Arabian Nights. The only difference was that, unlike that cynical Oriental, this king believed all the stories that he heard. It is hardly necessary to add that he lived in England. His face had not the swarthy secrecy of the tyrant of the thousand tales; on the contrary, his eyes were as big and innocent as two blue moons; and when his yellow beard turned totally white he seemed to be growing younger. Above him hung still his heavy sword and horn, to remind men that he had been a tall hunter and warrior in his time: indeed, with that rusted sword he had wrecked armies. But he was one of those who will never know the world, even when they conquer it. Besides his love of this old Chaucerian pastime of the telling of tales, he was, like many old English kings, specially interested in the art of the bow. He gathered round him great archers of the stature of Ulysses and Robin Hood, and to four of these he gave the whole government of his kingdom. They did not mind governing his kingdom; but they were sometimes a little bored with the necessity of telling him stories. None of their stories were true; but the king believed all of them, and this became very depressing. They created the most preposterous romances; and could not get the credit of creating them. Their true ambition was sent empty away.[3] They were praised as archers; but they desired to be praised as poets. They were trusted as men, but they would rather have been admired as literary men.

At last, in an hour of desperation, they formed themselves into a club or conspiracy with the object of inventing some story which even the King could not swallow. They called it The League Of The Long Bow; thus attaching themselves by a double bond to their motherland of England, which has been steadily celebrated since the Norman Conquest for its heroic archery and for the extraordinary credulity of its people.[4]

At last it seemed to the four archers that their hour had come. The King commonly sat in a green curtained chamber, which opened by four doors, and was surmounted by four turrets. Summoning his champions to him on an April evening, he sent out each of them by a separate door, telling him to return at morning with the tale of his journey. Every champion bowed low, and, girding on great armour as for awful adventures, retired to some part of the garden to think of a lie. They did not want to think of a lie which would deceive the king; any lie would do that. They wanted to think of a lie so outrageous that it would not deceive him, and that was a serious matter.

The first archer who returned was a dark, quiet, clever fellow, very dexterous in small matters of mechanics. He was more interested in the science of the bow than in the sport of it. Also he would only shoot at a mark, for he thought it cruel to kill beasts and birds, and atrocious to kill men. When he left the King he had gone out into the wood and tried all sorts of tiresome experiments about the bending of branches and the impact of arrows; when even he found it tiresome he returned to the house of the four turrets and narrated his adventure. 'Well', said the King, 'what have you been shooting?' 'Arrows', answered the archer. 'So I suppose', said the King smiling; 'but I mean, I mean what wild things have you shot?' 'I have shot nothing but arrows', answered the bowman obstinately. 'When I went out on to the plain I saw in a crescent the black army of the Tartars, the terrible archers whose bows are of bended steel, and their bolts as big as javelins. They spied me afar off, and the shower of their arrows shut out the sun and made a rattling roof above me. You know, I think it wrong to kill a bird, or worm, or even a Tartar. But such is the precision and rapidity of perfect science that, with my own arrows, I split every arrow as it came against me. I struck every flying shaft as if it were a flying bird. Therefore, Sire, I may say truly, that I shot nothing but arrows'. The King said, 'I know how clever you engineers are with your fingers'. The archer said, 'Oh', and went out.

The second archer, who had curly hair and was pale, poetical, and rather effeminate, had merely gone out into the garden and stared at the moon. When the moon had become too wide, blank, and watery, even for his own wide, blank, and watery eyes, he came in again. And when the king said, 'What have you been shooting?' he answered with great volubility, 'I have shot a man; not a man from Tartary, not a man from Europe, Asia, Africa, or America; not a man on this earth at all. I have shot the Man in the Moon'. 'Shot the Man in the Moon?' repeated the king with something like a mild surprise. 'It is easy to prove it', said the archer with hysterical haste. 'Examine the moon through this particularly powerful telescope and you will no longer find any traces of a man there'. The king glued his big blue idiotic eye to the telescope for about ten minutes, and then said, 'You are right; as you have pointed out, scientific truth can only be tested by the senses. I believe you'. And the second archer went out, and being of a more emotional temperament burst into tears.

The third archer was a savage, brooding sort of man, with tangled hair and dreamy eyes, and he came in without any preface, saying, 'I have lost all my arrows. They have turned into birds'. Then as he saw that they all stared at him, he said, 'Well, you know everything changes on the earth; mud turns into marigolds, eggs turn into chickens; one can even breed dogs into quite different shapes. Well, I shot my arrows at the awful eagles that clash their wings round the Himalayas; great golden eagles as big as elephants, which snap the tall trees by perching on them. My arrows fled so far over mountain and valley that they turned slowly into fowls in their flight. See here', and he threw down a dead bird and laid an arrow beside it. 'Can't you see they are the same structure. The straight shaft is the backbone; the sharp point is the beak; the feather is the rudimentary plumage. It is merely modification and evolution'. After a silence the king nodded gravely and said, 'Yes; of course everything is evolution'. At this the third archer suddenly and violently left the room, and was heard in some distant part of the building making extraordinary noises either of sorrow or of mirth.

The fourth archer was a stunted man with a face as dead as wood, but with wicked little eyes close together, and very much alive. His comrades dissuaded him from going in because they said that they had soared up into the seventh heaven of living lies, and that there was literally nothing which the old man would not believe. The face of the little archer became a little more wooden as he forced his way in, and when he was inside he looked round with blinking bewilderment. 'Ha, the last', said the King heartily, 'welcome back again!' There was a long pause, and then the stunted archer said, 'What do you mean by "again"? I have never been here before'. The King stared for a few seconds, and said, 'I sent you out from this room with the four doors last night'. After another pause the little man slowly shook his head. 'I never saw you before', he said simply; 'you never sent me out from anywhere. I only saw your four turrets in the distance, and strayed in here by accident. I was born in an island in the Greek Archipelago; I am by profession an auctioneer, and my name is Punk'. The king sat on his throne for seven long instants like a statue; and then there awoke in his mild and ancient eyes an awful thing; the complete conviction of untruth. Everyone has felt it who has found a child obstinately false. He rose to his height and took down the heavy sword above him, plucked it out naked, and then spoke. 'I will believe your mad tales about the exact machinery of arrows; for that is science. I will believe your mad tales about traces of life in the moon; for that is science. I will believe your mad tales about jellyfish turning into gentleman, and everything turning into anything, for that is science. But I will not believe you when you tell me what I know to be untrue. I will not believe you when you say that you did not at all set forth under my authority and out of my house. You other three may conceivably have told the truth; but this last man has certainly lied. Therefore I will kill him'. And with that the old and gentle king ran at the man with uplifted sword; but he was arrested by the roar of happy laughter, which told the world that there is, after all, something which an Englishman will not swallow.

206a Saturday article. This is no stuff for a Christian democracy on the eve of a half-holiday.] in *AD* is replaced by the following:
    genial essay.

Notes
1. *THE LONG BOW*: Reprinted in *AD*, pp. 227-34; and *DayNight*, pp. 45–8 (excluding the first paragraph).
2. *the last book by Mr. H. G. Wells ... fatigue*: Presumably *The War in the Air* (1908).
3. *sent empty away*: See Luke 1:53.
4. *inventing some story ... its people*: 'To pull the long bow' is to tell falsehoods or tall stories: an item of English slang now largely forgotten.

November 14, 1908.

THE ENGLISHMAN.

A very interesting paper has recently been published called 'The Englishman'.[1] I bought it in the street the other day. The editor appears to found his claim to be a representative Englishman upon the ground that he has quarrelled with all other Englishmen; and I do not say that his attitude is without its value. Modern society has come to be in such a condition that if you abuse everybody all round you can hardly avoid very often telling the truth. Nor do I particularly object to the occasional outbursts of mere Jingo romance which occur in the periodical. One writer, in his researches into history, has discovered a battle in the later Middle Ages which was called Crécy,[2] and another less generally known conflict called Poitiers,[3] at which, it appears, the English showed that they were unconquerable. He also says (as far as I can understand him) that at Waterloo England faced Europe in arms.

Now I do not quarrel with these sound schoolboy sentiments at all. They have nothing to do with real history. It is not really very important that schoolboys should learn history; it is very important that they should learn patriotism. It would, perhaps, be as irrelevant to put real history into this patriotic paper as to put it into a boy's adventure story. Such a paper is not, perhaps, the proper place for pointing out that the French Wars were a dynastic family quarrel; that Edward III was almost as much a Frenchman as the King of France, and that one splendid rearguard action fought by a retreating army five hundred years ago, does not show that the descendants of the victors are a race of Supermen.

****

And, perhaps, it is not even the proper place for contradicting a palpable lie, as that England fought Europe in arms. Evidently the English are mainly marked in history by the fact that they scarcely ever fought except with allies. If anyone fought Europe in arms it was obviously the French. But all this, though alphabetically simple, may be a shade too subtle for the just encouragement of national sentiment in the very young; therefore I do not insist that it shall be introduced into 'The Boy's Own Paper'[4] or into music-hall songs, or into the 'Englishman'; more especially as the 'Englishman' does show that it can face some of the faults of England.

The real quarrel I have with this periodical is based upon nothing but its cover. If we carefully study the cover of this magazine (designed, I daresay, by somebody who felt no interest in the magazine at all), we shall, I think, come rather close to the real criticism upon modern England. One general rule about Jingoism is that the more mild and peaceable it is the more poisonous and dangerous it is. If a man says, 'The power of England is that every army on earth flies shrieking from the mere shaking of her flag', the statement is innocent; for it can be disproved. But if a man says 'The power of England is in the quiet self-control and steady private righteousness of her people' then the boast is more false and perilous. For a man cannot positively disprove that you and I are quietly and steadily righteous – that is, unless he knows us very well indeed.

Now, the funny thing about the cover of the paper was this: that it represented the British Lion couchant (I wish to God that he were rampant and regardant; but they always draw him couchant and half asleep, and unfortunately they are right enough there). It represented, I say, the British Lion couchant upon a pile of stone steps, each marked in large letters with a British virtue. And the first British virtue that caught my eye was 'Sobriety'. Then I saw in a flash the solid fact about our solid self-satisfaction. Our patriotic boasting is not a loose and fantastic exaggeration: it is a strict and decorous lie. We do not overstate our virtues; we simply claim all the virtues, especially those which we obviously haven't got. There are a great many obviously important virtues which we have got. If patience is a virtue, God knows that the English people have got it. Kindness is undoubtedly a virtue, and they have got that. Men who know France and the Continent really well – men like Mr. Maurice Baring,[5] men as different from each other as Mr. George Moore[6] and Mr. Hilaire Belloc[7] – all agree on one thing, that the English popular fun and the English popular slang are really more hearty and human than the same thing in France and elsewhere. Therefore, if I had seen the British Lion reposing on a rock marked 'Slang' or marked 'Nonsense', I should really be inclined to admit that 'The Englishman' understood the Englishman.

****

But when it is suggested, even by unconscious pictorial symbol, that the English democracy reposes on a special basis of Sobriety, the rest of Europe looking at the statement would really hardly know what to say. We are justly renowned throughout the world as the one specially and almost permanently drunken nation. If we suggest that we are more sober than Frenchmen we might really just as well say that we are more musical than Germans. There is no reason why we should not say that we are more black than niggers. We might well, while we were about it, say we were nearer the North Pole than Esquimaux.

The ruinous self-satisfaction does not consist in saying that one is the best blossom on the tree. It lies in saying that one is the trunk of the tree. I would not mind even the boast of the old Englishman that he was stronger than others if he would only admit that others are taller, or handsomer, or more Christian, or more pure than he. But he will talk persistently of the need for Sobriety and never once mention that the Frenchman is more sober than the Englishman. He will talk persistently of the need of moral purity, and never once mention that the Irishman is more morally pure than the Englishman. The Englishman (I sincerely believe, and I most solemnly pray) will soon really find his own virtue. But he will only find it when he has consented to give up all the other virtues; by way of exchange.

Notes
1. *A very interesting paper ... 'The Englishman'*: The *Englishman*, edited by Charles Weld-Blundell (1845–1927), was a patriotic newspaper published between 1908 and 1911. Also in 1908 Weld-Blundell, in a book called *Are We a Stupid People?* (London: Kegan Paul, 1908), exhorted the English to teach the young 'to be earnest and sincere, faithful and dutiful, patriotic and loyal to their God, their family and their race' (p. 503). The book – a root-and-branch critique of contemporary politics – rather bears out Chesterton's impression that the author 'has quarrelled with all other Englishmen'. A Roman Catholic, Weld-Blundell owned land in Dorset and Lancashire. After much travel earlier in life, he took up art, politics and journalism in his forties.
2. *a battle ... Crécy*: Battle of Crécy (1346), in which Edward III of England defeated Philip IV of France.
3. *conflict called Poitiers*: Battle of Poitiers (1356) in which English and Gascon troops under the Black Prince defeated the army of Jean le Bon and took him prisoner after a downhill charge and rear offensive.
4. *'The Boy's Own Paper'*: The *Boy's Own Paper* was a weekly paper for boys published in England from 1879 to 1967 – initially by the Religious Tract Society and subsequently by other publishers with less emphatically moral editorial policies.
5. *Mr. Maurice Baring*: Maurice Baring; see 'Tommy and the Traditions', *DN*, 23 May 1908, p. 79, n. 7 above.
6. *Mr. George Moore*: see Mr. Gallienne Again', *DN*, 15 February 1901, Volume 1, p. 27, n. 5 above.
7. *Mr. Hilaire Belloc*: Hilaire Pierre René Belloc; see 'On Shooting at the Stars', *DN*, 6 August 1904, Volume 2, p. 270, n. 1 above.

November 21, 1908.

THE QUEER MEMORY.[1]

There is probably much truth in the popular notion that the strength of kings has largely consisted in the power of remembering faces. It is only fair to add that their strength has frequently consisted in the power of forgetting faces. But the vulgar legend, like most vulgar legends, is substantially correct. The man who specialises in the life of courts, where almost everything depends on personal influence, is not likely to be loose or forgetful about the element of personality.

Those of my readers who are not kings and queens (and these are a large and growing class) have nearly all of them had this difficulty of remembering names, faces, and identities. The reason is not obscure. Nearly all of us have to study some positive, but impersonal, thing; banking, or shooting bears, or astronomy, or the egg trade. But if a king wants to know about these (and I don't know why he should) he can have a special report prepared upon bankers and bad eggs and things of that kind. There is a definite official called the Astronomer Royal,[2] whose whole object in life (to judge by his title) must be to tell the King about astronomy. There is also, one may naturally infer, a Bear-leader Royal, whose business it is to entertain the Court with information about bears. But if you or I, with no official advisers, have to understand such things we must peg away very hard at very impersonal problems.

****

But kings can specialise in personality. Kings can think only about men. Premiers, especially when they are trying to work education compromises, must try (poor brutes) to think about Man. But at least most of us have that difficulty of remembering people's faces or names sufficiently for the purposes of politeness.

Personally I am in a curious position; it is neither their names, addresses, nor details of physique that I can remember. I always remember people by their opinions. I remember what the man said to me in some far-off argument which I must have had with him in the middle of Ludgate Circus. Therefore, if he says to me, with a sort of beaming cunning (as he almost always does), 'Now you don't know who I am, you know', then I can truthfully assure him that I do know. I know his most sacred thoughts, his central pillar of conviction, the very backbone of his soul. The trifling fact that I have not the faintest notion of his name, or what he is, or where I met him, the mere fact that in the popular phrase I do not know him from Adam (except by the costume), is in no sense an invalidation of my claim that I know him spiritually, as he would be known in Heaven.

But I find that in practice this is not well received. It does not soothe such a man to say to him: 'I don't know your name; but you are the man who believes that Mahomet was the real founder of Christianity'. For the social purpose of breaking the ice such an opening is not to be compared to that of the weather. It is true, after all, in the most solemn and universal sense, that nothing but the weather can break the ice. Somehow my method does not work. A person is not pleased when I say to him: 'I do not remember who you are; but I can tell you exactly what view of the Monroe Doctrine you had in the affair with Venezuela'.[3] Nor does it do when introducing the gentleman to somebody else to say: 'This is the gentleman who believes that the Duke of Wellington was in the pay of Napoleon Bonaparte. I have not the pleasure of knowing his name'. It ought to work out all right, like Parliamentary government, but somehow it doesn't. Hence it happens that my social tragedies in this respect increase rather than diminish; and men will not admit that I may reverence their intellects without remembering their surname.

****

The other day I came across a very strange bit of psychology in this connection. I will tell it as exactly and essentially as it can be told. I was walking slowly through the most magnificent of London parks (I will not condescend to name it), when a man passed me, walking quickly. I instantly recognised him as a man whom I had known years before at an art school; it was the more unquestionable because he had an unmistakable appearance, a long, strong body and a long, weak face. Having reached very rapidly the remote end of the avenue, he flung himself impatiently on to a seat, and lit a cigarette, as if waiting for somebody. I came nearer and nearer to him (as always happens in such cases), conscious of the need to salute him, and consciously unconscious until it was time to do so. But before it was the man sprang up and came heartily towards me. He was so glad to meet me again. He had always hoped to have that pleasure. I warmly reciprocated his enthusiasm, for besides the fact that a lost friend found is a prodigy, like a man raised from the dead, I remembered him as an earnest and interesting youth.

He had been one of those who are unbalanced by being just a little more afraid of vice than they are fond of virtue. Thus he was sensitive and fastidious even more than conscientious; and he was conscientious enough to kill twenty men. In short, he was one of those who will waste on the problem of slanting sunlight on a cactus plant so as to make it ideally comfortable more insatiable and over-driven devotion than would be required to destroy the whole horrible society in which we live

In short, as I have previously confessed, I remembered the man's opinions even if I had forgotten his name. I leant back luxuriantly on the wooden seat as one who falls into a familiar and friendly difference, and at the first words the man spoke I sat bolt upright again. He began by spitting on the path, and the first sentence he uttered involved an oath; these are small things to me, but I knew that they would have been very big things to him. I was so puzzled that I returned to my test of opinions, and asked him his opinion of the Licensing Bill, with which (as a whole) I agree,[4] though few of its supporters would agree with my agreement with it. His answer was so splendid and energetic that it cannot be printed here, or, I should imagine, anywhere else.

I was puzzled, because the fundamental fact in conviction does not often alter so entirely as that; so I said at random, alluding to one of his intimate friends at the art school, 'Do you ever meet Muggeridge now?' He opened on me vast and innocent grey eyes, and said with a sudden air of constraint, 'Muggeridge? ... We never knew any Muggeridge'. 'We jolly well did', I answered, 'if we were at the Slade School some fifteen years ago'. He stared for some seconds, and then said, quite simply, 'But we weren't. I met you on tour with an amateur company acting the "Mikado" at Manchester'.

We went into the question with considerable argumentative thoroughness, and at the end of it we agreed that as a matter of fact we had never met each other before. He had mistaken me for someone else; I had mistaken him for someone else. We parted with mutual esteem. But the real mystery remains; for what reason on earth (or rather in heaven or hell) should the two false recognitions have been independent and simultaneous. Why did two total strangers freely and instinctively treat each other as did friends? Had we been friends in some strange and alien world, and are there things that men are not meant to remember? My instinct is against speculations of that kind; so I come back to the mere fact. I have falsified certain facts in telling it, precisely because it is so true that if I told it as it was it might cause accidental and irrelevant pain. But the whole is a good study of the fact that realism is more fictitious than romance. For in this story it is only the ordinary part that I have altered. The extraordinary part is strictly true.

****

The strange man went away and left me sitting on the seat somewhat dazed about what deduction I should draw from it all. The only deduction that seemed directly cogent was that, after all, I was right in judging men by their convictions. As far as I could see, every fact and detail of the man's face and figure were the same as those of my old friend. But I saw that his soul was different before he had spoken three words. And I remembered vaguely that the few unforgotten facts in our life are facts of inspiration; facts which one has seen suddenly and yet seen solid, like square undiscovered cliffs exhibited under lightning. So I did what I always do now when I feel strongly and don't want to write an article; I wrote a Ballade to express my mixed emotions; and here it is printed for anyone who can endure such things:

> The mists that melt across the piers at Leith,
>   And all the soot that dances up the flue,
> And all the speeches of the Earl of Meath,[5]
>   And all the nutshells scattered at the Zoo,
> And all religions that are labelled new,
>   And all the smoke of every cigarette
> Even all things made, all but a very few
>   These things a man may easily forget.
>
> I may forget my name is Gilbert Keith,
>   Or my Museum ticket to renew,
> To pay my taxes, or to clean my teeth,
>   To shun the art of sitting down on glue;
> Yea, I may roam botanic gardens through
>   With eyes in a sublime abstraction set
> And knock the big pagoda down at Kew
>   These things a man may easily forget.
>
> But one last sunset upon Hampstead Heath,
>   A bar of music in the dusk and dew
> A silence of strong friends the boughs beneath,
>   And in that hush how like to gods we grew.
> Yea, all the immortal battle trumpets blew,
>   Though we must keep the rhyme by etiquette
> I will not say it, for it is not true,
>   These things a man may easily forget.
>
>   ENVOY.
>
> Princes, mark you, too, are mortal, and pursue
>   Your triumph rich with wreath and coronet,
> But please remember it is only you,
>   These things a man may easily forget.

Notes
1. *THE QUEER MEMORY*: Reprinted in *CR*, 17:2 (May 1991), pp. 147–50.
2. *Astronomer Royal*: a post created in 1675 by Charles II to resolve the urgent navigational problem of measuring longtitude.
3. *Monroe Doctrine ... Venezuela*: The Monroe Doctrine – formulated by US President James Monroe in his State of the Union Address in 1823 – is, in effect, that the New World and the Old should henceforth be distinct and separate spheres of influence. On the one hand, any further effort by European powers to establish colonies or interfere with states in the Americas would be treated as an act of aggression against the United States; on the other, the United States would not interfere with existing European colonies or meddle in the internal affairs of European countries. Chesterton is here referring to the 'Venezuela Crisis' of 1895: a territorial dispute between Great Britain and Venezuela in which, citing the Monroe Doctrine in justification, the United States had intervened to bring about an arbitration of the disputed territory.
4. *Licensing Bill ... I agree*: The Bill's objectives were to reduce the number licences for selling alcohol, with no obligation to compensate fully the interests damaged by non-renewal; and to take greater public control of the licensing system by restoring the power of magistrates to determine in what manner alcohol should be sold. Opponents of the Bill maintained that it would do little to advance the cause of temperance while giving new powers to the state to interfere in a trade about the details of which its officials knew little. It was rejected by the House of Lords on its second reading: see *Hansard*, HL Deb 26 November 1908 vol. 197 cc. 538–638. One can guess that Chesterton agreed with the effect of the Bill in curtailing the profits of the brewers.
5. *Earl of Meath*: Reginald Brabazon, twelfth Earl of Meath (1841–1929), was a politician and philanthropist. An ardent Conservative, Unionist and imperialist, Brabazon was the major force behind the establishment of Empire Day, an annual celebration of the British empire on Queen Victoria's birthday, 24 May. He was also a keen supporter of Lord Roberts's campaign for National Military Service (J. Springhall, *ODNB*). For Chesterton's withering response to Brabazon's initiative, see 'What is It?', *DN*, 29 May 1909, pp. 322–5 below.

November 28, 1908.

THE THING INDIFFERENT.[1]

We English will never get any further until we leave off boasting of being illogical. Illogicality is sometimes to be accepted as a burden, never to be erected as a crest. There is truth in everything. There is a truth even in modern science and machinery. But the curious thing is that modern machinery has not succeeded in teaching us the one truth which it really had to teach. The one important truth in mechanics is this: that the most idealistic work is the most practical work. A man making wheels for your motor-car makes them as ideally and perfectly round as he can. He would be a fool if he sat down in the middle of the road and cried because they never could be perfectly round in the sight of God. But he would be much more of a fool if he did not aim at exquisite mathematical roundness. He would be much more of a fool if he put the car on top of four shapeless shapes called in Euclid irregular polygons, and in popular language smashed window frames, and if he expected to win a race with a machine so constructed. Suppose he said 'I am no idealist or theorist; I have no time to waste over abstract calculations; you may say that one of my wheels looks like a drunken triangle and the other like an unfinished star fish; but I am going to win the race'. I do not somehow share his confidence of victory.

But I lament to observe that a Liberal leader has recently thus boasted of his illogicality, as a justification of the latest education policy.[2] I wonder whether it is any earthly good making a last attempt to introduce logic or light or any other intelligible thing into the education policy. Anyhow, I will make one attempt, and you will be glad to hear that it is my last. I believe that the whole education trouble has come from people trying to be loose and universal, not from people trying to be dogmatic and particular. We could all respect each other's faith; but it is too much to ask us to respect each other's doubt and hesitation. Millions of imaginative Nonconformists, with an instinct for old English history, might enjoy the Archbishop of Canterbury as an Archbishop. But they cannot enjoy him as a statesman. Every sane Churchman can believe in Dr. Clifford[3] as a great Baptist minister. It is when he says that he is only a citizen that they cannot believe him. This illogical amiability, this pretence that every man is umpire, has really been the curse of the whole affair. If everybody would clearly ask for what they would like in the abstract it might be possible for somebody to get something in the concrete. As it is, politicians are like stupid schoolmasters who should try to make the tangle of Euclid easier by drawing every circle on the black board as badly as possible. The boys find it hard enough to follow the train of thought even with good diagrams; they will not find it more 'human' and 'practical' when even the pictures are unreliable.

Now let us, as I say, by way of a desperate last attempt, draw the plain diagram of the Liberal position. The Liberal doctrine is this: that the English Government is not, as such, concerned with theology. Whatever may be right in nations religiously unanimous, our commonwealth has no creed and should have no concern with creeds. That is your position and mine. But unfortunately in the current welter of words this simple Liberal idea has got mysteriously mixed up with another idea which is entirely different. The idea that the State should ignore creeds has got mixed up with the idea that the State should distrust creeds – a totally different notion. I say that theology is a thing indifferent to politics, as I say that the colours of the sunrise are things indifferent to Euclid. They may be more important than Euclid. They are. But Euclid is emphatically one of the things that are twopence plain and a penny coloured; colours of the sunrise would really spoil him.

One might say, perhaps, that politics is the form of society and religion is its colour. But, at any rate, they are different things. Now, though the morning clouds have nothing to do with Euclid, you would not be very angry if a boy looking out of a window while he was learning Euclid happened to see a morning cloud. And if it were convenient for other reasons you would let him stand for half an hour watching the morning cloud; because you are sure that clouds can do no harm. But if anyone suggests 'the right of entry' you will cry out, 'Denominationalism in the Schools!'[4] 'The Priest in the Classroom!' because you are not sure that creeds can do no harm. You are sure that they always must do harm. In short, the truth can be shortly and substantially stated. Creeds are things indifferent to the Liberal state. But to you they are not indifferent.

Some pious people shrink from this expression that the Government has no concern with creeds, because they think that in some dim way it is dethroning religion from that supreme position which it must occupy to any intelligent man who believes in its occupying any position. But this is a mere mistake arising from the modern reaction against the anarchy of the doctrine of Manchester.[5] The modern world believes in a wild and foolish thing called 'The swing of the pendulum'; which means that because for the last ten years you have been mad on petting tigers, for the next ten years you must be mad on torturing them. Thus the modern spirit says, 'You would be a Materialist and deny that a saint could cure a man's feet of corns; you shall now jolly well be a Christian Scientist and deny that there are any feet to be cured'. In the same way, because a few rich men in whiskers chose to suggest that it would be much nicer if there were no laws, and chose to call this proposal the science of economics, because of this, a huge reaction called Collectivism has overwhelmed us, and people are now talking as if everything important in human life must be connected with the organ of government; therefore they are shocked to hear that religion should not be so connected because it sounds to them like saying religion is not very important.

But in reality the most important things of all are nearly all of them things which are outside the Government; for instance, love and marriage. What wife a man chooses and what god he worships are much more important than any Budget or any battleship. The difference is in the efficiency of the organ; we feel that the Government will presumably have an educated and informed taste in taxes and armaments; whereas the Government's taste in gods might be poor, and its taste in wives deplorable.

Therefore I should regard any attempt to employ [the?] public power of money in the matter of courtship and marriage exactly as I regard it in the case of the imposition of a theology. If the Government altered or spoilt the schools in order to give amorous opportunities to the nicest of the masters and mistresses, I should think they were stepping outside their function. If they laid out the grounds in romantic lanes and laid on artificial moonlight I should say they were wasting public money. If they had tests for teachers, which obliged them all to be troubadours, if no teacher could gain a place unless he could play the guitar or produce a packet of love-letters, I should think it distinctly unfair. Even if the Government spent money on balls and evening parties with the sole object of bringing the sexes together, I should say the Government was not minding its own business. So I would say of love, and so I would say of religion; it is not the function of the Government to encourage either of them; nor do they (generally speaking) require much encouragement.

But suppose the situation were like this; suppose we were engaged in [a] complicated commercial treaty for some buildings or machinery about which we were really trying to make a genial compromise; and suppose it were suggested that while the Government gained these buildings for its own public objects, dances and balls should still be held in them, for the ordinary purpose of conditioning with dignity and civilization the way of a man with a maid.[6] And suppose some people jumped up and cried out, 'What, will you introduce the poison of romance into a public building! What, will you have the Lover in the schools! What, shall our innocent populace be split up by emotional jealousies and fanciful selections!' We should reply, I imagine, 'Oh, I beg your pardon. I didn't know you hated love. I thought you only meant that it was no direct duty of government. I didn't know you disliked the idea of people getting married. I thought you merely held (as I do) that it is not the best occupation of the Cabinet or even for the County Council'.

It follows that upon this abstract problem of the right of entry the ultimate argument must turn. I agree that the Government has nothing to do with creeds, just as a botanist has nothing to do with whales. But when you say it, I think you mean it as a philanthropist has nothing to do with beggars. A philanthropist will have nothing to do with beggars even if he meets them in hell. It is a matter of principle with him. But a successful botanist might very well allow in his school-room a well-behaved whale once a week, if by doing this he could secure big subscriptions for botany.

Notes
1. *THING INDIFFERENT*: See Romans 14 (Rubric, King James Version): 'Men may not contemn nor condemn one another for things indifferent; but take heed that they give no offence in them'.
2. *a Liberal leader ... education policy:* Presumably Chesterton is referring to Asquith's statement during the debate on the second reading of the (McKenna) Education Bill on 26 November, 1908 – that the question of religious education should be considered 'not from the point of view of whether it is ideally the best solution of a difficult political problem, but whether it does contain the elements of a reasonable and workable settlement'. The speeches on this subject are printed in full at *Hansard*, HC Deb 26 November 1908 vol 197 cc. 707–824. See also 'The Education Bill', *The Times*, 27 November 1908, p. 9. The Bill failed because of strong Nonconformist objections.
3. *Dr. Clifford*: John Clifford; see 'Lord Halifax and Dr. Clifford', letter to the editor, *DN*, 20 September 1902, Volume 1, pp. 386–7, n. 2 above.
4. *'right of entry ...Denominationalism in the Schools!'*: See 'Something to Avoid', *DN*, 28 April 1906, Volume 3, pp. 356–7, n. 2 above.
5. *doctrine of Manchester*: i.e. of 'Manchester liberalism' – the 'laissez faire' doctrine of unregulated economic activity – particularly associated with the Manchester textile industry.
6. *way of a man with a maid*: See Proverbs 30:18–19: 'There be three things which are too wonderful for me, yea, four which I know not: the way of an eagle in the air; the way of a serpent upon a rock; the way of a ship in the midst of the sea; and the way of a man with a maid'.

December 5, 1908.

HOW I FOUND THE SUPERMAN.[1]

Readers of Mr. Bernard Shaw and other modern writers may be interested to know that the Superman has been found. I found him; he lives in South Croydon. My success will be a great blow to Mr. Shaw, who has been following quite a false scent, and is now looking for the creature in Blackpool; and as for Mr. Wells's notion of generating him out of gases in a private laboratory I always thought it doomed to failure. I assure Mr. Wells that the Superman at Croydon was born in the ordinary way, though he himself, of course, is anything but ordinary.

Nor are his parents unworthy of the wonderful being whom they have given to the world. The name of Lady Hypatia Smyth-Browne (now Lady Hypatia Hagg) will never be forgotten in the East End, where she did such splendid social work. Her constant cry of 'Save the children!' referred to the cruel neglect of children's eyesight involved in allowing them to play with crudely painted toys. She quoted unanswerable statistics to prove that children allowed to look at violet and vermilion often suffered from failing eyesight in their extreme old age; and it was owing to her ceaseless crusade that the pestilence of the Monkey-on-the-Stick was almost swept from Hoxton. The devoted worker would tramp the streets untiringly, taking away the toys from all the poor children, who were often moved to tears by her kindness. Her good work was interrupted, partly by a new interest in the creed of Zoroaster,[2] and partly by a savage blow from an umbrella. It was inflicted by a dissolute Irish apple-woman, who, on returning from some orgy to her ill-kept apartment, found Lady Hypatia in the bedroom taking down some oleograph, which, to say the least of it, could not really elevate the mind. At this the ignorant and partly intoxicated Celt dealt the social reformer a severe blow, adding to it an absurd accusation of theft. The lady's exquisitely balanced mind received a shock; and it was during a short mental illness that she married Dr. Hagg.[3]

Of Dr. Hagg himself I hope there is no need to speak. Anyone even slightly acquainted with those daring experiments in Neo-Individualist Eugenics, which are now the one absorbing interest of the English democracy, must know his name and often commend it to the personal protection of an impersonal power. Early in life he brought to bear that ruthless insight into the history of religions which he had gained in boyhood as an electrical engineer. Later he became one of our greatest geologists; and achieved that bold and bright outlook upon the future of Socialism which only geology can give. At first there seems something like a rift, a faint, but perceptible, fissure, between his views and those of his aristocratic wife. For she was in favour (to use her own powerful epigram) of protecting the poor against themselves; while he declared pitilessly, in a new and striking metaphor, that the weakest must go to the wall. Eventually, however, the married pair perceived an essential union in the unmistakably modern character of both their views; and in this enlightening and comprehensible expression their souls found peace. The result is that this union of the two highest types of our civilization, the fashionable lady and the all but vulgar medical man, has been blessed by the birth of the Superman, that being whom all the labourers in Battersea are so eagerly expecting night and day.

****

I found the house of Dr. and Lady Hypatia Hagg without much difficulty; it is situated in one of the last straggling streets of Croydon, and overlooked by a line of poplars. I reached the door towards the twilight, and it was natural that I should fancifully see something dark and monstrous in the dim bulk of that house which contained the creature who was more marvellous than the children of men. When I entered the house I was received with exquisite courtesy by Lady Hypatia and her husband; but I found much greater difficulty in actually seeing the Superman, who is now about fifteen years old, and is kept by himself in a quiet room. Even my conversation with the father and mother did not quite clear up the character of this mysterious being. Lady Hypatia, who has a pale and poignant face, and is clad in those impalpable and pathetic greys and greens with which she has brightened so many homes in Hoxton, did not appear to talk of her offspring with any of the vulgar vanity of an ordinary human mother. I took a bold step and asked if the Superman was nice looking.

'He creates his own standard, you see', she replied, with a slight sigh. 'Upon that plane he is more than Apollo. Seen from our lower plane, of course...' And she sighed again.

I had a horrible impulse, and said suddenly, 'Has he got any hair?'

There was a long and painful silence, and then Dr. Hagg said smoothly, 'Everything upon that plane is different; what he has got is not ... well, not, of course, what we call hair ... but ...'

'Don't you think', said his wife, very softly, 'don't you think that really, for the sake of argument, when talking to the mere public, one might call it hair?'

'Perhaps you are right', said the doctor after a few moments' reflection. 'In connection with hair like that one must speak in parables'.

'Well, what on earth is it', I asked in some irritation, 'if it isn't hair? Is it feathers?'

'Not feathers, as we understand feathers', answered Hagg in an awful voice.

I got up in some irritation. 'Can I see him, at any rate?' I asked. 'I am a journalist, and have no earthly motives except curiosity and personal vanity. I should like to say that I had shaken hands with the Superman'.

The husband and wife had both got heavily to their feet, and stood embarrassed.

'Well, of course, you know', said Lady Hypatia, with the really charming smile of the aristocratic hostess. 'You know he can't exactly shake hands ... not hands, you know ... The structure, of course ...'

I broke out of all social bounds, and rushed at the door of the room which I thought to contain the incredible creature. I burst it open; the room was pitch dark. But from in front of me came a small sad yelp, and from behind me a double shriek.

'You have done it, now!' cried Dr. Hagg, burying his bald brow in his hands. 'You have let in a draught on him; and he is dead'.

As I walked away from Croydon that night I saw men in black carrying out a coffin that was not of any human shape. The wind wailed above me, whirling the poplars, so that they drooped and nodded like the plumes of some cosmic funeral.

'It is, indeed', said Dr. Hagg, 'the whole universe weeping over the frustration of its most magnificent birth'. But I thought that there was a hoot of laughter in the high wail of the wind.

Notes
1. *HOW I FOUND THE SUPERMAN*: Reprinted in *AD*, pp. 129–34; and *CW*, 11, pp. 359–62.
2. *Zoroaster*: Zoroaster or Zarathustra, was the ancient Iranian philosopher and prophet who, many centuries before Christ, founded the dualist religion called Zoroastrianism of Mazdaism. His appearance here is in rather oblique reference to Nietzsche's *Also sprach Zarathustra: Ein Buch für Alle und Keinen* (*Thus Spake Zarathustra: a Book for All and None*) (1883–5) – a feature of which is the appearance of Nietzsche's idea that the goal and end of human development is the *Übermensch* or 'Superman'.

3. (*Lady Hypatia Hagg*) ... *married Dr. Hagg*: Lady Hypatia and Dr Hagg are caricatures of the kind of earnest scientific reformers that Chesterton dislikes so much; but it is difficult not to detect in this sketch of Dr Hagg a glimpse of Herbert Spencer. Lady Hypatia may conceivably be Beatrice Webb in disguise.

December 12, 1908.

ON BLUFF.

There seems to be a strange weakening in the whole habit and science of intellectual war. And, like most things that decay, it begins, as it were, to die at both ends. Thus in the same way religion generally breaks up into scepticism and superstition simultaneously. Thus our age of doubt has seen the growth of Christian Science, which is worse even than unchristian science. Thus, again, the old dignity and decency of patriotism has been threatened by two heresies, one which says that you should love all other countries and conquer them, while the other says that you should love all other countries and let them conquer you. Somewhat similar has been the fate of the true idea of fighting, whether physical or mental. Most current attempts at the thing are full of timidity or of bullying; and these two are in truth the same being only the allotropic forms of the same great modern morbidity, the habit of admiring Power rather than Valour. That word valour, by the way, is in itself a stirring sermon. It means putting one's full value into the struggle or settlement; the almost exact translation of valour is 'being in it for all you are worth'.

****

On most political platforms, in most newspapers and magazines, I observe that there are at present only two ideas, either to avoid controversy or to conduct it by mere bluff and noise. If a man writes a letter to the 'Daily Express', let us say, rubbing in some illogicality or cruelty in Ireland or India, the 'Daily Express' does one of two things. It either ignores the letter and writes a leading article about Lap Dogs, or it calls the man a pro-Boer and a sentimentalist, and describes him as tearing the Union Jack with his teeth and dancing with demoniac joy while the Germans are sacking London – all of which has quite as little to do with the subject as the lap dogs themselves. The idea of fighting, of answering the argument by a suitable counter-argument, even if it be a sophistry, has evidently vanished from the editorial mind. Evasion and violence are the only expedients. A man must be deaf to his opponents' arguments; he may be deaf and silent, and this is called dignity; or he may be deaf and noisy, and this is called 'slashing journalism'. But both these things are equally remote from the fighting spirit, which involves an interest in the enemy's movements in order to parry or to pierce them. The good controversialist is a good listener; he is learned in the arguments of his adversary, he wishes to have every word of the speech which he is to answer. But the large Imperial controversialist of the 'Daily Mail' order really might as well be answering one speech as another, because he is not really answering anything. The object of fighting is to hit, not merely to hammer. The swordsman who can only keep up a clatter with his own sword on the other sword is as weak as he who drops his own sword and runs away from the other. And most of the gladiators of our Press at present are of one type or the other.

One principle strangely forgotten is this, that the art of controversy, like any other art, however wild in form, parody, or allegory, or farce, must have some ultimate relation to truth. The common, modern trick of attempting to bluff a man out of his reputation is both unscientific and unsoldierly. It is weak as war.

****

For instance, I saw the other day in some paper which dislikes Socialists some such sentence as this: 'Mr. Bernard Shaw is going to lecture on "Woman"; we do not suppose anyone wants to hear what Mr. Shaw happens to think on this subject, etc'. Now if the writer had jeered at Mr. Shaw merely for having red hair, it would have been much more forcible and effective than this. It would have borne some relation to truth. Some people do dislike red hair; and everybody knows that Mr. Shaw has got red hair. But everybody knows that Mr. Shaw is not a person whose views evoke no curiosity. Everybody knows that some people do like to hear what he thinks; that he can easily fill a hall with such people. The sneer, having no connection with any facts at all, does not irritate even for an instant. Mr. Shaw is left smiling, as Mr. Carnegie[1] would be left smiling if you taunted him with his poverty, or the King if you told him that he was boycotted by the illustrated magazines.

All this is part of that unchivalrous and even unmilitary idea of bullying, of using bombastic terrors in order to avoid a conflict which is at this moment the highest turret of the tall hypocrisies of Europe. Europe is full of the idea of bluff, the idea of cowing the human spirit with a painted panorama of physical force. We see it in the huge armaments which we dare to accumulate, but should hardly dare to use. We see it in the enormous biological theories which are not sufficiently proved to convince scientific men, but which are already used to terrify ordinary men. We see it in the ghastly Barmecide banquet of modern finance; in the Stock Exchange, where men buy and sell, so as to shake continents, the things that do not even exist. For the soul of all our commerce is that the peasant says (being often a greedy fellow), 'I have grown a turnip; will you give me a shilling?' Whereas the broker says, 'If I had ten thousand turnips would you borrow ten thousand shillings and buy them?' It is all the spirit of the bully, of the man who, instead of strengthening himself, labels himself strong. For in spite of Charles Lamb the popular phrase is profoundly true, the real bully is always a coward.[2] For the bully is the man who acts on the assumption that he will not have to fight.

****

I do not like hovering and lingering threats of armaments; nor do I like hovering and lingering threats of riot. If people want to have a revolution let them have it and let it have the advantage of a revolution, that of being drastic and decisive. But a mere parade of possible war seems merely a perpetual anarchy. Revolution creates government; but anarchy only creates more anarchy. This is my principal prepossession against the ladies who broke up the meeting for female suffrage.[3] If women choose to learn rifle shooting, to kill the police, to seize the treasury, and to rule England, then they will become a government like any other; it will be first war and then peace. But my objection to the Suffragettes is not that they are violent, but that they are vague; it is not that they fight, it is that they do not fight well. A fight of its nature has an end. But there is no reason why this sort of weak uproar should have any end for ever.

Notes
1. *Mr. Carnegie*: Andrew Carnegie; see 'The Mystery of the Middle Ages', *DN*, 16 October 1908, p. 190, n. 15 above.
2. *in spite of Charles Lamb ... a coward*: see Lamb, 'Popular Fallacies, 1: That a Bully is Always a Coward' (in *Last Essays of Elia* (1833)): 'This axiom contains a principle of compensation, which disposes us to admit the truth of it. But there is no safe trusting to dictionaries and definitions. We should more willingly fall in with this popular language, if we did not find *brutality* sometimes awkwardly coupled with *valour* in the same vocabulary'.
3. *the ladies who broke up the meeting for female suffrage*: Women from the Women's Social and Political Union disrupted a meeting at the Royal Albert Hall on 5 December 1908, organized by the Women's Liberal Federation. The principal speaker – David Lloyd George, Chancellor of the Exchequer – took two hours to deliver a speech in support of woman's suffrage that should have taken twenty minutes: 'Mr. Lloyd George and Woman Suffrage: Disorderly Scenes', *The Times*, 7 December 1908, p. 6a.

December 19, 1908.

AFTER THE MILTON CELEBRATION.[1]

It is a difficulty in celebrations and centenaries and such things that one generally has to make up the observations before and one generally feels the emotions afterwards. During the whole of a long and happy life I have been systematically late for everything; and I often have the proper sentiments of an occasion some little time after it. I burst with Christmas benevolence somewhere about the beginning of February; I write impulsive lyrics on spring during the autumn; and I begin really to love my great-great-grandmother several days after her birthday. I, therefore, feel impelled upon the present occasion to recall your thoughts to the subject of the Milton celebration, which you supposed, with such unthinking glee, to be altogether done with.[2] My only excuse is that the subject is one of the few upon which real emotion grows after [a?] consistent course of thought. Of all poets Milton is the one whom it is the most difficult to praise with real delicacy and sincerity of definition. Of all poets Milton is the one whom it is most easy to praise with mere facile phraseology and conventional awe. And as it is one of the most difficult subjects in the world, what could be more appropriate for my present purpose, when I am dictating desperately to a typewriter in order to catch a train?

There is one thing about Milton which must have been generally observed – that he is really a matured taste, a taste that grows. Shakespeare is really for all ages, for all the seven ages of man. I was fond of Shakespeare when I crept unwillingly to school, and I am fond of him now when I can be more vividly described as a lean and slippered pantaloon.[3] And I do not mean that as a child I was fond of his romantic tales merely; I was fond of his poetry, especially when it was entirely unintelligible. The open and rolling rhythm seemed to be speaking plainly even when I could not comprehend it. The huge heraldic imagery of red and gold was obvious, though I could not take it in. Members of my family who collect coincidences have assured me that I was small enough to run along the street and fall on my nose in the very act of saying the lines:

> Do not for ever with thy veilèd lids
> Seek for thy noble father in the dust.[4]

Lines like

> Revisit'st thus the glimpses of the moon,[5]

or like

> Still climbing trees in the Hesperides[6]

were not only good poetry, they were good children's pictures like the cow who jumped over the moon, or the number of red herrings that grow in a wood.

But Milton at his best is absolutely nothing to childhood. I do not mean that children cannot enjoy Milton; children can enjoy the Post Office directory. That is the kingdom of heaven; to enjoy things without understanding them. But I say that children cannot enjoy the Miltonism of Milton; the thing that no one but Milton can do. A boy does not appreciate that wonderful and controlled style, which, like a well-managed war-horse, even capers and caracoles rather by restraint than impetus. A boy does not feel the lift of those great lines, as of a great eagle leaving the nest,

> That with no middle flight presumes to soar
> Above the Aonian mount.[7]

I think a great part of the trouble which the ordinary mind has in appreciating Milton (or, rather, Milton in pleasing the ordinary mind, for please remember that the popular mind is much more important than Milton) lies in the mistake of always describing him as a pure and classical writer. Really he was a highly complex and in some ways too modern writer. The perfectly classical can be understood by anybody. No charwoman would say that the tale of Ulysses coming back in rags to the woman who had been faithful to him was not a touching tale. No dog fancier in the street would be indifferent to the death of Argus.[8] No man in the street could ever say upon his conscience that the Venus of Milo was not a fine woman.[9]

It is the secondary and distorted art which really and suddenly loses the sympathies of the people. The charwoman would fail in seeing the peculiar pathos of Mr. Robert Elsmere,[10] who wanted to be a curate and also an agnostic. The dog fancier would be justly indifferent to the rhetoric of the numerous modern animal lovers who could not look after a dog for a day. And the man in the street will not admit that the women of Aubrey Beardsley are fine women,[11] because they are not. The tastes of the man in the street are classical.

And if Milton were really as straightforward as Homer or the Elgin Marbles he would be, in practice, uproariously popular. The real reason that he cannot make his glory quite as broad as it is undoubtedly deep and high is that there was in him something of the modern individualist, something of the social schismatic. He had that weird and wicked ambition of the modern artist; he wanted 'to think for himself'. But Dante and Dickens wanted to think for other people also.

Milton stands between the very social society in which Dante lived and the very social society which Dickens always desired and occasionally experienced, with that fastidious isolation which belongs to art in our time and belonged to religion in his time. He is the seventeenth-century individualist. He is the perfect Calvinist; the man alone with his God. He is also the perfect artist; the man alone with his art.[12] No man, perhaps, has ever had such power over his art since the arts of humanity were made. And yet there is something that makes one turn to the firesides of the 'Pickwick Papers,' and even to the fires of the Purgatorio.

Notes

1. *AFTER THE MILTON CELEBRATION*: Reprinted as 'The Taste for Milton,' *HA*, pp. 75–7, commencing at 'Of all poets Milton is the one whom it is the most difficult to praise with real delicacy and sincerity of definition'. The final sentence of the first paragraph is omitted.
2. *Milton celebration ... done with*: The tercentenary of Milton's birth was on 9 December. The celebrations were led by the British Academy and events were planned to take place at the Academy's home, Burlington House, in the City of London, and at various gatherings throughout the capital. There was also an exhibition of Milton's work at the British Museum: 'The Milton Tercentenary', *The Times*, 7 December 1908, p. 10a.
3. *lean and slippered pantaloon*: see Shakespeare, *As You Like It*, II.vii.
4. *Do not for ever ... dust*: Hamlet, I.ii.
5. *Revisit'st ... of the moon*: Hamlet, I.iv.
6. *Still climbing ... Hesperides*: Love's *Labours Lost*, IV.iii.
7. *That with no middle flight ... Aonian mount*: Milton, *Paradise Lost*, book 1, ll.13–15.
8. *death of Argus*: see Homer, *Odyssey*, book 17.
9. *Venus of Milo ... fine woman*: i.e. the famous 'armless' statue of Venus (probably) by Alexandros of Antioch (fl. 80 BC) now in the Louvre, Paris.
10. *Mr. Robert Elsmere*: Robert Elsmere is the eponymous hero of the novel by Mary Augusta Ward (1851–1920), published in 1888. Robert Elsmere is a clergyman who, under the influence of the Oxford Philosopher T. H. Green, loses his faith, despite the continuing orthodoxy of his wife. Unable to continue his work in the Anglican Church, he dedicates his life to social service and secular preaching.
11. *The women of Aubrey Beardsley are fine women*: see 'The Optimism of Byron', *DN*, 2 December 1901, Volume 1, p. 286, n. 3 above.
12. *He is the seventeenth-century individualist ... alone with his art*: On Chesterton's view of the isolation of Milton's art, see 'The Influence of Dogmatism', *DN*, 25 June 1904, Volume 2, p. 250, n. 8 above.

December 26, 1908.

THE CHRISTMAS BOXES.

If the link of tradition should be lost in modern life, I suppose many future philosophers and historians will be mystified as to what we meant by Boxing Day. I am not sure that we even know ourselves; and it is impossible to predict what they will make out of it. Perhaps the Socialists will say that it was originally Baxing Day, a day on which one endeavoured, as far as possible, to go on like Mr. Belfort Bax.[1] Perhaps the Liberals will still retain the legend that it was called Buxing Day because of the extraordinary burdens it threw on the department of Mr. Buxton.[2] But even for us it is not at all clear what is the exact reason for calling the day after Christmas Boxing Day; it is certainly not a day on which the average sensual man finds himself physically inclined for boxing. That it has some relation to Christmas boxes is sufficiently evident; but even this does not explain the whole situation. First of all it does not explain why the day after Christmas should be named after Christmas presents; in the present condition of the post, if we began to pack up our Christmas presents on Boxing Day, we should probably be well advised if we made them Easter eggs. And it does not explain the more searching and spiritual question of why Christmas presents should be called boxes at all.

****

On both of these subjects I obtained a certain light in a conversation with a friend of mine which took place a few days before Christmas. He is an artistic bookbinder by trade, and lives in one of those long streets full of gaunt and yet garish villas which lie on the other side of Clapham Common. In all our modern industrial development there is the note of a dehumanised monstrosity; our millionaires and our mendicants are like the stunted dwarfs and toppling giants in a fair. We are a museum of freaks with no spectators; and this unnatural spirit breaks out even in our architecture. Our houses are either giant houses like the flats of New York or dwarf houses like the villas of Brixton. That there is a normal human size for a family house has been entirely forgotten. But these little houses beyond Clapham Common carried yet a step further the parallel of Barnum freaks; for they were semi-detached villas. They were built in the revolting image of the Siamese twins.[3] The man who lived in such a modern house, or rather half-house, was not isolated, like a brave man, in his family fortress; nor was he welded into a manly and military community like man in a monastery or a barracks. He was linked by a link of brick, as loathsome as the Siamese link of flesh, to one other accidental man, generally to a man whom he disliked.

All such gloomy considerations as these were indeed poured out to me by the artistic bookbinder himself, who had no religion in particular, and was therefore subject to depression, especially just before Christmas. We were engaged in tying up Christmas parcels and presents for all his outlying nephews and nieces, and rows of rectangular objects covered with brown paper and string lay ranged like a regiment in front of us.

'How on earth do you expect us', said my friend bitterly, 'to care about your Christmas pudding and your Christmas piety. Whether the thing ever was genuine or only a maudlin fictitious memory in sulky old feudalists like Walter Scott, whether or no there was ever a happy reality, it is plain enough that it is not a reality now. Compare the Christmas that is preached to us with the meaningless 25th of December that is forced on us. You offer the Yule Log to people who are forced for economy to have asbestos stoves. You praise plum pudding to people whose work has not left them the digestion for it even if their wages had left them the money. Oh! I'm not talking about the poor, we are not poor in this street. If we were we should have a jollier time. But we should be poor if we tried to have any one of the things that have ever given a day's pure pleasure to Christian or to Pagan men'.

I said nothing, but tightened string round a last of five cardboard boxes of the same size that stood covered with brown paper in a row on the table before me. As I twisted the last knot I suddenly saw as in a kind of vision the meaning of the word Christmas box. I thought in how many houses, even of that little hurried civilization my friend was fiercely denouncing, the mere sight of those square sealed or string[-]secured brown parcels would make children, whose anticipations were already celestial, find a heaven above heaven. That very compactness, that very concealment, were among the primary elements of the ecstasy. Even the pleasure of playing with a toy is less than the pleasure of unpacking it. To Santa Claus, as of all the worldly deities of mankind, the great word could be said 'Verily thou art a god that hidest thyself'.[4] That was the sufficient explanation; a Christmas present is called a Christmas box because the box is so much more important than the present.

****

My friend the artistic bookbinder was continuing his acrid but not irrational soliloquy. 'Look at the street we live in. Look at the ridiculous naked railings, a mere iron row of spikes running in front of us – as if anyone could want to get into our houses. Look at the houses themselves, which stand two and two, and two and two all the way down for half a mile. These semi-detached villas are worse than monotony. They are monotony repeating itself. Great heavens! Is humanity a humdrum output of twins?'

I was still looking at the row of brown paper cubes, and my eye was for some reason hypnotised with them. Most of them I knew contained mechanical toys, coloured and complex bricks, Japanese villages, and the like; some, I fear, contained books.

'Look at the houses', he went on savagely, 'or rather don't look at them. Or rather look at them, but don't call them houses. Those are not houses as one talks of a man's house in any human prose or poetry. Those are not houses; those are hutches; those are boxes – '

'Yes; now I understand', I cried, startled into speech. 'Yes, the houses are boxes. They are Christmas boxes'.

'What do you mean?' he asked.

'Look at that row of square brown houses in the street', I said. 'Are they an inch squarer or a shade browner or a bit more ugly than that row of brown boxes? And yet how that row of boxes will madden the children with a merriment and curiosity almost beyond that of this earth. And why? Because there is inside them some jumping metal monkey, or some pig that stands on his head again and again. Suppose there were inside those boxes a jumping stockbroker, whose movements, however offensive, were not mechanical – a pig who might do other things beside stand on his head?'

'What on earth are you up to?' he asked.

'I am going outside', I answered. 'I am going along the streets to unpack all my Christmas presents in all the streets. And I am going to find the monkey inside'.

Notes
1. *Mr. Belfort Bax*: Ernest Belfort Bax (1854–1926), was a Marxist theoretician and activist. Influenced by German thinkers, Bax sought to elaborate on the ethical, religious and metaphysical aspects of socialism after Marx's death. In 1884, he and William Morris were instrumental in establishing the Socialist League as a breakaway organization from Hyndman's Social Democratic Federation, jointly editing its organ, *The Commonwealth* with Morris. He rejoined the SDF in 1889, editing its journal, *Justice*. He remained at war with Christianity and also with the institutions and conventions of bourgeois society throughout his life. His abstract and laboured style denied him popular support. His books include *The Religion of Socialism* (1885) (S. Pierson, *ODNB*).

2. *Mr. Buxton*: Sydney Charles Buxton (1853–1934), was an English Liberal politician; he became Viscount Buxton in 1914 and Earl Buxton in 1920. At the time of this article he was Postmaster General.
3. *the Siamese Twins*: The reference here is to *the* Siamese twins because Chesterton is thinking specifically of Chang and Eng Bunker, the original 'Siamese Twins' whose birth in 1811 was the first properly recorded instance of conjoined twins. They both died in 1874. Chesterton's use of the word 'revolting' and, later in the paragraph, 'loathsome' in relation to these unfortunate people is uncharacteristic of him.
4. *'Verily ... hidest thyself'*: Isaiah 45:15.

December 30, 1908.

A BOOK OF THE DAY.

The Democracy of Dickens.[1]

'Charles Dickens: The Apostle of the People'. By Edwin Pugh. New Age Press. 5s. net.

When a thing is as thoroughly great as the work of Dickens we must be content to admire it without agreeing about it. It is right that there should be as many Dickenses as there are Dickensians. To take but one instance of the wide octave stretched by the hand of that master: Dickens is one of the few things Mr. Bernard Shaw warmly admires. And yet Dickens is also the idol and emblem of all the things of the people Mr. Shaw most hates and despises: the domestic sentimentalists, the old playgoers, the lovers of brandy and turkey and all the conventions of conviviality. So arresting is the shrewdness, the vitality and what may be called the comic clairvoyance of Dickens, that Mr. Shaw can even forgive him his sympathy with popular happiness. And at the same time the port winey old English gentleman is so melted by Dickens' geniality and good-feeling that he forgives him for having been a keen critic and a public spirited citizen. This is real greatness; to be adored by antagonistic people for inconsistent reasons.

Books about Dickens must follow this rather wild plan. Mr. Swinburne, who prefers the Elizabethan energy to everything, has maintained admirably the general proposition that Dickens is a volcano, and not an extinct volcano.[2] Mr. George Gissing made a much needed plea for Dickens as a realist, indicating his thousand tones and touches of cool observation and intimate social irony.[3] Mr. Edwin Pugh[4] is not therefore to be blamed if he devotes a book to only one aspect of Dickens, especially if, unlike Gissing and the others, he avows his restriction on the title page. Mr. Pugh's book is called 'Charles Dickens: The Apostle of the People'. It is designed to show that Dickens believed in political democracy, and would have believed in Socialism if he had heard of it, or at least understood it. The first proposition cannot be doubted. The second cannot be proved, but together they make up the material of an able and attractive book; a book which has at least the one thing that is wanted in books just now, the note of the trumpet, the note of dogma and challenge.

Healthy Prejudices.

Mr. Pugh, one of the new Socialists, does really possess one of the virtues of the old Radicals like Dickens, a virtue which it is very hard to define exactly because it is so definite, as definite as the sense of smell. It is not enough to call it the fighting spirit; it is an inch or two nearer to call it the instinct for fair fight. Roughly, it consists of two qualities: holding on in defiance of the omens, and knowing by instinct where one's real enemy is. It is that instinct which leads one to distrust Mr. Rockefeller's ideals of purity and poverty.[5] It is that instinct which saved some of us from being crushed by the cataract of eulogies on Kipling[6] and Cecil Rhodes.[7] Its enemies are always called 'Prejudice'.

Of this honourable pugnacity Mr. Pugh's book is full. He has a thoroughly healthy prejudice; a prejudice on the side of the poor. His instincts, which are chivalrous instincts, tell him at once that the chances are a hundred to one that the poor man's sins have been overstated and the rich man's sins concealed. All clear-sighted souls, from the time of Christ, have seen that in spiritual matters there ought to be one law for the rich and another for the poor. Spiritually, the rich are suspect: there is a prima facie case against them. The man who may have been a robber must show himself a saint. Mr. Pugh's book is full of this feeling, and, therefore, plenty of people will say that it is full of prejudice. Plenty of people will say, and have some justification in saying, that it is full of crude and melodramatic appeals to the gallery. As Mr. Pugh and I should agree that the gallery is the most important part of the theatre this will not disturb us. Mr. Pugh says that for him the word Gentleman 'smacks of all abominations'. He suggests, with most sound and crushing truth, that the poor are much more polite and ceremonial than the rich. For urging that fact alone I could forgive him all his errors.

Anti-Pickwick.

And now comes the queer and mysterious fact about Mr. Pugh. He has been heartily and humanly right about all the bitter or angry or pathetic side of democracy; and then suddenly he goes quite wrong about all the side of democracy that is hearty and human. He does not like Pickwick. He complains of its blatant objectivity – which means that Mr. Pickwick looked funny when he ran after his hat. He complains of its 'almost entire lack of spirituality', which means that Pickwick was only a good man in the sight of God, and did not want to 'aspire' like an egotistical theosophist. He condemns its 'flippant, light-hearted disregard of vital issues'; as if the perpetuation of such Englishmen as Pickwick and Sam Weller were not now the only vital issue in England. As for his other accusation against Pickwick, 'the gay, cynical carelessness of its pervading tone', it makes me want to talk to Mr. Pugh like a father, if not like a Dutch uncle. Let me assure him, with all-shattering emphasis, that no cynic from Creation to Judgement has been, or can be, gay. Pickwick and Sam Weller were gay and careless because they were good men: Mr. Pugh, with all his virtues, must toil to attain the Pickwick standard: he must take care that he also may at last be equally careless.

The only thing that irritates in Mr. Pugh's book is this irritation of his against the spirit of Pickwick, the spirit of the old Dickens. One may feel the same suspicion of Mr. Pugh's refinement which Mr. Pugh justly feels of the word 'gentleman'. I do not mean to write a rude or 'slating' review; or else I should, in so many words, call Mr. Pugh a gentleman. He offers Dickens as 'The Apostle of the People', and yet all the parts of Dickens he dislikes are the popular parts. All those elements that disgust Mr. Pugh, the clowning and caricature, the preposterous figures, and the practical jokes, Mr. Pickwick getting into the wheelbarrow and Tony Weller hardly getting into his waistcoat – all this is simply the life and laughter of the actual English people. One has only to go down the Battersea Park-road on a Saturday night to hear it. Mr. Pugh, who is so largely right in his book, is at least supremely right in his title. Dickens was the apostle of the people – especially on the points upon which Mr. Pugh disagrees with him.

Notes
1. *The Democracy of Dickens*: Reprinted in *CR*, 17:2 (May 1991), pp. 151–3.
2. *Mr. Swinburne ... extinct volcano*: Swinburne, 'Charles Dickens', *Quarterly Review*, 196 (1902).
3. *Mr. George Gissing ... social irony*: See 'An Edition of Dumas', *DN*, 2 January 1907, Volume 4, p. 131, n. 5 above.
4. *Mr. Edwin Pugh*: Edwin William Pugh (1874–1930), was a novelist, short story writer and critic. Born into a theatrical family in London, Pugh was employed as a clerk in a solicitor's office for eight years before becoming a writer. He became part of the 'Cockney school of writers' that included William Pett Ridge (see 'The Beauty of Noise', *DN*, 18 August 1906, Volume 4, p. 40, n. 5 above) and Arthur Morrison (see 'The Green Eye of Goona, *DN*, 23 September 1904, Volume 2, pp. 297–300 above). However, it has been claimed that his portrait of East End life was over-sentimental; unlike Morrison, it seems, he ignored its darker side. He also wrote for periodicals and magazines, including the *New Age*, where he set forth his socialist views in 1907 and 1908. His works include his first collection of short stories, *A Street in Suburbia* (1895), and his first novels *The Man of Straw* (1896) and *Drum: A Cockney Boy* (1898) (D. Atkinson, *ODNB*).

5. *Mr. Rockefeller's ideals of purity and poverty*: For John Davison Rockefeller, see 'The Fault of the System', *DN*, 18 January 1908, p. 12, n. 3 above.
6. *Kipling*: Rudyard Kipling; see 'A Kipling Reader', *DN*, 21 February 1901, Volume 1, p. 31, n. 3 above.
7. *Cataract of eulogies ... Cecil Rhodes*: for the provisions of Rhodes's will that stimulated the 'cataract of eulogies', see 'The Rich Man', *DN*, 21 July 1906, Volume 4, pp. 12–13, n. 6 above.

January 2, 1909.

THE SACRED SUSPICION.

We were all born upon a battlefield. That is, we were all born in a beautiful but a bewildering place. If one could imagine that a single conflict could go on for so long that babies were brought forth during the progress of it, it is obvious that those babies would find much in the military movements to attract or to seduce them; that long before they learnt anything of the country or the quarrel they would be pleased to see the wind waving the banners like wings of scarlet or the light turned to crooked lightning upon burnished breastplate or helmet.

So it is with us all in this field of spiritual warfare on which we were born. We have all made mistakes; we have all been misled by the colours of some uniform or the shape of some flag. We have fought for accidents against essentials; we have supported a colour against a creed. Because we were Red Republicans we have helped the redcoats to destroy the republics. Because we wanted justice to some black man we have supported everything that was blackest, from the Black Brunswickers of the Holy Alliance[1] to the Black Hundred of the Russian reaction.[2] Associations quite as accidental and absurd as these fanciful colours have led many a good Liberal to support the South African War or the indeterminate sentence[3] or the ceaseless misgovernment of Ireland. The tyrants of South Africa called themselves Progressives, and millions of Englishmen immediately offered to progress along with them; and they did progress until they were stopped, like Lord Methuen,[4] and had to fall back, like Consols.[5] The tyrants of Ireland said that they represented the freer and more civilized race in Ireland; and many Englishmen actually believed them. The tyrants in our present prisons and workhouses say that they are acting upon the latest scientific and humanitarian principles, and apparently we believe them also, in spite of the evidence of almost every human being who has been in their hands. I suppose we are waiting for some tyrants who will call themselves tyrants.

****

Indeed, the strongest instance of all this intellectual confusion arising out of names and badges is the case of English confidence in the constabulary. We are the only nation which has a special and almost supernatural confidence in the mere machinery of its government. You might say that the Dutch and the Italians have not much in common; but they have something in common; they distrust the police. You might say that the Americans are not very like the Russians; but the Americans are like the Russians in distrusting their police. The only country where the police are perpetually protected and flattered is the only country where one wealthy class still almost completely controls the Government. For an official in an oligarchy will not directly insult a member or potential member of that oligarchy. Even an official is not such a fool as that.

Now, when one says that policemen often lie, often shirk, often do detestable injustice, it is always offered as a primary answer that the accuser is attacking the police. If it were so, I should care little; we shall have to attack things stronger than police if we are to make anything of this poor old country of ours. But surely even the charge of attacking the police is absurd. If I say that a greengrocer, being a man, may be tempted to cheat, I am not accused of being a bitter enemy of all greengrocers. If I say that a hairdresser may, like any other man, be heartless to his wife or his apprentices, I am not supposed to assert that all hairdressers have no heart. The magisterial and political system of this country is only accused of being on the ordinary level of all things worked by human hands; that it is not substantially better than Tammany Hall[6] or the House of Commons. We do not accuse the police of being inhuman. We accuse them of being human. We say that in that trade, as in every other, there are the ordinary temptations to tyranny, or weakness, or corruption. But the whole English political world, which merely means all the wealthy people in England, shakes and shudders to its foundation at the mere suggestion that the police are human at all. And if this is so with the policeman, who, after all, is a plain man and drops his h's, it is much more so in the case of the great magistracy, which models all England in accordance with its own capricious mind.

****

The other day a wealthy woman was let off, not only without punishment, but without exposure. Her name was suppressed by the magistrate; a thing that would not be done for any ordinary man unjustly accused of any extraordinary crime.[7] If the kindest man in Battersea were accused of torturing children, if the bravest man in the British Army were accused of running away from a cow, his name would appear along with his acquittal. In this case the magistrate was satisfied with the assertion that the victim was suffering from anaemia. Anaemia does not seem to be the sort of malady that would make anyone leap up to commit acts of pillage. I think my own family would be startled if I sprang up at the dinner table, clutched my throat for an instant, and then crying in a dreadful voice 'Anaemia!' rushed out of the room, careered round the neighbourhood, and stole seven diaries and sixteen umbrellas.

Just about the time that I heard this astonishing story of how bloodlessness leads people first to take the property that is not their own, and then to hide the surname that is, I also heard of a case in Battersea, in which a poor fellow, caught out in a first theft which was quite unsuccessful, was solemnly sworn to by the police as a hardened and habitual criminal. I knew the contrary to be the case; as I know that I wear boots. But what can one do? The thing is always going on and will always go on; until we rediscover the meaning of the word tyrant.

But one can at least distrust this mere mesmerism by terms and titles. We can look at men's faces instead of looking at their uniforms. We can decide for ourselves whether the visage of the criminal is a shade more or a shade less stupid and brutal than that of the judge who condemns him. If a magistrate accepts anaemia as an excuse for theft, we can at least decide, not only that he does not understand the word anaemia, but also that he does not understand the word magistrate.

Notes
1. *Black Brunswickers of the Holy Alliance*: The Black Brunswickers was a volunteer force raised and commanded by Frederick William, Duke of Brunswick-Wolfenbüttel (1771–1815) to fight in the Napoleonic Wars. The name comes from their black uniform. Duke Frederick William was killed at the Battle of Quatre Bras on 16 June 1815.
2. *Black Hundred of the Russian Reaction*: The Black Hundred (more usually called The Black Hundreds) was a counter-revolutionary organization that supported the Tsarist regime against the revolutionary movement in Russia in the early twentieth century.
3. *the indeterminate sentence*: See 'A Theory of Tyrants', *DN*, 13 June 1908, p. 89, n. 8 above.
4. *Lord Methuen*: Paul Sanford, third Baron Methuen; see 'The Toy Theatre', *DN*, 2 February 1907, Volume 4, p. 150, n. 2 above.
5. *Consols*: see 'The Temple of Everything', *DN*, 24 March 1903, Volume 2, p. 39, n. 3 above.
6. *Tammany Hall*: Tammany Hall, also called the Society of St Tammany, the Sons of St Tammany or the Columbian Order, was founded in 1786, originally as a patriotic and charitable organization. From the 1790s to the 1960s it was, in effect, the political machine of the Democratic Party in New York City. From the middle of the nineteenth century Tammany Hall became synonymous with dubious and corrupt political practices.
7. *The other day ... extraordinary crime*: On 30 December, *The Times* reported that a charge of theft had been brought against a female student who had been forced to give up her studies due to a bad form of anaemia. She pleaded guilty to stealing diaries and two umbrellas from the Army and Navy Stores on 22 September. Although she had the

means of payment with her and was of a highly respectable family, she succumbed to what her counsel described as a 'sudden temptation'. Although the magistrate admitted that it was difficult to distinguish her case from others, he was inclined to be lenient: p. 2d.

January 9, 1909.

ON PERSONALITIES.

It is an interesting question why the word 'personal' in our language should commonly mean something unpleasantly personal. If a man has uttered 'personalities' it does not merely mean personalia. If, when I had delivered some lecture or other, the whole audience cried in one deafening chorus, 'The blaze of Mr. Chesterton's wit is only excelled by the beauty of his countenance and the athletic grace of his form', that would be a distinctly personal criticism. But I do not think it would be fair if it were reported in the newspapers merely by the statement 'The audience indulged in some very personal remarks about the lecturer'. A man may be kicked out for being a libeller or for being a lover; but both libeller and lover are equally personal. I should be personal if I said of Mr. Balfour that he was loose and lounging; but it would be equally personal to say that he is tall and elegant. This curious English use of the word 'personality' puts between our fingers a thread that will lead ultimately to the heart of that labyrinth, the modern Government of England.

****

There are only two theories of government, personal government and impersonal government. A republican is merely a man who wants England to be governed by England. A royalist is simply a man would rather take his chance with one Englishman; there are strong arguments on both sides. One of the arguments against monarchy is that the one Englishman often happens not to be an Englishman, and sometimes happens not to be a man. One of the arguments against democracy is that it is so hard for it to remain democratic; it tends to get into the hands of persons who are a great deal too impersonal, doctors and inspectors, and well-known authorities, and God knows what.

But I for one believe in democracy for five hundred reasons, of which this is one (I think it is No. 57), that when all is said and done, the most healthy and vigorous sense of personality exists under impersonal, that is to say, republican government. France and America are utterly different; and they differ from England in different ways, and resemble her in different ways. France and England are ancient and chivalric. France and America are Protectionist. England and America are Protestant.

But there is one thing common between the old republic of permanent peasants and the new republic of very temporary millionaires. The one thing common is the beautiful and satisfying fact that in both republics politics are furiously personal. The one splendid thing to be said for America is that though the Americans did produce Rockefeller they do at least calumniate him. The attacks on him are vast and violent, and therefore bear some relation to his own vast and violent spoliations. We have many such men in England who are never attacked at all.

****

Similarly, the great glory of the French Republic is exactly that which most of its English defenders definitely repudiate and dislike. It is the fact that in the French Republic a President is not treated with sleek and snobbish tenderness like a mere King; but is regarded as a fighting citizen and the leader of the system, and as such is exposed to the personal anger of the fanatics.

That, then, is one reason why I believe in democratic or impersonal government; because under impersonal government you have an insistence on personalities. Under personal government you have the suppression of personalities; we live under personal oligarchical government; and therefore, we have an indefensible amount of impersonality and namelessness in all the branches of our working system.

That is where the curious paradox comes in. We worship names; we are governed by names; and for that reason we suppress names in a police court.[1]

****

There is considerable danger that the recent and righteous irritation against certain decisions by police magistrates in the matter of the suppression of names[2] should be turned into a mere attack on those particular magistrates; whereas it ought to be useful in opening our eyes to the open indecency of the whole system of oligarchy.

As a matter of mere emotion I sympathise with the magistrates; I think I know exactly how they feel. The magistrate allowed the lady to plead anaemia as a reason for anonymity. It sounds odd; but I am sure I understand the most secret and sacred feelings of that magistrate. He saw in front of him the kind of woman whom he often met and whom he knew to be capable of nervous extravagances and plunges of passion. His own aunt, his own sister, his own grandmother, may have had the nervous ecstasies and agonies which sometimes result in going wrong.

Or, let me take an easier case from a recent issue of 'The Morning Leader' which reports how four country gentlemen managed to get fined for being drunk and disorderly without being accused or even mentioned by name.[3] Here again my spirit, with ruthless sympathy, steals its way into the inmost heart of the J.P.'s. The magistrate said to himself, 'Why, my boy Jack got drunk six times at Oxford; I was drunk myself once or twice when I was there. And shall I blast before all England people who look just like my son, for acting just like my son?'

Thus we see that the very ecstasy of personality leads to impersonality; the importance of names leads to the suppression of names. There are a great many excuses for this view; in fact, there is really only one objection to it.

The only objection to it is that there is unfortunately such a thing as the English people. If the English lords and ladies were living on a small island all by themselves I am not sure that their casual and kindly method, the method of remembering faces and forgetting names, might not be a tactful and genial solution. But the objection is this: Only once a month does a magistrate see anyone even resembling himself in the dock; only once a year, perhaps does he see anyone wearing his own class clothes and talking with own class voice. And then he lets him off.

He does not do this because he is a coward or a snob; he is often quite brave and not specially snobbish. He does it because for the first time in his whole professional career he has a case in front of him which he understands. He knows nothing about the motives of ordinary burglary; he never has known anything about them. He has heard that burglars break into houses, as he has heard that savages boil missionaries; he can no more conceive himself as a burglar than as a cannibal. But when he sees a lady or gentleman before him, he is startled with an inspired and unexpected feeling of knowing his business. This feeling of suddenly knowing his business naturally throws him for a moment off his balance. For years past he has been dealing with mortal flesh and immortal souls as if they were so much cheese or mutton, carting them off to prison by the ton, and never thinking further about it. Then suddenly he sees someone who might be his own uncle, and then he sees everything else. He sees the whole hideous explosion of public punishment; he sees the cold compassion of friends, he sees the sneers of housemaids. In short, he sees for the first time what he is doing. But this which may be the salvation of him is the destruction of English government. We may at least raise the question – might it not be well to have the crimes of the poor judged by somebody who knows something of the poor, of their torturing temptations, and their terrible self-respect? But if we had that we should certainly have a violent revolution.

Notes
1. *we suppress names in a police court*: See 'The Sacred Suspicion', *DN*, 2 January 1909, pp. 242–3, n. 7 above.
2. *recent and righteous irritation ... names*: not identified.
3. *a recent issue of 'The Morning Leader' ... mentioned by name*: not identified.

January 16, 1909.

THE THREE TEMPLES.[1]

The quaint old folk-tale which I have to tell was not told me by my old dusky nurse in the West Indies; it is not still repeated by the old wives in Westmoreland [sic], though no doubt it will be on Saturday when the Northern edition of this newspaper appears. The legend is but little known; in fact, it is not known at all because I have not quite made it up yet. The only thing I am sure about in connection with it is its rich and abysmal moral significance and the truth with which it traces the three stages through which Art commonly or at least often passes.

Let me hasten to affirm with energy that I do not say 'must pass' or 'necessarily passes'. No more poisonous trash has been talked in our time than that which represents the life of a nation as just like the life of an animal, with inevitable early vigour, incurable decay, and fixed day of death.[2] You might just as well say that a nation has horns or a tail. It is a stupid material metaphor – which does not apply. A society can be sluggish in its ninth year, and buck up in its nineteenth or its nineteenth hundred; it depends on the will of its living citizens. There are pseudo-sociologists who will gravely explain to you that Australia came of age at some particular time, or that France must die at some other time. I wonder they do not explain at what time Australia lost her first teeth. I shall not be surprised if they state at what time France went bald.

To talk like this is simply to be the dupe of an animal figure of speech; in fact, as a nation always consists of so many million new babies, it always consists of so many million potential decadents or potential reformers. I do not mean therefore that the art of a great people must pass through these stages of growth and zenith and collapse; but I mean that it often has and it always may. The first stage is an impulse which is often accepted; the second is a discovery that is often made; the third is a disaster which is not always avoided. We can refuse any of the stages; but unless we definitely exert our will we generally pass through them.

But let us get back to the fairy tale, for I know no other way of expressing the idea.[a]

I.

Once upon a time there lived upon an island a merry and innocent people, mostly shepherds and tillers of the earth. They were republicans, like all primitive and simple souls; they talked over their affairs under a tree, and the nearest approach they had to a personal ruler was a sort of priest or white witch who said their prayers for them. They worshipped the sun, not idolatrously, but as the golden crown of the god whom all such infants see almost as plainly as the sun.

Now this priest was told by his people to build a great tower, pointing to the sky in salutation of the Sun-god; and he pondered long and heavily before he picked his materials. For he was resolved to use nothing that was not almost as clear and exquisite as sunshine itself; he would use nothing that was not washed as white as the rain can wash the heavens, nothing that did not sparkle as spotlessly as that crown of God. He would have nothing grotesque or obscure; he would not have even anything emphatic or even anything mysterious. He would have all the arches as light as laughter and as candid as logic. He built the temple in three concentric courts, which were cooler and more exquisite in substance each than the other. For the outer wall was a hedge of white lilies, ranked so thick that a green stalk was hardly to be seen; and the wall within that was of crystal, which smashed the sun into a million stars. And the wall within that, which was the tower itself, was a tower of pure water, forced up in an everlasting fountain; and upon the very tip and crest of that foaming spire was one big and blazing diamond, which the water tossed up eternally and caught again as a child catches a ball.

'Now', said the Priest, 'I have made a tower which is a little worthy of the sun'.

II.

But about this time the island was caught in a swarm of pirates; and the shepherds had to turn themselves into rude warriors and seamen; and at first they were utterly broken down in blood and shame; and the pirates might have taken the jewel flung up for ever from their sacred fount. And then, after years of horror and humiliation, they gained a little and began to conquer because they did not mind defeat. And the pride of the pirates went sick within them after a few unexpected foils; and at last the invasion rolled back into the empty seas and the island was delivered. And for some reason after this men began to talk quite differently about the temple and the sun. Some indeed, said, 'You must not touch the temple; it is classical; it is perfect; since it admits no imperfections'. But the others answered, 'In that it differs from the sun, that shines on the evil and the good and on mud and monsters everywhere. This temple is of the noon; it is made of white marble clouds and sapphire sky. But the sun is not always of the noon. The sun dies daily; every night he is crucified in blood and fire'.

Now the priest had taught and fought through all the war, and his hair had grown white, but his eyes had grown young. And he said, 'I was wrong and they are right. The sun, the symbol of our father, gives life to all those earthly things that are full of ugliness and energy. All the exaggerations are right; if they exaggerate the right thing. Let us point to heaven with tusks and horns and fins and trunks and tails so long as they all point to heaven. The ugly animals praise God as much as the beautiful. The frog's eyes stand out of his head because he is staring at heaven. The giraffe's neck is long because he is stretching towards heaven. The donkey has ears to hear – let him hear'.[3]

And under the new inspiration they planned a gorgeous cathedral in the Gothic manner, with all the animals of the earth crawling over it, and all the possible ugly things making up one common beauty, because they all appealed to the god. The columns of the temple were carved like the necks of giraffes, the dome was like an ugly tortoise; and the highest pinnacle was a monkey standing on his head with his tail pointing at the sun. And yet the whole was beautiful, because it was lifted up in one living and religious gesture as a man lifts his hands in prayer.

III.

But this great plan was never properly completed. The people had brought up on great wagons the heavy tortoise roof and the huge necks of stone, and all the thousand and one oddities that made up that unity, the owls and the efts and the crocodiles and the kangaroos, which hideous by themselves might have been magnificent if reared in one definite proportion and dedicated to the sun. For this was Gothic, this was romantic, this was Christian art; this was the whole advance of Shakespeare upon Sophocles. And that symbol which was to crown it all, the ape upside down, was really Christian; for Man is the ape upside down.

But the rich, who had grown riotous in the long peace, obstructed the thing, and in some squabble a stone struck the priest on the head and he lost his memory. He saw piled in front of him frogs and elephants, monkeys and giraffes, toadstools and sharks, all the ugly things of the universe which he had collected to do honour to God. But he forgot why he had collected them. He could not remember the design or the object. He piled them all wildly into one heap fifty feet high; and when he had done it all the rich and influential went into a passion of applause and cried, 'This is real art! This is realism! This is things as they really are!'[a]

248–9a   'The quaint old folk-tale ... expressing the idea.] In *AD* is replaced by the following:

Alone at some distance from the wasting walls of a disused abbey I found half sunken in the grass the grey and goggle-eyed visage of one of those graven monsters that made the ornamental water-spouts in the cathedrals of the Middle Ages. It lay there, scoured by ancient rains or striped by recent fungus, but still looking like the head of some huge dragon slain by a primeval hero. And as I looked at it, I thought of the meaning of the grotesque, and passed into some symbolic reverie of the three great stages of art.

250a   ... things as they really are!] In *AD* is followed by two additional paragraphs:

That, I fancy, is the only true origin of Realism. Realism is simply Romanticism that has lost its reason. This is so not merely in the sense of insanity but of suicide. It has lost its reason; that is its reason for existing. The old Greeks summoned godlike things to worship their god. The mediaeval Christians summoned all things to worship theirs, dwarfs and pelicans, monkeys and madmen. The modern realists summon all these million creatures to worship their god; and then have no god for them to worship. Paganism was in art a pure beauty; that was the dawn. Christianity was a beauty created by controlling a million monsters of ugliness; and that in my belief was the zenith and the noon. Modern art and science practically mean having the million monsters and being unable to control them; and I will venture to call that the disruption and the decay. The finest lengths of the Elgin marbles consist of splendid horses going to the temple of a virgin. Christianity, with its gargoyles and grotesques, really amounted to saying this: that a donkey could go before all the heroes of the world when it was really going to the temple. Romance means a holy donkey going to the temple. Realism means a lost donkey going nowhere.

The fragments of futile journalism or fleeting impression which are here collected are very like the wrecks and riven blocks that were piled in a heap round my imaginary priest of the sun. They are very like that grey and gaping head of stone that I found overgrown with the grass. Yet I will venture to make even of these trivial fragments the high boast that I am a mediaevalist and not a modern. That is, I really have a notion of why I have collected all the nonsensical things there are. I have not the patience nor perhaps the constructive intelligence to state the connecting link between all these chaotic papers. But it could be stated. This row of shapeless and ungainly monsters which I now set before the reader does not consist of separate idols cut out capriciously in lonely valleys or various islands. These monsters are meant for the gargoyles of a definite cathedral. I have to carve the gargoyles, because I can carve nothing else; I leave to others the angels and the arches and the spires. But I am very sure of the style of the architecture and of the consecration of the church.

Notes
1. *THE THREE TEMPLES*: Reprinted as 'Introductory: On Gargoyles', in *AD*, pp. 1–7. Chesterton added new material at the end, using the theme of the fable to introduce to the reader the essays that comprised *Alarms and Discursions*.

2. *I do not say 'must pass' or 'necessarily passes'... fixed day of death*: A possible reference here is Arthur de Gobineau's *On the Inequality of the Races of Man* (1855), which advanced a theory of inevitable racial degeneration from Aryan and Teutonic purity caused by miscegenation. Gobineau's pessimism was fuelled by anxiety about the decline of the French aristocracy, which he regarded as ethnically German, and the ascendancy of a mongrelized plebeian class. His work increased in popularity in France in the 1880s when it went through a second edition, due to the discrediting of democracy and French 'self-abasement' in the wake of German defeat: J. W. Burrow, *The Crisis of Reason: European Thought, 1848-1914* (New Haven, CT: Yale University Press, 2000), p. 107.

3. *ears to hear – let him hear*: See Matthew 11:15.

January 23, 1909.

THE PERIL OF THE COINCIDENCE.

The biggest danger immediately in front of us is one which we do not see; that is why it is the biggest danger. A false history and foolish metaphysics have managed to lodge in most men's heads the incurable conception, that popular self-government is something which belongs specially to advanced civilization, while aristocracy is peculiar to primitive ages with obvious ideas.

Now, the truth is that we are growing more and more aristocratic as we grow more and more civilized; that is, civilized in the modern sense, which mostly concerns machinery. Democracy is easiest under plain and primary conditions, where all the citizens can shout in the marketplace, or all the fathers of the tribe talk under a tree. You can always give the power to the many if they are not too many. It is with the need for envoys, representatives, executive officers that the devil of oligarchy creeps in; for some very sound political philosopher observed the devil is a gentleman.[1] He was flung from heaven because of his intolerably gentlemanly deportment.

In our complex and cosmopolitan conditions, where so many things are done by telegraph or telephone, there must be a great deal of privilege and even despotism. After all, there can only be one man at the other end of the telephone. As a private person I am glad of this, because I have a telephone; but as a sociologist (and don't you forget it) I am bound to confess that it involves an extreme individualism and the absence of any collective spirit or collective cry. After all, you can't have a mob shouting down a telephone. And it is even difficult to express the precise note or intensity of prolonged shouts and yells in a telegram. When we read in most newspaper reports that 'Loud cheers' followed some ordinary observation as that Natal is more important than England, or that men who have bought peerages have proved themselves above corruption, it is commonly difficult to know whether the applause was the deafening clamour that shakes a building or merely that hearty, but indistinct, murmur which greets an admitted truth.

****

The more we have to work by instruments the further we get from the breath and pulsation of the people; and it is obvious that in theory there might almost be a perfection of machinery which would deprive the mass of men of what power they at present possess. I am not going to dispute that miry and trampled area of argument about whether industrial machinery really deprives men of work; it is enough for me that it certainly deprives them of importance. There is a dreadful potential democracy even on a ship. The men could mutiny and refuse to work the ship. But suppose that a ship could be wound up like a clock to go for a whole voyage, the men might mutiny all day long amid general approval. The concentration of power at one or two handles or buttons may, perhaps, make it easier for working men to idle; but it makes it much harder for them to strike.

That is a fine word, 'strike', one of the few forcible words left in politics; but in practice the thing itself is often less forcible. It is vain for the poor man to strike unless the rich man can be struck. Of course it is a matter of degree; no scheme, however scientific, is utterly independent of its subordinates. But in practice the degree is very marked. The engineer of a steamboat would have more chance of getting to port with a divided crew than a Cambridge coxswain would have of winning the boat race with a divided crew. Similarly you could keep an unpopular factory going much longer than an unpopular expedition for hunting or fishing, because in a factory it is so much easier to manipulate things so as to give the minority the powers of the majority. In short, it may or may not be certain that machinery lowers the economic state of democracy; but it is quite certain that it lowers its political pride and power. Machines may save labour; but they do not save Labour Parties. We shall probably all live to see military science, one of the most recent and scientific of the sciences, employed to resist the power of the human mass; and whether or no workmen were wise to smash machines, they would certainly have been wise to smash machine guns.

****

I see the pale and eager face of my friend the scientific Socialist peering at me as I have often seen it at lectures and debates; and I can see his lips fervently forming the words 'Democracy . . . capture. . . industrial machine'. But that is unfortunately my whole meaning. A democracy cannot capture a machine in the sense that it might capture a field or a vineyard or a granary. I repeat that it is a matter of degree; doubtless a field cannot be worked well without knowledge and discipline. But an electrical apparatus cannot be made to move at all without the autocracy of an expert; there will be a hundred men with a vague tradition of the spade and plough for one man who will know which handle to turn or which button to press. You can even argue with the man at the plough; but you must not speak to the man the wheel. If you doubt this general distinction, imagine that you and I were cast upon a promising desert island. Should we, as ordinary intelligent citizens, try to erect a Manchester electric factory, or should we try, by some fable from our fathers, to till the soil?

This anti-democratic dilemma does exist, and all Democrats of sincerity and originality have felt it, Rousseau, Cobbett, Walt Whitman. There are two ways of getting over it; one in saying (as I am strongly inclined to say) that man is happier as well as more democratic in smaller and simpler societies, and that to these the sanity of experience will return. Another is to say that this tyranny of the mechanical expert is one of the dangers of modern life only because it is one of the eternal dangers of human nature; that it cannot be obviated all together, but that it can be guarded against by an enormous increase of democratic law and intervention in highly civilized states. Both these answers are reasonable. But it is not in either of them that I see the danger averted; nor, indeed, is it in the mere machinery and scientific civilization that I see the danger. The real danger lies in a certain horrible coincidence.

****

The danger is this. When social reformation comes along its present lines, from the Socialists or somebody like them, it will find it necessary to establish a working hierarchy with a great many specialists and people controlling departments. But it happens (by the horrible coincidence) that the system of this country is already a hierarchy, with people controlling departments, landlords, agents, commercial magnates. That is one of the most obvious arguments of the Socialist. He says, 'It is idle to talk of whether property shall be concentrated. It is already concentrated; only it is not concentrated for the public good'.

But these big owners are, by a universal chorus of modern magazines and newspapers, saluted as the strongest and most sagacious figures of their time. This millionaire, we are told, gained his power by sheer pluck, that one by sheer grit, the other (one often hears) by sheer Christianity. In the same way one duke is called the best of landlords, another the strongest of diplomatists, another the most quiet and capable of politicians. There, then, are the holes in the new machine gaping for lords and masters; and there are a set of men perpetually praised to the populace for their lordship and mastery. I will bet any ordinary pair of boots that when the revolution comes these men step out of their shoes in order to step into them again, or do not step out of them at all. Mr. Guggenheim[2] has made a huge income by his boldness and foresight; he will be paid that huge income, or something like it, to use his boldness and foresight for the community. Lord Stonehenge owns half a county, and is good to the villagers; he will be paid the worth of half a county as a State official if he will go on being good to them. I seriously believe that the storm of Socialism will roar and pass, and leave our whole oligarchy standing.

Notes
1. *some very sound political philosopher ... the devil is a gentleman*: Shelley, 'The Devil' (from *Peter Bell the Third* (1819)); see 'The Beauty of Noise', *DN*, 18 August 1906, Volume 4, p. 40, n. 4 above.
2. *Mr. Guggenheim*: Solomon R. Guggenheim (1861–1949), was an American businessman, art collector and philanthropist; in 1937 he established the Solomon R. Guggenheim Foundation for the promotion of modern art.

January 27, 1909.

A BOOK OF THE DAY.

A String of Novelists.

'Great English Novelists'. By Holbrook Jackson. Grant Richards. 3s.6d. net.

The need to compress or concentrate does good to a sensible writer, and it absolutely destroys a silly one. If each paragraph had to be cut down to the one sentence that was necessary, we should soon find out whether any of the sentences were necessary at all. A policy can be put into a telegram; a political evasion in its nature requires a column of 'The Times'. There has to be a lot of it because there is nothing. It cannot be cut down to its essentials, because it has none. For this reason I am strongly in favour of capable and ardent young men being given literary jobs which are too big for them. And Mr. Holbrook Jackson,[1] who is a capable and ardent young man, has (I am glad to say) been given a job that is too big for anybody.

Mr. Grant Richards is bringing out a series of series: 'Great English Poets', 'Great English Painters', and here 'Great English Novelists'. Mr. Jackson has been forced to write in the space of one small book the truth about Defoe,[2] Lord Beaconsfield,[3] Smollett,[4] George Meredith,[5] Dickens, Sir Edward Bulwer Lytton,[6] Fielding,[7] Thackeray,[8] and Scott;[9] and he has been obliged to do all this under the heavy disadvantage of not being a fool or a conventional charlatan. If he were a smooth, fashionable dunce or knave, he could of course run over all the names quite easily. Defoe would have written the best of books for boys, Disraeli would be the English patriot who discovered the primrose and the Empire, Smollett would be a little known author whose indecency we have happily outgrown, Meredith would be a novelist once ridiculously unintelligible, but venerable now that he has white hair and does not write novels; Dickens would be widely popular but vulgar and sentimental, Fielding would be 'coarse', Thackeray would be 'cynical', and Scott (for all one dare shudderingly conjecture) might be 'the wizard of the North'.

Much in Little.

By this method, by always reading the newspapers and never reading the novels, Mr. Jackson might have got through his novelists in splendid style, and at a stunning rate of speed. But Mr. Jackson does not give one this impression; he gives the impression that he would really like to stop and think out each of his subjects thoroughly. We feel that he could have made the whole book out of each of his chapters, and yet I am not sure that it would have been such a good book. I fancy, as I have said above, that compression is good for any honest writer, even when the compression is part of an almost impossible scheme. If a man has really something to say about Defoe, it may bring out his powers to have to say it in ten pages. If he has nothing to say about Defoe, it may take him ten volumes to say it.

Now it was really unreasonable to ask Mr. Holbrook Jackson or anybody else to deal adequately in this space with names some so mighty and all so miscellaneous. And yet there are places where he profits by the impossibility; and I think there is more good criticism crammed tight into this book than any that was spread loose through his book on Bernard Shaw,[10] where he could splash about in the featureless future. The form forces upon him a certain sobriety and fulness of statement; that of a man trying to tell the truth as shortly as possible. I take an instance from the first page at which I open. After regretting the gloom of Puritanism, he adds this note of its useful office: 'In the first place, by discountenancing any art but that which contributed in some perceptible way to the moral life of the time, it cleared the field of that dense mass of frivolous and pedantic matter which had for many years impeded the growth of healthy literature'.

The Virtue of Being Hurried.

Now that is a modest, close-packed, and convincing statement of what was really effective in the Puritanism of Bunyan[11] and Defoe. There are a thousand writers, who have not read a line of the seventeenth century who would pour you out poetical prose by the gallon about how the Puritans stood alone in fighting for a higher view, a holier vision, a purer conception of life. All that is lying or ignorance; the Puritans did not stand for virtue against the world; the Catholics and the Cavalier mystics had ideals possibly higher, certainly quite as high. But it is true that the spirituality of Crashaw[12] and Browne[13] was entangled with the affected fantasticality of a dying literary taste; and it is true that Bunyan and Defoe were making a manlier English. This does not prove that Puritanism was right, or that Defoe was right; all that is a much larger question. But it does prove that Mr. Holbrook Jackson is right; he has avoided current verbiage, and marked the real strength of the Puritan and the real weakness of the Cavalier literature. He has done it very possibly, because he was cramped and hurried.

Just as Mr. Jackson would have liked to write a book on every one of his novelists, so I should like to write an article upon almost every one of Mr. Jackson's paragraphs. The only comment, I fancy, that really cries for utterance is one upon the old matter of the morality of Fielding. Here Mr. Jackson touches for a moment the modern or advanced spirit, and instantly loses his intelligence. He seems to make an attempt to connect the energy of Fielding with an anarchy which, as he says, 'anticipates the attitudes of such moderns as Henrik Ibsen and Friedrich Nietzsche'. He says of Tom Jones: 'It is an affirmation of the goodness of life against Richardson's affirmation of the goodness of mere morals'. And again, 'One is almost convinced by the argument of Fielding's fine enthusiasm for life and his epic tolerance, that virtue and instinct may be identical'.

Now the truth is that all the 'modern' notion that virtue is the same as instinct is a notion not possible to Fielding, because it is a notion not possible to a virile man. Mr. Holbrook Jackson does not really entertain it any more than I do. A man is hardly worth calling a man if he has not had a great many incidental instincts which he knows quite well were not the same as virtue. A man with a strong mind and a strong body knows well which should command. Fielding did not think that Tom Jones had done wisely: Tom Jones did not think that Tom Jones had done wisely. He specifically says, in the book, that he has not. Fielding thought what all the high and humane moralists have thought; that you must have a man before you can have a saint. There must be the materials of healthy temptation before there is any healthy triumph. If thy right hand offend thee, cut it off.[14] But you must have a tolerably strong left hand to cut it off with.

Notes

1. *Mr. Holbrook Jackson*: Holbrook Jackson (1874–1948), was an author and editor. With A. R. Orage, he became joint editor of the *New Age* in 1907, editor of the *Beau* in 1910, and acting editor and then editor of *T. P's Weekly*, 1911–14. Chesterton reviewed sympathetically his nuanced study, *The Eighteen Nineties: A Review of Art and Ideas at the Close of the Nineteenth Century* (London: Grant Richards, 1913), in 'The Decay of the Decadents', *New Witness*, 20 November 1913, reprinted in *CR*, 14:4 (November 1988), pp. 509–14. His many other works included *Edward Fitzgerald and Omar Khayyam* (1899), *The Eternal Now: A Book of Verses* (1900), *William Morris: A Biography* (1908), *Romance and Reality* (1911), and *William Caxton* (1933). For a perceptive analysis of the literary relationship between Chesterton and Jackson over many years, see Owen Dudley Edwards, 'Holbrook Jackson in Chestertonian Context', *CR*, 14:4 (November 1988), pp. 567–90.
2. *Defoe*: Daniel Defoe (*c.* 1659–1731), was an English novelist, journalist and pamphleteer; he was a prolific author under a variety of pen-names, but is now chiefly remembered

for three novels: *Robinson Crusoe* (1719), *Moll Flanders* (1724) and *A Journal of the Plague Year* (1722).

3. *Lord Beaconsfield*: Benjamin Disraeli, Earl of Beaconsfield; see 'Mr. Gallienne Again', *DN*, 15 February 1901, Volume 1, p. 27, n. 4 above.
4. *Smollett*: Tobias George Smollett (1721–71), was a Scottish poet and author. His first novel, *The Adventures of Roderick Random* (1748), raised public awareness of medical conditions in the navy. It was preceded by two verse satires, *Advice* (1746) and *Reproof* (1747). The most genial of his later novels was *Humphrey Clinker* (1771), centred on a Welsh family's tour of Scotland. A talented caricaturist, he influenced Scott, Melville, Thackeray and Dickens.
5. *Meredith*: George Meredith; see 'The British Academy', *DN*, 4 September 1902, Volume 1, pp. 378–9, n. 9 above.
6. *Sir Edward Bulwer Lytton*: Edward George Earle Lytton Bulwer-Lytton, first Baron Lytton; see 'Gossip: Good and Bad', *DN*, 13 September 1905, Volume 3, p. 192, n. 5 above.
7. *Fielding*: Henry Fielding; see 'The "Good Man" of the Eighteenth Century', *DN*, 22 March 1901, Volume 1, p. 66, n. 7 above.
8. *Thackeray*: William Makepeace Thackeray; see 'The Soul of Charles II', *DN*, 16 July 1901, Volume 1, p. 129, n. 6 above.
9. *Scott*: Sir Walter Scott; see 'The Curse of Collins', *DN*, 1 March 1901, Volume 1, p. 39, n. 16 above.
10. *his book on Bernard Shaw*: *Bernard Shaw: A Study* (London: Grant Richards, 1908).
11. *Bunyan*: John Bunyan; see 'A New Study of Swinburne', *DN*, 12 February 1901, Volume 1, p. 14, n. 6 above.
12. *Crashaw*: Richard Crashaw; see 'A Step of Progress', *DN*, 14 July 1906, Volume 4, p. 8, n. 3 above.
13. *Browne*: William Browne (c. 1590–1645), was an English poet. Influenced by Spenser, and in turn an influence on Milton and Keats, Browne's poems are mainly pastoral; they are notable for their rich and flowing style. His chief works are *Britannia's Pastorals* (1613–16), *The Shepheard's Pipe* (1614), and *The Inner Temple Masque* (1615). *Britannia's Pastorals* is dedicated to his patron, William Herbert, third Earl of Pembroke.
14. *If thy right hand ... cut it off*: Cf. Matthew 5:30.

January 30, 1909.

THE HEROIC THAT HAPPENED.[1]

Some little time ago Mr. Bernard Shaw, faced with the frightful difficulty of explaining how a man of his intelligence could be anything nowadays but an orthodox Christian, invented (as is his wont) a really new argument, good or bad. The old-fashioned blasphemers (who are the most lovable of men) had always denounced Bible stories as silly stories; they were too clumsy and faulty to be believed. But Mr. Shaw said of the central Bible story, not that it was too faulty to be believed, but that it was too faultless to be believed. He rejected it not because it was imperfect, but because it was perfect. He declared that the story of Calvary was to be discredited precisely because it was sublime, because it was pointed and poetic. Things so artistic as that (he said in effect) do not happen.[2]

I am not concerned here to offer any of the many minor criticisms which might be made upon this view. I might remark for the hundredth time upon the hundredth example of the fact that the enemy of Christianity is always eating his own words and deserting his own standard; that the attack on that faith can only be kept up even for three generations by each one of its accusers repudiating the last accusation, by every son of scepticism disowning his own father. I might also suggest that if the Superman ever came on earth Mr. Shaw would not complain if he talked naturally in poetry – if he asked for the mustard in an impromptu sonnet. If it be imaginable that the Superman on earth might speak poetry, it is surely not unlikely that God on earth might act poetry.

But I am not now entangled in any of these considerations. It is only one much more innocent aspect of Mr. Shaw's theory that I propose to attack. He said that a certain tale is probably unhistorical because it is dignified and dramatic, a thing with an artistic climax. I am concerned to point out that Mr. Shaw said this because he had not really read or understood human history; because he has allowed his great genius and sympathy to be suffocated with the materialism of a mean modern environment. The truth is that the things which astonish us in the tremendous tale of the Passion are things which not only would happen at a Divine crisis, but which have happened at every genuine human crisis. It is only in epochs of exhaustion and mere pottering about with problems that they do not occur. Mr. Shaw, when he suggested that the Passion was too artistic to happen, really meant that it was too artistic to happen in the Fabian Society or in the London School of Economics. But in history it did happen. It happened again and again.

****

We talk of art as something artificial in comparison with life. But I sometimes fancy that the very highest art is more real than life itself. At least this is true: that in proportion as passions become real they become poetical; the lover is always trying to be the poet. All real energy is an attempt at harmony and a high swing of rhythm; and if we were only real enough we should all talk in rhyme. However this may be, it is unquestionable in the case of great public affairs. Whenever you have real practical politics you have poetical politics. Whenever men have succeeded in wars they have sung war songs; whenever you have the useful triumph you have also the useless trophy.

But the thing is more strongly apparent exactly where the great Fabian falls foul of it, in the open scenes of history and the actual operation of events. The things that actually did happen all over the world are precisely the things which he thinks could not have happened in Galilee, the artistic isolations, the dreadful dialogues in which each speaker was dramatic, the prophecies flung down like gauntlets, the high invocations of history, the marching and mounting excitement of the story, the pulverising and appropriate repartees. These things do happen; they have happened; they are attested, in all the cases where the soul of man had become poetic in its very peril. At every one of its important moments the most certain and solid history reads like a historical novel.

****

A peasant girl, called half-witted, did promise to defeat the victors of Agincourt; and did it; it ought to be a legend, but it happens to be a fact.[3] A poet and a poetess did fall in love and eloped secretly to a sunny clime; it is obviously a three-volume novel; but it happened.[4] Nelson did die in the act of winning the one battle that could change the world. It is a grossly improbable coincidence; but it is too late to alter it now. Napoleon did win the Battle of Austerlitz; it is unnatural; but it is not my fault. When the general who had surrendered a republican town returned saying, easily, 'I have done everything', Robespierre did ask, with an air of inquiry, 'Are you dead?'[5] When Robespierre coughed in his cold harangue, Garnier did say, 'The blood of Danton chokes you.'[6] Strafford did say of his own desertion of Parliament, 'If I do it, may my life and death be set on a hill for all men to wonder at'.[7] Disraeli did say, 'The time will come when you shall hear me.'[8]

The heroic is a fact, even when it is a fact of coincidence or of miracle; and a fact is a thing which can be admitted without being explained. But I would in conclusion, merely hint that there is a very natural explanation of this frightful felicity, either of phrase or action, which so many men have exhibited on so many scaffolds or battlefields. It is merely that when a man has found something which he prefers to life, he then for the first time begins to live. A promptitude of poetry opens in his soul of which our paltry experiences do not possess the key. When once he has despised this world as a mere instrument, it becomes a musical instrument; it falls into certain artistic harmonies around him. If Nelson had not worn his stars he would not have been hit. But if he had not worn his stars he would not have been Nelson; and if he had not been Nelson he might have lost the battle. It is all quite natural; nothing requires any explanation; except Nelson – except why a man should feel most alive when he is doing his best to die.

Notes

1. *THE HEROIC THAT HAPPENED*: Reprinted in *LL*, pp. 143–6.
2. *But Mr. Shaw said of the central Bible story ... do not happen*: not identified.
3. *A Peasant girl ... a fact*: Jeanne [Jehanne] d'Arc (Joan of Arc); see 'The Sentimentalism of Zarathustra', *DN*, 15 December 1906, Volume 4, p. 115, n. 3 above.
4. *A Poet and a Poetess ... but it happened*: The reference is to Robert Browning and Elizabeth Barrett, who married in August 1846 despite the opposition of Elizabeth's father. They did not actually elope (they were married in St Marylebone Parish Church in London), but they immediately left England for Italy, where they remained more or less permanently until Elizabeth's death in 1861.
5. *Robespierre did ask ... Are you dead*: See Hilaire Belloc, *Robespierre: a Study* (New York: Charles Scribner's Sons, 1901), p. 264.
6. *Garnier ... chokes you*: Antoine Marie Charles Garnier (Garnier de l'Aube), (1742–1805), was a French Deputy. See Belloc, *Robespierre*, p. 348.
7. *Strafford ... wonder at*: not identified.
8. *Disraeli ... you shall hear me*: Disraeli's maiden speech in the House of Commons in December, 1837 (on Irish elections) was a notorious flop; it ended with the words: 'though I sit down now, the time will come when you will hear me'. See W. F. Monypenny and G. E. Buckle, *The Life of Benjamin Disraeli*, rev. G. E. Buckle, 2 vols, 2nd edn (London: John Murray, 1929), vol. 1, p. 409.

February 6, 1909.

THE VOTE AND THE VOTARY.

In that entertaining paper, 'The New Age', I see that I am described this week as 'a poet suffering from Gallic Anglo-mania' who 'sees England through French spectacles as the land of "home" in excelsis'.[1] This is rather funny; since, as a matter of fact, I see England as the land of homelessness in excelsis; I see it as the one Christian country where domesticity has been practically destroyed by territorial and commercial lusts. An Englishman's house is not his castle; the Englishman (as I have suggested elsewhere)[2] is almost the only European whose house is not his castle. He has been driven out of it by mercantile megalomaniacs into the street or into the workhouse. His despoilers offer him the most wonderful things in exchange, including the British Empire and the Superman, but they will not give him back his own house. All of them assure him that a home is an extinct superstition. Some of them assure him that he is really happiest in the street. That is called Individualism. Others assure him that he is really happiest in the workhouse. That is called Socialism.

****

In the same article, however, there is another observation, which arrests my eye. The article is called 'Unedited Opinions'; it is not surprising that they are unedited, because they are written by the editor. It is partly about female suffrage, but it is not that aspect of it to which I refer just now. Female suffrage might be very right or very wrong, and the following paragraph, appearing in a Socialist paper, would still be portentous.

'But do you really think women care about the vote at all?'

'Did the majority of men care about the vote? No matter about the majority. It is the minority that counts. We want to make conditions to suit a noble minority, and then to let the majority who cannot survive perish. Why not?

Didn't brains enable the first men to survive when the mammoth and mastodon died? And it is the same in spiritual affairs. Men of imagination produce secular changes in the climate of the soul. The incapable have every right to protest, and to die protesting. I deny nobody his right to protest ... I'm more concerned about the feeling of the spiritual few than about the feelings of the material many. You don't hesitate to feed a dog on a bone; why should we hesitate to sacrifice dead souls to living souls?'

In other words, the writer of this passage wishes to have universal suffrage because he does not believe in democracy.[3] Because the majority is generally wrong, he wishes to extend the machinery of majorities. Because the minority is superior he wishes to extend the only human form of government which denies that the minority is superior. Superficially (I say it without offence), one would suppose that he was mad; but I happen to know that he is a highly intelligent man. What is the explanation of such self-evidently suicidal vagaries of thought?

The explanation is that democracy has become a superstition without ceasing to be a truth; just as religion often became a superstition without ceasing to be a truth. We hear often enough from the modern world that there is no real good in worshipping God when you do not love God. What good is there, I should like to know, in enfranchising the people when you do not trust the people? We often hear that priests and bigots despise the Christ while they worship the Cross. What shall we say of these people who despise the voters while they worship the vote? Of the writer in 'The New Age' I happen to know other and far more lively things. But as regards that paragraph I say that he is a dead ritualist. He is still worshipping the machinery of popular government while he has permitted himself to forget, or be persuaded out of, every moral or mental sympathy which ever made anyone ask for popular government. He has forgotten why anyone ever gave votes to this majority 'of the material many', this majority which does not count. But though he has forgotten why the votes were given, he still wants to go on giving them. He wants to give them in a quite new and quite different case. The last and boldest experiment of democracy is to be made by people who, by their own account, do not know what democracy is all about. 'The New Age' writer is anti-democratic to a degree which literally would not have been allowed in any other age. The more evil of the old Pontiffs may have treated men like dogs. But they would not have been suffered to describe them as dogs; still less would they have been suffered to describe them as bones just fit for dogs. The author of that remarkable metaphor is the only man who has gone one degree better in detestation of popular self-government than Foulon when he said, 'Let them eat grass'.[4] Even Foulon did not say, 'Let them be eaten by dogs'. Foulon, in the French Revolution, was hanged from a lamp-post with grass stuffed into his mouth. The well-meaning 'New Age' philosopher, in the

French Revolution, would have been hung from a lamp-post with a dog's bone stuck in his throat.

****

How comes it that so able and honest a man can be so heartily and sincerely anti-popular, and yet be fighting (and fighting with fire and candour) on behalf of what is considered the popular side in politics? The fact, strange as it is, is not without historical parallel. Ours is pre-eminently an age of superstition; that is, an age in which words, however true, are repeated by rote. In other ages of superstition it may be remarked that the very moment when some idea was most undermined and hollowed away was the very moment when people tried to build on it the most towering and oppressive piles. Thus, shortly before the Reformation, the very moment when the Church was most questioned as a matter of theory, even by its own popes and princes, was the very time when it was most taken for granted as a matter of high payments and heavy routine. Just in the same way do these wild individualists who call themselves Socialists rear a perpetually climbing turret of democratic extension upon a perpetually crumbling cliff of democratic belief.

Notes
1. *In that entertaining paper ... in excelsis*: A. R. Orage, 'Unedited Opinions', *NA*, 4 February 1909, p. 301.
2. *as I have suggested elsewhere*: the 'elsewhere' to which Chesterton refers has not been identified; but in 1910, in *What's Wrong with the World* (part 1, chapter 9) he says: 'Burke, a fine rhetorician, who rarely faced realities, said, I think, that an Englishman's house is his castle. This is honestly entertaining; for as it happens the Englishman is almost the only man in Europe whose house is not his castle'.
3. *the writer of this passage ... does not believe in democracy*: Orage argued that the Suffragettes were among the few in society who were making a bid for freedom in the broadest, not merely political sense. Opponents of female suffrage – both women and men such as Chesterton – merely 'desire[d] to see continued a race of wives, prostitutes, and old maids'. The passage in Orage's article that Chesterton omitted is as follows:
    "'But would you ignore the protests of the obsolescent majority?'
    'Without a qualm, if I could: with qualms if I couldn't; but I should ignore them all the same. Women who do not want the vote want nothing. They are hopelessly satisfied, and therefore hopelessly unsatisfactory. The past belongs to them, but the future never. They must be frozen out of existence; or, as is more likely, scorched out.
    'You are pretty brutal, I must say'.
    'Not at all. I am more concerned ..."'
    The passage may have provoked the introduction to the essay that followed, 'Simmons and the Social Tie', *DN*, 13 February 1909, pp. 268–71 below.
4. *Foulon ... grass*: Joseph-François Foulon de Doué (1715–89) was appointed Controller-General of Finances by Louis XVI in 1789. The attribution to him of 's'ils ont faim, qu'ils

broutent l'herbe' (by Jules Michelet, *Histoire de la revolution française* (1847), 1:183-184) is probably apocryphal, but he was the object of great popular hatred and lynched by the mob at the Hôtel de Ville on 22 July 1789.

February 13, 1909.

SIMMONS AND THE SOCIAL TIE.[1]

It is a platitude, and none the less true for that, that we need to have an ideal in our minds with which to test all realities. Thus I have selected Mrs. Buttons, a charwoman in Battersea, as the touchstone of all modern theories about the mass of women. Her name is not Buttons; she is not in the least a contemptible nor entirely a comic figure. She has a powerful stoop and an ugly, attractive face, a little like that of Huxley[2] – without the whiskers, of course. The courage with which she supports the most brutal bad luck has something quite creepy about it. Her irony is incessant and inventive; her practical charity very large; and she is wholly unaware of the philosophical use to which I put her.

But when I hear the modern generalisations about her sex on all sides I simply substitute her name, and see how the thing sounds then. When on the one side the mere sentimentalist says, 'Let woman be content to be dainty and exquisite, a protected piece of social art and domestic ornament', then I merely repeat it to myself in the other form, 'Let Mrs Buttons be content to be dainty and exquisite, a protected piece of social art, etc'. It is extraordinary what a difference the substitution seems to make. And on the other hand, when some of the Suffragettes say in their pamphlets and speeches, 'Woman, leaping to life at the trumpet call of Ibsen and Shaw, drops her tawdry luxuries and demands to grasp the sceptre of empire and the firebrand of speculative thought' – in order to understand such a sentence I say it over again, in the amended form: 'Mrs. Buttons, leaping to life at the trumpet call of Ibsen and Shaw, drops her tawdry luxuries and demands to grasp the sceptre of empire and the firebrand of speculative thought'. Somehow it sounds quite different. And yet when you say Woman I suppose you mean the average woman; and if most women are as capable and critical and morally sound as Mrs. Buttons it is as much as we can expect, and a great deal more than we deserve.

****

But this article is not about Mrs. Buttons; she would require many articles. I will take a less impressive case of my principle, the principle of keeping in the mind an actual personality when we are talking about types or tendencies or generalized ideals. Take, for example, the question of the education of boys. Almost every post brings me pamphlets expounding some advanced and suggestive scheme of education; the pupils are to be taught separate; the sexes are to be taught together; there should be no prizes; there should be no punishments; the master should lift the boys to his level; the master should descend to their level; we should encourage the heartiest comradeship among boys, and also the tenderest spiritual intimacy with masters; toil must be pleasant and holidays must be instructive; with all these things I am daily impressed and somewhat bewildered.

But on the great Buttons principle I keep in my mind and apply to all these ideals one still vivid fact; the face and character of a particular schoolboy whom I once knew. I am not taking a mere individual oddity, as you will hear. He was exceptional, and yet the reverse of eccentric; he was (in a quite sober and strict sense of the words) exceptionally average. He was the incarnation and the exaggeration of a certain spirit which is the common spirit of boys, but which nowhere else became so obvious and outrageous. And because he was an incarnation he was, in his way, a tragedy.

I will call him Simmons. He was a tall, healthy figure, strong but a little slouching, and there was in his walk something between a slight swagger and a seaman's roll; he commonly had his hands in his pockets. His hair was dark, straight, and undistinguished; and his face, if one saw it after his figure, was something of a surprise. For while the form might be called big and braggart, the face might have been called weak, and was certainly worried. It was a hesitating face, which seemed to blink doubtfully in the daylight. He had even the look of one who has received a buffet that he cannot return. In all occupations he was the average boy; just sufficiently good at sports, just sufficiently bad at work to be universally satisfactory. But he was prominent in nothing, for prominence was to him a thing like bodily pain. He could not endure, without discomfort amounting to desperation, that any boy should be noticed or sensationally separated from the long line of boys; for him, to be distinguished was to be disgraced.

Those who interpret schoolboys as merely wooden and barbarous, unmoved by anything but a savage seriousness about tuck or cricket, make the mistake of forgetting how much of the schoolboy life is public and ceremonial, having reference to an ideal; or, if you like, to an affectation. Boys, like dogs, have a sort of romantic ritual which is not always their real selves. And this romantic ritual is generally the ritual of not being romantic; the pretence of being much more masculine and materialistic than they are. Boys in themselves are very sentimental. The most sentimental thing in the world is to hide your feelings; it is making too much of them. Stoicism is the direct product of sentimentalism; and schoolboys are sentimental individually, but stoical collectively.

For example, there were plenty of boys at my school besides myself who took a private pleasure in poetry; but red-hot iron would not have induced most of us to admit this to the masters, or to repeat poetry with the faintest inflection of rhythm or intelligence. That would have been anti-social egoism; we called it 'showing off'. I myself remember running to school (an extraordinary thing to do) with mere internal ecstasy in repeating lines of Walter Scott about the taunts of Marmion or the boasts of Roderick Dhu,[3] and then repeating the same lines in class with the colourless decorum of a hurdy-gurdy. We all wished to be invisible in our uniformity; a mere pattern of Eton collars and coats.

****

But Simmons went even further. He felt it as an insult to brotherly equality if any task or knowledge out of the ordinary track was discovered even by accident. If a boy had learnt German in infancy; or if a boy knew some terms in music; or if a boy was forced to feebly confess that he had read 'The Mill on the Floss'[4] – then Simmons was in a perspiration of discomfort. He felt no personal anger, still less any petty jealousy; what he felt was an honourable and generous shame. He hated it as a lady hates coarseness in a pantomime; it made him want to hide himself. Just that feeling of impersonal ignominy which most of us have when someone betrays indecent ignorance, Simmons had when someone betrayed special knowledge. He writhed and went red in the face; he used to put up the lid of his desk to hide his blushes for human dignity, and from behind this barrier would whisper protests which had the hoarse emphasis of pain. 'O, shut up, I say ... O, I say, shut up ... O, *shut* it can't you?' Once when a little boy admitted that he had heard of the Highland claymore Simmons literally hid his head inside his desk and dropped the lid upon it in desperation; and when I was for a moment transferred from the bottom of the form for knowing the name of Cardinal Newman,[5] I thought he would have rushed from the room.

His psychological eccentricity increased; if one can call that an eccentricity which was a wild worship of the ordinary. At last he grew so sensitive that he could not even hear any question answered correctly without grief. He felt there was a touch of disloyalty, of unfraternal individualism, even about knowing the right answer to a sum. If asked the date of the battle of Hastings, he considered it due to social tact and general good feeling to answer 1067. This chivalrous exaggeration led to bad feeling between him and the school authority, which ended in a rupture unexpectedly violent in the case of so good-humoured a creature.

He fled from the school, and it was discovered upon inquiry that he had fled from his home also.

I never expected to see him again; yet it is one of the two or three odd coincidences of my life that I did see him. At some public sports or recreation ground I saw a group of rather objectless youths, one of whom was wearing the dashing uniform of a private in the Lancers. Inside that uniform was the tall figure, shy face, and dark, stiff hair of Simmons. He had gone to the one place where everyone is dressed alike – a regiment. I know nothing more; perhaps he was killed in Africa. But when England was full of flags and false triumphs, when everybody was talking unmanly trash about the whelps of the lion and the brave boys in red, I often heard a voice echoing in the under-caverns of my memory, 'Shut up ... O, shut up ... O, I say, shut it'.

Notes
1. *SIMMONS AND THE SOCIAL TIE*: Reprinted in *AD*, pp. 49–55.
2. *Huxley*: Thomas Henry Huxley; see 'George MacDonald and His Work', *DN*, 11 June 1901, Volume 1, p. 103, n. 2 above.
3. *The lines of Walter Scott ... Roderick Dhu*: Roderick Dhu is chief of the Clan Alpine in Scott's *The Lady of the Lake* (1810).
4. *The Mill on the Floss*: George Eliot, *The Mill on the Floss*, 3 vols (1860).
5. *Cardinal Newman*: John Henry Newman; see 'Russell of Killowen', 18 November 1901, Volume 1, p. 271, n.4 above.

February 20, 1909.

THE DIVINE DETECTIVE.[1]

Every person of sound education enjoys detective stories, and there are even several points on which they have a hearty superiority to most modern books. A detective story generally describes six living men discussing how it is that a man is dead. A modern philosophic story generally describes six dead men discussing how any man can possibly be alive. But those who have enjoyed the *roman policier* must have noted one thing, that when the murderer is caught he is hardly ever hanged. 'That', says Sherlock Holmes, 'is the advantage of being a private detective'; after he has caught he can set free.[2] The Christian church can best be defined as an enormous private detective, correcting that official detective – the State. This, indeed, is one of the injustices done to historic Christianity; injustices which arise from looking at complex exceptions and not at the large and simple fact. We are constantly being told that theologians used racks and thumbscrews, and so they did. Theologians used racks and thumbscrews just as they used thimbles and three-legged stools, because everybody else used them.[a] The Church did, in an evil hour, consent to imitate the commonwealth and employ cruelty.[b]

But if we open our eyes and take in the whole picture, if we look at the general shape and colour of the thing, the real difference between the Church and the State is huge and plain. The State, in all lands and ages, has created a machinery of punishment, more bloody and brutal in some places than others, but bloody and brutal everywhere. The Church is the only institution that ever attempted to create a machinery of pardon. The Church is the only thing that ever attempted by system to pursue and discover crimes, not in order to avenge, but in order to forgive them. The stake and rack were merely the weaknesses of the religion; its snobberies, its surrenders to the world. Its speciality – or, if you like, its oddity – was this merciless mercy; the unrelenting sleuthhound who seeks to save and not slay.

****

I can best illustrate what I mean by referring to two popular plays on somewhat parallel topics, which have been successful here and in America. 'The Passing of the Third Floor Back' is a humane and reverent experiment, dealing with the influence of one unknown but divine figure as he passes through a group of squalid characters. I have no desire to make cheap fun of the extremely abrupt conversions of all these people; that is a point of art, not of morals; and, after all, many conversions have been abrupt. This saviour's method of making people good is to tell them how good they are already; and in the case of suicidal outcasts, whose moral backs are broken, and who are soaked with sincere self-contempt, I can imagine that this might be quite the right way. I should not recommend this method for authors or members of Parliament, because they would so heartily agree with it.

Still, it is not altogether here that I differ from the moral of Mr. Jerome's play.[3] I differ vitally from his story because it is not a detective story. There is in it none of this great Christian idea of tearing their evil out of men; it lacks the realism of the saints. Redemption should bring truth as well as peace; and truth is a fine thing, though the materialists did go mad about it. Things must be faced, even in order to be forgiven: the great objection to 'letting sleeping dogs lie' is that they lie in more senses than one. But in Mr. Jerome's 'Passing of the Third Floor Back' the redeemer is not a divine detective, pitiless in his resolve to know and pardon. Rather he is a sort of divine dupe, who does not pardon at all because he does not see anything that is going on. It may, or may not, be true to say, 'Tout comprendre est tout pardonner'.[4] But it is much more evidently true to say, 'Rien comprendre est rien pardonner', and the Third Floor Back does not seem to comprehend anything. He might after all be a quite selfish sentimentalist, who found it comforting to think well of his neighbours. There is nothing very heroic in loving after you have been deceived. The heroic business is to love after you have been undeceived.

****

When I saw this play it was natural to compare it with another play which I had not seen, but which I have read in its printed version. I mean Mr. Rann Kennedy's 'Servant in the House',[5] the success of which sprawls over so many of the American newspapers. This also is concerned with a dim, yet evidently divine, figure changing the destinies of a whole group of persons. It is a better play structurally than the other, but there is nothing aesthetic or fastidious about it. It is as much or more than the other sensational, democratic, and (I use the word in a sound and good sense) Salvationist.

But the difference lies precisely in this – that the Christ of Mr. Kennedy's play insists on really knowing all the souls that he loves; he declines to conquer by a kind of supernatural stupidity. He pardons evil, but he will not ignore it. In other words, he is a Christian, and not a Christian Scientist. The distinction doubtless is partly explained by the problems severally selected. Mr. Jerome practically supposes Christ to be trying to save disreputable people; and that, of course, is naturally a simple business. Mr. Kennedy supposes Him to be trying to save the reputable people, which is a much larger affair. The chief characters in 'The Servant in the House' are a popular and strenuous vicar, universally respected, and his fashionable and forcible wife. It would have been no good to tell these people they had some good in them – for that was what they were telling themselves all day long. *They* had to be reminded that they had some bad in them – instinctive idolatries and silent treasons which they always tried to forget. It is in connection with these crimes of wealth and culture that we face the real problem of positive evil. The whole of Mr. Blatchford's controversy about sin was vitiated throughout by one's consciousness that whenever he wrote the word 'sinner' he thought of a man in rags. But here, again, we can find truth merely by referring to vulgar literature – its unfailing fountain. Whoever read a detective story about poor people? The poor have crimes; but the poor have no secrets. And it is because the proud have secrets that they need to be detected before they are forgiven.

272a them.] in *MM* is followed by:

> Christianity no more created the mediaeval tortures than it did the Chinese tortures; it inherited them from any empire as heathen as the Chinese.

272b The Church ... employ cruelty.] in *MM* opens a new paragraph.

Notes
1. THE DIVINE DETECTIVE: Reprinted in *MM*, pp. 235–40.
2. 'That', says Sherlock Holmes ... *free*: Probably a reference to 'The Adventure of Charles Augustus Milverton', in *The Return of Sherlock Holmes* (1905).
3. *The Passing of the Third Floor Back ... Mr. Jerome's play*: The play – published in 1908 – was an attempt by Jerome K. Jerome to produce a serious work in contrast to much of his other writing (D. Atkinson, *ODNB*). It was made into a film twice (in 1918 and 1935).
4. *Tout comprendre est tout pardonner*: This expression is usually attributed to Leo Tolstoy (*War and Peace* (1868), vol. 1, part 1, ch. 28), but it is probably much older as a proverb, and other versions of it occur; e.g. in Goethe, *Torquato Tasso* (1790), II.i.1113: 'Was wir verstehen, das können wir nicht tadeln'.
5. *Mr. Rann Kennedy's 'Servant in the House'*: Charles Rann Kennedy (1871–1950), was an English dramatist, actor and producer who was born and educated in the Midlands. After an early career in commerce, he took to the stage; he first appeared in New York in 1903 and became an American citizen in 1917. His plays were concerned with moral problems. *The Servant in the House* was published in 1908.

February 27, 1909.

WAS DICKENS A SOCIALIST?

There is much that is supercilious and something even that is silly, about the boast made by some authors that they 'never reply to critics'. It depends, or ought to depend, upon whether the author has anything to say. A poet might have created the most superb poem and received the most imbecile review; and still he would have nothing to say. If a critic had written 'As for Mr. Milton's notion of English verse, we need only quote the exquisitely ugly and idiotic line:

> "While the still morn went out with sandals gray",[1]

our readers will scarcely desire to hear any more of such stuff' – if a critic had written thus of Milton, then certainly Milton would have been unwise in replying; for there would have been nothing to reply. Good poetry is all a matter of taste. But suppose a critic had said of Milton, 'He wishes to make us Republicans, like the Turks', or 'His account of the Garden of Eden gravely differs from that given in the Book of Exodus', then I think John Milton might have been excused if he wrote in reference to the mere facts, and pointed out that there was no Eden in Exodus and no Republic in Turkey.

And as a large number of the book reviews which I have read (and written) were sprinkled with statements of a similar accuracy, I for one know too much to blame any author for mere egotism when he protests against a review. It is egotistical of you to complain of merely aesthetic misunderstanding of your poem. For you cannot really talk about your poem; therefore, you must be talking about yourself. But you could talk about a clear fact without talking either about yourself or your poem; and talking about facts is to be encouraged, especially in a scientific age in which it is mostly forbidden. But there is another occasion upon which a poet or other writer should be welcomed when he answers the critic; and that is at the opposite extreme. A poet should not defend his poem, but he should always defend his theory of poetry; or his theory of anything.

The two things that justify retort are a small fact and a big truth. For both are outside oneself. Milton might justly have fought about the pronunciation of Tiresias or about the doctrine of Calvin; for God governed in defiance of Milton, and the dead Greeks spoke in spite of him. The little fact and the big truth were alike outside his own mere personality; therefore, he could have argued about them. But he could not have argued about 'Paradise Lost'; it was not worth it. It is not worth the slightly vulgar condescension of replying to criticism; nothing but conviction is worth that. It is, when all is said, slightly undignified to answer a criticism. Now a man's dignity is much more important than his poems. But his opinions (if he really has any) are much more important than his dignity.

****

I therefore make no excuse for commenting in this column on a reply made to a review which I wrote on another page of this paper – a review of Mr. Edwin Pugh's work on Charles Dickens.[2] Mr. Pugh begins, indeed, upon the old fastidious note of Matthew Arnold and others – 'This is the first time in my life that I have fallen to the temptation to reply to my critics'. Why should not Mr. Pugh reply to his critics? Why should Mr. Pugh 'fall' even in replying to me? We have both written books on Dickens, and both books consist chiefly of lectures on the French Revolution and the future of modern England. I may think that, in going over my manuscript, I introduced occasional allusions to Dickens with more dexterity and art. Mr. Pugh may think that his rare allusions to Dickens were even more felicitous. But we shall not quarrel about egotistical affairs of that sort. We are both on the broad road. We both think Dickens more important than art, and we both think democracy more important than Dickens.

The point on which we disagree is this: that Mr. Pugh thinks that the democratic sentiment, obviously strong in Dickens, amounted to a moral sympathy with what is called Socialism. To this I replied, obviously enough, that there is nothing specially democratic about Socialism at all. Socialism (I could repeat it as a schoolboy much better than my Greek Iambics) is the assumption by the State of all the means of production, distribution, and exchange. The State might be a despotic State; it might be an aristocratic State; it might be a Papal State. But if it owned and distributed all essential capital it would be a Socialistic State. I am quite well acquainted with all the sound arguments which connect such a State with unity or efficiency or progress; but I cannot see what connects it with Dickens. Socialism would certainly stop the present anarchy; but Dickens did not especially object to anarchy. Dickens objected to tyranny; and a good half of the tyrants he denounced were Socialist tyrants; that is, State and Municipal tyrants. I pointed out that Bumble and Mr. Tite Barnacle were officers of State appointment, paid and controlled by the Commonwealth, and were therefore in the ultimate sense Socialists.³ To this Mr. Pugh replies 'they were nothing of the kind; they were flunkeys'. Quite so; but why is it un-Socialistic to be a flunkey – so long as you are a State flunkey. The State might own the means of production, and still desire, in a passion of poetic maternity, to produce flunkeys. The State might own the means of distribution, and still manage, with the most exquisite efficiency, to distribute flunkeys. The King's flunkeys are national flunkeys. The Lord Mayor's flunkeys are municipal flunkeys. What conceivable reason have we for supposing that the mere fact of wages being paid out of the Treasury would eliminate precedence or servility, when we know that these things are rampant among the very people who are paid out of the Treasury? Of course, one may be a Socialist and wish it to be democratic. My friend Mr. Donaldson⁴ wishes it to be Catholic; and another friend (whom I will not name) wishes it to be polygamous. But Socialism, as such, is not polygamous, is not Catholic, and is not democratic. Socialism is simply the proposal that the Government, instead of taxing all property equally or unequally, should secure all property, and distribute it equally or unequally. And when it comes to the next Cecil (who will show a marvellous talent for military analysis) or the next Churchill (who will have made the subject of Australia his own) I think you will find that the distribution will be unequal; that the dreary history of human jobbery will be drearily renewed. You will say 'But they can vote against Cecil if they like'. I answer, with some sadness, 'But they could do that now'.

****

This matter is worth the pause of a moment; because Dickens is one of the few full and undivided voices that remain to us; one of the few men who speak simply and strongly out of their own feelings, which are the final facts. He was neither a Socialist nor an Individualist, which is certainly worse. He was a man who saw that men abused their advantages over men; the advantage of having wit, like Mr. Skimpole, the advantage of having whiskers, like Mr. Mantalini, the advantage of having rank, like Sir Leicester Dedlock, the advantage of having money, like Mr. Bounderby, the advantage of being a Socialist official, like Mr. Tite Barnacle or Bumble. That is the true instinct of Liberalism; the instinct of potential revolt; the instinct of splendid and immortal suspicion. Whatever will be powerful may by tyrannical; we shall remember that and you have not heard the last of us. After all Socialist legislation there will remain a certain organ, a large and watchful eye, the great satiric eye of Dickens, which will see the face of Barnacle as plainly among your Socialist officers as it now sees the face of Gradgrind⁵ among your Anarchist employers.

Notes
1. *'While the still morn ... gray'*: From *Lycidas* (1637):

   Thus sang the uncouth swain to th' oaks and rills,
   While the still morn went out with sandals grey;
   He touched the tender stops of various quills,
   With eager thought warbling his Doric lay

2. *a review which I wrote on another page ... Charles Dickens*: see 'The Democracy of Dickens', *DN*, 30 December 1908, pp. 236–9 above.
3. *Bumble and Mr. Tite Barnacle ... Socialists*: Mr Bumble is the beadle in *Oliver Twist*; Mr Tite Barnacle is one of the Barnacle family that (in *Little Dorrit*) controls the Circumlocution Office, one of the principles of which is 'never, on any account whatever, to give a straightforward answer'. A puzzling feature of this paragraph is that neither in 'The Democracy of Dickens' nor in his book on Dickens does Chesterton actually say the things that he here attributes to himself.
4. *Mr. Donaldson*: Frederick (sometimes Frederic) Lewis Donaldson (1860–1953), was an English Anglo-Catholic priest and Christian socialist; he served as Canon of Westminster from 1924 to 1951.
5. *Mr. Skimpole ... Gradgrind*: Harold Skimpole and Sir Leicester Dedlock are characters in *Bleak House*; Alfred Mantalini, whose real name is Alfred Muntle, is in *Nicholas Nickleby*; Bounderby and Gradgrind are in *Hard Times*.

March 6, 1909.

THE NEW TESTS.

The fellow who is always asking for 'facts,' and says he does not care about 'theories' is a very unbusinesslike fellow, not to be trusted with a purse or a perambulator. He is unbusinesslike for many reasons, but among them this – that, fixing his eye on the facts, by which he means the external shapes of things and ignoring any principle in them, he becomes unable to recognise the same principle when it appears under some new shape. He is like a man who watches so carefully for rain that he cannot see the snow. Or he is like a man so narrow and cautious in keeping caterpillars that he lets them all escape as butterflies. He cannot see the old thing under a new disguise; he expects the enemy's face with such eager hatred that he never notices his mask.

One case of this can be noticed in connection with that political and religious problem about which we Liberals have torn everything to tatters for the last twenty years; what we called the imposition of Tests.[1] The phrase, of course, like all political phrases, sometimes became a rather shapeless shibboleth, and it is necessary from time to time to restate the solid, Radical doctrine in the matter. Of course, it is not tests in themselves that are wrong. We must have tests for teachers as we have tests for cabmen; but the test for a cabman is that he can drive a cab, and the test for a teacher is that he can teach whatever we want taught.

Everything depends upon what office we are proposing to fill; if it is a public office it should not have a sectional test. It is illiberal to say that no one but a Wesleyan may be Commander-in-Chief; but it is not illiberal to say that no one but a Wesleyan may be President of the Wesleyan Conference. It is intolerant to say that only a Catholic may be a policeman; but it is not intolerant to say that only a Catholic may be a Pope.

What Liberalism has always disliked, in short, is not tests, but irrelevant tests; it has disliked the power, whatever it was, to step beyond its plain and admitted functions and begin to encourage and discourage other and more enormous human affairs. It must not do anything more even if it is something more important. If the Postmaster-General is a sincere Pantheist (which I do not for a moment suggest), he must regard Pantheism as including everything, or what becomes of poor old Pan? But he ought not therefore to insist on Pantheism in all the postmen. If Mr. Haldane[2] is an Upstanding Glassite (which I neither affirm or deny), he must mean that all heaven and earth are covered by the religion of a Mr. Glass; that is what one means by having a religion. But Mr. Haldane's recruits, however Upstanding, need not all be Glassites.[3]

In brief, we have borne witness for a hundred years to this principle: government is an important thing, religion is a much more important thing, yet it does not follow that it is good for either of them that the first should impose the second.

****

But if we concede this, what shall we say of what follows, of what is happening now? If there are some things, habits, tastes, and points of view which even responsible statesmen should not enforce, what are we to say when irresponsible tradesmen enforce them? If we should protest against the ancient human republic, which is our only home, forcing us to be Christian Scientists or Vegetarians, what shall we say of the same sort of commandment if it comes only with the divine authority of Crosse and Blackwell or Marshall and Snelgrove?[4] Shall we allow the cobbler to go beyond his last when we have already forbidden the King to go beyond his sceptre?

You would smile if I suggested that Liberals might impose upon their employees the obligation of being Republicans. You might even laugh if I indicated that the firm of Mr. William Whiteley[5] might insist on a mystic celibacy. But things not unlike these are actually being done. That power to control thoughts, moralities, and tones of life which we would not give to the Commonwealth itself, crowned with the auctoritas of the people, we are actually giving to every twopenny firm, to every ephemeral business that can scrape together enough money to enslave a score or two of men.

Two detestable examples of this loose and lawless persecution have appeared of late. An insurance firm has agreed to bring pressure on its servants to force them to enter the Army;[6] and a gas company has brought pressure upon all its servants to prevent them from entering public-houses.[7] Now, if the British Commonwealth, by its own high democratic authority, chooses to establish Conscription, let it establish Conscription. If it chooses to establish Total Prohibition let it establish Total Prohibition. Neither course accords with the English Liberal tradition; but both courses may accord quite well with the dignity and consistency of the English Government.

But it is altogether intolerable that the very autocracy which is too great for the public grasp should be permitted to the private grasp. If conscription or prohibition are too daring even for a whole people, they must be perfectly impudent in one wealthy person. I for one would rebel against this style of coercion with mere laughter and contempt; and quite apart from the questions involved in it. I might risk my life at command of the complete society to which I belong; but it would be too absurd to risk my life at the command of the Alliance Company, which only exists to insure it. I might cut off my beer by a great national consensus; but it would be too ludicrous to cut off the beer at the mere command of men whose only political quality is that they can turn on the gas.

A world in which society made a systematic tariff and scheme of life for everyone would be perfectly dignified, though slightly dull. But that pianoforte makers should forbid the use of tobacco; that jam factories should insist on the wearing of sandals; that one hatter should make a hundred vegetarians; that one successful Christian Science cheesemonger should ruin half the doctors in his neighbourhood; all that is a chaos of caprice and tyranny which is not to be borne. In the old times employers, even if wicked, were sane; but now they have grown rich and are therefore slowly going mad. The only question is how long and how far we shall submit to their madness. Now I, for one, can endure mania, but not monomania. I object to being governed by a special aristocracy of lunatics. If we are to go mad, for God's sake let us all go mad together.

Notes

1. *imposition of Tests*: Chesterton is referring to the dispute over religious tests for the recruitment of teachers in rate-aided schools. In the last – failed – attempt to find a settlement agreeable to all sides in 1908, the Prime Minister referred to twelve or thirteen years of warfare after the consensus brought about by the Education Act of 1870 began to break down: see 'The Thing Indifferent', *DN*, 28 November 1908, p. 221, n. 2 above. The tests would have been abolished if the 1908 Bill had succeeded.
2. *Mr. Haldane*: Richard Burdon Haldane, Viscount Haldane; see P. W. W., '"G. K. C." at Home', *DN*, 13 December 1907, Volume 4, p. 377, n. 5 above.
3. *Glassites*: Glassites were a Christian sect founded in Scotland in about 1730 by a minister of the Church of Scotland called John Glas (1695–1773). Robert Sandeman, who established the sect in America under the name Sandemanians, was Glas's son-in-law.
4. *Crosse and Blackwell or Marshall and Snelgrove*; for Cross and Blackwell, see 'The Battle of the Standard', *DN*, 12 November 1904, Volume 2, p. 319, n. 9 above; for Marshall and Snelgrove, see 'In Topsy-Turvy Land', *DN*, 8 December 1906, Volume 4, p. 107, n. 2 above.
5. *Mr. William Whiteley*: Evidently, despite having taken such an interest in the man who shot him (see 'On Hanging a Man', 30 March 1907, Volume 4, p. 189, n. 2 above), Chesterton has forgotten that Mr Whiteley is no more.
6. *An insurance firm ... enter the Army*: In early February, the Board of the Alliance Assurance Company had decided that as of 1 March, all new employees would be required to give an undertaking that they would join the Territorial Force, a reserve army that was

introduced in 1908. The decision of the Company was commended by R. B. Haldane, Secretary of State for War: *The Times*, 6 February 1909, p. 9b.

7. *a gas company ... entering public-houses*: not identified.

March 13, 1909.

THE REAL MOB.

Though much has been said in this column about political democracy, I am not a bigot in favour of that mere political machinery. I can imagine life livable [*sic*] under many other forms of polity, despotism, militarism, bureaucracy, or priestcraft. There is only one form of government which I absolutely refuse to endure; and that is government by the educated classes. Government by the educated classes simply means the tyranny of all those frivolous prejudices which have nothing to do with real life over all those brutal or painful prejudices that have something to do with it.

Thus the poor have a prejudice against the workhouses, probably an exaggerated prejudice; but a prejudice founded on some first-hand experience. But the educated have a prejudice in favour of a mere word, the word 'Municipal', which may cover anything from Plato's Republic to Bumble. Thus the poor somewhat blindly and recklessly suspect the hospitals; but not half so blindly and recklessly as the rich trust the hospitals. Thus the lower classes submit to send their sons to Board Schools, though they grumble at them. But their position is at least more sensible than that of the educated, who exalt and deify the Board Schools, but would never consent to send their children to them. The bias of the uneducated is a bias true at least so far as it goes; it is not always a truth, but it is always a fact; that is, it is a fragment of experience.

But the bias of the educated has often no root in realities at all. It may easily be a mere error; a mistake made in some book. I would rather trust a twelfth-century peasant telling me about pigs than a twelfth-century Crusader telling me about salamanders; yet the knight would certainly be the more educated of the two. So I would rather hear Mr. Will Crooks[1] telling me about one Jew in the East End than Mr. Carl Joubert[2] telling me about all the Jews in the East. A theory may possibly be *entirely* valueless, but a fact can never be.

***

The truth is that an aristocracy is in certain points pre-eminently a vulgar thing; it has two characteristics which we associate with vulgarity – the pursuit of mere novelties and a swiftness and superficiality of judgment. One racks one's brain vainly to imagine where people got the idea that an aristocracy was a guardian of old customs and old institutions. It must be a false generalisation from the French noblesse, who were smashed so completely that they forgot their own tradition, and believed what they read in history books – an absurd habit. Now that the French aristocracy does not exist it is haughty, heraldic, and antiquarian. When the French aristocracy did exist, when it was powerful and genuine, then it was pushing, sceptical, eager, atheistic, and in love with all innovations. Now that French counts are only citizens they want to be aristocrats; when they really were aristocrats, they wanted to be moderns. And everywhere else, including this country, the upper class is positively vulgar in its pursuit of the latest thing. A real duchess of the controlling sort would no more appear with last year's philosophy than with last year's hat. The truth is that all those charges which oligarchs have always made against the masses are especially true of an oligarchy – impatience, fickleness, fast and furious decisions. An aristocracy is a real rabble, a genuine mob, with all the vices of a mob, and this additional vice – that it is much easier to madden a small mob than a large one.

****

The House of Lords, for instance, is a real mob. People can still be found, even in the upper class itself, who defend the House of Lords; but they are commonly people of whom one must hope that some knowledge of a better world compensates for their peculiar ignorance of this one.[3] These innocents advance the argument that a Second Chamber is a good thing because it delays and discusses legislation. So it might be, if it did anything of the sort. But it does not. If there is one sin of which the House of Lords is wholly innocent it is that of delaying legislation. If there is one merit that the House of Lords cannot claim, it is that of discussing things at length. It swallows laws; and it spits them out; but it does both in a great hurry.

The House of Lords is not a slow stagnant unyielding sort of institution. It is, on the contrary, a very headlong, breathless, and American sort of institution; as might be expected from the pushing City men and parvenu lawyers who go so increasingly to compose it. But even that part of it which really is aristocratic is also rapid and reckless. A Bill like the Licensing Bill, for instance, is discussed in a various and detailed way in a million decent homes; it is discussed in the Commons to the point of tedium. But the jolly rabble in the Upper House will have no such pedantic dissections; they make very short work of the thing. The Lords have never resisted any Tory measure, even when it was manifestly of a sort which a Second Chamber exists to reconsider – a hasty Jingo measure, a hasty coercion measure, or a hasty No-Popery measure. But this is the smallest part of the case. The case is that our Second Chamber has never specially delayed, has never specially discussed any measure. It has always behaved like a mob; it has lynched them or carried them in triumph.

Indeed, it was among the vainest of the fantasies of men to think that they could erect against the mob the barrier of an aristocracy. That is itself a crowd, small, fierce, vague, and full of all the fevers of a crowd. The only barrier against the mob is the people. Only the actual public body itself is strong enough, actual enough, ancient enough, and if you will, stupid enough to arrest the sudden charge of a sophistry or the tireless teasing of fashions and fads. If you have a new religion which says that God is a pessimist or a new morality which says that mushrooms should have votes, you stand a very good chance of knocking down two or three marquises or going home with a good bag of earls. It is with the coalheaver that you will be closeted for a considerable time.

Notes
1. *Mr. Will Crooks*: Will Crooks (1852–1921), was a politician and devout Christian who, with George Lansbury, was a pioneer of the Socialist and Labour movement in Poplar and became the first Labour mayor in London in 1901.
2. *Mr. Carl Joubert*: Carl Joubert (d. 1906), was an English journalist and author of several books on Russia and Judaism; Chesterton is probably referring to his *Aspects of the Jewish Question: Zionism and Antisemitism* (1906).
3. *People of whom one must hope ... peculiar ignorance of this one*: Perhaps he is referring to the 'Lords Spiritual': the twenty-six Anglican bishops who sit as of right in the House of Lords and who may be supposed to have 'some knowledge of a better world'.

March 20, 1909.

ON ARTIFICIALITY.

One of the words that worry and betray us is the word 'artificial'; there ought only to be the word 'insincere'. It does not specially matter whether a thing is made by man or Nature; the question is whether it is made to deceive. A wooden leg is artificial; but it is not insincere. A chameleon is disgustingly insincere; but he is not artificial. If a lady tinted her cheeks to an exquisite peacock green it would be artifice, but scarcely vanity. But over and above this obvious distinction there is a further fact of evident philosophy. We talk of men easily mistaking the false for the true, the artificial for the natural.

But it is quite as easy to mistake what is true for what is plainly false and artificial. Natural things look so unnatural. You are proud of not being deceived into thinking the golden wig of some duchess is hair. But remember that a child always thinks the hair of a negro is a wig; for the excellent reason that it looks like one. It does: it seems a system of careful curls, like a doormat made and kept by old maids. Because he is a barbarian he looks too tidy. It is the same with tropical birds, which look like toy birds, with tropical flowers and fruits which look literally as if they were modelled out of wax. All unfamiliar colours give us the sensation of having been smeared upon the outside of a thing; and if we had seen less of them, it may be we should regard all things as painted. The proverb that the devil is not so black as he is painted is, perhaps, an expression of this incredulity about natural colours. Many sages, if they saw it for the first time, would say that the grass was not so green as it was painted; that the sky was not so blue as it was painted. They would accuse the rose of rouging a little. For, indeed, the colours of this cosmos which is our country are so frank and fierce that to people of tender sensibility they must appear garish and theatrical. I should not blame a modern artist if he felt that the starlit sky was a very vulgar and irregular show of spangles. I should, of course, take the earliest opportunity of removing him from my commonwealth; but I should not blame him. I have a rooted suspicion that most of these modes and periods which were called artificial were not artificial in the least; but bore witness to an essential truth.

Take any example you prefer. Take that pastoral notion praised by Theocritus,[1] by Virgil,[2] and by Pope.[3] When confronted with this the modern Englishman smiles a fat, superior smile, and produces what he calls 'The Real Shepherd', as against what he calls 'The Ideal Shepherd'; the dancing and piping peasant of the eclogues and elegies. The modern Englishman produces the actual English shepherd, who drives or drifts after other men's sheep on the Sussex Downs or the Yorkshire Dales: a beery, bloated, stunted yokel and says 'This is the natural shepherd'. But he is wrong. This is the artificial shepherd; this is the creation of elaborate political and economic art. A fastidious aristocracy framed and proportioned that figure; the men who stole the Abbey lands whipped him (literally) into shape; the enclosure of commons enclosed him more and more in an artistic frame; he was long rubbed down and polished by the squires; and the last touch was given to him by the hunger of the Forties[4] and the far-off madness of the city. So that now he is what is called in art a finished product; he is pretty nearly done with. But if you go to other countries which have not the privilege of being owned by a few proprietors, you will find that the shepherd of fact is not so very unlike the shepherd of fancy: the shepherd of Virgil and Pope. There is sin and sorrow in Italy; for the matter of that there is sin and sorrow in Virgil. But the Italian peasant does dance, he does sing in series, he does fling his body into all the free attitudes of the hunter or the lover that are arrested for us in traditional sculpture. The beautiful shepherd is the real shepherd; it is the ugly, heavy, grimy shepherd who is a product of civilization; it is the dirty shepherd who is a mere work of art.

There is another instance that has often struck me of the old literary or artistic forms which are called artificial, but which are in truth singularly realistic. Read those old Elizabethan or Cavalier love lyrics which are always fantastically complaining of the 'coldness' of a woman; which monotonously compare her eyes to ice or her bosom to snow. Read those remarkable sonnets which attempt to compliment a woman by calling her cruel and heartless.[5] And then, having done that, ask any honest man whether he does not suffer from such arctic intervals; and ask any honest woman whether she does not sometimes depend upon an armour of ice. Then modern novelists write realistic studies of feminine 'temperament'; little quiet everyday episodes, in which the woman rolls on the floor and foams at the mouth or throws vitriol or elopes with a Brahmin.[6] But there is really far more psychological accuracy in the old smooth stanzas about Lydia and Chloe; for a certain negative cruelty, a certain sudden appearance of heartlessness and hollowness, is really the worst weapon of a woman.

As I think of those unjustly contemned graces, I feel as if I were growing more elegant every minute, and am more than half inclined to powder my hair.

Powder is a good example of the honest artifice, which is not deception; old dandies whitened their hair as if in symbolic reverence for old age; modern dandies dye their hair in insolent assertion of youth. There are only two things in that old style of speech and habit on which I am still an infidel. I do not want trees clipped into cocks and hens; and I never saw a lady 'trip' – that is, not without falling down. But for this, I am just now a complete 18th century Man of Sensibility; with a diamond and a dewy tear, and I have even expressed my feelings in my favourite metre, which you will please to note is an artificial one:

> If sometimes I have stopped and sighed
> In the full tide of mirth and glee,
> If, while I made a butter-slide,
> Or took a bishop on a spree.
> Quite without warning, suddenly,
> The torrent of my tears is shed,
> I shall be better presently,
> I cry because Queen Anne is dead.
>
> Sleeps Hector on Scamander side,
> And Harold by the Sussex sea,
> And Egypt's awful eyes undried,
> Above the bones of Antony.
> And he whose name was anarchy,
> Attila, keeps his bloody bed
> Under a well-clipt garden tree,
> I cry because Queen Anne is dead.
>
> I see dead poets in their pride,
> Simp'ring, with snuff, and sipping tea,
> Dick Steele, the hot and humble-eyed,
> Pope, strutting with deformity.
> One cassocked in a dean's agree,
> Who shakes his doomed and dreadful head,
> Oh, what is England, where is she?
> I cry because Queen Anne is dead.
>
> ENVOI
>
> Prince, when your slaves by your decree
> Pour down my nostrils boiling lead,
> *They* do not wring a moan from me,
> I cry because Queen Anne is dead.

Notes

1. *Pastoral notion ... Theocritus*: 'Pastoral' or 'bucolic' literature, briefly described, treats in an idealized or 'romantic' manner rural subjects and the lives of country people. The *Idylls* of the third-century Greek poet Theocritus are the earliest examples.
2. *Virgil*: Virgil's ten *Eclogues* are an adaptation into Latin forms of the genre of Theocritus; their influence is felt in more or less all Italian and English pastoral poetry from the fourteenth to the eighteenth century.
3. *Pope*: Alexander Pope's *Pastorals* were among his earliest poems, written when he was sixteen in emulation of Virgil's *Eclogues*; they first appeared in the sixth part of Jacob Tonson's *Poetical Miscellanies* some five years after their composition, on 2 May 1709.
4. *hunger of the Forties*: i.e. the economic depression of the 1840s – the 'Hungry Forties': in 1839 there was a serious slump in trade, leading to a steep increase in unemployment exacerbated by poor harvests in 1839–41 and by the fact that the Corn Laws kept the price of bread artificially high. The 1840s radically changed the character of rural life in England.
5. *Read those old Elizabethan or Cavalier ... cruel and heartless*: Many examples of what Chesterton has in mind can be found in *Cavalier and Courtier Lyrists* (ed. W. H. Dircks, with notes by E. Sharwood Smith; London and Newcastle-upon-Tyne: Walter Scott Publishing Company, 1891) and *The New Oxford Book of Seventeenth Century Verse* (ed. A. Fowler; Oxford: Oxford University Press, 1991).
6. *The modern novelists ... Brahmin*: This is presumably a comment on overwrought modern fiction in general; but among the things that Chesterton has in mind may be George Gissing's *The Nether World* (1889) and Conan Doyle's story 'The Adventure of the Illustrious Client' (in *The Case Book of Sherlock Holmes*).

March 27, 1909.

ON KEEPING A DOG.[1]

Cynics often speak of the disillusioning effects of experience, but I for one have found that nearly all things not evil are better in experience than in theory. I found love with a small *l* more thrilling than Love with a large one, and when I saw the Mediterranean it was bluer than the colour blue. In theory, for example, sleep is a negative thing, a mere cessation of life. But nothing will persuade me that sleep is not really quite positive, some mysterious pleasure which is too perfect to be remembered. It must be some drawing on our divine energies, some forgotten refreshment at the ancient fountains of life. If this is not so, why do we cling to sleep when we have already had enough of it; why does waking up always seem like descending from heaven upon earth? I believe that sleep is a sacrament; or, what is the same thing, a food.

※※※

Here, however, I only want to maintain that the real experience of things is often much better than our poetic anticipation of them; that peaks are often higher than they look in pictures and truths more terribly true than they appear in copy-books. Take, for example, the innovation which I have of late introduced into my domestic life; he is a four-legged innovation in the shape of an Aberdeen terrier. I have always imagined myself to be a lover of all animals, because I have never met any animal that I definitely disliked. Most people draw the line somewhere. Lord Roberts dislikes cats; the best woman I know objects to spiders; a Theosophist I know protects, but detests, mice; and many leading humanitarians have an objection to human beings.

But I cannot recall ever having shrunk from an animal; I do not mind a slug, however slimy he is, nor a rhinoceros, however much his horn is exalted. When I was a little boy I used to keep a pack of snails as representing what I thought the proper pace of hunting. Thus I fell into the mistake common to many modern universalists and humanitarians. I thought that I loved all God's creatures, whereas the only point was that I did not hate them. I did not dislike the camel for having a hump or the whale for containing blubber. But I could not seriously have supposed that the time would ever come when a whale's blubber would move my heart with a quiver of affection; or that I should know one camel's hump among others as one knows the profile of a beautiful woman. This is the first of the extraordinary effects of having a dog, upon one who has never had one before. One loves an animal like a man instead of merely accepting an animal like an optimist.

****

But then, again, if the dog is loved he is loved as a dog; not as a fellow-citizen, or an idol, or a pet, or a product of evolution. The moment you are responsible for one respectable animal, that moment an abyss opens as wide as the world between cruelty and the necessary coercion of animals. There are some people who talk of what they call 'Corporal Punishment', and class under that head the hideous torture inflicted on unfortunate citizens in our prisons and workhouses; and also the smack one gives to a silly boy or the whipping of an intolerable terrier. You might as well invent a phrase called 'Reciprocal Concussion' and leave it to be understood that you included under this head kissing, kicking, the collision of boats at sea, the embracing of young Germans, and the meeting of comets in mid-air.

That is the second moral value of the thing; the moment you have an animal in your charge you soon discover what is really cruelty to animals, and what is only kindness to them. For instance, some people have called it inconsistent in me to be an anti-vivisectionist and yet to be in favour of ordinary sports. I can only say that I can imagine myself shooting my dog, but cannot imagine myself vivisecting him.

But there is something deeper in the matter than all that, only the hour is late, and both the dog and I are too drowsy to interpret it. He lies in front of me curled up before the fire, as so many dogs must have lain before so many fires. I sit on one side of that hearth, as so many men must have sat by so many hearths. Somehow this creature has completed my manhood; somehow, I cannot explain why, a man ought to have a dog. A man ought to have six legs; those other four legs are part of him. Our alliance is older than any of the passing and priggish explanations that are offered of either of us; before evolution was, we were. You can find it written in a book that I am a mere survival of a squabble of anthropoid apes; and perhaps I am. I am sure I have no objection. But my dog knows I am a man, and you will not find the meaning of that word written in any book as clearly as it is written in his soul.

It may be written in a book that my dog is canine; and from this it may be deduced that he must hunt with a pack, since all canines hunt with a pack. Hence it may be argued (in the book) that if I have one Aberdeen terrier I ought to have twenty-five Aberdeen terriers. But my dog knows that I do not ask him to hunt with a pack; he knows that I do not care a curse whether he is canine or not so long as he is my dog. That is the real secret of the matter which the superficial evolutionists cannot be got to see. If traceable history be the test, civilization is much older than the savagery of evolution. The civilized dog is older than the wild dog of science. The civilized man is older than the primitive man of science. We feel it in our bones that we are the antiquities, and that the visions of biology are the fancies and the fads. The books do not matter; the night is closing in, and it is too dark to read books. Faintly against the fading firelight can be traced the prehistoric outlines of the man and the dog.

Notes
1.   *ON KEEPING A DOG*: Reprinted in *LL*, pp. 147–50.

April 3, 1909.

THE THREE FOOLS.

I do not know whether everybody remembers, as everybody ought to remember, the old fairy tale which is called in England 'The Three Sillies', but which in Grimm is called, I think, 'Hans and Alice', or some such name. One never knows, however, in these days how far ignorance has spread, so, in case anyone is really in darkness on this point, I will briefly recount this sublime and philosophical tale.[1]

****

A young squire fell in love with the daughter of a poor peasant, and was eagerly entertained at the cottage supper, during which the daughter went down into the cellar to draw the beer. When she had turned on the tap she caught sight of a chopper hanging on the wall, and this immense and mystical thought rushed upon her mind. 'Suppose I do marry and have a beautiful child, and then one morning a chopper falls on his head', whereupon she sat down with flowing tears in front of the flowing ale.

Upstairs the young man tried to make himself agreeable, but could not help his eyes straying towards the door in expectancy of the lady, and possibly of the drink. Observing this, the mother went downstairs and was astonished to find her daughter sobbing and the beer running away. To her, however, the daughter, in a broken voice, pointed out how dreadful it would be if, in the remote future, a chopper should fall on the head of her hypothetical child. Whereupon the mother (in fine contrast to the unsympathetic mothers of our modern soulful heroines) sat down on a stool and cried too.

The talk between the two gentlemen upstairs became jerky and embarrassed. They remarked on the weather, on the imminence of a German naval victory, and similar topics, till at last the master of the house could bear no more, and rushed downstairs to see what was the matter. To him also the grave potentialities of the chopper were explained. After a moment's struggle with his manly feelings, he also burst into tears at the mere possibility of such an occurrence.

The young man upstairs whistled and looked at albums for some little time, and eventually made his way down to the cellar, where he saw the father, mother, and daughter sitting in a row, and mingling their tears with the rising flood of ale which was by this time overflowing the apartment. In a style slightly and excusably staccato, he asked the meaning of this family group. Then, like three witches, they lifted up their awful voices, full of that deep, irrational rationality of doubt and doom which is in the Greek tragedies and the Northern tales, and told him how they had realised that all happiness might be a lure of fate, how any human wish may walk towards destruction, and how even heroic love like his might end only in the golden head of some child above whom hung the hideous and appointed axe. The young man considered them for a few minutes, and then spoke, with an air of finality, as follows: 'I love your daughter, and I will not give her up yet; but this is what I will do. I will gird on my sword and mount my horse, and I will ride over the whole world for a year and a day, seeking every dark place, every cave or crypt or madhouse or lost tribe. And if in the whole world I can find three greater fools than you, I will come back, and our wedding bells shall ring'. With these haughty and highly creditable words the young man went away. And the rest of the story describes how he found one man who tried to fish the moon out of the lake, another who tried to keep spring by chaining up the cuckoo, etc., etc., and so came back and married the mystical and fatalist young lady, and lived happily ever afterwards, having found that she was not the greatest fool in the world.

****

It has always seemed to me that this fairy tale has in it the whole soul of fact; the unquestionable solidity of the great stories; it is not like a modern tale, a mere 'aspect'; it has the three dimensions of man: breadth which is liberality, and depth which is reality, and height which is religion. How fair and solid and many-sided it is I can only express by saying that almost any modern author, however great, would have made the story more narrow and one-sided.

Let us suppose, for instance, that story told by Maeterlinck[2] and by Rudyard Kipling.[3] With what magical instinct, with what faint but faultless sympathy, Maeterlinck would follow and appreciate the unbegotten apprehensions of the three fools. Maeterlinck would have exquisite understanding of the cosmic panic of the poor girl who felt suddenly that her own intoxication of happiness might be merely drugging her to danger. Maeterlinck knows better than any other modern pagan that every step along the road of life is the last step over a precipice. He could have given us all that in the story; and then his strength would have stopped. Exactly what Maeterlinck could not possibly give us, if he tried for a thousand years, is the splendid explosion of common sense at the end, the complete and colossal revolt of the healthy young man who wonders if the whole cosmos contains such idiots as these three followers of Maeterlinck. That ending is like that sudden smashing of a coloured window, letting in fresh air. Yes, fate is something; it is a sentiment inside certain environments and atmospheres. But free will is the fact outside.

On the other hand, if Mr. Kipling had told the story, its human universality would have been lost on the other side. He would have represented the dreamers, not as people to be laughed at, but as people to be loathed; as Bandar-log;[4] as degenerates tumbling down into a hopeless abyss of the unfit. But perhaps the shortest way of putting the matter is to say that in Mr. Kipling's story the young man would have ridden away from his betrothed and never come back at all.

****

I had intended this article to be about War Panics;[5] but I find that it is about much more enduring and important things; that is, about old wives' fables, or, in my own case, the fables of an old husband. In any case, this is the main lesson of the old unwritten literature of the world. To be able to relax and to recover; to be able to laugh and then to be serious; or (more important still) to be able to be serious and then to laugh. Or you can put in yet another way the old argument and balance between fancy and fact; to be able to dream and yet able to wake up. The followers of Maeterlinck, the modern mystics, cannot wake up. The followers of Kipling, the modern realists, cannot even go to sleep, which is even worse for their health.

Notes
1. *the old fairy tale ... philosophical tale*: The story that Chesterton has in mind is called 'Die kluge Else' ('Clever Alice'; some translators say 'Clever Elsie'), number 34 in *Kinder- und Hausmärchen* (1812).
2. *Maeterlinck*: Maurice Polydore Marie Bernard, Count Maeterlinck: see 'The Good Man of the Eighteenth Century', *DN*, 22 March 1901, Volume 1, p. 67, n. 14 above.
3. *Rudyard Kipling*: see 'A Kipling Reader', *DN*, 21 February 1901, Volume 1, p. 31, n. 3 above.
4. *Bandar-log*: 'Bandar log' is what Kipling calls monkeys in *The Jungle Book* (1894); it means 'Monkey people' in Hindi.
5. *War Panics*: Chesterton will resume this theme in the following article, 'Panic', *DN*, 10 April 1909, pp. 296–9 below.

April 10, 1909.

PANIC.

―――――

The reason that I cannot get on with Marcus Aurelius,[1] with certain ethical societies, and with the general trend of rationalist morality, is, I think, ultimately this – that they all make the morality a mere question of moderation and degree. They recognise no positive evil except excess. Murder is only fighting too much; inconstancy is only flirting too much. There is a proper limit of flirting, let us say two ladies or twenty-three and a half ladies, and beyond that the thing becomes progressively bad, like over-eating. I do not say that they adopt this example, but they do adopt this principle. Now the evil that lies in wait for us all seems to me to be of quite a different kind, of a very positive kind. The original impulse to fight or flirt is very often quite healthy; but the moral madness that the thing may breed does not creep upon us like a paralysis, but often leaps on us like a tiger. The difference between the instinct and the evil is more like the difference between sunshine and sunstroke.

A man may kill another man excusably in some monstrous crisis; but if he kills five men his ruin is not that he has killed too many men. His ruin is that he has become a murderer – one to whom destruction is endurable and normal. If a man has flirted with twenty-three and a-half women, it is not his condemnation that he has flirted with too many women. His condemnation is that he has become a flirt; that is, a fool, and (I use the phrase gravely and theologically) a damned fool. The evil lies in becoming something evil; one may do it at the thousandth transgression – or at the first. 'What shall it profit a man' ran the great saying – 'if he gain the whole world and lose his own soul?'[2] Losing one's own soul is not a matter of degree, of eating or drinking too much; no, nor of burgling, and forging, and burning down houses too much. Losing one's own soul means (as its words imply) becoming somebody else; and somebody much nastier.

****

It is in this spirit that I should also approach the problem of alarm in moral and political affairs. Just as there exist at the beginning an innocent love and an innocent battle, so there exists at the beginning an innocent fear. Just as it is not primarily insane to run after a girl, so it is not primarily insane to run away from a bull. Sometimes it is quite good for your health. But if you yield much to the emotion you will find yourself, at a somewhat more leisurely trot, running away from a cow. And at last, when you fly screaming down the Strand pursued by a contemptuous guinea-pig, you will realise, not that you have carried fear too far, but that you have definitely become a coward.

So it is with the larger types of spiritual or sociological fear. It is natural to be afraid of the dark; children are, and all the best poets and philosophers. It is natural to be afraid of the sea; sailors are horribly afraid of it. But if you indulge that dread deliberately, and in a certain way, you will find that you are no longer a child nor a sailor, nor a poet, nor anything human; Nature will have got on your nerves, and you will be a pessimist. You will only be fit to be chained up in some university to give godless lectures to grinning and absent-minded boys. Or, again, it is natural to employ a practical caution for one's country; to balance evident forces, to avoid needless sacrifices, to retain a coaling station, to secure a treaty, to protect a vulnerable place. But if you see shadows and expect shocks everywhere, if you are always thinking of something stronger than yourself, if you feel and talk in terms of a timid materialism, if you always refuse a chivalrous adventure, and always make the most of a safe one; if, in short, caution has gone crazy in you, then the curse has fallen on you; you are no longer a healthy poltroon; you are already an Imperialist.

****

England is now divided with the dispute, whether a certain campaign of national defence is of this morbid kind, or is of a more manly type of prudence.[3] I do not wish to answer that question in detail; but I wish to suggest that there are certain tests by which I think it can be answered. I mean that if we wish to know whether this movement, or any movement, is mere panic in the demoralising sense, the best thing we can do is to ask the following three questions about it:

First: Is the alarm in any way related to a legend; to something belonging to the past and not the present? Is it a fearful bogey because a familiar bogey? Historical parallels can alone express what I mean. When Walpole went into the mad war with Spain,[4] when Cromwell earlier made the same mistake,[5] with more excuse, England's soul was still overshadowed by the almost Roman Empire of Spain which had hung like thunder above Elizabeth. The Lion and Castle of

King Philip's shield were still the awful emblems of the prince of this world that they were when his Brobdingnagian ships nearly sailed up the English rivers: the lion a very devouring lion, a castle an impregnable castle.[6] England had no notion that Spain had really grown weak; that the Lion of Aragon by this time was a rather mangy beast; that the Castle of Castille [sic] was something of a Castle in Spain. The past overpowered them; they still thought Spain the world, though the glory of France was at its noon and that of Prussia already dawning.

****

Now, without handling too coarsely so delicate a matter, we may say, I think, that the general notion of Germany's frightful force is a Legend; a vivid but untested impression from a comparatively remote past. This fancy of a Prussia made of iron is the echo and memory of the fact that nearly half a century ago Prussia won the last big war with great rapidity, and surprised people by defeating France.[7] This surprised people because France was then the established terror of Europe, because France in her turn half a century before had ground the Prussians to atoms.

It seems to me that these forty or fifty year legends do not generally come off. If I wanted to exercise a strong and sagacious sort of vigilance I should keep my eye on any spot except the spot where the last cannon ball happened to come through. But, on the other hand, if I wanted a demagogue panic of 'nous sommes trahis'[8] then I should take great care to raise it about the nation which wore the flattered though faded laurels of the last war. This is my first reason for doubting the existing agitation. A real international expert would probably have his eye on some new conqueror. But a demagogue must keep his eye on some old and vulgarised conqueror.[9]

****

The second test I should employ is this: Is there anything vast or megalomaniac about the imagery and the examples of such a movement? On any practical expedition, say a picnic or a lifeboat or a bank, the thing that is really needed at any given instant is quite likely to be something very small, though very important. A picnic may be spoilt for want of a corkscrew: that is sane. But if a man said, 'We must have large hampers, larger hampers, largest hampers', I should feel that insane. Grace Darling's rowing boat[10] might be useless for want of one oar; but not for want of longer and longer oars. A bank may desperately desire the presence of one clerk; but not the presence of one very tall and fat clerk. Any insistence on size makes me suspicious. It is so obviously meant for the imagination abruptly awakened. It is so unlikely to be the one little thing really wanted.

Third and last, I should ask if those who are raising the alarm about things that can be done swiftly, with a stroke of the pen, are equally active about the much more strenuous things that must be slow. Have they dared to insist that our foul cities make their citizens unfit for war as much as peace? Have they had the moral courage to point out the inevitable lack of physical courage? To make all English ships Dreadnoughts means writing on a piece of paper. To make all English men Dreadnoughts means a long, laborious, and perilous business. Of which do they talk most?

Notes

1. *Marcus Aurelius*: Marcus Aurelius Antoninus; see 'The Return of the Angels', *DN*, 14 March 1903, Volume 2, p. 26, n. 4 above.
2. *What shall it profit ... soul*: see Matthew 16:26; Mark 8:36.
3. *England is now divided ... type of prudence*: Chesterton is referring to the 'Naval Scare' of 1909. Germany, in a supplementary naval law of 1908, had proposed to lay down the keels of four Dreadnoughts (heavy battleships) in that year, four more in 1909, and to develop plans for more in 1910. This alarmed the British Admiralty and some Members of Parliament who saw in the German fleet an immediate threat to the British Empire. At the urging of the First Sea Lord, Lord Fisher, Reginald McKenna, First Lord of the Admiralty, introduced his navy estimates to Parliament on 16 March 1909, proposing that eighteen battleships of the Dreadnought class be built – six in each of the years 1909–11. In this he was opposed by Lloyd George and Winston Churchill and supported by Asquith and Lord Grey.
4. *Walpole ... Spain*: The 'War of Jenkins's Ear', 1739–48, was ostensibly provoked by a series of incidents, one of which was an injury to Captain Robert Jenkins, whose ear had been cut off during the boarding of his vessel by Spanish coastguards in 1731. In reality the war arose from disputes over the Asiento Treaty of 1713 by which Britain had been given a thirty-year right to sell slaves in Spanish America.
5. *Cromwell ... mistake*: The Anglo–Spanish War of 1654–60 was actuated chiefly by commercial motives and fought from 1657 onwards in alliance with France.
6. *The Lion and Castle ... impregnable castle*: In 1588 the Spanish fleet – the 'Spanish Armada' – sailed against England under the command of the Duke of Medina Sidonia. The purpose of the Armada was to carry an army under the Duke of Parma across the Channel to England with the intention of dethroning Queen Elizabeth I.
7. *echo and memory ... defeating France*: a reference to the Franco–Prussian War of 1871.
8. *nous sommes trahis*: An exclamation attributed to Jean-Paul Marat in 1789.
9. *It seems to me ... vulgarised conqueror*: This paragraph suggests none of the fear of Germany that Chesterton claimed retrospectively to have experienced during an earlier visit to that country; see 'The Great Simplicity', *DN*, 27 July 1907, Volume 4, p. 269, n. 2 above.
10. *Grace Darling's rowing boat*: Grace Horsley Darling (1814–42), was an English heroine. The daughter of the lighthouse keeper at Longstone, one of the Farne Islands in Northumberland, she and her father risked their lives to rescue nine people from the *Forfarshire* when she was wrecked near the lighthouse in 1838.

April 17 1909.

THE PROTECTION OF THE BIBLE.[1]

It is a matter of great gratification that an official voice in practical education has spoken in favour of that exclusion of all theologies from the national schools for which many have long pleaded.[2] It is a policy promoted, generally speaking, by the most lucid and magnanimous of all parties. Some, and I am one of them, do not wish theology to interfere with education. Some, and I am again one of them, have the greatest horror of education presuming to interfere with theology, which is so much more living and exciting a subject. And a very interesting question is undoubtedly raised by the distinction which Dr. Clifford[3] draws between the teaching of theology and the teaching of the Bible. The question of whether the Bible can be taught merely as literature is a question that raises the whole riddle of things that have two meanings, a big meaning and a small meaning. Can the Koran be treated as literature? Yes, anywhere except in Islam. Can the Bible be taught as pure literature? Yes; anywhere except in a Protestant country.

There are several popular misconceptions about this educational aspect of Scripture. One quite curious mistake is this. It is always somehow assumed that if the Bible is taken out of the schools it will be taken out in the interest of those who do not believe in it. This is a complete mistake. Those who do not believe in it are exactly the people who have no reason to object to it. It is the people who do believe in it who have a right to get restless. A reasonable Freethinker need not have the faintest objection to his child learning a chapter of Isaiah, merely as literature. In so far as he is reasonable, he will agree that it is literature, and in so far as he is a Freethinker, he will agree that it is only literature. The man who is hardly used by such teaching of the Bible is precisely the orthodox man, the man to whom Isaiah means first and foremost the blood-stirring prophecy of a world-shattering event. I should not mind my children learning Icelandic folk-lore. Nor should I mind them learning Jewish folklore – if it is only folklore. I should not mind children being told about Mahomet, because I am not a Mohammedan. If I were a Mohammedan I should very much want to know what they were told about him.

Therefore, in the struggles of which Dr. Clifford is so largely the centre, I sympathise with secular education, but not because [my] sympathy is with the new-fashioned Puritan who wishes the Bible to be treated as literature. My sympathy is with the old-fashioned Puritan, who does not want the Bible to be treated as literature, because he happens to have a religion which is about the most interesting thing a man can have. It is the old-fashioned theologians who ought to insist on secular education. It is the orthodox Puritans who ought to want the Bible kept out of the schools. The truth can, indeed, be put in a kind of dilemma. Either the Bible must be offered as something extraordinary or as something ordinary. If it is offered as something extraordinary, that is certainly unfair to the agnostics and the doubters. If it is offered as something ordinary, that is grossly and atrociously unfair to the theologians and the believers.

I am often assured, and I give all respectful consideration to the assurance, that the teachers find no difficulty with simple Bible teaching. If this means that children of five and six do not start theological sessions in the schoolroom I can well believe it. If it means that boys of eight or nine do not pay much attention to their religious lessons or to any of their other lessons, that also a stretch of imagination enables one to entertain. If it means that the wretched children in our Board schools are too bored or too tired or too hungry to ask a single intelligent question in the course of sixty lessons I will believe that also if the experts assure me of it.

But I fear I can only admit the negative success of such a system for reasons that throw grave doubt on its positive success. If Bible instruction is a success, then Board school instruction is a failure. If no child ever says of a Bible story, 'Please, teacher, did that really happen?' if no teacher ever feels impelled to tell the children a little of what he thinks himself about things so tremendous as the coming of the Cross or the mystery of the Jewish people, then something has gone wrong between pupil and teacher, and we are not educating at all. There really seem to be only three possibilities in connection with the matter, and they all have objections against them of the most ultimate and iron sort, objections of principle. Suppose a child says, 'Did Jesus really come out of the grave?' Either the teacher must answer him insincerely, and that is immorality, or he must answer him sincerely, and that is sectarian education, or he must refuse to answer him at all, and that is first of all bad manners and a sort of timid tyranny; and it is, moreover, gross and monstrous idolatry. It is something darker and more irrational than a religion – it is a silence. The Bible is worshipped without even being proclaimed. Its priests must not offer even a reason for placing it beyond reason.

Dr. Clifford expresses a hope that secular education need not mean the elimination of all faith, all prayer, or (in effect) of all religion. But surely secular education should mean this, if only in justice to the Secularists. I do not think I am misinterpreting Dr. Clifford if I put his view thus: There should be a faith, but not a creed. Well, it happens that a creed is the Latin for a faith. I would as soon say 'I will not have une foi, but I will have a faith'. How can there be faith without something to have faith in; how can there be prayer without something to which to pray? I for one cannot conceive how the Nonconformists can follow a line so destructive to both sides of their great historic effort. For the Bible compromise is false both to the civic idea of liberty and to the Protestant idea of the Bible. If Dr. Clifford insists on this retention he will have surrendered on both points to the free-thinkers. He will allow the Bible to be taught in a totally agnostic sense. And yet he will leave the agnostics a real grievance, an excuse for using against him also the weapons of passive resistance. He first gives up the Book to his enemies, and then allows them to throw it at his head.

Notes
1. *THE PROTECTION OF THE BIBLE*: Reprinted in *CR*, 22:3 (August 1996), pp. 289–92.
2. *official voice ... long pleaded*: a reference to the presidential address by Mr. C. Hole to the National Union of Teachers at its annual conference in Morecambe, 12 April 1908; see 'National Union of Teachers', *The Times*, 13 April 1909, p. 5c. Dr John Clifford criticized his remarks in a letter that he circulated to various newspapers including *The Times*, 'The Education Question: The Secular Solution', 15 April 1909, p. 8b. Clifford continued to advocate the use in education of 'portions of the Bible suited to the capacity of the children, such use to be literary, historical, ethical and spiritual; but never in any way theological or ecclesiastical'. The context of the dispute was the establishment of an 'Education Settlement Committee' after the failure of the Education Bill in November 1908 to resolve continuing disputes about the role of religion in state education.
3. *Dr. Clifford*: John Clifford; see 'Lord Halifax and Dr. Clifford', letter to the editor, *DN*, 20 September 1902, Volume 1, pp. 386–9, n. 2 above.

April 24, 1909.

A CAB RIDE ACROSS COUNTRY.[1]

Sown somewhere far off in the shallow dales of Hertfordshire there lies a village of great beauty, and I doubt not of admirable virtue, but of eccentric and unbalanced literary taste, which asked the present writer to come down to it on Sunday afternoon and give an address. Now it was very difficult to get down to it at all on Sunday afternoon, owing to the indescribable state into which our national laws and customs have fallen in connection with the seventh day. It is not Puritanism; it is simply anarchy. I should have some sympathy with the Jewish Sabbath, if it were a Jewish Sabbath, and that for three reasons; first, that religion is an intrinsically sympathetic thing; second, that I cannot conceive any religion worth calling a religion without fixed and material observances; and third, that the particular observance of sitting still and doing no work is one that suits my temperament down to the ground.

But the absurdity of the modern English convention is that it does not let a man sit still; it only perpetually trips him up when it has forced him to walk about. Our Sabbatarianism does not forbid us to ask a man in Battersea to come and talk in Hertfordshire; it only prevents his getting there. I can understand that a deity might be worshipped with joys, with flowers, and fireworks in the old European style. I can understand that a deity might be worshipped with sorrows. But I cannot imagine any deity being worshipped with inconveniences. Let the good Moslem go to Mecca, or let him abide in his tent, according to his feeling for religious symbols. But surely Allah cannot see anything particularly dignified in his servant being misled by the time-table, finding that the old Mecca express is not running, missing the connection at Bagdad [*sic*] or having to wait three hours in a small side station outside Damascus.

So it was with me on this occasion. I found there was no telegraph service at all to this place; I found there was only one weak thread of train-service. Now if this had been the authority of real English religion, I should have submitted to it at once. If I believed that the telegraph clerk could not send the telegram because he was at that moment rigid in an ecstasy of prayer, I should think all telegrams unimportant in comparison. If I could believe that railway porters when relieved from their duty rushed with passion to the nearest place of worship, I should say that all lectures and everything else ought to give way to such a consideration. I should not complain if the national faith forbade me to make any appointments of labour or self-expression on the Sabbath. But, as it is, it only tells me that I may very probably keep the Sabbath by not keeping the appointment.

****

But I must resume the real details of my tale. I found that there was only one train in the whole of that Sunday by which I could even get within several hours or several miles of the time or place. I therefore went to the telephone, which is one of my favourite toys, and down which I have shouted many valuable, but prematurely arrested, monologues upon art and morals. I remember a mild shock of surprise when I discovered that one could use the telephone on Sunday; I did not expect it to be cut off, but I expected it to buzz more than on ordinary days, to the advancement of our national religion. Through this instrument, in fewer words than usual, and with a comparative economy of epigram, I ordered a taxi-cab to take me to the railway station. I have not a word to say in general either against telephones or taxi-cabs; they seem to me two of the purest and most poetic of the creations of modern scientific civilization. Unfortunately, when the taxi-cab started, it did exactly what modern scientific civilization has done – it broke down. The result of this was that when I arrived at King's Cross my only train was gone; there was a Sabbath calm in the station, a calm in the eyes of the porters, and in my breast, if calm at all, if any calm, a calm despair.

There was not, however, very much calm of any sort in my breast on first making the discovery; and it was turned to blinding horror when I learnt that I could not even send a telegram to the organizers of the meeting. To leave my entertainers in the lurch was sufficiently exasperating; to leave them without any intimation was simply low. I reasoned with the official. I said: 'Do you really mean to say that if my brother were dying and my mother in this place, I could not communicate with her?' He was a man of literal and laborious mind; he asked me if my brother was dying. I answered that he was in excellent and even offensive health, but that I was inquiring upon a question of principle. What would happen if England were invaded, or if I alone knew how to turn aside a comet or an earthquake? He waved away these hypotheses in the most irresponsible spirit, but he was quite certain that telegrams could not reach this particular village. Then something exploded in me; that element of the outrageous which is the mother of all adventures sprang up ungovernable, and I decided that I would not be a cad merely because some of my remote ancestors had been Calvinists. I would keep my appointment if I lost all my money and all my wits. I went out into the quiet London street, where my quiet London cab was still waiting for its fare in the cold and misty morning. I placed myself comfortably in the London cab and told the London driver to drive me to the other end of Hertfordshire. And he did.

****

I shall not forget that drive. It was doubtful whether, even in a motor-cab, the thing was possible with any consideration for the driver, not to speak of some slight consideration for the people in the road. I urged the driver to eat and drink something before he started, but he said (with I know not what pride of profession or delicate sense of adventure) that he would rather do it when we arrived – if we ever did. I was by no means so delicate: I bought a varied selection of pork-pies at a little shop that was open (why was that shop open? – it is all a mystery), and ate them as we went along. The beginning was sombre and irritating. I was annoyed, not with people, but with things, like a baby; with the motor for breaking down and with Sunday for being Sunday. And the sight of the northern slums expanded and ennobled, but did not decrease, my gloom: Whitechapel has an Oriental gaudiness in its squalor; Battersea and Camberwell have an indescribable bustle of democracy; but the poor parts of North London ... well, perhaps I saw them wrongly under that ashen morning and on that foolish errand.

It was one of those days which more than once this year broke the retreat of winter; a winter day that began too late to be spring. We were already clear of the obstructing crowds, and quickening our pace through a borderland of market gardens and isolated public-houses, when the grey showed golden patches and a good light began to glitter on everything. The cab went quicker and quicker. The open land whirled wider and wider; but I did not lose that sense of being battled with and thwarted that I had felt in the thronged slums. Rather the feeling increased, because of the great difficulty of space and time. The faster went the car, the fiercer and thicker I felt the fight.

The whole landscape seemed charging at me – and just missing me. The tall shining grass went by like showers of arrows; the very trees seemed like lances hurled at my heart, and shaving it by a hair's breadth. Across some vast, smooth valley I saw a beech-tree by the white road stand up little and defiant. It grew bigger and bigger with blinding rapidity. It charged me like a tilting knight, seemed to hack at my head, and pass by. Sometimes, when we went round a curve of road, the effect was yet more awful. It seemed as if some tree or windmill swung round to smite, like a boomerang. The sun by this time was a blazing fact; and

I saw that all Nature is chivalrous and militant. We do wrong to seek peace in Nature; we should rather seek the nobler sort of war; and see all the trees as green banners.

****

I gave my address,[a] arriving just when everybody was deciding to leave. When my cab came reeling into the marketplace they decided, with evident disappointment, to remain. Over the lecture I draw a veil. When I came back home I was called to the telephone, and a meek voice expressed regret for the failure of the motor-cab, and even said something about any reasonable payment. 'Payment!' I cried down the telephone. 'Whom can I pay for my own superb experience? What is the usual charge for seeing the clouds shattered by the sun? What is the market price of a tree blue on the sky-line and then blinding white in the sun? Mention your price for that windmill that stood behind the hollyhocks in the garden. Let me pay you for ...' Here it was, I think, that we were cut off.

3a   I gave my address]. In *TT* (2) this is replaced by the following: I made my speech

Notes
1.   *A CAB RIDE ACROSS THE COUNTRY*: Reprinted in *TT* (2), pp. 159–66.

May 8, 1909.

THE PILLORY.

Perhaps one of the few really democratic institutions ever created was the pillory. I do not say that it was a humane institution, though it was certainly more humane than our system of silent imprisonment.[1] But being humane has nothing to do with being democratic. You may have humane and inhumane democracies, just as you may have humane and inhumane despots.

The point is that the pillory was a real appeal to the people; if it was cruel, it was because the people were cruel, or perhaps justly indignant. The people threw dead cats (the less humanitarian, I believe, threw live cats), but they could throw bouquets and crowns of laurel if they liked. Sometimes they did. The argument about the old public punishments cuts both ways. The publicity was an additional risk for the Government as well as an additional risk for the prisoner, and this is specially true of the executions for treason. It was no small thing that half a million men might possibly treat as a martyr a man whom the King was treating as a murderer; that the prince had to concede to every obscure ruffian exactly what that ruffian probably wanted most – fame. The judges had to put a man in history even while they put him out of existence; they were obliged to give a dog a good name and then hang him. The death of rebels in arms (if we were so lucky as to have any) would be a much smoother and easier matter now. A modern Sidney[2] or Montrose[3] would be strangled with hateful secrecy by officials in a little room; and the people would never have the chance of seeing whether he looked a finer man than his foes.

****

I could never agree with those who thought that the making of the death penalty private was a step in progress or pity. On the contrary, if we could see all the things that go on in our prisons we should no longer permit them; and (to speak in the style foolishly called Irish) if there were public executions there would be no executions. Or, at least, there would not be any except in those awful and exceptional instances of treason or tyranny in which vengeance is, indeed, only a wild justice. When the mob hung Foulon from the lamp-post with his false mouth stuffed full of grass, I think it was at worst a venial sin; because to say of poor people, 'Let them eat grass'[4] was a mortal sin, a sin of the abyss. But to hang a man secretly seems to me a dirty, Oriental sort of trick, a thing for the harem and the divan. Even the hangman has a sort of personal dignity – nay, personal delicacy – which might be considered. And the least we can do for the hangman is to be able to call him the public executioner. But our hangman is nothing so healthy, honest, and European as the public executioner. He is only the Bearer of the Bowstring.

****

But the natural fascination of the gallows has led us away from our true subject, which is the pillory. My attention was drawn to this neglected moral instrument by a fragmentary fact which I read somewhere the other day (I could find the reference if necessary), which showed that in simpler times the pillory was not only democratic in its methods, but essentially democratic in its aims. Not only was the punishment of the pillory decided by the right persons – that is, by the ordinary persons – but the punishment was often actually directed towards the right person – which means, of course, the person who was wrong.

There was a law in the Middle Ages that any man who should do exactly what the Wheat King has recently done – that is, make a corner in wheat[5] – should stand in the pillory for several hours. It is a ceaseless and senseless discussion to urge one age against another; in all ages man is a great thing defeated by being also a small thing. That phrase which people thought so intolerably pathetic when applied to Coleridge is the definition of him and of every other man – an Archangel a little damaged.[6] We need not dig up our ancestors either to worship them or to hang them on the gallows.

But if anyone wants to feel the full difference between our ultra civilized State and a simpler one, if anyone wants to imagine in what respect a mediaeval community was free from our particular entanglements, let him simply connect those two terms, let him simply call up that one picture. Let him shut his eyes and see the Wheat King in the pillory. Conceive the man whose exploit we speak of as one of the ordinary victories of finance, whom even his enemies interview with a certain respect[,] whom current literature calls 'strong' and 'Napoleonic', whose ceaseless injustice is called splendid enterprise, and whose belated mercy is solemnly called magnanimity.

Imagine him as he is, with all his imploring telephones and all his congratulatory telegrams. And then imagine him as he stood in what you call a barbarous age under what you call a superstitious religion; held high above the street in a great wooden man-trap, so that the nice question of where financial unfairness begins might be decided with dead cats and carrots by the actual people who had been hurt by him, whose pitiful last pence fell just short of the high-priced loaf, or whose dead children had cried for his corn in vain. Imagine that astounding contrast when next you are inclined to think of all tyrannic power as ancient or all popular expression as modern. The Wheat King in the pillory may be brutality; but it is certainly democracy.

****

It is worth while to insist just now on this possibility that we may literally fall below our fathers in popular feeling. The recent discussions on the Budget show sinister signs of that particular sort of stiffening which makes a slate brittle, it breaks because it cannot bend. Lord Hugh Cecil, I hear, has just written to 'The Times', saying that the Budget is bad because it uses taxation as a tool for moral reproof.[7] It is the custom to call Lord Hugh Cecil Mediaeval; this ought to clear his character for ever of that charge. If you had said to any mediaeval philosopher that he must not tax with a moral intention, he would have replied, unanswerably, and in rich, mediaeval Latin, 'Why the deuce not?' If there is one thing that I should have expected a good Anglo-Catholic to maintain it is that the evils of civilization are mainly due to sin, and should be corrected with a sense of sin. Let us leave it to the quiet, meek materialists to trace all ills to forces and balances, average and percentage. Lord Hugh Cecil and I ought to be tracing them where they are to be traced, to the seven deadly sins, to the avarice and pride and sloth and gluttony of everybody, and especially of ourselves.

I, at least, am much more mediaeval than Lord Hugh Cecil; for I believe, as the mediaevals did, that the only authority of government is moral, that the chief object of government is to get the most wicked man, the oppressor of the poor, into the pillory.

Notes
1. *our system of silent imprisonment*: See 'A Theory of Tyrants', DN, 13 June 1908, p. 89, n. 8 above.
2. *Sidney*: Algernon Sidney; see 'Tommy and the Traditions', DN, 23 May 1908, p. 79, n. 3 above.
3. *Montrose*: James Graham, fifth Earl and first Marquess of Montrose (1612–50), was a Scottish Royalist soldier. A Presbyterian, he became a Covenanter in reaction against the high-handed treatment of the Scottish Church by Charles I. But, troubled by the extreme Covenanters in the national movement, he went over to the King in 1641. He

rallied the loyalist Highland clans to Charles, although his efforts to quell revolt in the Lowlands were unsuccessful. He was hanged at Edinburgh in 1650.

4. *Foulon ... Let them eat grass*: See 'The Vote and the Votary', *DN*, 6 February 1909, pp. 266–7, n. 4 above.

5. *Wheat King ... corner in wheat*: The reference here is probably to James A. Patten (1852–1928), the American financier and grain merchant who attempted to corner the wheat crop in 1909. He and his associates apparently secured control of more than 23,000,000 bushels of wheat, thereby forcing up the price of wheat and flour. He also operated his business in Liverpool. See D. Greising and L. Morse, *Brokers, Bagmen, and Moles: Fraud and Corruption in the Chicago Futures Markets* (New York: John Wiley & Sons, 1991).

6. *That phrase ... Archangel a little damaged*: In a letter to Wordsworth on 26 April 1816, Charles Lamb said of Coleridge: 'His face when he repeats his verses hath its ancient glory, an Archangel a little damaged'. See E. V. Lucas (ed.), *The Works of Charles and Mary Lamb*, 7 vols (London: Methuen, 1903–05), vol. 5: *The Letters of Charles and Mary Lamb*, 1796–1820, no. 230.

7. *Lord Hugh Cecil ... tool for moral reproof*: The letter attacked Lloyd George's tax on unearned increment as based on a spurious distinction between 'deserving' and 'undeserving' income; in this respect, there was the danger of a Chancellor of the Exchequer 'undertaking the functions of an angel of retribution': 'Unearned Increment', *The Times*, 6 May 1909, p. 9d. For Cecil, see 'The Secular Solution', *DN*, 12 May 1905, Volume 3, p. 101, n. 6 above.

May 13, 1909.

A BOOK OF THE DAY.

An American View of Mystics.

'Studies in Mystical Religion'. By Rufus M. Jones, M:A, D Litt. Macmillan and Co. [1909]. 12s.

It is to be hoped that most of us realise by this time that the one magnificent thing about history is that it does not repeat itself; that it is incalculable. Vague and visionary prophecies are sometimes, though not very often, fulfilled; but scientific prophecies are always wrong. The most striking example of this is the intellectual development of America. We have gained from America exactly the things that we never expected from America; such things as Mr. Whistler[1] and a delicate school of draughtsmanship and a great deal of good society verse, ornamental and even aristocratic. But the most surprising thing of all is that the new American school of thought in history is interested, of all things in the world, in mysticism. Benjamin Franklin,[2] in his dreams (if he allowed himself to have any), may possibly have felt a terrible premonition that he was going to give birth to Mr. Rockefeller;[3] but I am quite sure that he never saw with the prophetic eye so wild a vision as Mr. William James.[4]

Mr. Rufus Jones,[5] who has written a most interesting study of those mystics in Christian history who were either opposed to or apart from the main bulk of working Christianity, is a follower of Professor James both in his detachment from the official Church and his interest in the mystical mind. This very valuable book is in substance something very like a rebuke of the mediaeval Church, not for being too mystical, but for not being mystical enough. It is very queer to notice the way in which the war changes. A little while ago the great attack on mediaeval religion was that it was so weird and unworldly that it neglected the needs and instincts of the man in the street. But the young American professors have started a new game; which is that it was so hard and practical that it neglected the best dreams of the man in the cloister. The old cry was that the Pope was too [spiritual] to listen to the Emperor. The new cry is that the Pope was too materialist to listen to St. Francis.[6]

The Candour of the Mystics.

The book contains abundant material of the best historical and literary sort. The extracts from the letters of St. Catherine of Siena[7] to the Pope are alone worth a book to hold them; those wonderful letters in which she writes to him as if he were a little boy; calls him Christ upon Earth, but advises him to correct his self-will. In fact, nothing is more interesting in Mr. Rufus Jones's interesting compilation of facts than the fact that some of the boldest protests against pontifical abuse come from the orthodox mystics, and not the heretical ones. The heresiarch seems to care chiefly for his heresy; it is generally the ordinary saint who snubs the ordinary pontiff. To tell only one of Mr. Jones's stories: The Pope introduced St. Dominic[8] to the gold and marble of the Vatican, saying gaily: 'You see St. Peter cannot now say, "Silver and gold have I none"'. 'No', answered St. Dominic, 'and neither can he now say "'Rise and walk"'.

I think the only error in Mr. Rufus Jones's estimate of the mystics can be summed up in the fact that he does not sufficiently realise that there is a bad spirituality as well as a good spirituality. He investigates a number of very dim and obscure sects, who professed to have certain peculiar paths of their own to heaven; but in many of them (and, indeed, in many of the greater mystics also) it is much more evident that the path is picturesque, new and secret, than that it is the path to heaven. To my poor feelings the path seems to lead suspiciously downwards sometimes. For instance, many of these mediaeval eccentrics, even one of the noblest of them, Tauler,[9] seemed to have professed a doctrine which they called the doctrine of the Divine Dark;[10] which certainly sounds very nice. Some of the more orthodox bishops, however, seem to have found it not quite so nice; and from what I can make out of what it was I am inclined to agree with them. It seems to have been the doctrine that God has no special qualities; that you cannot use an adjective about him. The quick mediaeval logic would at once interpret this as meaning that God was not any more good than he was bad; that is, that virtue and vice do not really exist on the highest plane. And I am not surprised if a hard-working mediaeval bishop, who already had his hands full in trying to persuade the king not to have six mistresses and the baron not to hang sixty vassals – I am not surprised, I say, if he found the doctrine of the Divine Dark considerably more dark than divine.

Was it Devil-Worship?

And Mr. Rufus Jones certainly leaves out of account an important consideration. To speak plainly, if we are to discover of any group of men whatever, Jesuits or Freemasons, Theosophists or Thugs, whether there was in their worship any element of devil-worship, of the poetry of evil, it will not do merely to look at the idealistic language of their leaders and public utterances. It has always been a definite mark of diabolism that its language was splendid and pure. For the heart of all evil religion is fear. And the sacrament of fear is flattery. For this reason the old pagans called the Furies the Gracious Ones.[11] For this reason many modern peasants called their goblins good people because they believe that they are bad people. It is the common-sense of all diabolism that if you worship Satan you worship him as God. Now Mr. Rufus Jones admits by implication that there was some basis for the general opinion that some of these wild sects, especially the Anabaptists and the Family of the Lord,[12] were, to say the least of it, eccentric in practice as well as in theory. This impression may be true or false; but Mr. Jones does not wash it away with floods of fine words about love and spiritual liberty quoted from their books and teachers. Mr. Jones, in a really suggestive phrase, urges that the true mystic goes by experience. In this matter it happens that it is possible to go by experience. The language of the Anabaptists was doubtless idealistic, but not more so, I should guess, than the cries that go up under the car of Juggernaut[13] or the family prayers read before the assembled wives of Brigham Young.[14] If we have nothing but tall talk to turn away the imputation the Family of Love in Westphalia may have been uncommonly like the Abode of Love at Clapton.[15]

Notes

1. *Mr. Whistler*: James Abbott McNeill Whistler; see 'Two Great Tories', *DN*, 1 August 1903, p. 106, n. 2 above.
2. *Benjamin Franklin*: Benjamin Franklin (1706–90), was an American statesman who played a pivotal role in drawing up the Declaration of Independence.
3. *Mr. Rockefeller*: John Davison Rockefeller; see 'The Fault of the System', *DN*, 18 January 1908, n. 3, p. 12 above.
4. *Mr. William James*: William James (1842–1910), was an American psychologist, philosopher and physician; older brother of the novelist Henry James, he wrote extensively on psychology, mysticism and religious experience, and the philosophy of pragmatism. Chesterton here probably has in mind his book called *The Varieties of Religious Experience* (1902). He was one of the earliest psychologists to investigate the properties of mood-altering substances (he claimed – in an essay called 'Subjective Effects of Nitrous Oxide', *Mind*, 7 (1882) – that it was only when he was under the influence of nitrous oxide that he was able to understand Hegel).
5. *Mr. Rufus Jones*: Rufus Matthew Jones (1863–1948), was an American Quaker historian and theologian who wrote extensively on Quakerism, religion and mysticism; he was editor of the *Friends' Review*, 1893–1912.
6. *St. Francis*: St Francis of Assisi; see 'The Mystery of the Mystics', *DN*, 30 August 1901, Volume 1, p. 175, n. 9 above.

7. *St. Catherine of Siena*: St Catherine of Siena; see 'The Fear of the Past', 7 December 1907, Volume 4, p. 369, n. 7 above. She carried on a long and remarkably intimate correspondence with Pope Gregory XI: see S. Noffke (ed.), *The Letters of St. Catherine of Siena*. (Binghamton, NY: Center for Medieval and Early Renaissance Studies, State University of New York at Binghamton, 1988). She was canonised by Pope Pius II in 1461.
8. *St. Dominic*: Saint Dominic (variously called Dominic of Osma, Dominic de Guzmán and Domingo Félix de Guzmán) (1170–1221), was a Spanish priest and founder (*c*. 1215) of the Dominican Order (more correctly the Order of Preachers – *Ordo Praedicatorum*). He was canonized in 1234 by Pope Gregory IX.
9. *Tauler*: Johannes Tauler (*c*. 1300–61), was a German Dominican friar and mystic associated with (though he did not found) the lay mystical group known as The Friends of God (*Gottesfreunde*).
10. *Divine Dark*: The 'Divine Dark' – expressed very briefly – is the idea that God lies beyond all the categories of reason: the mind can say only what God is not, never what He is; it is only by abandoning its own sense of selfhood that the soul can penetrate the Divine Dark and attain a mystical knowledge of God. The idea is associated in the fourteenth century especially with the Dominican mystics Eckhart von Hochheim ('Meister Eckhart') (*c*. 1260–1327) and Johannes Tauler, but as a feature of Christian mysticism it probably originates with the anonymous late fifth-century author traditionally called Dionysius the Areopagite,
11. *the old pagans ... the Gracious Ones*: In Greek mythology the Ἐρινύες (Erinyes – 'the angry ones') or Εὐμενίδες (Eumenides – 'the gracious ones') personify vengeance and anger. See, for example, Aeschylus, *Oresteia* ll. 788–1047; Homer, *Iliad* 14:274–79; 19:259–60; Virgil, *Aeneid* 7:324, 341, 415, 476.
12. *Anabaptists ... Family of the Lord*: i.e. the radical Christian reformers of the sixteenth century who rejected traditional Christian practice (including infant baptism) in favour of a literal and often millenarian interpretation of the gospel. For a lucid description of the various minority social and religious movements that arose out of the Protestant Reformation see N. Cohn, *The Pursuit of the Millennium* (Oxford: Oxford University Press, 1957).
13. *car of Juggernaut*: 'Juggernaut' is an English corruption of the Sanskrit word Jagannatha, which means 'Lord of the Universe'. Chesterton is referring to the annual procession, at the Jagganath Temple in Puri, of large chariots carrying the statues of Jagannath, Subhadra and Balabhadra. The erroneous belief that the faithful fling themselves, or are encouraged to fling themselves, under the wheels of these chariots originates with Sir John Mandeville's *Travels*. The adoption by synecdoche of the word Juggernaut to mean 'a large vehicle' is comparatively recent.
14. *Brigham Young*: Brigham Young (1801–77), was an American religious leader. He was President (from 1847 until his death) of the Church of Jesus Christ of Latter-day Saints, more usually called Mormons. He was the founder of Salt Lake City and the first governor of the Utah Territory of the United States. He is reputed to have had fifty-five wives, though there is apparently reason to suppose that this is an exaggeration.
15. *Abode of Love at Clapton*: The Abode of Love is a rather extravagant ecclesiastical building at Upper Clapton (now used by the Georgian Orthodox Church) built in 1892 by a sect called the Agapemonites. The Agapemonites, founded by Henry James Prince (1811–99), appear to have been energetically committed to a doctrine of free love. After a good deal of scandal the sect went into decline in the late 1920s after its then leader, who had declared himself immortal, died.

May 15, 1909.

ALONE IN A CELL.

My own political philosophy is very plain and humble; I can trust the uneducated, but not the badly educated. Very broadly speaking, these two things correspond, as a rule, to the respective spirits of popular governments and of class government. A mob is generally uneducated; an aristocracy is generally badly educated. Boys in the slums learn no Latin; boys at Eton and Harrow learn to pronounce it wrong. The uneducated Englishman cannot understand the Irishman, and there is an end of it. But the educated Englishman is told that he does understand the Irishman, and of that monstrous confusion there seems no end at all. It is a fine thing, no doubt, to have a liberal education, but in the English upper class a liberal education always means a Tory education. It is a great pleasure, no doubt, to learn geography and the use of the globe; but what is the good of it when one is taught that the only use of a globe is to paint it red? When the refined class of the country learns a history that is vulgar Jingoism and a philosophy that is fourth-rate science, give me the unrefined class. Coal heavers at least have not twisted and tortured their own minds until they believe that a monkey is a man, or that a Colonial is an Englishman.

****

But there are some instances in which an aristocracy cannot be quite precisely defined as a badly educated class. There are many cases in history in which the aristocrats rise almost to the level of the purely uneducated; in which they stand for a certain rough truth or naturalness, especially in comparison with the elaborate public opinion of our time. I particularly admire, in comparison, with modern methods, the way which the old barons had of throwing people into prison. As some very serious people seem to read this column — I cannot imagine why – I will hasten to state that I do not regard Front-de-Boeuf[1] as an admirable character.

I only say that I can understand him a great deal better than I can understand the authors of our present penal system. What you did, I take it, when you were a feudal tyrant of the Dark Ages was this: you got hold of some personal enemy who was a permanent problem in your life. He was always harrying your farms, or worse still, he was always telling the truth about your personal character, and as the libel law had not then been perfected as at present the rich man could not always crush the poor man in a court of justice. You collared this man, and if you had some odd or mystical objection to having him chucked into a grave you had him chucked into a dungeon. In either case your motive was the same: to prevent him running about and behaving in his own inimitable style. Having put him in a black hole somewhere in the castle you then got drunk and forgot all about him. In short, you behaved like an irresponsible beast; but you could claim something of the oblivion and the innocence of one who is a beast and irresponsible. Your servants fed the man as carelessly as they liked; but also as kindly as they liked. If one of the attendants chanced to favour him, no one wanted to intercept the favours; if he could bribe a jailor to bring him wine nobody had the slightest objection, or indeed any feeling in the matter beyond a vague hope that he might drink himself to death. The object of his imprisonment was not to do him good, but simply to prevent him doing someone else harm. If he could find any fun in his unpleasant cell he was quite welcome to it.

The stories of the amusements of prisoners are innumerable, of how they trained spiders or made friends with mice or wrote verses on the wall. But make this largest and fullest allowance of what might have happened or did occasionally happen in the old dungeons. Suppose that the jailors were by some accident kind, or that the cell was by some accident sunlit. Suppose that by a piece of glorious good fortune the place was overrun with spiders and mice. The essential abomination remains; the essential shame of the feudal lord remains, even if he drowned it in wine; the essential agony of the captive remains, even if he could sometimes forget it among spiders. That agony was loneliness; that shame was having made a man lonely.

****

That is enough to cover with a curse the ancient solitary confinement. But what in the name of heaven (or, rather, in the opposite name) are we to say of modern solitary confinement? In our modern prisons we elaborately and horribly prepare this inhuman solitude; and then we take the most complete and successful care that it shall not be interrupted even by any of those merciful accidents which could find their way into the old foul dungeon. The modern prisoner is not only isolated by design, but is guarded against any pitiful pleasure that might fall on him by chance.

Make a list of the numerous attested incidents of history which prove that the old prisons were in one way or another not inaccessible to relief, and you will find that in every one of them such relief is now impossible. A prisoner in the sixteenth century made a lifelong friend of a mouse, but modern prisons are far too clean and hygienic to admit any living thing. A prisoner in the Middle Ages was fed by a woman who came to the window of his cell; but there are no such windows to our cells. We have committed a crime worse than that of our fathers, because more complete; there was far less responsibility on the old rulers who made imprisonment possible than on the modern rulers who have made it inevitable. In this matter of solitary confinement there lies on us all the extra burden of proof which belongs to those who have made their system finally and fanatically perfect. The old tyrant only wanted his enemy inside, so that he should not be outside. We wish the man to be inside for the sake of being inside. We do not forget him; we think about him, and still leave him there. The blackest of the old barons only wished his foe to be friendless because it meant being helpless; but we take one man out of a herd of men already helpless, and we impose on him friendlessness because it is friendlessness; we impose solitude intentionally as a psychological torture. We pretend that our punishment is ameliorative. We make a revolting profession that we are really thinking about this soul which we hang in hell. Really, there are degrees in everything, even in oppression and humbug. I can put up with the people who only wish to keep a man quiet and manage to drive him mad; but the stomach of a Christian turns at the people who drive him mad in order to make him moral.

****

I notice about this institution, as about many other modern police methods, this interesting fact: that nobody seems to know what the thing is supposed to do. In what way is the ruffian or anarchist understood to be affected by it? Is he supposed to learn the sociable virtues in solitude? Is he supposed to be civilized by being as dumb as a dog and as lonely as a lost buccaneer? Punishment is not merely vindictive, nor is it merely utilitarian; it is a reaction and an expiation. All crime is a kind of despotism; and the sin against the Holy Ghost[2] is the attempt to be the superman. All punishment is a sort of righteous rebellion; the revolt of all men against the man who thinks he is the only man in the world. It is the whole sin of the anarch that he thinks he is alone. And we actually try to correct it by making him really alone. I fear that there is really in this punishment an idea more horrible; a conception far more frightful than cropping the man's ears, putting out his eyes, or lopping off his hands or feet. I fear it is meant (perhaps half-consciously) that he should lose that inner strength which is the source alike of sin and virtue; and come with his fingers and his hairs all numbered, but something less than a man.

Notes
1. *Front-de-Boeuf*: Reginald Front-de-Boeuf is a brutal villain in Scott's *Ivanhoe*; he presides over the castle of Torquilstone where Saxon prisoners are incarcerated.
2. *sin against the Holy Ghost*: Cf. Matthew 12:31–2; Mark 3:29; Luke 12:10.

May 22, 1909.

A GREAT MAN.[1]

People accuse journalism of being too personal; but to me it has always seemed far too impersonal. It is charged with tearing away the veils from private life; but it seems to me to be always dropping diaphanous but blinding veils between men and men. The Yellow Press is abused for exposing facts which are private; I wish the Yellow Press did anything so valuable. It is exactly the decisive individual touches that it never gives; and a proof of this is that after one has met a man a million times in the newspapers it is always a complete shock and reversal to meet him in real life. The Yellow Pressman seems to have no power of catching the first fresh fact about a man that dominates all after impressions. For instance, before I met Bernard Shaw I heard that he spoke with a reckless desire for paradox or a sneering hatred of sentiment; but I never knew till he opened his mouth that he spoke with an Irish accent, which is more important than all the other criticisms put together.

Journalism is not personal enough. So far from digging out private personalities, it cannot even report the obvious personalities on the surface. Now there is one vivid and even bodily impression of this kind which we have all felt when we met great poets or politicians, but which never finds its way into the newspapers. I mean the impression that they are much older than we thought they were. We connect great men with their great triumphs, which generally happened some years ago, and many recruits enthusiastic for the thin Napoleon of Marengo[2] must have found themselves in the presence of the fat Napoleon of Leipzic.[3]

I remember reading a newspaper account of how a certain rising politician confronted the House of Lords with the enthusiasm almost of boyhood. It described how his 'brave young voice' rang in the rafters. I also remember that I met him some days after, and he was considerably older than my own father. I mention this truth for only one purpose: all this generalisation leads up to only one fact – the fact that I once met a great man who was younger than I expected.

****

I had come over the wooded wall from the villages about Epsom, and down a stumbling path between trees towards the valley in which Dorking lies. A warm sunlight was working its way through the leafage; a sunlight which though of stainless gold had taken on the quality of evening. It was such sunlight as reminds a man that the sun begins to set an instant after noon. It seemed to lessen as the wood strengthened and the road sank.

I had a sensation peculiar to such entangled descents; I felt that the treetops that closed above me were the fixed and real things, certain as the level of the sea; but that the solid earth was every instant failing under my feet. In a little while that splendid sunlight showed only in splashes, like flaming stars and suns in the dome of green sky. Around me in that emerald twilight were trunks of trees of every plain or twisted type; it was like a chapel supported on columns of every earthly and unearthly style of architecture.

Without intention my mind grew full of fancies on the nature of the forest; on the whole philosophy of mystery and force. For the meaning of woods is the combination of energy with complexity. A forest is not in the least rude or barbarous; it is only dense with delicacy. Unique shapes that an artist would copy or a philosopher watch for years if he found them in an open plain are here mingled and confounded; but it is not a darkness of deformity or death. It is a darkness of life; a darkness of perfection. And I began to think how much of the highest human obscurity is like this and how much men have misunderstood it. People will tell you, for instance, that theology became elaborate because it was dead. Believe me, if it had been dead it would never have become elaborate; it is only the live tree that grows too many branches.

****

The trees thinned and fell away from each other, and I came out into deep grass and a road. I remember being surprised that the evening was so far advanced; I had a fancy that this valley had a sunset all to itself. I went along that road according to directions that had been given me, and passed the gateway in a slight paling beyond which the wood changed only faintly to a garden. It was as if the curious courtesy and fineness of that character I was to meet went out from him upon the valley; for I felt on all these things the finger of that quality which the old English called 'faerie'; it is the quality which those can never understand who think of the past as merely brutal; it is an ancient elegance such as there is in trees. I went through the garden and saw an old man sitting by a table, looking smallish in his big chair. He was already an invalid, and his hair and beard were both white; not like snow, for snow is cold and heavy, but like something feathery, or even fierce; rather they were white like white thistledown. I came up quite close to him; he looked at me as he put out his frail hand, and I saw of a sudden that his eyes were startlingly young. He was the one great man of the old world whom I have met who was not a mere statue over his own grave.

He was deaf and he talked like a torrent. He did not talk about the books he had written; he was far too much alive for that. He talked about the books he had not written. He unrolled a purple bundle of romances which he had never had time to sell. He asked me to write one of the stories for him, as he would have asked the milkman, if he had been talking to the milkman. It was a splendid and frantic story, a sort of astronomical farce. It was all about a man who was rushing up to the Royal Society with the only possible way of avoiding an earth-destroying comet; and it showed how even on this huge errand the man was tripped up at every other minute by his own weaknesses and vanities; how he lost a train by trifling or was put in gaol for brawling. That is only one of them; there were ten or twenty more. Another, I dimly remember, was a version of the fall of Parnell;[4] the idea that a quite honest man might be secret from a pure love of secrecy, of solitary self-control. I went out of that garden with a blurred sensation of the million possibilities of creative literature. The feeling increased as my way fell back into the wood; for a wood is a palace with a million corridors that cross each other everywhere. I really had the feeling that I had seen the creative quality; which is supernatural. I had seen what Virgil calls the Old Man of the Forest; I had seen an elf. The trees thronged behind my path; I have never seen him again; and now I shall not see him, because he died last Tuesday.[5]

Notes
1. *A GREAT MAN*: Reprinted in *TT* (2), pp. 131–6.
2. *thin Napoleon of Marengo*: In the Battle of Marengo (14 June 1800) French forces drove the Austrians out of Italy; the victory reinforced Napoleon's position in France as First Consul.
3. *fat Napoleon of Leipzic*: The Battle of Leipzig, also called The Battle of the Nations (16–19 October 1813), was one of Napoleon's most decisive reversals, leading immediately to the invasion of France by the forces of the Sixth Coalition; in the following year he was forced into exile.
4. *fall of Parnell*: Charles Stewart Parnell; see 'The Poetry of Race', *DN*, 10 July 1901, Volume 1, p. 124, n. 7 above.
5. *he died last Tuesday*: He was George Meredith, who lived at Boxhill in Surrey.

May 29, 1909.

WHAT IS IT?

Last Monday I went about disconsolate, trying to find out what it was. It held up the traffic, it crowded some of the streets, it discommoded the passers-by, yet it did not seem to excite them. I asked a number of people what it was all about, and they did not know. Some of them called it 'Empire Day';[1] but it might have been dedicated to the Chinese Empire for any trace there was in it of English custom and English popular feeling. It was not the day of a great battle or a religious festival, or anything that brought a picture to the mind. Most of the men I talked to had never heard of it in their lives; it had been suddenly and silently imposed upon them from above. It was less philosophic than Trafalgar Day, and far less national than 'Guy Fawkes' Day'. Two or three Canadians send complimentary telegrams to each other, a few of the simpler or the more vulgar Conservatives hang out flags, a number of little boys with sticks and guns defy the world in Hyde Park, and then Lord Meath[2] gets up and says that it does not mean Jingoism and vainglory. I wish it meant anything so clear. I understand Jingoism and vainglory; but I cannot make head or tail of Empire Day. That little boys should have guns is quite right and proper – toy guns, of course; you can buy them quite cheap in the old-fashioned toyshops, painted a bright reddish brown, and with a hammer that will really fire off caps. But why should they only have them once a year, and what has it got to do with the Colonies? What is it? Who made it? What does it celebrate? Why have we got to bother about it?

****

As I found that the English people knew no more about 'Empire Day' than I did, I turned anxiously to its official exponents. I bought an Imperialist paper and read the reports of the speeches given at that great bazaar or Imperial mart over which Mr. Kiralfy[3] and other rugged Britons preside. I read reverently the report of a speech by Sir Gilbert Parker; but whether Sir Gilbert Parker's eloquence so excited the reporter that he did not get it down quite right, or whether the occasion so excited Sir Gilbert that he did not say it quite right, the words quoted from him only plunge me deeper in my mystification. 'It [the Imperial idea] was chilled', exclaimed the orator passionately, 'by the cold blasts of indifference and the dislike of those small souls who could not see beyond Beachy Head or the Grampian Hills, men who cared so much for all the world that they cared less for their own race, whose opposition to individualism made them impatient even of nationality and ravaged it in its tender youth; but it put forth its strength and thrust its roots deeper in the soil, resisting the spoiler.'[4]

In unravelling rhetoric of this high and abstruse order one must carefully and even patiently arrange one's ideas. It seems that there are a set of people with small souls who never look beyond Beachy Head or the Grampians, and these people are so fond of the whole world beyond those boundaries that they like it better than their own race.

That does not seem quite clear. Let us try it another way. There are men so fond of the whole world that they never look beyond Beachy Head ...

No; that does not seem right either. And what is it that is ravaged in its tender youth? Can it be Beachy Head? Or Individualism perhaps? Is Sir Gilbert Parker under the impression that the national sentiment of England is still in its tender youth? Or is he thinking of his own Canadian home; and did some Little Englander attempt to ravage him at an early age? I am a very old-fashioned Englishman myself; it was considerably on this side of the Grampian Hills that my father fed his flocks; and my small soul so clings to custom and prejudice that if I did dare for one moment to look beyond Beachy Head I should not expect to see Canada, but, if anything, France. I therefore feel that there is some sort of mysticism in Canadian Imperialism which my heavy island spirit cannot follow. So I gave up the prose and tried the poetry.

****

I was fortunate enough to find in the same newspaper a poem which was actually written in order to answer my anxious query. The reader can imagine with what a throb of pleasure I found that a patriotic song sung at the St. Mary's School, Peckham, had for its very first line the words that I had been repeating to myself all day long:

> What is the meaning of Empire Day?
>   Why do the cannon roar?
> Why does the cry 'God Save the King'
>   Echo from shore to shore?

The real official answer is given in the chorus, which I read therefore with an almost dry-throated eagerness. The true reply to the riddle is, it seems, as follows:

> On our Nation's 'Scroll of Glory'
>   With its deeds of daring told,
> There is writ the story
>   Of our heroes bold in the days of old.
> So, to keep their deeds before us,
>   Every year we homage pay
> To our banner proud, that has never bowed,
>   And *that's* the meaning of Empire Day.⁵

So that's all right; and now you know as much about it as I do or anybody else. The italics are, I am proud to say, not mine.

****

Only when I think for an instant of a few of those idle songs that have been written by the small souls between Beachy Head and the Grampians, I cannot but think the lyric quoted above a singular and even portentous object. We hardly attempt to familiarise the poor with those English verses which will last longer than England. But we eagerly and elaborately instruct them in this bombastic doggerel, which has all the marks of being illiterate without even the air of being sincere. If we must rant why cannot we rant literature like our fathers before us; why cannot the children sing Garrick's 'Hearts of Oak'⁶ or Thomson's 'Rule Britannia',⁷ or repeat the swaggering speeches out of 'Henry V'.? Let the boys read something written in English, the songs of Dibdin⁸ or the tales of Captain Marryat.⁹ These songs and speeches [i e of the bombastic doggerel type?] are not written in English but in Imperialese. They are in the true sense vulgar. Vulgarity does not consist in treating respectable things derisively, as in the old English writers. Real vulgarity consists in taking contemptible things seriously, as that song was taken at Peckham.

Along with this faint plea for literature I may perhaps make a yet fainter plea for logic. Our souls, being small, are easily satisfied, and to us in this little island such names as Milton or Newton naturally seem large. But naturally Sir Gilbert Parker, taking in at one glance a mighty horizon, seeing New Zealand beyond the Grampians and Newfoundland beyond Beachy Head, sees also a literature that eclipses Milton and a philosophy that soars higher than Newton. He sees the literature and philosophy from our Colonies, which is already enchanting the world. But I think that we English, in our old academic way, might be allowed to insist that the charges against us should make some sense when put together in a sentence. I really wish Sir Gilbert Parker would make up his mind whether our crime consists in thinking about the rest of the world or in not thinking about it. It seems to pass the obvious powers even of a small soul to be continually and disgracefully inside his country and also continually and disgracefully outside it. It must be one or the other; and I suppose in the long run the Imperialists will settle it somehow. I should prefer to be inside my country; they will probably prefer to be outside. But I think they should explain their meaning, with as few contradictions as possible.

Notes
1. *'Empire Day'*: See 'The Queer Memory', *DN*, 21 November 1908, p. 217, n. 5 above.
2. *Lord Meath*; Reginald Brabazon, twelfth Earl of Meath; see n. 1, above.
3. *Mr. Kiralfy*: Imré Kiralfy (formerly Königsbaum) (1845–1919), was a dancer and impresario; born in the Austro-Hungarian empire, Kiralfy's family was forced to flee Hungary following the failure of the revolution of 1848. As well as large dance-based spectacles, he specialized in directing exhibitions. After performing in Paris and the United States, he came to Britain in 1891 with *Nero, or the Fall of Rome*, which he had produced in New York. He returned in 1893 to recreate the Earl's Court Exhibition Centre as a replica of Chicago's 'White City'. He worked closely with the British Empire League: he and his sons played a major role in the development of the Imperial International Exhibition Centre at the new White City at Shepherd's Bush, which opened in 1908. The architecture of both White Cities had a strong imperial flavour (J. Pes, *ODNB*).
4. *The report of a speech by Sir Gilbert Parker ... resisting the spoiler*: 'Empire Day', *Morning Post*, 25 May 1909, p. 7. The speech was made at the unveiling of the King's statue at White City, a monument that filled the central arch of the Imperial Tower. For Sir (Horatio) Gilbert George Parker, baronet, see 'Some Good Short Stories', *DN*, 12 March 1906, Volume 3, p. 323 n. 8, above.
5. *What is the meaning of Empire Day ... And that's the meaning of Empire Day*: A slightly different version of this song is reproduced in R. Roberts. *The Classic Slum: Salford Life in the First Quarter of the Century* (Manchester: Manchester University Press, 1971), p. 113.
6. *Garrick's 'Hearts of Oak'*: 'Heart of Oak' (1759) is the official march of the Royal Navy and several other Commonwealth navies. It was composed by the eighteenth-century actor David Garrick and set to music by William Boyce.
7. *Thomson's 'Rule Britannia'*: 'Rule, Britannia' was composed by James Thomson (1700–48) and set to music by Thomas Arne (*c.* 1740); it has, along with 'Land of Hope and Glory', become an unofficial national anthem. Chesterton referred admiringly to the song again in 'Liberty', *DN*, 21 August 1909, Volume 6, p. 32 below.
8. *the songs of Dibdin*: Charles Dibdin (bap. 1745, d. 1814), was an English actor, composer and writer. His talent as a writer of ballads won recognition as Britain resumed war with France in June 1803. For the next six months he was commissioned by the Government to publish eight *British War Songs* per month 'suitable for ships, camp and home'. But his output was much wider, some 900 songs altogether, including 'Poor Jack', 'Tom Bowling' and 'Push the Grog About', many of which became part of the folk tradition (J. A. Gillaspie, *ODNB*).
9. *Captain Marryat*: Frederick Marryat; see H. M. Wallis, 'The Sin of Torture', letter to the editor, *DN*, 27 August 1908, p. 152, n. 4 above.

June 5, 1909.

THE ANGRY OPTIMIST.

I have just been reading with huge pleasure, I will not say with downright gaiety, my friend Mr. C. F. G. Masterman's last book, 'The Condition of England'.[1] Some people regret that Mr. Masterman's admirable English is set to a somewhat wailing tune; but I have not the slightest objection to Mr. Masterman being a pessimist, though (as you will see) I draw the line when he tries to make out that I am one. It is literally true that he can do in English literature a great thing that nobody else can do. He can see men as a mass and yet see them as a mass of men. Many others can describe individuals, and many others can describe mere averages and statistics. Mr. Sidney Webb can give me a map; but a map is always inaccurate. I remember that in early youth I thought the whole of Scotland was light mauve because it was so in an atlas. Mr. Bernard Shaw, again, can give me a picture, but the picture is always a portrait, and rather frequently a portrait of Bernard Shaw.

There are only two men alive who can describe what Mr. James Douglas[2] cleverly called a 'manscape', a moving forest of men, each individual, like the walking forest that went to Dunsinane.[3] Those two men are H. G. Wells and C. F. G. Masterman. And Mr. Masterman is even the greater of the two in this respect; that he is not modern at all, that he sees this shapeless and mysterious army moving from a divine creation to some divine doom. In any case, he is one of the two men who can create not a map but a live map. One looks at the shapes and colours of the counties and provinces, and the colours move and mix like the loathsome colours on the live back of a snake. It is not a pleasant metaphor, nor are Mr. Masterman's metaphors. I am proud to say that he has not thought of this one.

But Mr. Masterman, not content with his nightmare omniscience, has descended to personalities, and has especially made a remark about me which would have roused more abject individuals to protest. He attempts to maintain that I am no longer an optimist, which seems to mean a happy man. But I will quote:

> Mr. Chesterton, again, first entered the arena of controversy in another spirit, crashing upon the stage sword in hand, and with a breath of jolly fresh air, offering to lead all humanity to the downfall of Doubting Castle.[4] His challenge and defiance were to all pessimisms and life denials, to all who refused to affirm that to-day was the first of days, and every dawn a miracle. The slums of the cities were stupendous; the suburbs sublime. Each fat red pillar-box was a symbol of enchantment. Dragons' eyes glared from the lights of engines, and the lampposts shouted, like the Sons of God, for joy that they were made.[5] But to-day, in our solitary and splendid optimist, the rejoicing has already been sicklied o'er with the pale cast of doubt.[6] The music of his rustic flute has kept not for long its happy country tone, and has taken a stormier note from the tempest-tossed children of mankind.[7] So the sunlight fades on the vision of a people which … lies deferential and prostrate before an oligarchy of rich men, who only cannot be bought because they have sold themselves already.

This is a dreadful situation; rather like that in which Burke cried out to Fox in the House of Commons, 'Our friendship is at an end'.[8] Mr. Masterman is really rather like Burke in the rich roll of his sentences, in his sad and sweeping view of civilization, in his fear that we are sloping towards a whirlpool. I am like Fox only in fatness and affection for my friends. And it is in the hope that some middle way may be effected to avoid this awful breach that I offer my remaining observations.

****

Let me state, with all possible violence, that to-day is the first of days, and that everyone who does not see it must be mad. Let me lay down once more as dogma that every fat red pillar-box is a symbol of enchantment, and whoever cannot feel it is in danger of hell fire. Dragons' eyes do glare; I often see them. Lampposts do shout; I often hear them. The slums are stupendous; are there not men in the slums? The suburbs are sublime; what other word would you use of places where the very image of God burns inside a box of brick? I never walk down one of these mean streets of Mr. Masterman's vision, or one of those long lanes which for him have no turning, without feeling that every separate house might be stuck on the spike of a peaked mountain to be worshipped of all the creatures of the earth.

In my idle youth I said that the suburbs were fairyland; but that was the mere light prophecy and instinct of innocence. Now I know that the suburbs are fairyland, because I have lived in one of them. I once had a sort of fancy that a fire on the hearth was a good red goblin, the god of the house; but now I know it as a simple domestic fact. I once conjectured that perhaps a chair was a kind of wooden quadruped who would allow a man to ride on it without moving; but now I am certain; I have tested the fact.

I am far more flaming with the poetry of common things than I ever was before; I am certain, more certain, than I can say, that men could make their Paradise out of pots and pans and three-legged stools. In short, as Mr. Masterman says, I enter sword in hand offering to lead all humanity to the downfall of Doubting Castle.

But why even in a fairy tale is one sword in hand? And why did the great allegorist exhibit even hesitation as something entrenched; why is even Doubting a Castle? Surely it is for this simple reason: that there is something that is spiritually destructive to the surprise and splendour of these things. There is something that is in favour of lampposts, but against the magic of lampposts. There is something that is for engines but against the childish poetry of engines. There is something that is for pillar boxes, but against the meaning of pillar boxes. There is something that makes industrial suburbs, but does not admire them, while I admire them, but would not have the responsibility of making them.

In short, I will make this concession only of my defeat as an optimist. There is something that makes small clerks rather quicker than I can learn to love them. But what is this force that makes the lamp-post anything less than flaming or the suburban citizen anything less than a man? Is it not simply the growth of a certain cowardice and corruption in high places, and can one defend the lamp-post better than by attacking those who are too rich to spare any money for it? My dislike of the rich class that rules Britain is first and last a dislike of people who are making impossible for the masses this vivid and supernatural vision of their daily life. I am quite certain that the land would be lovable but for the landlords. I am quite sure that the house would be holy but for the house rents. I am quite sure that an artificial oligarchy stands between us and very simple appreciations.

In fine, I am still ready to lead humanity to the downfall of Doubting Castle; only now I know where it is.

Notes
1. *my friend C. F. G. Masterman's last book ... 'The Condition of England'*: The Condition of England (London: Methuen, 1909). For Charles Frederick Gurney Masterman; see 'For Persons of the Name of Smith', *DN*, 28 November 1902, Volume 1, pp. 440–1, n. 2 above.
2. *Mr. James Douglas*: James Douglas; see 'Anti-Puritanism' (Editorial), 21 May 1906, Volume 3, p. 371, n. 4 above.
3. *Dunsinane*: See 'Walking Tours', *DN*, 23 September 1901, Volume 1, p. 200, n. 2 above.
4. *Doubting Castle*: Doubting Castle is the home of the Giant Despair in the first part of Bunyan's *Pilgrim's Progress*. Christian and Hopeful are imprisoned there and beaten and starved until, using a key called Promise, they escape.
5. *shouted ... for joy that they were made*: See Job 38:7.
6. *sicklied o'er ... doubt*: See *Hamlet*, III.i:

And thus the native hue of resolution
Is sicklied o'er with the pale cast of thought,
And enterprises of great pith and moment
With this regard their currents turn awry,
And lose the name of action.

7. *tempest-tossed children of mankind*: see Matthew Arnold, 'Thyrsis' (1861):

What though the music of thy rustic flute
Kept not for long its happy, country tone;
Lost it too soon, and learnt a stormy note
Of men contention-tost, of men who groan,
Which tasked thy pipe too sore, and tired thy throat –
It failed, and thou wage mute!

8. *Burke cried out to Fox ... 'Our friendship is at an end'*: Chesterton has in mind's Burke's reply to Fox after the debate on the Quebec Bill in the House of Commons on 6 May 1791. Having disagreed with him fundamentally, Fox assured Burke that 'there is no loss of friendship'. Burke answered: 'I regret to say there is. I have indeed made a great sacrifice; I have done my duty though I have lost my friend'. See J. Prior, *Life of the Right Honourable Edmund Burke* (London: Henry G. Bohn, 1854), p. 329.

June 12, 1909.

THE CASE FOR MACAULAY.[1]

We have all heard of prophets and poets being unpopular; and also of unpopularity as a thing that may purify the soul. But there is this further and rather odd fact – that every great man must go through a period of unpopularity, not while he is alive, but shortly after he is dead. That after eclipse is essential because in that is settled the difference between temporary and eternal oblivion. The prophet and the quack are alike admired for a generation, and admired for the wrong reasons. Then they are both forgotten, for no reason at all. But if the man is a mere quack he never returns. If he is a great man he returns, and he returns for the right reasons.

We need not dwell on the obvious instances of this. Dr. Johnson was enthroned as a cold arbiter, and dethroned as a cold arbiter.[2] Now he has been restored as a most hot and human Christian soul, and Christians can never forget him. Dickens was adored for Little Nell, and then despised for Little Nell. It is only when Little Nell is quite dead and out of the way that he can be sufficiently adored for Dick Swiveller.[3] Of these once popular figures there is one who has not yet recaptured his popularity. Just as a little while ago it was thought cultured to sneer at Dickens, so it is still thought cultured to sneer at Macaulay.[4] Perhaps I had come myself to be too much under that cloud of disillusion; for when I opened Macaulay's History by accident the other day I was startled by the unmistakable roll of rich style and real greatness in the thing.

****

Macaulay's popularity was shallow; he was popular for the wrong reasons. The wit of those ringing and arresting sentences is constantly coarse and unfair, though I wish it were more often remembered that this old lucid cleverness really had to be clever; whereas our vague culture is quite free to be stupid. Wit is lower than humour; but sham humour is much easier than sham wit. You can pretend that you have made an atmosphere; you cannot pretend that you have made a pun. Similarly many a modern professes that his style has the nameless charm of Newman, because he could not possibly invent one clever antithesis of Macaulay. Still, Macaulay's mere wit and logic are shallow, and would not make him great. What is it, after all, that makes him great?

This, I think, makes him great and even eternal, that he had the high passion of history. He understood the word glory; the glory of man as a thing like the glory of God. The only difference between the warrior and the poet is that the warrior seeks this thing in the future and the poet or the historian in the past. Macaulay had the music of history in him, just as Walter Scott had it. He was passionately traditional. There is one unquestionable test of this: he was frightfully fond of proper names. Some of the best lines of Scott's poetry consist entirely of the names of places. Some of the strongest sentences of Macaulay hang wholly on words like Milton or Rome.

****

There is something that is higher than impartiality, and Macaulay possessed it; poetical justice; the living impartiality of the imagination rather than the dead impartiality of the reason. He sometimes made good men bad and bad men good in the heat of political prejudice; but he always made them men, and even great men. He slandered his opponents, but he did not belittle them. He had a high pleasure in mixing with heroic affairs; he liked to crowd his stage with men of stature and presence; he had a warlike sort of wish to see villains worthy of his heroes. Though he was not enough of a Christian to love his enemies, he was enough of a heathen to admire them, and a heathen is the next best thing. Take the case of the celebrated Graham of Claverhouse, afterwards Lord Dundee.[5] Macaulay starts, by prejudice or purpose, indecently or even insanely against the man. He is really unreasonable in the whole affair of the Covenanters. Claverhouse, I imagine, was an ordinary officer of Dragoons, a type that does not always specialise in the Christian virtues, in the later 17th century, a time when the Scotch nobility and gentry were cynical and gross. It was his merely military duty to put down a rebellion of men whom you may call prophets or maniacs according to taste, but who were utterly exceptional, ruthless, and beyond common reason; who gave no quarter in battle, and wished to persecute every other religion on earth. I daresay Claverhouse did wrong; just as any bull-necked English officer would probably do wrong in dealing with some swarm of alien fanatics that ride with the Mahdi or the Mad Mullah. But that is all. Macaulay gives a picture of harmless and laborious peasants trampled down in blood by a monstrous fiend in top-boots, who dances on them apparently for fun. In the first few pages about John Graham, Macaulay describes a beast rather than a man.[6] Whether he was like that in real life we need not elaborately discuss. One thing is certain: that he does not remain like that in Macaulay's 'History'.

As soon as Dundee begins to play his great part at the very crisis of the English kingship, an extraordinary impression begins to grow. Macaulay begins to like him. Macaulay is mad for the Revolution; and he becomes quite fond of Dundee because he came so near to frustrating the Revolution. Macaulay is glad with every cell of his brain that James II. should go. Yet he is thrilled with every drop of his blood when the arresting voice of Graham calls James like a trumpet to remain. When Dundee is mounted, and rides down the street, Macaulay's prose moves to the tune of Walter Scott. Stroke after stroke changes the beast to a prince of chivalry. Macaulay talks of the calm magnanimity of this monster. He goes out of his way to mention that he reproved the rapine of the clans; that he held heroic language in the council of the chiefs; and that on the eve of his last battle he asked for peril as a favour, that he might show that he was a soldier as well as a general. When the claymores come cleaving their way down Killiecrankie, Macaulay is almost a Jacobite. The last words of the great persecutor of the Covenant are lofty and unselfish; and in death he is as pure as Hector. I know no more singular change of tone in the description of one man.[7]

This is a striking instance of what I may call the abstract enthusiasm of Macaulay. He had a passion for the cause; but he also had a passion for the subject, for the period and everybody in it. A stranger and stronger case still is that of Marlborough. If ever there was a moral dwarf, a spiritual monkey, it was he. He was a lump of littleness just large enough to be seen. He combined all despicable qualities in combinations hitherto untried. He was a thrifty profligate. He was an unpatriotic militarist. He sold his sister and his country not madly, like a gambler, but quite quietly and explanatorily, like an old maid bargaining with a cabman. It is almost incredible that any man, or even any animal, should be such an object of contempt. And yet Macaulay is so carried away with the great Whig Crusade, the great story that he is telling, that when dealing with one who played a large part in it, he cannot help making the man magnificent, although the part was base.[8] He tells all the truths about Marlborough that I have cited, without the least doubt or favour; and yet he gives the impression that he has been describing a great man.

I have heard that somebody has started something else which is called scientific history,[9] and I once tried to read it. It appears to avoid the dangers of describing great men by the bright and simple solution of not describing men at all. By this method the historian looks down on all the movements of men as if they were ants. If I want truth I must confess that I prefer Macaulay. I prefer to look up at men as if they were angels, even if they are angels of darkness.

Notes

1. *THE CASE FOR MACAULAY*: Reprinted in *HA*, pp. 107–11.
2. *Dr. Johnson ... dethroned as a cold arbiter*: Samuel Johnson; see 'The Good Man of the Eighteenth Century', *DN*, 22 March 1901, Volume 1, p. 66, n. 5 above. Though Dr Johnson enjoyed a generally high reputation during his life and after his death, Macaulay and others – notably the Romantic Poets, who especially disliked his views on Milton – thought ill of him. His reputation as a critic was fully restored only in the twentieth century. See S. Lynn, 'Johnson's critical reception', in G. Clingham, *The Cambridge Companion to Samuel Johnson* (Cambridge: Cambridge University Press, 1997), p. 245.
3. *Dickens was adored ... Dick Swiveller*: Chesterton is referring to *The Old Curiosity Shop*.
4. *Macaulay*: Thomas Babington Macaulay; see 'A Handbook of Tennyson', *DN*, 5 August 1901, p. 150, n. 4 above.
5. *Graham of Claverhouse, afterwards Lord Dundee*: John Graham of Claverhouse, first Viscount of Dundee; see 'Bigotry and Intolerance', *DN*, 18 February 1905, Volume 3, p. 40, n. 7 above.
6. *In the first few pages about John Graham ... man*; see The *History of England, from the Accession of James II*, 5 Vols (1848–55), vol. 1, ch. 4.
7. *As soon as Dundee begins ... one man*: see *The History of England*, vol. 3 (1855), ch. 13.
8. *A stranger and stronger case still ... although the part was base*: See 'Charity: A Dream', *DN*, 5 August 1905, Volume 3, p. 160, n. 3 above.
9. *scientific history*: See 'History Versus the Historians', *DN*, 25 July 1908, p. 115, n. 6 above.

June 14, 1909.

A BOOK OF THE DAY.

Who Was Junius?

'Junius Unveiled'. By James Smith. Dent. [1909]. 2s 6d.

Mr. James Smith[1] is confident, not so much that he can prove, but, that he has proved, that 'Junius'[2] was Edward Gibbon,[3] the historian. It is a remarkable thing that in these discussions about identity the least convincing things are always the facts. I mean that a general atmospheric probability may really be suggested; but the details, which should be solid, seem particularly thin. The idea may be almost an inspiration; it is the arguments that are mere coincidences. So it is certainly with Mr. Smith and his theory that Gibbon wrote the Letters of Junius. The moral arguments which he does not urge are really stronger than the material arguments that he does urge. There is, I think, a certain spiritual (or rather unspiritual) resemblance between Junius and Gibbon. There is at least a resemblance as compared with the spiritual abyss which separates Junius from some of the other candidates, as, for example, Burke.[4] Mr. Smith carefully assures us that Burke voluntarily denied having written the letters. This is a good instance of the futility of a fact compared with a character. The truth is that Burke could never have been sneak enough to write the Letters of Junius. But if he had been sneak enough to write them he might easily have been sneak enough to deny it.

But he did not write them. I know he did not. Gibbon was at least like Junius in this – that he has all a rationalist's dislike of authority, combined with all a scholar's dislike of popular control. Both of them distrusted kings, detested priests, and literally loathed the people. Mr. Andrew Lang has written of Mr. Smith's hypothesis: 'I hope Gibbon was not Junius; for Junius was no gentleman'.[5] But this is the sentimental use of the term. In the strict and social sense

Junius seems as much a gentleman as Gibbon; more of a gentleman than Gibbon. His sympathies were aristocratic; his tone was scholarly; he had all the perilous ease that comes from pride. But Mr. Lang, I think, means by gentleman a generous man. Junius was not particularly kind or chivalrous; but neither was Gibbon. Everything about Gibbon personally seems smug and small, from his frigid jilting of the girl he loved to his enduring fear of the great popular movements. He was a great man with a small heart. There have been in human history two flaming hopes and fulfilments, which, though both rooted in human fraternity, have often collided, and are still dividing mankind: they were Christianity and the French Revolution. Almost every man with a soul has been in arms either for a combination of them or for one of them against the other. Gibbon had a poisonous hatred of both.

The Method of Mr. Smith.

Thus along lines of character one could really approximate the two personalities. But it is exactly when Mr. Smith begins to give his detailed proof that the whole thing begins to dissolve into accident or vagueness. For instance, Mr. Smith employs a method of which the Bacon-Shakespeare enthusiasts are very fond, and an uncommonly bad method it is. It consists of printing lists and tables of parallel quotations from the two writers involved, in each of which there is a trick of phrase or two or three words the same. This is useless nonsense, for in almost every case it is just as likely that two writers would use such terms as that one writer should carefully repeat them. Here is an instance. Mr. Smith quotes from Junius, 'He was neither an object of derision to his enemies nor of melancholy pity to his friends'. He then quotes from Gibbon, 'He never lost the confidence of his friends nor the esteem of his enemies'. Now this antithesis of friends and enemies might occur to anyone from a Jesuit to a Red Indian, and to say that the opposition is crisply and lucidly put is only to say that it was written in the eighteenth century. Mr. Smith might as well say that both Junius and Gibbon probably wore three-cornered hats and buckles on their shoes.

He quotes again from Junius, 'He determined to quit a Court whose proceedings and decisions he could neither assent to with honour nor oppose with success', and from Gibbon, 'Julian expressed his intention of resigning the purple, which he could not preserve with honour, but which he could not abdicate with safety'. There is a similarity in the antithesis, but it is the similarity of a whole age and school. I would undertake to find sentences balanced exactly like that in every writer of that tradition from Dr. Johnson to Macaulay, in Hume,[6] in Burke, in Robertson,[7] in Bishop Butler, in Madame D'Arblay.[8] In the same way some people prove that an Elizabethan judge wrote the comedies of an Elizabethan playwright, because both of them made bad Elizabethan puns or had heard of Jupiter and Juno.

Coincidences.

Of course, Mr. Smith has many other arguments besides this parallelism of style, but they are most of them open to the same objection; that they are too sweeping, too universal, to be true. Thus both Junius and Gibbon had an extravagant contempt for the Roman Catholic Church; but the whole England of the eighteenth century had it, though it was softened to sadness in two great spirits – Burke and Johnson. A Whig oligarchist like Junius would be bound to have it whoever he was. Or again, it is true, as Mr. Smith says, that Gibbon and Junius both regarded Wilkes[9] with undue indulgence. But everybody regarded Wilkes with undue indulgence. He is one of the most mysterious cases of a nameless magic of personality. Even the men who desired his death liked his society. Men like Sandwich[10] were his false friends, but never exactly his enemies. Dr. Johnson, who had fifty good reasons and fifty thousand bad reasons for hating the demagogue could not sit through dinner with him without making friends.[11]

The strongest, because the most special, of Mr. Smith's coincidences are the exceptional knowledge of French and military matters and the silence of Junius during one of the domestic troubles of Gibbon. But these things, though not universal, are not unique. The social atmosphere of the eighteenth century was such that many gentlemen, if not most gentlemen, might specialise in French or soldiering, and when one thinks of the thousand causes, from intellectual doubt to physical laziness, which may lead a literary man to drop his work for a few months, it is not necessary to seek for any tragic secret in the gaps of Junius. Mr. Smith has not, as he seems to fancy, proved a case. But he has suggested a possibility, where many another man has only suggested an impossibility. Junius cannot have been Burke; he may have been Gibbon. But in all these things we must go by the truth taken as a whole, not by the facts taken in detail. The only valuable sort of learning is learning to see all the facts at once, as all the features are united and suspended in one unforgotten face.

Notes
1. *Mr. James Smith*: Nothing is known of Smith other than that he was Australian. The book under review here is his only entry in the British Library catalogue.
2. *'Junius'*: 'Junius' was a pseudonym used by the contributor of a series of letters to the *Public Advertiser* from 21 January 1769 to 21 January 1772. The letters were written in elegant polemical opposition to the ministries of Grafton, Lord North and the Duke of Bedford. They revealed close political secrets and private scandals. Their authorship is still unknown, but the likeliest candidate seems to be the English politician and pamphleteer Sir Philip Francis (1740-1818): see A. Frearson, 'The Identity of Junius', *Journal for Eighteenth-Century Studies*, 7:2 (2008), pp. 211-27.

3. *Edward Gibbon*; see 'The Good Man of the Eighteenth Century', *DN*, 22 March 1901, Volume 1, p. 67, n. 18 above.
4. *Burke*: Edmund Burke; see 'The Good Man of the Eighteenth Century', *DN*, 22 March 1901, Volume 1, p. 67, n. 20 above.
5. *Mr. Andrew Lang ... no gentleman*: 'At the Sign of St. Paul's', *ILN*, 5 June 1909, p. 816. For Andrew Lang, see 'The Madness of the Omarites', *DN*, 7 March 1901, Volume 1, p. 47, n. 7 above.
6. *Hume*: David Hume; see 'Whatever Happened to Rational Persons', *DN*, 12 December 1903, Volume 2, p. 168, n. 7 above.
7. *Robertson*: William Robertson (1740–1803), was a Scottish antiquary and author. His *History of Ancient Greece* appeared in 1768 and *A North Briton Extraordinary* – a riposte to John Wilkes – in the following year. Robertson met Johnson and Boswell at Cullen House in Banffshire in 1773. Robertson was Deputy Keeper of the Parliamentary records in Scotland, and his edition of the Acts of the Scottish Parliament, *The Parliamentary Records of Scotland*, was published a year after his death (P. Cadell, *ODNB*).
8. *Madame D'Arblay*: Madame D'Arblay is the married name of the English novelist, diarist and playwright Frances Burney (1752–1840), also called Fanny Burney (she married a French exile, General Alexandre D'Arblay, in 1792). Her novels – *Evelina* (1778), *Cecilia* (1782), *Camilla* (1796) and *The Wanderer* (1814) – depict the lives of the English aristocracy in a mordant satirical vein. She was well thought of by such contemporary literary figures as Samuel Johnson, Edmund Burke and David Garrick.
9. *Wilkes*: John Wilkes; see 'A Glimpse of My Country', 9 March 1907, Volume 4, p. 177, n. 6 above.
10. *Sandwich*: John Montagu (1718–92), fourth Earl of Sandwich, was a politician and musical patron. As Secretary of State for the states of Northern Europe in 1763, Montagu took up the prosecution of John Wilkes, whose newspaper had accused the King of lying, from his inept predecessor. His action brought Wilkes to financial ruin. Wilkes's supporters accused Sandwich of betraying a friend, although their closeness has been questioned (N. A. M. Rodger, *ODNB*).
11 *Dr. Johnson ... without making friends*: The dinner to which Chesterton refers took place on 15 May 1776; it was contrived by Boswell and reported with some amusement in vol. 3 of his *Life of Johnson*.

June 19, 1909.

THE MYSTERY OF A PAGEANT.[1]

Once upon a time, it seems centuries ago, I was prevailed on to take a small part in one of those historical processions or pageants which happened to be fashionable in or about the year 1909.[2] And since I tend, like all who are growing old, to re-enter the remote past as a paradise or playground, I disinter a memory which may serve to stand among those memories of small but strange incidents with which I have sometimes filled this column. The thing has really some of the dark qualities of a detective story; though I suppose that Sherlock Holmes himself could hardly unravel it now, when the scent is so old and cold and most of the actors, doubtless, long dead.

This old pageant included a series of figures from the 18th century, and I was told that I was just like Dr. Johnson.[3] Seeing that Dr. Johnson was heavily seamed with small-pox, had a waistcoat all over gravy, snorted and rolled as he walked, and was probably the ugliest man in London, I mention this identification as a fact and not as a vaunt. I had nothing to do with the arrangement; and such fleeting suggestions as I made were not taken so seriously as they might have been. I requested that a row of posts should be erected across the lawn, so that I might touch all of them but one, and then go back and touch that. Failing this, I felt that the least they could do was to have twenty-five cups of tea stationed at regular intervals along the course,[4] each held by a Mrs. Thrale[5] in full costume. My best constructive suggestion was the most harshly rejected of all. In front of me in the procession walked the great Bishop Berkeley, the man who turned the tables on the early materialists by maintaining that matter itself very possibly does not exist. Dr. Johnson, you will remember, did not like such bottomless fancies as Berkeley's, and kicked a stone with his boot, saying, 'I refute him so!' Now (as I pointed out) kicking a stone would not make the metaphysical quarrel quite clear; besides, it would hurt. But how picturesque and perfect it would be if I moved across the ground in the symbolic attitude of kicking Bishop Berkeley! How complete an allegoric group; the great transcendentalist walking with his head among the stars, but behind him the avenging realist *pede claudo*,[6] with uplifted foot. But I must not take up space with these forgotten frivolities; we old men grow too garrulous in talking of the distant past.

This story scarcely concerns me either in my real or my assumed character. Suffice it to say that the procession took place at night in a large garden and by torchlight (so remote is the date), that the garden was crowded with Puritans, monks, and men-at-arms, and especially with early Celtic saints smoking pipes, and with elegant Renaissance gentlemen talking Cockney. Suffice it to say, or rather it is needless to say, that I got lost. I wandered away into some dim corner of that dim shrubbery, where there was nothing to do except tumbling over tent ropes, and I began almost to feel like my prototype, and to share his horror of solitude and hatred of a country life.

In this detachment and dilemma I saw another man in a white wig advancing across this forsaken stretch of lawn; a tall, lean man, who stooped in his long back robes like a stooping eagle. When I thought he would pass me he stopped before my face, and said, 'Dr. Johnson, I think. I am Paley'.[7]

'Sir', I said, 'you used to guide men to the beginnings of Christianity. If you can guide me now to wherever this infernal thing begins you will perform a yet higher and harder function'.

His costume and style were so perfect that for the instant I really thought he was a ghost. He took no notice of my flippancy, but, turning his black-robed back on me, led me through verdurous glooms and winding mossy ways, until we came out into the glare of gaslight and laughing men in masquerade, and I could easily laugh at myself.

And there, you will say, was an end of the matter. I am (you will say) naturally obtuse, cowardly, and mentally deficient. I was, moreover, unused to pageants; I felt frightened in the dark and took a man for a spectre whom, in the light, I could recognise as a modern gentleman in a masquerade dress. No; far from it. That spectral person was my first introduction to a spectral incident which has never been explained and which still lays its finger on my nerve.

I mixed with the men of the 18th century; and we fooled as one does at a fancy-dress ball. There was Burke[8] as large as life and a great deal better looking. There was Cowper[9] much larger than life; he ought to have been a little man in a night-cap, with a cat under one arm and a spaniel under the other. As it was, he was a magnificent person, and looked more like the Master of Ballantrae[10] than Cowper. I persuaded him at last to the night-cap, but never, alas, to the cat and dog. When I came the next night Burke was still the same beautiful improvement upon himself; Cowper was still weeping for his dog and cat and would not be comforted; Bishop Berkeley[11] was still waiting to be kicked in the interests of philosophy. In short, I met all my old friends but one. Where was Paley? I had been mystically moved by the man's presence; I was moved more by his absence. At last I saw advancing towards us across the twilight garden a little man with a large book and a bright attractive face. When he came near enough he said, in a small, clear voice, 'I'm Paley'. The thing was quite natural, of course; the man was ill and had sent a substitute. Yet somehow the contrast was a shock.

By the next night I had grown quite friendly with my four or five colleagues; I had discovered what is called a mutual friend with Berkeley and several points of difference with Burke. Cowper, I think it was, who introduced me to a friend of his, a fresh face, square and sturdy, framed in a white wig. 'This', he explained, 'is my friend So-and-So. He's Paley'. I looked round at all the faces by this time fixed and familiar; I studied them; I counted them; then I bowed to the third Paley as one bows to necessity. So far the thing was well within the limits of coincidence. It certainly seemed odd that this one particular cleric should be so varying and elusive. It was singular that Paley, alone among men, should be sometimes tall and sometimes short, should swell and shrink and alter like a phantom, while all else remained solid. But the thing was explicable; two men had been ill and there was an end of it. Or there should have been an end of it; only I went again the next night, and a clear-coloured elegant youth with powdered hair bounded up to me, and told me with boyish excitement that he was Paley.

For the next twenty-four hours I remained in the mental condition of the modern world. I mean the condition in which all natural explanations have broken down and no supernatural explanation has been established. My bewilderment had reached to boredom when I found myself once more in the colour and clatter of the pageant, and I was all the more pleased because I met an old school-fellow, and we mutually recognised each other under our heavy clothes and hoary wigs. We talked about all those great things for which literature is too small and only life large enough; red hot memories and those gigantic details which make up the characters of men. I heard all about the friends he had lost sight of and those he had kept in sight; I heard about his profession, and asked at last how he came into the pageant.

'The fact is', he said, 'a friend of mine asked me, just for to-night, to act a chap called Paley; I don't know who he was ...'

'No, by thunder!' I said, 'nor does anyone'.

This was the last blow, and the next night passed like a dream. I scarcely noticed the slender, sprightly, and entirely new figure which fell into the ranks in the place of Paley, so many times deceased. What could it mean? Why was the giddy Paley unfaithful among the faithful found?[12] Did these perpetual changes prove the popularity or the unpopularity of being Paley? Was it that no human being could support being Paley for one night and live till morning? Or was it that the gates were crowded with eager throngs of the British public thirsting to be Paley, who could only be let in one at a time? Or is there some ancient vendetta against Paley? Does some secret society of Deists still assassinate anyone who adopts the name?

I cannot conjecture further about this true tale of mystery; and that for two reasons. First, the story is so true that I have had to put a lie into it. Every word of this narrative is veracious except the one word Paley. And, second because I have got to go into the next room and dress up as Dr. Johnson.

Notes

1 THE MYSTERY OF A PAGEANT: Reprinted in *TT* (2), pp. 257–63.
2 *historical processions ... 1909*: This was the English Church Pageant held at Fulham Palace from 10 to 16 June 1909, with cheap performances repeated for some days after; a photograph of Chesterton dressed up as Dr Johnson appeared in the *Illustrated London News* on the same day as this article: 'Our Note Book', p. 880. For an account of the forces behind Edwardian pageantry, see P. Readman, 'The Place of the Past in English Culture, c. 1890–1914', *Past and Present*, 186 (February 2005), pp. 147–99.
3 *Dr. Johnson*: Samuel Johnson; see 'The Good Man of the Eighteenth Century', *DN*, 22 March 1901, Volume 1, p. 66, n. 5 above.
4 *I requested that a row of posts ... along the course*: Dr Johnson's odd rituals and tics – apparently evidence of Obsessive Compulsive Disorder or Tourette's Syndrome – are recorded by Boswell, as is his fondness for tea and his 'refutation' of Berkeley mentioned a few lines later. For an explanation of his peculiarities of behaviour see, for example, J. M. Pearce, 'Doctor Samuel Johnson: "the great convulsionary" a victim of Gilles de la Tourette's syndrome', *Journal of the Royal Society of Medicine*, 87:7 (1994), pp. 396–9.
5 *Mrs. Thrale*: Hester Lynch Thrale (née Salusbury; after her second marriage, Hester Lynch Piozzi) (1741–1821), was an English diarist, author and a close friend of Samuel Johnson; after his death she published *Anecdotes of the late Samuel Johnson* (1786).
6 *pede claudo*: 'Raro antecedentem scelestum deseruit pede poena claudo' ('Though lame of foot, punishment rarely deserts the criminal') (Horace, *Odes* V.ii.31–2)
7 *Paley*: William Paley (1743–1805), was an English theologian, moralist and utilitarian. He was the author of *The Principles of Moral and Political Philosophy* (1785), but is now most remembered for his *Natural Theology, or Evidences of the Existence and Attributes of the Deity Collected from the Appearances of Nature* (1802). It was in the latter work that he proposed the 'watchmaker analogy' that exponents of creationism still cite with approval.
8 *Burke*: Edmund Burke; see 'The Good Man of the Eighteenth Century', *DN*, 22 March 1901, Volume 1, p. 67, n. 20 above.
9 *Cowper*: William Cowper; see 'Shooting at the Stars', *DN*, 6 August 1904, Volume 2, p. 270, n. 3 above.
10 *Master of Ballantrae*: R. L. Stevenson, *The Master of Ballantrae: A Winter's Tale* (1889), a novel that focuses on the divisions in a family of Scottish noblemen caught up in the Jacobite rising of 1745.
11 *Bishop Berkeley*: see 'The Good Man of the Eighteenth Century', *DN*, 22 March 1901, Volume 1, p. 67, n. 15 above.
12 *unfaithful among the faithful found*: A resonance of Milton. *Paradise Lost* 5:896–7:
So spake the Seraph Abdiel, faithful found
Among the faithless, faithful only he.

June 26, 1909.

THE EVIL DAY.

I have sometimes in this column ventured to hint a hazy doubt as to the complete satisfactoriness of the idea of Imperialism, and in other places I have even disputed the primary doctrines of Socialism, thereby risking ostracism by the Smart Set, who are all Socialists now. I think the time has come when I should say something in favour of Imperialism and Socialism, and it also happens, by a delightful coincidence, that I have actually thought of something favourable to say.

Anyone who wishes to do justice either to Imperialism or to Socialism should sharply remember the epoch in which they arose. I mean, of course, arose in this country and recently. They are both as old as human error. Sparta was Socialistic, and Babylon was Imperialist. Nay, the things are even pre-human. Ants are a sort of Socialists, and very unpleasant creatures they are; while the cuckoo seems to me a type of the perfect Imperialist. First, because he always says the same thing; and second, because he is proud of having deserted his offspring and left them lying about all over the world.

****

But this is to be an article in praise of Imperialism and Socialism. Let me fix that fact firmly in my mind. Now the great thing to be said for these two great exaggerations or heresies (and every heresy is a truth taught out of proportion) is that they were both rebellions against the age in which I was born. The society against which they raised their voices was a very intellectual and artistic society. I have felt its atmosphere, and I truly think that if they had been silent the very stones would have cried out.[1]

This dark period began vaguely about 1870; that end of the great Liberal epoch, the year when Paris fell and when Dickens died. It spreads equally vaguely up to the retirement of Gladstone and the abandonment of Home Rule, the last Liberal crusade which was unmistakably Liberal and unmistakably dangerous. All that period was filled with emptiness. Oscar Wilde[2] was justly its greatest man; because he alone could really do levity upon a large scale. Its products include many men whom I count as my best friends – myself among others. But I can hardly think of one of them who would not have been both better and happier if he had been born in any other period from the Stone Age to the Reign of Terror. For almost all other ages have set one enthusiasm against another; but of this brief and black age only can it be said that it sneered at enthusiasm simply for being enthusiastic. All men had dreaded the lightning because it was destruction; but these disdained the lightning because it was the light.

It is idle presumably to speculate as to the causes of this queer interregnum and vacuum. The truth, I fancy, is this: that religion and politics (man's chief concerns, almost his only concerns) alternate in history, but are seldom absent simultaneously. A rude society may be rich in saints; or a time of frigid infidelity, such as the eighteenth century, may be heroic in politics. But at the particular point I speak of both these waves were spent. Liberty had become a legend, and France, its standard-bearer, was struck down. At the same time everyone had drunk in Darwin ceaselessly and silently; men absorbed the idea that we had come from the beasts, which rapidly and popularly transformed itself into the idea that we had not come very far.

I speak, of course, of vast ignorant impressions. To anyone acquainted with the true facts Sedan[3] was only one fight in an ever-fluctuating struggle around the Rhine. And Darwinism was only [a?] biological conjecture for overcoming some difficulties in the very ancient doctrine of evolution.

That was the fact; but it was not the impression. The impression was that heavy hands had shut the doors of man's two great outlets – liberty and faith; [the] one was blocked by Bismarck with his blood and iron,[4] and the other by Darwin with his blood and bones. The appearance of 1870 was that political materialism had broken political idealism for ever. And the appearance of 'The Descent of Man' was that it was really a descent of man – that man had been kicked off his pedestal on to the floor.

****

Whether for this cause or some other, the years of which I speak were years of yawning, they were like the hours of an afternoon 'At Home' in a rich house on a rainy day when nobody comes to call. Their poems and pictures showed a real genius in tracing the leaden tints and echoing the tuneless tones of an afternoon like that. One hardly heard anything but pessimism – except Art, which is worse. Now, whenever I wish to feel tender towards Imperialists or Socialists I always remember that at least their Union Jacks and their red ties interrupted the twilight of that infernal afternoon. At least people wanted us to do something, and not dawdle any more about the drawing room. Communists wanted us to go picnicing; patriots wanted us to go poaching. Both rebellions bore, indeed, the marks of the bad world in which they were born. Imperialism is heathen because it is a form of Nature-worship; the belief in luck as a star of cosmic benediction. The heathen wishes to worship strength, but the Christian to strengthen worship. And the Socialists suffered from their atmosphere in so far that they did not trust the soul sufficiently. They tended to say, 'Give us free meals, and we will show you free citizens'. Whereas in truth only citizens could ever obtain the meals.

But the materialism both of the Imperial and the Social revolt did not prevent them doing real good in breaking up the old hedonistic hothouse. Rudyard Kipling did show that romance could be found in coarse and laborious affairs. And the Socialists have at least done one excellent thing; they have brought back creeds into politics. A Socialist will say to you, 'I don't want to know whether you condescend to love humanity, or whether in your own opinion you have lofty ideals; I want to know if you agree with the State taking all the means of production'. For a creed is the sword of the spirit;[5] the only tool with which the mind can fight.

That empty time has been so utterly forgotten that many even who lived in it will hardly know of what I speak. Of its weary wits and philosophic dandies hardly one remains; some are dead; some have gone into exile; some have gone to pieces. Two I knew were of real genius, a genius which survived that season of ashes and went on burning into our own time. I had forgotten their link with the unlucky age, or I fancied that they had forgotten it. One of them was a small, vivid man, one of the black Scotch, with dark burning eyes and a high colour. He had been the most piercing lyrist of the old minor poets, but of late he had taken up newer notions, going in with Mr. Shaw for enormous images of the Superman or the last giants of evolution. His talk was all of expanding life and unceasing activity.[6] The other was a quieter and much cleverer man; one of the most perfectly clever men ever born. He was tall, slow, saturnine, an omnivorous observer, a very fastidious judge. His work was almost wholly in a world of cool and almost heartless comedy. He had a slight smile always on his face. He also has dropped the mere pessimism of the dark age, and was doing hopeful and constructive work in the creation of a new and more solid English drama.[7]

Those are the only two men who have come triumphant out of that strange old atmosphere. Each one of them during the last few months has died by his own hand.[8]

Notes

1. *silent ... the very stones would have cried out*: see Luke 19:40.
2. *Oscar Wilde*: Oscar Fingal O'Flahertie Wills Wilde (1854–1900), was a seminal writer of the Irish literary renaissance, notable for his epigrammatic wit. He was educated at Trinity College, Dublin and Magdalen College, Oxford where he was influenced by Walter Pater and John Ruskin. He became central to the *fin de siècle* movement in both its aesthetic and decadent phases, providing the model for the satire on aestheticism in the Gilbert and Sullivan opera *Patience* (1881). His aestheticism found expression in social as well as literary criticism, particularly in his essay 'The Soul of Man Under Socialism' (1891). He achieved notoriety with his novel, *The Picture of Dorian Gray* (1891), a work with clear homosexual overtones. This was followed by a number of dramatic successes, including *Lady Windermere's Fan* (1892), *A Woman of no Importance* (1892) and *The Importance of Being Ernest* (1895). Performances of his play *Salomé* (1891) were forbidden by the Lord Chamberlain for its transgressions of Protestant belief. In 1895, Wilde was found guilty of gross indecency with two male prostitutes and imprisoned until 1897. Chesterton praised *The Ballad of Reading Gaol* that Wilde wrote during his imprisonment (O. Dudley Edwards, *ODNB*).
3. *Sedan*: i.e. the Battle of Sedan, 1–2 September, 1870, which was the decisive battle of the Franco–Prussian war. The Emperor Napoleon III was captured on 2 September and deposed by the forces of the Third Republic in Paris two days later.
4. *Bismarck ... blood and iron*: Otto Eduard Leopold von Bismarck (1815–98), was a Prussian statesman who as Ministerpräsident (Prime Minister) of Prussia from 1862 to 1890 largely presided over the unification of Germany. The phrase 'Blut und Eisen' ('blood and iron') that is so commonly associated with him occurred in a speech to the Budget Committee of the Prussian Chamber of Deputies on 30 September 1862.
5. *creed is the sword of the spirit*: see Ephesians 6:17: 'And take the helmet of salvation, and the sword of the Spirit, which is the word of God'.
6. *One of them ... unceasing activity*: John Davidson; see 'Mr. Archer and his Poets', *DN*, 15 October 1901, Volume 1, p. 229, n. 6 above.
7. *The other ... solid English drama*: St John Emile Clavering Hankin (1869–1909), was an English essayist and playwright; his health began to decline in 1907 and he drowned himself in June 1909. Hankin contributed to the *Saturday Review*, the *India Daily News*, *The Times*, and *Punch* before turning to dramatic writing. In *Mr Punch's Sequels* (1901) he added supplementary acts to the great classics of English dramas; he parodied eminent writers in *Lost Masterpieces* (1904). His plays included *The Return of the Prodigal* (1905), *The Charity that Began at Home* (1906), and *The Cassilis Engagement* (1907). His work for the stage was of a 'realistic frankness'. He was partly influenced by Shaw but had a cynicism all his own (G. S. Woods, rev. K. Mullin, *ODNB*). Chesterton's praise of Hankin as having 'dropped the mere pessimism of the dark age' does not correspond to other appraisals of his work.
8. *Each on of them ... his own hand*: Davidson and Hankin were identified as the two unnamed figures in this article by A. L. Maycock, *The Man who was Orthodox: A Selection from the Uncollected Writings of G. K. Chesterton* (London: Dennis Dobson, 1963), p. 131.